Petersburg to Appomattox

MILITARY CAMPAIGNS OF THE CIVIL WAR

Volumes in the Military Campaigns of the Civil War series feature insightful original essays by leading scholars and public historians. Taking advantage of recent scholarship and drawing on the full range of primary sources, contributors to the series reexamine common assumptions about pivotal campaigns, the experiences of major figures and common soldiers involved in the fighting, the connection between strategy and tactics on the ground, and the political and social ramifications of battles on the respective home fronts. The series offers an ideal introduction to key ideas and debates in Civil War history.

Petersburg

to

Appomattox

THE END OF THE WAR IN VIRGINIA

Edited by Caroline E. Janney

THE UNIVERSITY OF NORTH CAROLINA PRESS

Chapel Hill

This book was published with the assistance of the
Fred W. Morrison Fund of the University of North Carolina Press.

© 2018 The University of North Carolina Press

Designed by Jamison Cockerham
Set in Arno, Cutright, and Scala Sans
by Tseng Information Systems, Inc.

Manufactured in the United States of America

The University of North Carolina Press has been a member
of the Green Press Initiative since 2003.

Jacket illustration: *Position of the Confederate Army When the Surrender
Was Announced,* from Alfred H. Guernsey and Henry M. Alden, *Harper's
Pictorial History of the Civil War* (Fairfax Press, 1866), 770.

LIBRARY OF CONGRESS CATALOGING-IN-PUBLICATION DATA
Names: Janney, Caroline E., editor.
Title: Petersburg to Appomattox : the end of the war in Virginia /
edited by Caroline E. Janney.
Other titles: Military campaigns of the Civil War.
Description: Chapel Hill : University of North Carolina Press, [2018] | Series:
Military campaigns of the Civil War | Includes bibliographical references and index.
Identifiers: LCCN 2017044384| ISBN 9781469640761 (cloth : alk. paper) |
ISBN 9781469640778 (ebook)
Subjects: LCSH: Appomattox Campaign, 1865. | Virginia — History — Civil War,
1861–1865.
Classification: LCC E477.67 .P47 2018 | DDC 973.7/38 — dc23
LC record available at https://lccn.loc.gov/2017044384

For

GARY W. GALLAGHER

Contents

Figures and Maps

◇ ◇ ◇ ◇
◇ ◇ ◇ ◇

Acknowledgments

I would like to thank each of the contributors to this collection. As with previous volumes, the authors include both public and academic historians. Many are veterans of this series. A handful are welcome new additions. All have been gracious and professional, and I am indebted to all of them. I likewise am grateful for the assistance of Patrick Shroeder, historian at Appomattox Court House National Historical Park, who graciously provided me with numerous sources and offered invaluable insight into the campaign.

My greatest debt is to Gary W. Gallagher. Gary began this series in 1994 with the *Third Day at Gettysburg and Beyond*. In the twelve years that followed, he edited eight more volumes covering most of the major campaigns of the Eastern Theater—all the while authoring several monographs, teaching undergraduates, mentoring graduate students, and editing the University of North Carolina Press's Civil War America series. Two years ago, I joined him in reviving the Military Campaigns of the Civil War series with *Cold Harbor to the Crater*—an experience that only furthered my admiration of his deep knowledge of the war and his expert editing. I remain exceptionally grateful for his steady guidance, encouragement, mentoring, and friendship. Working with him, whether as a graduate student or as a coeditor, has been the best professional choice I have ever made. It is to him that I dedicate this volume.

Petersburg to Appomattox

Introduction

Caroline E. Janney

Taking pen in hand on the evening of April 9, 1865, Capt. Henry A. Chambers of the 49th North Carolina could scarcely believe what he was about to write. "Today the 'Army of Northern Virginia,' the best army we Southerners have, was surrendered," he began. For a week he had pushed west watching the once great army crumbling around him, yet Chambers remained in disbelief. "Who would have ventured to prophesy this two years, aye, twelve or six or three or even one month ago," he wrote. All hope for independence had vanished. All that he and other Confederates treasured was lost. But what galled him more than anything at that moment was a deep humiliation. "Worse than all," he admitted, "is the fact that these worthless fellows whom we have so often whipped, whose cowardly backs we have so often seen, have at last by sheer force of numbers, numbers swelled by contributions from almost every race and color on the face of the globe, have compelled us to come to this, can now lord it over us and ours, can pass, with the airs of conquerors, through our camps, and hereafter, through our whole country." His hatred brimming from the tip of his pen, he hoped for some form of "terrible retribution" to befall "this motly crew who have waged upon us so unjust, so barbarous a warfare!"[1]

Chambers's call for vengeance stands in stark contrast to the romantic stories of Appomattox—of a peaceful and tidy end to the war, of the quiet dignity symbolized by the surrender. Indeed, the final campaigns of the Eastern Theater combined with Robert E. Lee's surrender to Ulysses S. Grant have been wrapped in mythology since 1865. Veterans and historians alike have focused on the inevitable defeat of the Confederacy and recalled the generous surrender terms set forth by Grant. Both the Confederacy's certain demise and the terms, they suggest, helped to facilitate peace and served as the foundation for sectional reconciliation. But like Chambers, the authors in this collection offer a more nuanced and ambiguous portrait of the war's final months. They remind us of the deep uncertainty among leaders within both the Union and Confederate armies in the late winter of 1865 and that the so-called road to Appomattox might not have been taken at all. Indeed, they reveal that much hope remained for Confederate independence even late into the war's last spring. Most important, they stress that the meaning of Appomattox was far from settled in 1865 — or even decades later.

Petersburg to Appomattox takes up the last winter and spring in Virginia. The previous volume in the Military Campaigns of the Civil War series examined the conclusion of the Overland campaign, beginning with Cold Harbor through the battle of the Crater on July 30, 1864. Along with essays on these battles, that volume covered some material that might well fit in this one, including essays on how Confederate soldiers and Petersburg civilians coped with the ten-month siege. This volume picks up with the winter of 1865. It does not cover in detail the tactical action that occurred between August 1864 and April 1865, but it does offer background on the armies during these months. Although focused in a significant degree on the Appomattox campaign, the essays embed what happened between April 2 and April 9 in the larger context — both before and after this final campaign of the Union Armies of the Potomac and the James and the Confederate Army of Northern Virginia.

The story of these last few months is well known. Throughout the fall of 1864 the Army of the Potomac, commanded by Maj. Gen. George G. Meade but accompanied by Lt. Gen. Ulysses S. Grant, and Gen. Robert E. Lee's Army of Northern Virginia remained nearly immobile outside of the besieged city of Petersburg. As fall gave way to winter, Grant continued to tighten his grip and extend his lines westward, forcing Lee to similarly extend the lines defended by his increasingly dwindling army.[2]

On March 2, 1865, Maj. Gen. Philip H. Sheridan routed what remained of Lt. Gen. Jubal A. Early's small Confederate army at Waynesboro, and Lee knew that Sheridan would soon be free to reinforce Grant at Petersburg. To the south, Maj. Gen. William T. Sherman's 60,000 western veterans were likewise advancing toward the Virginia border with hopes of joining Grant. Lee's only option was to break free from the lines and join forces with Gen. Joseph E. Johnston's command. In the early hours of March 25, Lee committed between 10,000 and 12,000 men to Maj. Gen. John B. Gordon, instructing him to punch through the Federal defenses at Fort Stedman before turning south and rolling up the Union lines as far as possible. Before dawn the Confederates had captured Fort Stedman, but initial success soon gave way to a bloody fiasco that resulted in 3,000–4,000 rebel casualties. "I fear now it will be impossible to prevent a junction between Grant and General

Caroline E. Janney

William T. Sherman," Lee wrote Confederate president Jefferson Davis on March 26, adding, "nor do I deem it prudent that this army should maintain its position until the latter shall approach too near."[3]

Grant took advantage of the disastrous attack on Fort Stedman in part by sending Sheridan (who had now joined the Army of the Potomac) to attack Lee's right flank on March 29. Anticipating such a course, Lee ordered the divisions of Generals George E. Pickett and Fitzhugh Lee to protect Five Forks "at all hazards."[4] If the crossroads fell, Lee would be forced to abandon the defenses of Petersburg. When Sheridan attacked on April 1, the outnumbered Confederate left flank collapsed, costing Lee's beleaguered army another 5,000 men.

The Union victory allowed Grant to order an all-out assault against Petersburg on April 2. When the Sixth Corps achieved a decisive breakthrough along the Confederate defenses west of the city, Lee had no other choice but to withdraw. Abandoning Petersburg meant that Richmond, too, would be lost. "I advise that all preparations be made for leaving Richmond tonight," Lee telegraphed the War Department that morning. While Lt. Gen. Richard S. Ewell's soldiers set fire to government stores and property, Davis and his entourage evacuated the capital city via train bound for Danville. On April 3, Union troops marched into the former Confederate capital, and the following day President Lincoln arrived to tour the smoldering city.[5]

Following the evacuations of Richmond and Petersburg, Lee's army tramped westward, hoping to connect with Johnston along the Virginia and North Carolina border. More than 60,000 Confederates streamed out of the capital and the Petersburg trenches with plans to reconvene at Amelia Court House thirty-five miles west of Richmond, where they expected to find trainloads of much-needed rations.[6] Instead, due to Lee's failure to designate where the rations should be sent, his army found only ammunition awaiting them. With both man and beast desperate for food, the army halted to forage the countryside and await General Ewell's straggling column, thus allowing Sheridan's cavalry and three infantry corps to come perilously close. On April 5, Sheridan's men cut the Richmond & Danville Railroad near Jetersville, prompting Lee to alter his plans and head due west. Still, the Union army remained in close pursuit. The next day, three Union corps captured approximately 8,000 of Lee's men and destroyed their wagon train at Sailor's Creek. An exacerbated Lee exclaimed, "My God! Has the army been dissolved?"[7]

Lee's remaining forces slogged west toward Farmville, where they hoped to find provisions before turning south toward Keysville and the Richmond

& Danville Railroad. But all along its path the army that had held the heights at Fredericksburg and stormed the ridges of Gettysburg left signs it was disintegrating—littering the roads with broken wagons, ambulances, artillery carriages, discarded muskets, and haversacks. Thousands of stragglers dropped out of line, some simply collapsing along roadbeds and others wandering listlessly through Virginia's budding spring woods. But the signs were there for all to see. From his headquarters in Farmville, on the evening of Friday, April 7, Grant issued a note under a flag of truce inviting Lee to surrender. "The results of last week must convince you of the hopelessness of further resistance," Grant began. "I feel that it is so, and regard it as my duty to shift from myself the responsibility of any further effusion of blood by asking of you the surrender of that portion of the Confederate army known as the Army of Northern Virginia." Although one of his aides suggested he ignore the note, a fatigued Lee responded by asking what the terms might be. The following day, suffering from a severe headache, Grant informed Lee that his only condition was that the men and officers surrendered would be disqualified from taking up arms against the U.S. government until properly exchanged, offering to meet with the Confederate leader to arrange more definitively the terms. But Lee was not quite ready to submit.[8]

The capture of Confederate supplies on the afternoon of April 8 and the battle at Appomattox Station that followed proved critical in giving the Federal cavalry key positions on Palm Sunday, April 9. Early that morning, Confederate generals John Gordon and Fitzhugh Lee readied their men just west of Appomattox Court House to break past Sheridan's cavalry. The now ravenous rebels managed a final push against the Union horsemen, rallying each other on with one last spine-tingling rebel yell. But upon cresting a ridge west of the village they encountered infantry from Maj. Gen. Edward O. C. Ord's Army of the James (including two brigades of African American soldiers), followed closely by Maj. Gen. Charles Griffin's Fifth Corps. Confederate hopes of breaking through the lines vanished. Only a contingent of 1,500 to 2,000 Confederate cavalry managed to escape the Union cordon and ride toward Lynchburg.[9]

Although most of the men who remained in Lee's lines did not realize that the army was now trapped, Lee had decided to accept Grant's offer. As he readied himself to ride out and meet Grant, one of the general's most trusted lieutenants urged him not to surrender. Tell your men to disperse, to scatter to the woods and bushes with their rifles, and take up guerrilla warfare, he advised. But Lee would have none of this proposed bushwhacking. If he followed the suggested course, his men would have no rations and would be

Caroline E. Janney

under no discipline. They would be forced to rob and plunder to survive and the country would be filled with lawless bands, leading only to more retaliation from the Union army. This was not an option.[10] As much as he loathed surrendering his army, Lee knew that accepting Grant's offer was the only way to restore peace.

Meeting in the parlor of Wilmer McLean's home, the two commanders who had faced one another on the bloody fields of the Wilderness, Spotsylvania, Cold Harbor, and Petersburg shook hands. After a bit of small talk, Grant bent over a small, oval table with a cigar in his mouth to pen the surrender terms: officers and men could return to their homes "not to be disturbed by U.S. authority so long as they observe their paroles and the laws in force where they may reside." The arms, artillery, and public property of the army were to be turned over to the Union forces, but officers would be allowed to keep their personal sidearms and baggage. Lee asked for an addition. He explained to Grant that the Confederates had supplied their own cavalry and artillery horses, and he asked that they might be able to keep their mounts to return home and resume farming. Grant readily agreed. The generals spoke briefly about prisoner exchange and rations for the Confederates.[11] At three o'clock, they rose and shook hands, and Lee departed.[12] Ninety minutes later, Grant telegraphed Washington: "General Lee surrendered the Army of Northern Virginia this afternoon on terms proposed by myself."[13]

As with all previous volumes in the Military Campaigns of the Civil War series, *Petersburg to Appomattox* does not provide a narrative of all the strategic and tactical action or an analysis of all the command decisions made between the summer of 1864 and April 1865. Instead, some of the contributors bring new light to bear on familiar topics, while others explore less well-known aspects of the final fighting in Virginia. Together these essays remind readers of the contingent nature of Union victory in the spring of 1865 and examine the ways in which the outcome at Appomattox continued to resonate years and even decades later. While the authors do not offer a single coherent argument or consensus on all aspects of the war's final months, collectively they challenge many assumptions about the ways in which the war came to an end and the meaning that has become attached to Appomattox.

Central to this understanding is a reminder that Union victory on the battlefield was not inevitable. It is well worth remembering that in the previous three years, the Army of the Potomac had managed only one clear victory—and that in its own territory at Gettysburg. In the lead essay, William W. Bergen argues that such a turnaround occurred only once Grant was able to institute his own aggressive brand of warfare with the Armies of the James and the Potomac—once he finally, and completely, took command. But such was not an easy task. Unlike Lee, who had command of a single army—and had led that army for two years by the time of the Overland campaign—as general in chief, Grant commanded all the Union forces while accompanying an unfamiliar army in an unfamiliar region. He would first need to get to know his various armies and commanders and, equally important, break the culture of caution that had developed in the Union's largest and most visible army, the Army of the Potomac. Finally freed from political constraints after the presidential election in November 1864, Grant appointed army and corps commanders who matched his style and temperament, thus enabling him to shape the Union forces that would succeed in one final campaign. Surveying the challenges Grant faced between March 1864 and the following spring, Bergen's essay is a powerful reminder of the ways in which partisan politics, personalities, and battlefield success all proved deeply entangled.

Susannah J. Ural's essay shifts the focus from entire armies to a single brigade during the last year of the war. In the spring of 1864, Hood's Texas Brigade was recovering from a difficult winter of desertions under the guidance of a junior officer corps who restored discipline in the ranks, furnished new uniforms and food, and oversaw the return of wounded, captured, or otherwise absent men. Morale in the ranks soared—as did the unit's pride. But just as the brigade regained its strength, it embarked on one of the bloodiest periods of the war. The Overland campaign's devastating casualties left many to wonder if there were enough men to sustain the Texas Brigade. Hunkered down in the siege lines around Petersburg during the autumn, the brigade faced calls from Richmond for consolidating understrength regiments and worrisome news from the Texas home front. Denied furloughs home that winter, the men might have deserted en masse. But they did not. Through detailed portraits of individual soldiers and explorations of the Texas home front, Ural explains why the soldiers of this unit remained fiercely committed to Lee, the Army of Northern Virginia, and each other even as the Confederacy crumbled around them in the winter and spring of 1865.

Five Forks is often described as one of Confederate general George Pickett's most egregious failures. At best, historians have blamed the routing on an unfortunate natural phenomenon that prevented the division commander from hearing the sounds of battle while enjoying a fish fry with fellow officers Thomas Rosser and Fitzhugh Lee. Others have been less generous, condemning Pickett for a dereliction of duty that rendered the battle an easy victory for Union forces. Peter S. Carmichael's essay, however, reveals that neither of these interpretations is wholly accurate. Placing the battle in the larger context of Robert E. Lee's plans for a spring campaign, Carmichael concludes that while Pickett and Fitz Lee deserve much of the blame for the calamity at Five Forks, the Confederate loss was not entirely their fault. Robert E. Lee's loss of operational control of the right flank coupled with his poorly worded orders to hold the Forks "at all hazards"—a boggy terrain, which rendered it nearly impossible to move man or horse—likewise contributed to the defeat. "Operational oversight from Lee's headquarters could have brought attention to this issue and likely averted disaster, though not defeat," Carmichael explains. Yet by the early twentieth century, the Lost Cause had worked to absolve Robert E. Lee of blame for any shortcomings — including Five Forks. Responsibility for the routing would fall squarely on the shoulders of his subordinates — and a few unfortunate shad.

Wayne Wei-Siang Hsieh's essay turns attention to the Union cavalry that Pickett encountered at Five Forks. Specifically, it explores how Philip H. Sheridan's operations during the Appomattox campaign represented the culmination of an evolutionary process of the Union cavalry arm in the East from 1861 though the spring of 1865. Sheridan's aggressive style of command and gradual maturation proved central to its success. There were other senior cavalry officers in the Army of the Potomac who might have commanded the Cavalry Corps in 1864, including Alfred Pleasonton or David McMurtrie Gregg. But Sheridan's ascendancy and his leadership style ultimately restored a measure of fluidity to military operations in Virginia that had evaporated in the Overland campaign. With an independent command in the Shenandoah Valley during the fall of 1864, Sheridan had deployed infantry in conjunction with the cavalry units, many of which carried Spencer repeating carbines — a tactic that would prove key as Federal forces pursued Lee's army the following spring. As Hsieh points out, Appomattox was not the foreordained triumph of a Union cavalry armed with state-of-the-art weapons but rather the product of finally coordinating cavalry and infantry in battle.

The war might not have ended with a surrender of Lee's army at Appomattox, William C. Davis reminds us. In fact, there had "always been multiple paths to peace," including an armistice, which might have left slavery dead but the Confederacy still intact. Or individual states might have held conventions and sought their own end to the war. Indeed, in the late winter of 1865, the newly appointed Confederate secretary of war John C. Breckinridge believed that the war was lost, reunion was all but inevitable, and with Lee's endorsement the Confederate Congress might press Jefferson Davis to sue for peace. For months prior to Appomattox, Lee, Breckinridge, and Assistant Secretary of War John A. Campbell strategized on how the Confederacy might avoid an absolute military subjugation. As late as April 2, Breckinridge and Campbell were devising a new peace strategy, and on April 7 Lee and the secretary of war discussed how they might yet prevent outright surrender. Highlighting the interplay between the military and political goals of the war, Davis's essay places Lee's exchanges with Grant between April 7 and 9 into context: if Lee could stall as long as possible and convince the Union general to agree to an armistice, perhaps the Confederacy might yet survive, or at the very least the Union would be forced to make significant concessions.

If Grant and Lincoln had agreed to an armistice, the story of the Confederate records — or more precisely, the destruction of Confederate records — that Keith Bohannon uncovers might not have occurred. During the last year of the war, Confederate record keeping had become haphazard and incomplete at best, with company and regimental record books in a disorderly state. But disarray was not the same as destruction, which was the fate of both Confederate governmental and army records during the first week of April 1865. In early March, War Department employees had managed to relocate two boxcars full of materials from Richmond to Danville, but in the wake of the capital's evacuation on the night of April 2, clerks bundled and set fire to great piles of official documents while thousands of other records fell victim to the flames that charred the city. Army records fared little better, Bohannon explains. Despite U.S. Secretary of War Edwin M. Stanton's instructions on April 5 to collect and forward all captured Confederate letters, papers, correspondence, and other documents to Washington, Grant remained focused on subduing Lee's army — not on preserving Confederate archives. In the unrelenting push west, Federal troops captured and burned scores of wagons, including dozens of headquarters wagons at Sailor's Creek alone. Even after Lee's capitulation on April 9, Grant and his lieutenants made no concerted effort to preserve or collect Confederate papers. While Bohannon faults neither the Union high command nor Confederates for the massive destruction of records, he reminds us that the paucity of official military correspondence and reports makes it extremely difficult to fully recover the story of those final days of Lee's command.

Defining what constitutes both the "final days" and "Lee's command" in early April 1865 is in large part the subject of my essay. While Appomattox serves as shorthand for the end of Lee's army and by extension the war, perhaps as much as one-third of the Army of Northern Virginia did not surrender in the small village. Some of the approximately 20,000 men absent from the surrender had dropped out of the ranks during the arduous push west, a

Caroline E. Janney

significant portion of the cavalry and many artillerists had escaped the Union cordon on April 9, and still others had refused to await formal parole after it was clear that the army had been defeated. While nearly 30,000 of Lee's soldiers stacked their arms and awaited parole at Appomattox, this chapter tells the story of those who were not there — of those who insisted that the rebellion was not yet dead and hoped to continue the fight, of others who attempted to make their way home while avoiding Union lines, and of the thousands who ultimately decided it was in their best interest to turn themselves in to Union provost marshals throughout the region in order to receive paroles. In the days, weeks, and even months after Appomattox, both the Union high command and the Appomattox absentees would struggle with the extent to which April 9 indeed marked the end of rebellion for thousands of Confederates.

The next two essays turn to ruminations on Appomattox and some of its key actors in the postwar era. Stephen Cushman takes us back to Sheridan through the lens of the general's memoirs. While Sheridan's memoirs have not enjoyed the popularity of those written by Grant and William T. Sherman, Cushman argues that they reveal considerable literary merit, offering readers "richly textured glimpses of moments and subjects that have no counterparts in Grant's and Sherman's accounts." Equally important, Cushman considers Sheridan's stylistic choices and highlights the striking ways the general's leadership style shone through his prose. A close examination of the memoirs exposes Sheridan's frank self-justification, critiques of his fellow officers, self-censorship, and firm but constant vigilance for the welfare of his men. Indeed, this window into Sheridan's personality helps explain his choices during the Appomattox campaign. As Cushman notes, "If Sheridan had been dutifully subordinate, in both letter and spirit, he might not have taken part in the Appomattox campaign at all; or, to put it differently, if Sheridan had been dutifully subordinate, the Appomattox campaign, as we know it, would not have unfolded when it did, the way it did."

Elizabeth R. Varon's essay closes the collection by exploring a powerful tradition among African Americans — a strong belief that Lee's defeat marked the demise of slavery. The essay elucidates how that belief took shape in the moment of Union victory and the myriad ways it found expression in the postwar era. Varon demonstrates that the enshrinement of Appomattox as a "freedom day" rested on three interconnected claims: "that the Union army's victory over Lee dramatized the manly heroism and agency of African American soldiers; that the surrender brought many slaves their first consciousness and experience of liberation; and that the magnanimous terms of surrender that Lt. Gen. Ulysses S. Grant offered Lee symbolized the promise of racial reconciliation between whites and blacks." Lee's surrender figured as a prominent symbol in the bitter and protracted debates over race, Reconstruction, and reunion.

While this volume closes the war in the Eastern Theater chronologically, there are two volumes that remain to complete the Military Campaigns of the Civil War series, one each on First and Second Manassas/Bull Run.

NOTES

1. T. H. Pearce, ed., *Diary of Captain Henry A. Chambers* (Wendell, N.C.: Broadfoot's Bookmark, 1983), 262 (diary entry April 9, 1865).

2. For the best overviews of the final campaigns, see William Marvel, *Lee's Last Retreat: The Flight to Appomattox* (Chapel Hill: University of North Carolina Press, 2002); Gary W. Gallagher, "An End and a New Beginning," in *Appomattox Court House*, by the U.S. National Park Service (Harpers Ferry, W.Va.: Division of Publications of the National Park Service, 2003), 27–81; Burke Davis, *To Appomattox: Nine April Days, 1865* (New York: Hold, Rinehart, and Winston, 1959); Chris M. Calkins, *The Appomattox Campaign, March 29–April 9, 1865* (Lynchburg, Va.: Schroeder, 2008); and Perry D. Jamieson, *Spring 1865: The Closing Campaigns of the Civil War* (Lincoln: University of Nebraska Press, 2015).

3. Earl J. Hess, *In the Trenches at Petersburg: Field Fortifications and Confederate Defeat* (Chapel Hill: University of North Carolina Press, 2009), 245–46; Marvel, *Lee's Last Retreat*, 9–11; Gallagher, "An End and a New Beginning," 36; Lee to Jefferson Davis, March 26, 1865, in *The Wartime Papers of R. E. Lee*, ed. Clifford Dowdey and Louis H. Manarin (Boston: Little, Brown, 1961), 916–18.

4. For more on the source of Lee's quote, see footnote 23 of Peter S. Carmichael's essay in this volume.

5. Hess, *In the Trenches at Petersburg*, xx; Jamieson, *Spring 1865*, 123; Edward G. Longacre, *The Cavalry at Appomattox: A Tactical Study of Mounted Operations during the Civil War's Climactic Campaign, March 27–April 9, 1865* (Mechanicsburg, Pa.: Stackpole Books, 2003), 109.

6. For more on the numbers, see my essay in this collection, "We Were Not Paroled," n. 6.

7. James M. McPherson, *The Civil War Era* (New York: Oxford University Press, 1988), 847–48; Gallagher, "An End and a New Beginning," 57; Robert M. Dunkerly, *To the Bitter End: Appomattox, Bennett Place, and the Surrenders of the Confederacy* (El Dorado Hills, Calif.: Savas Beatie, 2015), 5–6.

8. Bruce Catton, *A Stillness at Appomattox* (Garden City, N.Y.: Doubleday, 1954), 369–80; James M. McPherson, *Battle Cry of Freedom: The Civil War Era* (New York: Ballantine Books, 1988), 847–48. Confederate chaplain William Wiatt estimated that at least 25,000 to 30,000 men deserted before reaching Appomattox. Alex L. Wiatt, ed., *Confederate Chaplain William Edward Wiatt: An Annotated Diary* (Lynchburg, Va.: H. E. Howard, 1994), 237 (diary entry April 9, 1865).

Caroline E. Janney

9. Gallagher, "An End and a New Beginning," 65–66; Calkins, *Appomattox Campaign*, 159–64.

10. Edward Porter Alexander, *Fighting for the Confederacy: The Personal Recollections of General Edward Porter Alexander*, ed. Gary W. Gallagher (Chapel Hill: University of North Carolina Press, 1989), 531–33.

11. McPherson, *Battle Cry*, 848–50; James M. McPherson, *Ordeal by Fire: The Civil War and Reconstruction* (New York: Knopf, 1982), 482; *The Papers of Ulysses S. Grant*, ed. John Y. Simon and others, 32 vols. to date (Carbondale: Southern Illinois University Press, 1967–), 14:377–78.

12. McPherson, *Battle Cry*, 848–50; Bruce Catton, *The Centennial History of the Civil War, Volume Three: Never Call Retreat* (New York: Doubleday, 1965), 454.

13. *Personal Memoirs of U. S. Grant*, 2 vols. (1885; repr., Old Saybrook, Conn.: Konecky and Konecky, 1992), 2:633.

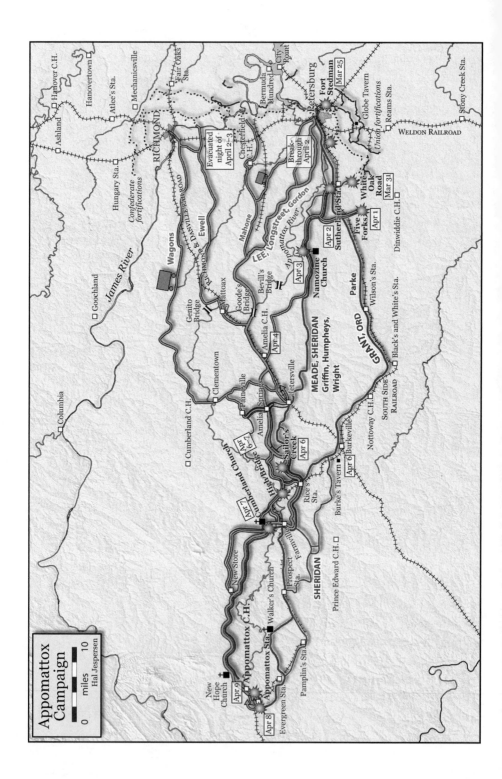

Grant *Finally* Takes Command

How the Race to Appomattox Was Won

William W. Bergen

The enduring popular image of Ulysses S. Grant is of a taciturn, humorless, even colorless general who nonetheless became one of the most effective commanders in history. Though remembered for wearing "an expression as if he had determined to drive his head through a brick wall, and was about to do it," to his staff Grant was an amiable fellow with a droll sense of humor.[1]

Grant resorted to mischief late on the first Tuesday in November 1864. On that election night, Grant and his staff gathered round their campfire awaiting returns. While such gatherings were routine at the general in chief's City Point, Virginia, headquarters, that evening's news held singular significance. Staff members listened as their chief read aloud election results handed him by the telegraph operator. Well into the night Grant recited one gloomy report after another, and many went to bed believing President Abraham Lincoln had been defeated in his bid for a second term. Only after most were asleep did Grant divulge that he had been kidding: Lincoln had been reelected.[2]

Grant's playful mood reflected confidence that Lincoln's victory would hasten the war's end. Now that the president would not be so constrained by the political considerations that had limited the general in chief's authority in selecting subordinates, Grant could look forward to more leeway in shaping his command structure. While Grant would exercise that new discretion in several of the far-flung military districts he commanded, his changes to the Army of the Potomac and the Army of the James stand out. These changes remade those armies and led directly to the swift surrender of the Confederate Army of Northern Virginia—and with its demise, the end of the Confederacy. The new U.S. army and corps commanders who won the race to Appomattox Court House were handpicked by Grant, and their aggressiveness, competence, and determination sharply contrasted with their predecessors' cautious and often bumbling performance. Various political factors had prevented these generals' promotions, and as a group they tended to be profane, loud, and belligerent, a style much different from that of their calmly determined chief. Yet they formed an effective team who won a swift and complete victory. Together they demonstrate that, in those final weeks, Grant finally took command.

In the retelling of the war's final days, it is easy to miss how the stillness at Appomattox came with astounding suddenness: armies Grant directed during his final campaign performed close to perfectly, forcing the surrender of the Army of Northern Virginia less than ten days after the fall of Petersburg and Richmond. Such a victory seems preordained given the contrast in the size and physical condition of the opposing armies, but the U.S. forces' conquest was achieved deep in enemy territory and against an army that had triumphed many times despite the Union's material and manpower advantages. The Appomattox surrender is all the more remarkable because at the core of the victorious forces was an army that, in three years of bloody fighting in the Eastern Theater, had won only one major, clear-cut victory, and that on its own ground at Gettysburg.

Grant's success in the Appomattox campaign can be traced to his being able to imbue his 1865 armies with his own brand of aggressive warfare, a development largely produced by changing their leadership and culture. That Grant required nearly a year to reshape these armies can be attributed to three interrelated factors: first, Grant lacked familiarity with the Army of the Potomac and other Virginia forces; second, the Army of the Potomac's culture of caution took time to overcome; third and most crucial, politics limited Grant's choices for subordinates until after Lincoln's reelection.[3]

The new general in chief's challenges in March 1864 are too often underemphasized. When analyzing the bloody road that began in the Wilderness and ended at Appomattox, historians are irresistibly drawn to comparing Grant and General Robert E. Lee, the war's two foremost generals, men who seem to embody the essence of their respective regions. In the shorthand the battle narrative form requires, chroniclers usually write of a commander doing one thing followed by the opposing commander reacting by doing another. Personalizing the armies in this way carries the implicit presumption that both commanders enjoyed equivalent control over their armies, and therefore a general's skill is often decisive in determining the winner. But for Grant and Lee this shorthand masks a crucial difference: during the Overland campaign, Lee exercised far more control over his army than Grant did over the Army of the Potomac.

One formal difference is often overlooked: Grant, as general in chief, commanded all U.S. armies in the field and did not command directly the Army of the Potomac, whereas until the war's final weeks, Lee's command was usually confined to the force he created, the Army of Northern Virginia. But other differences are profound. Lee, famously described as "audacity personified," had commanded his army for nearly two years by early 1864, and he had managed to imbue in his subordinates his own penchant for aggressive initiative. Because of his success and because political influence was muted in the Confederate command system, Lee had chosen nearly all of his subordinates almost entirely on the basis of merit.[4]

Grant's position was far different. Upon arriving in Virginia in the spring of 1864, he found himself among strangers and indirectly leading an army with a distinctive—and a much more political—ethos than his former commands. Besides a few old army friends, he knew no one in the Army of the Potomac. Worse, Grant was viewed with skepticism if not resentment: that he had been promoted to lieutenant general and that he would choose to accompany the Army of the Potomac reflected Washington's lack of confidence in the army's leadership. Grant knew the challenges that commanding an unfamiliar army would entail. In August 1863, after the capture of Vicksburg, Grant deflected overtures that he replace the Army of the Potomac's commander, Maj. Gen. George G. Meade. After the proposal fizzled out, Grant expressed relief, writing that transferring to the Army of the Potomac would have caused him "more sadness than satisfaction. . . . Here I know the officers and men and what each Gen. is capable of as a separate commander. There I would have all to learn." Besides, Grant continued, designating a westerner to command the Army of the Potomac would cause difficulties "with those who have grown up, and been promoted with it." But in early 1864, Grant found himself promoted to a position where he had "all to learn."[5]

The task was more difficult than Grant could have imagined. Armies acquire cultures fostered by their leaders that, once created, are self-sustaining. The Army of the Potomac had acquired its ethos from its creator, Maj. Gen. George B. McClellan, and his influence remained strong in the spring of 1864, some eighteen months after his dismissal. A charismatic leader and an outstanding organizer, McClellan had selected most of the army's senior officers. To them he left two legacies. One was a caution that exceeded all reason. McClellan's apprehensions about what Lee could and would do, plus implausibly inflated estimates of enemy numbers, became habits of thinking. Few generals were castigated for being too prudent or deliberative, an attitude reinforced by Lee's ability to inflict defeats seemingly at will. It would require time, an election, and considerable turnover in top generals to overcome this culture.[6]

The second legacy was an appetite and aptitude for political scheming. McClellan had fostered an attitude that taught senior commanders to be suspicious of politicians in general and of the Lincoln administration in particular. Yet, even as these mostly West Pointers abhorred appointments based on political influence, they often sought support from sympathetic politicians. Factions had formed, with some generals working to undermine their peers and, often, their superiors. The usual goal was to garner promotion for themselves. This maneuvering extended to all officers, with even second lieutenants liable to find themselves passed over for promotion in favor of those with political influence. In short, the army Grant now oversaw was, in the words of its celebrated chronicler Bruce Catton, "badly clique-ridden, obsessed by the memory of the departed McClellan, so deeply impressed by Lee's superior abilities that its talk at times almost had a defeatist quality."[7]

When the new general in chief established his headquarters in Culpeper, Virginia, in March 1864, the opening of the Overland campaign was barely eight weeks away. Rather than focusing on learning about the Army of the Potomac in its winter camps, Grant necessarily concentrated on his wider duties. He traveled frequently during that time to Washington and elsewhere and corresponded daily with commanders in all the U.S. military departments in nearly every Northern state, plus six in the Confederacy. The plan he devised would win the war, but adjusting to his new responsibilities afforded scant time to get to know the Army of the Potomac. In the fifty-eight days between being assigned as general in chief on March 9 and the opening battle of the Overland campaign, Grant spent fewer than forty nights in Culpeper.[8]

One incident during the battle of the Wilderness demonstrates how little Grant knew about his new command. When he gave his first operational order to the Army of the Potomac, to "pitch in" to confront Confederate forces along the Orange Turnpike, Grant knew nothing of the ground, the capabilities of the Union's lead division, or its commander, Brig. Gen. Charles Griffin. When that attack failed, Griffin galloped to headquarters to protest, loudly and profanely, that his attack had not received sufficient support. His tirade was directed not at his peers or immediate superior but at army commander Meade, who, though a man known for his own volcanic temper, remained calm. Grant and his staff were shocked, and after a still angry Griffin departed, Grant approached Meade. "Who is this Griffith?" Grant asked, and suggested that he be put under arrest. Meade corrected his chief: "It's Griffin, not Griffith, and that's just his way of talking." For Meade, such outbursts were evidently routine. But Grant was so unacquainted with his new forces that he did not recognize a division commander's name and thought that Griffin warranted arrest for insubordination. Grant was a clear-headed, calm leader who valued loyalty and teamwork, and Griffin's eruption showed how the culture of the Army of the Potomac differed starkly from the armies Grant had heretofore known.[9]

In contrast to piecemeal U.S. advances made in previous springs, the novice general in chief devised a coordinated plan to attack the Confederacy at several points simultaneously. Grant's most trusted lieutenant, Maj. Gen. William T. Sherman, would lead his armies south toward Atlanta. Grant would accompany Meade's army as it headed southeast toward Richmond. Unfortunately, Lincoln's need to ensure his reelection put the rest of Grant's scheme in the hands of political generals of questionable competence. Maj. Gen. Nathaniel Banks, a Democrat and former Speaker of the House of Representatives who hoped to be nominated for president that summer, was assigned to seize Mobile, Alabama, one of the few remaining Confederate ports. Weeks before the campaign was to begin, however, Banks embarked on the ill-fated Red River campaign, more a politically motivated move designed to bolster the fledgling U.S.-sponsored state government than a military necessity. The invasion bogged down, and it would be months before Banks's forces could threaten Mobile. In Virginia, politics compelled Grant to entrust two politicians with key parts of his plan. Maj. Gen. Franz Sigel, a popular figure among the sizable German American electorate, was to advance up the Shenandoah Valley to tie up Confederate forces there. He came to grief at New Market in May, allowing crucial reinforcements to reach Lee during the Overland campaign. The other effort, a drive up the James River to threaten Richmond, was assigned to Maj. Gen. Benjamin Butler and his Army of the James. A favorite of Radical Republicans and War Democrats, Butler considered running for president in 1864. Partly to head him off, the Lincoln administration had sounded him out that spring to see if he would be interested in being vice president or secretary of war. Butler demurred, hoping to enhance his political prospects on the battlefield. In what became known as the Bermuda Hundred campaign, however, Butler failed to accomplish much of anything.[10] Had Sigel and Butler performed adequately, the Overland campaign might have resulted in a U.S. triumph that spring.

While politics undermined Grant's plan in Virginia, he found success elsewhere. In August, operating with a token army force, Rear Admiral David

Farragut effectively closed Mobile Bay by forcing his way past the forts guarding the harbor. And Grant's trust in Sherman was not misplaced; Atlanta fell on September 2. These two victories, plus Maj. Gen. Philip H. Sheridan's success that fall in the Shenandoah Valley, the scene of several lopsided defeats for U.S. forces, helped ensure Lincoln's reelection.[11]

The political realities that constrained Grant's choices for subordinates were made clear almost immediately. When he arrived in Washington, Grant assumed from various published and private sources that the Lincoln administration wished to replace Meade. He was surprised to find that, to the contrary, Lincoln and the secretary of war, Edwin Stanton, though disappointed in Meade's perceived lack of aggressiveness, nonetheless favored his retention. Why that was so illustrates the political winds that buffeted the Army of the Potomac. An 1835 graduate of West Point, Meade had fought in the Mexican War but served nearly his entire prewar years as a topographical engineer and lighthouse designer. Excelling in brigade and division command early in the war, by 1863 Meade had risen to head of the Fifth Corps. He fought well at Chancellorsville and afterward declined to take part in a cabal that sought to dislodge Joseph Hooker as army commander. With Hooker acting erratically during the weeks before Gettysburg, however, Meade was ordered to take command of the army.[12]

Meade's skillful handling of the army at Gettysburg earned him deserved acclaim, but the Lincoln administration grew progressively more impatient with what it perceived to be Meade's lack of aggressiveness. Worse, during the winter of 1863–64, the U.S. Congress Joint Committee on the Conduct of the War held extensive hearings designed to undermine Meade and his subordinates. Dominated by Radical Republicans advocating harsher means of prosecuting the war, the committee heard testimony from generals whom Meade had sacked for cause as well as from Meade himself and his subordinates. Leaks to newspapers falsely suggested that Meade had wanted to retreat from Gettysburg on the first day of that battle. Hearing enough, committee members met with Lincoln to urge Meade's replacement. Lincoln, sensing that the committee's influence was waning, refused. Also buttressing the army commander's standing was strong support from Republicans in politically crucial Pennsylvania, Meade's home state; Lincoln would risk offending those interests were he to accede to the committee's wishes.[13]

Now relatively secure in his position, Meade worked with Stanton to reorganize the Army of the Potomac to reduce the number of corps from five to three. The reorganization allowed Meade to shed three inefficient corps commanders while providing a promotion for Maj. Gen. Gouverneur Warren, who had shined at Gettysburg and had temporarily commanded the Second Corps.

Before his promotion, Grant had stipulated he would command from the field, and he initially thought he would be accompanying his western armies. He soon realized, however, that he needed to accompany the Army of the Potomac so as to blunt political interference. This decision put Meade in an awkward and thankless command arrangement. Though Meade periodically bristled at perceived and real slights he suffered at Grant's hands, he handled his duties with characteristic professionalism. Still, by midsummer Grant recognized that Meade's effectiveness had been undermined by his testiness and that relations with his subordinates had frayed. Believing Meade and the Army of the Potomac might benefit from a change, Grant suggested transferring him to command in the Shenandoah Valley. Lincoln, however, apparently refused on the same grounds that he had resisted Meade's replacement as army commander. Having spent political capital to retain Meade, Lincoln did not want to be perceived as acquiescing in a reassignment that could be seen as a demotion—especially so close to the election. Meade would continue to serve loyally in the final weeks of the Petersburg and Appomattox campaigns, and though quite ill during the pursuit, he performed well in ways that reflected his innate sense of duty.[14]

Historian Mark Grimsley has suggested that the underlying friction between Grant and Meade stemmed not from their personal relationship but from their different approaches to command. "By temperament and experience," Grimsley writes, "Grant possessed a *coping* style of generalship, that is, a style aimed at shaping any outcome toward a desired objective." Meade, by contrast, believed that good generalship was based in "*control*—to use resources and manipulate variables so as to guarantee success." Because battles often, by definition, disrupt that control, the default reaction is toward safety, to revert to avoid losing. Like Meade, many other Army of the Potomac generals believed in this approach, which was taught to them by McClellan. It is no accident that in the race to Appomattox, Meade was eventually reduced to commanding just two of his corps while junior but more aggressive commanders were tasked with getting in front of Lee.[15]

Shortly after the 1864 election Grant visited Washington for consultations, and he moved quickly to take advantage of what he hoped would be more flexibility in choosing subordinates. While there he wrote Stanton to recommend dismissing nine major generals and thirty-one brigadier generals of volunteers; in subsequent correspondence over the next two weeks, Grant added another major general and two brigadiers to the list. He would not "insist upon such action being taken," Grant told Stanton, but "the public interest will be benefited by it." He suggested that for many of the cases "it might be advisable to notify, so as to give them the opportunity of resigning if they elect to do so." Because he knew few on the list of forty-three generals, Grant probably relied on War Department staff officers as well as on Sherman and Sheridan for the names. While eight on the list were U.S. Military Academy graduates, most were not, and nearly all had obtained their rank through political connections. Many were serving in administrative roles or awaiting orders, and Grant may have sought to create vacancies to be filled by those deserving promotion. The results of the proposed purge proved disappointing—only eight of these generals resigned or were removed before May 1865, and some of these departed through normal attrition. Grant's efforts did not seriously harm their reputations; nearly all the generals were mustered out with brevet promotions.[16]

Why Grant's recommendations yielded so few results is unknown. Certainly bureaucratic inertia played a role—replacing that many officers could not be accomplished quickly. The lack of action may also reflect the generals' enduring usefulness in occupying inconsequential commands, as Lincoln still needed political support for his final term. Finally, Grant's scant acquaintance with most on the list suggests he might not have felt strongly about dismissing many of them.

In compiling such a long list, Grant may have been looking for cover for his determination to sideline three prominent names on that list— major generals John A. McClernand, Franz Sigel, and William Rosecrans. McClernand, whom Grant had dismissed for insubordination during the Vicksburg campaign, resigned his commission almost immediately after the election ostensibly on the grounds of ill health. Though once politically influential, McClernand had lost whatever sway he once had by campaigning for McClellan during the election and might have jumped before he was pushed. Grant's effort to dismiss Sigel was less successful. After the New Market debacle, Sigel clung to a minor administrative command and enjoyed a moment of success in defending Harpers Ferry against a Confederate probe in July 1864. Shelved from that post shortly after, Sigel did not again command troops. But if he was asked to resign his major generalship, he refused, and he only relinquished his rank several weeks after Appomattox. Grant was able to remove Rosecrans from his post as commander of the Department of the Missouri—a removal long sought by Grant but in vain, apparently because of Rosecrans's continued political influence. When asked by Stanton what command Rosecrans might be given, Grant was blunt: "Rosecrans will do less harm doing nothing on duty. I know of no department or commander deserving such punishment as the infliction of Rosecrans upon them." Rosecrans waited in Cincinnati for orders that would never come, and he resigned his commission in December 1865.[17]

If Grant's lack of success in thinning the general ranks was disappointing, he was not deterred during the winter of 1864–65 from working to appoint other generals in key commands who would be more aggressive and responsive to his orders. He had already sidelined Banks by creating a new Division of West Mississippi and having him report to its commander, Maj. Gen. Edward R. S. Canby. After the election Banks wrote to Lincoln asking for Canby's recall, but Lincoln demurred, saying Grant, "whom I must hold responsible for military success," did not see the need for such a change. Grant employed a similar tactic in creating a new Military Division of the Missouri to be headed by Maj. Gen. John Pope. Sent to command the Department of the Northwest after his debacle at the battle of Second Manassas, Pope performed credibly in fighting Native Americans and, more important to Grant, had responded with alacrity to calls for reinforcements throughout 1864. In late November, Grant summoned Pope to City Point for consultations, a visit that went largely unnoticed. Grant first offered him the Department of the South, but Pope refused, not wanting to command what was mostly an army of occupation. In early February, Pope assumed command of the new division, which included the Department of the Northwest. On March 21, 1865, Grant expanded Pope's command to include the Department of Arkansas and urged an aggressive campaign against Confederates by "subsisting entirely off the Country." Grant added that "movements now in progress may end in such results within a few weeks as to enable me to send you forces enough for any campaign you may want to make, even to the overrunning of the whole of Texas." That Grant wrote such a message on the eve of the Appomattox campaign reflects his determination to ensure that the Confederate forces would be pressed on all fronts in 1865.[18]

Not mentioned in Grant's correspondence in the postelection weeks was removing inarguably his chief local liability, Benjamin Butler, the politically influential but incompetent commander of the Army of the James. The two men had operated in close proximity since the beginning of the siege of Petersburg in June 1864. Because Butler outranked Meade, Grant seldom left Petersburg during the siege as Butler would be left to act as overall commander in his absence. Grant's relationship with Butler had begun well; after their first meeting in early 1864, Grant noted Butler's "clear-headedness and capacity." But by summer it was clear that Butler was militarily inept as well as a disruptive influence, and Grant had tried to circumscribe his role by limiting him to administrative duties. This effort failed, however, because of War Department bungling as well as Butler's own wiliness and political sway. In August, several War Democrats, despairing of Lincoln's reelection, began discussing nominating Butler as a presidential candidate, and he antagonized Grant's staff and others by bragging about it. A late November report that Butler was to become secretary of war so worried Grant that he sought assurances from Washington that the rumor was untrue. Butler finally gave Grant an opening to sack him when he bungled an attack on Fort Fisher near Wilmington, North Carolina, in late December 1864. His reelection now behind him, Lincoln assented to Grant's request to relieve Butler. Grant waxed almost philosophical in a letter to an old friend: "The failure at Fort Fisher was not without important and valuable results."[19]

For Butler's successor, Grant turned to Maj. Gen. Edward O. C. Ord. An 1839 West Point graduate, Ord rose to prominence in 1862 in the Western Theater, where he earned Grant's confidence. Promoted to corps command during the siege of Vicksburg, Ord was among the few generals Grant brought east with him. What the new general in chief saw in Ord remains unknown, as he had shown a penchant for political and personal infighting, had compiled a mixed record in combat, and possessed a self-centered temperament at odds with Grant's. Though a senior major general, Ord's Maryland birth, well-known Democratic loyalties, and wife's family background fostered political opposition to his advancement, and he was not likely to be promoted to army command before Lincoln's reelection. After a period of largely self-inflicted underemployment in early 1864, Ord assumed corps command under Butler in July but was wounded just weeks later. Once recovered, Ord took over the Army of the James in early January 1865 and energetically reorganized his command, sweeping away several of Butler's favorites and instituting a rigorous schedule of drills and inspections. Whatever his liabilities, Ord was a decided improvement over Butler, and his performance during the Appomattox campaign was nearly flawless.[20]

Changes were also needed among the armies' corps commanders. While the most senior, and least able, of these, Maj. Gen. Ambrose Burnside, remained officially in command of the Ninth Corps until after the election, he left the army for good in August 1864. Brave, amiable, and, in an army of ambitious intriguers, honest and straightforward, everyone liked Burnside. Yet he remained incompetent: inattentive to detail, stubborn and peevish in the heat of battle, too loyal to underachieving subordinates, and always, in

Burnside's own words, trusting to luck. Few generals' careers had compiled as thoroughly a mixed record. Ordered to the command of the Army of the Potomac in November 1862 after twice refusing entreaties to take it voluntarily, Burnside promptly led his forces to disaster at the battle of Fredericksburg. He revived his reputation somewhat by taking and holding Knoxville in 1863. Brought back east with his Ninth Corps in early 1864, Burnside had fought without distinction during the Overland campaign. Granted leave two weeks after he thoroughly mismanaged the attack at the battle of the Crater in July 1864, Burnside headed home to rest and see to his personal affairs. Once his leave expired and it became clear he would never return to command the Ninth Corps, Burnside lobbied for another assignment, and Lincoln, among others, tried to be helpful. In November, Lincoln proposed that Burnside return to departmental command in Kentucky. Grant initially assented but reconsidered, writing Washington that upon "reflection I think it a bad selection." At least one other attempt to place him also fizzled, and in January a member of Grant's staff wrote Burnside that the general in chief would not even see him when he came to City Point as "[Grant] has at present no command to which he can assign you, or duty on which to order without making changes it's not desirable to be made." Grant's demurral may have been hardened by some of Burnside's political backers' attempts to place the blame for the Crater disaster on Meade and Grant. By late March, Burnside was reduced to writing to Stanton that he was ready to serve as "a subordinate commander or aide-de-camp, or as a bearer of dispatches." There is no record of a reply, and Burnside resigned his commission less than a month later.[21]

Burnside's replacement was his longtime subordinate Maj. Gen. John Parke. Graduating second in the West Point class of 1849, Parke spent his prewar career in the engineers. Well-liked by everyone, he commanded a brigade and then a division in the Ninth Corps and served as its chief of staff for much of the war. Parke had also led two divisions of the corps during the latter stages of the siege of Vicksburg, where he had earned Grant's respect. However, Parke may not have been Grant's first choice. In December, Grant repeatedly wrote to chief of staff of U.S. armies, Maj. Gen. Henry W. Halleck, suggesting that Parke be sent to serve under Canby and that Maj. Gen. Frederick Steele be transferred to command the Ninth Corps. Steele was Grant's West Point classmate, and the two had worked effectively together during the Vicksburg campaign. Grant dropped the idea only when he learned that Canby wanted Steele to command one of his corps. So Parke, a quiet but effective administrator, was assigned to command the Ninth Corps. Though not given a major role in the Appomattox campaign, he handled his responsibilities well and without the drama that always seemed to surround Burnside.[22]

Maj. Gen. Winfield Scott Hancock of the Second Corps, next in seniority, departed in November. Hancock had led the corps since Gettysburg, compiling a solid albeit bloody record, and was generally seen as Meade's obvious successor. While the timing probably was linked to the election—the politically connected Hancock may have been kept in place so as to not affect balloting in his native Pennsylvania—his relief had little to do with politics. Hancock went willingly; the wound suffered at Gettysburg still caused him considerable pain. Moreover, he had been deeply embarrassed by a one-sided rout of the Second Corps at the battle of Reams Station in late August. So distraught was Hancock on that occasion that he exclaimed, "I pray to God I may never leave this field." Stanton, with Grant's concurrence, crafted a new command for him, a veterans corps to be formed by men returning to the service once their enlistments had expired. Stanton hoped that Hancock's fame and prestige would encourage such reenlistments. Ailing and weary of infighting in the army, Hancock wanted a separate command, and he recognized that his Second Corps, once the pride of the army, would need considerable rebuilding to restore its effectiveness, leadership he no longer felt he could provide. Hancock left without fanfare on Thanksgiving Day.[23]

His replacement was Maj. Gen. Andrew A. Humphreys, Meade's chief of staff. A precise and thoroughgoing regular, Humphreys was an engineer who excelled in staff and combat command. An 1831 West Point graduate, Humphreys stood out, thought one observer, for his "distinguished and brilliant profanity." During the pursuit of Lee in April 1865, he displayed determination and decisiveness, as his second division commander, Brig. Gen. William Hays, found out. On the morning of April 6, Humphreys set out to inspect the division's preparations to pursue Lee's fleeing troops. Instead of finding the regiments ready to march, the division lay in its camps with no orders given to prepare to advance. Infuriated, Humphreys rode to division headquarters, where he found Hays asleep. Humphreys immediately relieved Hays, an act that would wreck his career. This incident illustrates how the culture of the 1865 version of the Army of the Potomac differed from the past. Heretofore, commanders were seldom reprimanded, let alone removed, for being dilatory. Grant had changed that. Humphreys acted unilaterally, apparently without checking with superiors, reflecting a confidence in his own discretion and sureness that Grant would back his action.[24]

Also promoted in early 1865 was Maj. Gen. John Gibbon. Designated commander of the newly created Twenty-fourth Corps of the Army of the James, Gibbon was long overdue for an elevation. A North Carolina native, Gibbon was an 1847 West Point graduate, and when the war came he broke with his family to side with the United States. Tough, blunt, "cold steel" Gibbon had served effectively at every level of command. Despite this, his Southern birth and lack of political sponsors delayed his promotion. An outspoken supporter of George McClellan for president—he even passed out McClellan campaign literature to his division—Gibbon was hardly one who would have been promoted before the election. Yet he formed his new command into an effective fighting force that would figure prominently in the final action at Appomattox.[25]

With the departure of Hancock and Burnside, General Warren became the army's senior corps commander. Assigned to the Fifth Corps in March 1864, Warren had an inconsistent record, and both Grant and Meade had considered replacing him. Second in his 1850 West Point class, Warren had served with distinction as a regimental and brigade commander and in early 1863 became the army's chief topographical engineer. Warren was moody, perhaps even clinically depressed at times, and increasingly prone to question orders and to criticize his superiors, once testifying to the Joint Committee that several fellow corps commanders were not up to their job. By the time the Appomattox campaign had begun, Warren's standing with Meade and Grant was shaky. Chronically oblivious to how others viewed him, Warren's status as the army's senior New Yorker may have kept him in place while the presidential election was undecided.[26]

Warren's dismissal came after his corps was assigned temporarily to serve under Sheridan for the advance that culminated in the battle of Five Forks on April 1, 1865. The two did not get along: Warren, the intellectual Easterner; Sheridan, the scrappy son of immigrants, Midwesterner, and poor student. Warren's advance to link up with Sheridan in an assault on Five Forks appeared slow, and Grant gave Sheridan the verbal authority to relieve Warren, which Sheridan did at the end of the fighting on April 1. Fifteen years later, a court of inquiry found that Warren's relief had been unjustified in findings released three months after Warren's death. Warren never understood that he had been sacked not so much for his actions at Five Forks—where he did as well as could be expected—but because Grant had lost confidence in his ability to lead a corps during the final push. "This was the first time in the history of the Army of the Potomac," noted Bruce Catton, "that a ranking commander had been summarily fired because his men had been put into action tardily and inexpertly. Sheridan had been cruel and unjust—and if that cruel and unjust insistence on driving, aggressive promptness had been the rule in this army from the beginning, the war probably would have been won two years earlier." With Grant in full command, 1865 was shaping up differently, and that someone as senior as Warren was so summarily dismissed sent a powerful signal to officers of all ranks about expectations for the coming campaign.[27]

It is difficult to fault Sheridan's choice for Warren's successor. Passing over the senior division commander, who was generally considered incompetent, Sheridan appointed Brig. Gen. Charles Griffin, the same officer Grant had suggested arresting after his outburst at the battle of the Wilderness. A graduate of the class of 1847, Griffin was serving as an instructor of artillery at West Point when the war began. He fought with distinction as a battery commander at First Bull Run and became a brigadier of infantry in 1862. Griffin's admiration of McClellan, his political positions, and his marriage to a Southern woman aroused the suspicions of the Joint Committee, and this kept him from being promoted. Griffin was sharp-tongued, hot-tempered, overbearing, and generally disliked, but he was the sort of hard-charger Grant needed in April 1865. That Griffin was elevated to corps leadership over the senior division commander and despite his unpopularity with his fellow officers indicated to the army that unrelenting aggressiveness was expected.[28]

Warren's dismissal made Horatio Wright the longest-serving corps commander in April 1865. An engineer graduating second in his West Point class of 1841, Wright had never led troops prior to the war. He spent the conflict's first two years in minor operations off the Eastern Seaboard and as a departmental commander in Ohio. In March 1863 the Senate, apparently pegging him as among those too cautious for top command, refused to approve his promotion to major general. Transferring to division command in the Army of the Potomac, Wright arrived just after the battle of Chancellorsville. He was promoted to command of the Sixth Corps (and finally earned the rank of major general) following John Sedgwick's death at the hands of a sniper at Spotsylvania, but his inexperience showed during his first months leading the corps. During the summer and fall of 1864, however, Wright emerged as a solid commander in the Shenandoah Valley campaign and would demonstrate a new aggressiveness during the Appomattox campaign.[29]

Few, if any, of Grant's principal subordinates contributed more to the success of the Appomattox campaign than did his protégé Philip H. Sheridan. In a war with many unlikely meteoric promotions, Sheridan stands out. An 1853 West Point graduate, Sheridan had been suspended for a year after a quarrel with one of his classmates. Graduating in the bottom third of his class, he compiled a surprisingly varied experience fighting Indians in the years before the war, earning a citation for gallantry from then general in chief Winfield Scott, but was only a newly promoted first lieutenant when the war began. After briefly leading a Michigan cavalry regiment, he rose quickly to command an infantry division in the Army of the Ohio and later in the Army of the Cumberland. Sheridan performed superbly at Stones River, fought better than most at Chickamauga, and led part of the force that carried Missionary Ridge at the climax of the battle of Chattanooga. That assault, and his aggressive pursuit of retreating Confederates, caught Grant's eye, and Sheridan became the most prominent general Grant transferred east in early 1864.[30]

Sheridan compiled a mixed, if not mediocre, record as commander of the Army of the Potomac's Cavalry Corps during the Overland campaign, and his aggressive swagger antagonized many in the Army of the Potomac, including Meade. When the two hot-tempered generals clashed over the use of cavalry during the opening stages of the battle of Spotsylvania, Grant sided with Sheridan, Meade's subordinate, a result at odds with the general in chief's reaction to Griffin's insubordinate outburst just days earlier. Reassigned in August to command the newly formed Army of the Shenandoah, Sheridan's September and October victories at Third Winchester, Fisher's Hill, and Cedar Creek helped ensure Lincoln's reelection.[31] In early March 1865, Sheridan's cavalry headed south from Winchester to cause more damage and to possibly join Sherman's advancing army in North Carolina. Finding his way south blocked by high water and burned bridges, Sheridan swung wide to the east and reached Petersburg a mere week before the battle of Five Forks.[32]

Sheridan's arrival completed the roster of senior commanders who would fight during those final weeks of the war. Comparing senior generals commanding in April 1865 with those in place a year earlier reflects the changed political landscape. The geographic distribution of the native states of army and corps commanders who marched into the Wilderness in 1864 differed dramatically from the concentrations seen in 1865. In early 1864, eight states were represented in the upper ranks: Illinois (Grant), Ohio (Sheridan, Quincy Gilmore), Pennsylvania (Meade, Hancock), Connecticut (Sedgwick, then Wright), Massachusetts (Butler), New York (Warren), Rhode Island (Burnside), and Vermont (William Farrar Smith). By April 1865, that arrangement had shrunk to five states: Illinois (Grant), Ohio (Sheridan, Griffin), Pennsylvania (Meade, Humphreys, Parke, Gibbon), Connecticut (Wright), and Maryland (Ord). Two of these, Ord and Gibbon, were born south of the Mason-Dixon Line; that, and their political views, had attracted

the suspicions of congressional Radicals and inhibited their advancement before the election. Promotions prior to 1865 for Humphreys and Gibbon, both
Pennsylvanians, were unlikely so long as their fellow Keystone Staters Meade
and Hancock occupied top commands. Burnside's retention as nominal head
of the Ninth Corps after the election probably reflected his general political support and his popularity in New England. Wright's promotion following Sedgwick's death at Spotsylvania was not a given—he was not even the
senior general in the corps—but being, like Sedgwick, a Connecticut native
might have influenced his promotion.[33]

Every postelection command change represented an improvement. All
were seasoned officers and West Point graduates, and collectively they were,
for the first time, at least equal to Lee's carefully constructed high command.
Measured by class standing at West Point, they were an accomplished group.
Meade, Humphreys, Parke, and Wright graduated close enough to the top of
their classes to be assigned to the engineers. Among the remaining corps and
army commanders, and finishing just below the engineers, were artillerists
Ord, Gibbon, and Griffin. Only Grant and Sheridan ranked so low as to be
assigned to the infantry upon graduation from West Point.[34]

Throughout the winter of 1864–65, Grant never ceased giving direction to commanders in other theaters, urging them to keep up the pressure.
In December, Grant focused on Maj. Gen. George H. Thomas at Nashville
as that city faced a threat from the Confederate Army of Tennessee. Once
Thomas's Army of the Cumberland was reinforced, Grant came close to sack-
ing Thomas because of his failure to promptly attack. Grant sent several increasingly pointed messages to Thomas, whose few and terse replies gave
little sign he understood his superior's concerns. But Thomas's meticulous
preparation paid off, as his army completely routed the Confederate army at
the battle of Nashville in mid-December. Grant's dispatches revealed a near-
obsession with getting Thomas to move aggressively to defeat and then finish off Lt. Gen. John Bell Hood's army. "Much is now expected," Grant wired
Thomas after his Nashville victory. Often unfairly critical, the telegrams reflected a lack of trust between the two commanders rooted in their previous
service together. It also illustrated the general in chief's reflexive aggressiveness and determination to ensure Confederate defeat.[35]

Much was likewise expected in the East. South of Petersburg, Warren
was leading a risky raid on the Weldon Railroad. Grant was trying to prod
Sheridan into launching a major raid on the Virginia Central Railroad, entreaties Sheridan resisted, but the general in chief did not compel his favored
subordinate to follow his instructions. The major concern in the weeks after

William W. Bergen

Lt. Gen. Ulysses S. Grant and his staff, City Point, March 1865.
(Library of Congress Prints and Photographs Division,
reproduction number LC-DIG-ppmsca-34086)

the election was the fate of Sherman's armies of Georgia and Tennessee. Grant had reluctantly assented to Sherman's plan to march from Atlanta to the sea, and, because it seemed risky, that advance began only after Lincoln's reelection. When his forces made it to Savannah seven weeks later, Sherman convinced Grant to allow him to advance overland through the Carolinas, a march he began in January 1865.[36]

Farther south, Grant ordered a devastating raid into central Alabama, pressed for the capture of the city of Mobile, and even sent a force to seize Tallahassee, Florida. After Fort Fisher fell, Grant transferred forces from Tennessee to capture Wilmington and other points on the North Carolina coast. Advancing toward the interior, these forces joined Sherman at Goldsboro, North Carolina, on March 23. In eastern Tennessee, Grant pressed Maj. Gen. George Stoneman into launching a major and successful raid in December. Grant ordered Stoneman out again in March 1865, and he wrecked more railroads and freed 1,400 U.S. prisoners of war at Salisbury, North Carolina. Not satisfied with the effective closure of Mobile, Grant rearranged forces to seize the city itself. By mid-March, however, Grant had grown dissatisfied with delays, writing Secretary of War Stanton that "I am very much dissatisfied with [the departmental commander, Maj. Gen.] Canby. He has been slow beyond excuse," adding that he wanted Sheridan to take his place as soon as he "could be spared."[37]

Still, for all his quiet confidence, Grant admitted in his memoirs that he was seldom as anxious as during those final weeks in Petersburg: "I felt that the situation of the Confederate army was such that they would try to make an escape at the earliest practicable moment, and I was afraid, every morning, that I would awake from my sleep to hear Lee had gone." Grant's anxiety stemmed, at least in part, from apprehensions about how swiftly the Army of the Potomac would react to Lee's withdrawal. His anxiety showed in a message sent to Parke in early February warning of the "possibility of an attack from the enemy at any time, and especially an attempt to break your center," and urging that "extra vigilance should be kept up both by pickets and the troops on the line. Let commanders understand that no time is to be lost awaiting orders if an attack is made in bringing all their reserves to the point of danger." As the roads began to dry in mid-March, Grant followed up with a directive to Meade: "From this time forward keep your command in condition to be moved in the very shortest possible notice, in case the enemy should evacuate or partially evacuate Petersburg."[38]

Throughout the winter of 1864–65, the Army of the Potomac and Army of the James held regular drills and inspections, rotated in and out of the

William W. Bergen

picket line, and marched to take part in largely inconclusive battles. In the late winter, brigades, divisions, and corps held formal reviews, so much a part of the Army of the Potomac's culture, albeit apparently not with the frequency and scale seen in earlier years. Aided by a reinvigorated command structure, the activity paid off during the Appomattox campaign.[39]

Still, much of the army was green and many of the new soldiers of poor quality. The 1865 version of the Army of the Potomac was much different from the one that had marched into the Wilderness in May 1864. Many veteran regiments had left the service in the spring, summer, and fall when their enlistments expired. A comparison of the Second Corps roster in May 1864 with one in March 1865 finds that of the seventy-nine regiments present at the Wilderness, more than a third had been mustered out over the next ten months and many of the rest had been consolidated or reduced to five or fewer companies. The famed 1st Minnesota, to cite an extreme example, had but two companies when it began the Appomattox campaign. Earlier in the war, the regiment would have been one of three or four that constituted a brigade; in their final campaign, the Minnesotans marched in a brigade made up of the remnants of ten regiments from seven states. Filling out the corps were various reinforcements, including several Heavy Artillery regiments fighting as infantry, new regiments, and some replacements joining veteran regiments.[40]

The Army of the James was in particular need of the rigor that Ord brought to it. Dubbed the "Army of Amateurs" by Edward G. Longacre, its foremost chronicler, the Army of the James suffered from a lack of professional leadership with only 30 percent of its generals being trained at West Point or having prewar military experience, less than half the percentage seen in the Army of the Potomac's leadership in 1864. To boost morale and corps identity, Ord and Gibbon established an army-wide inspection competition. Ord supported civilian relief agencies' efforts to promote the army's welfare, rigorously inspected the regimental camps himself, and devised a heavy work schedule to improve fortifications and communications. These efforts to boost soldiers' fitness would pay dividends during the footrace to Appomattox.[41]

Problems persisted, however, into 1865. Warren noted during a January engagement that "we are now getting to have an army of such poor soldiers that we have to lead them everywhere and even then they run away from us." During Warren's raid on the Weldon Railroad, one regiment reported that twenty new soldiers deserted to the Confederates. Some of these were later recaptured and hanged. Many regimental accounts testify to problems with bounty jumpers and deserters and witnessing their executions or other punishments. For all the triumphs seen in the final days of the war, problems persisted. On April 2, for example, one Sixth Corps brigade commander found that 60 percent of the men in the 61st Pennsylvania went missing as he was aligning his command for the predawn attack that finally broke Lee's lines around Petersburg. "As we started for the charge, [these 300 soldiers] disappeared and we never heard of them afterwards," the bitter colonel remembered.[42] Once Petersburg fell, Grant was clear in his orders to Meade: "Lee's Army is the objective point and to capture that is all we want." Grant was determined to get in front of, and not merely pursue, Lee. As if to emphasize this, Grant initially accompanied the Army of the James as it headed straight west, looking to prevent Lee from turning south. And it is striking that on the morning of April 9, in what was to become Grant's last operational decision made in the field, he left Meade's command to ride cross-country to join Sheridan's forces that had succeeded in getting in front of the Army of Northern Virginia.[43]

One last indication of how Grant made the Virginia forces his own can be seen in the campaign's final minutes. In the early morning mists of April 9, half of Lee's army started advancing west, hoping to break through the U.S. forces in their front to escape the gathering encirclement. Before them were cavalry commanded by Sheridan, Grant's protégé. Confederate generals recognized that if the horsemen were backed by infantry, surrender would be the only option. As the fighting started, and as the war took its last cruel casualties, the cavalry engaged the Confederate infantry, giving ground slowly, and then abruptly turned and trotted to the flanks. Behind them, on the distant ridge, blue-clad regiment after blue-clad regiment filed into line. Sheridan had bought the infantry time, but to get to that moment, several units had spent an incredible twenty of the last twenty-four hours marching. Ord's Army of the James led the way, hurrying with a determination and energy never seen with his predecessor, Benjamin Butler. "Your legs have done it, my men," a jubilant Ord shouted as he rode up and down his line. Helping Ord was his top subordinate, the hard-driving North Carolinian John Gibbon. Next on the scene was the Army of the Potomac's Fifth Corps under Charles Griffin, whose violent criticism of others so shocked Grant at the battle of the Wilderness.[44]

These generals' determination and cooperation without regard to rank—Ord was senior to Sheridan yet readily acceded to the cavalry commander's urgent summons—demonstrates they knew what their commander expected. All three owed their recent elevation to a general in chief largely free of political constraints. So freed, Grant sought out no-nonsense, tough, hard-charging regulars, and he found those qualities in Ord, Gibbon, and Griffin and in the man who bought them time and spurred them on, Sheridan. But the analysis does not stop there. Horatio Wright, the prudent engineer who had never commanded troops before the Civil War, displayed an aggressiveness that demonstrated he had learned from Sheridan and Grant. Andrew Humphreys had not commanded a corps before and had not led infantry since Gettysburg, yet his zeal and competence in the final campaign was matched by a physical energy that could not have been sustained by the tired and ailing Hancock. Though the Ninth Corps was not assigned a major role in the race to Appomattox, John Parke had reacted promptly and effectively to the seal the breakthrough at Fort Stedman. That victory may seem unremarkable, but Ambrose Burnside may well have botched the counterattack.

Accounts of the Appomattox campaign often emphasize the Army of Northern Virginia's low morale, the paucity of its supplies, and the poor physical condition of the Confederate soldiers to explain its surrender. Other scholars point to the approach of Sherman's forces, the limited strategic alternatives available to Lee, and the certainty of the Confederacy's inevitable defeat. While true, what too often goes unacknowledged is that those weaknesses and the overall strategic picture were due to Grant's determination to pressure the Confederacy from all points. It was his plan and subsequent orders that resulted in the fall of Atlanta and Sherman's subsequent marches through Georgia and the Carolinas, the loss of Virginia's Shenandoah Valley as a source of food and fodder, the pinning of Lee's forces to the Richmond and Petersburg defenses, the closing of the ports of Wilmington and Mobile, and, ultimately, Lincoln's reelection. The Army of Northern Virginia's poor morale and physical condition as well as Lee's limited options did not reflect bad fortune — they were the results of Grant's own actions. Nonetheless, the Confederate forces that left the defensive ring stretching from Richmond to the west of Petersburg remained formidable. Numbering some 56,000 effectives in February, Confederate forces faced more than twice their number in the opposite trenches. Once the lines were broken, however, U.S. forces were steadily reduced by garrison and railroad rebuilding duty — about 80,000 men left the trenches to chase after Lee — and the Union armies were waging a pursuit deep in enemy territory and ranging ever farther from their base. While Confederate defeat may seem inevitable today, the Army of Northern Virginia was operating in its own territory and had beaten longer odds in the past. What remains most striking, and was not inevitable, was how quickly and effectively Lee's entire command was forced to surrender.[45]

Bringing Lee's army to bay so swiftly and decisively reflected Grant's preferred method of warfare, an approach he once summarized in characteristically staccato sentences: "Find out where our enemy is. Get at him as soon as you can. Strike at him as hard as you can and as often as you can, and keep moving on." After three years of inconclusive combat, Grant had destroyed the Confederacy's will to resist in just eleven months. Lee's army was the third one he had forced to surrender, a feat equaled by few commanders in all recorded history. Yet key to Grant's final triumph was the 1864 election results, which gave Grant more power as general in chief. The rank and file seemed to understand what was stake in that election: a majority of the soldiers rejected the beloved founder of the Army of the Potomac, George McClellan, in favor of Abraham Lincoln. That electoral victory marked the end of the McClellan influence in the army and allowed Grant to appoint his top lieutenants with little regard to political considerations. Together they changed the culture of the Army of the Potomac.[46]

Grant never let up. It was Grant who, even after the election, marshaled the forces that permitted Thomas to destroy the only other sizable army of the Confederacy. It was Grant who, when the first attack on Fort Fisher failed, replaced the commander, tried again, and triumphed, closing the last sizable port in the South. It was Grant who, with the Confederacy clearly back on its heels in early 1865, did not let up, launching raids into the Deep South and into western Virginia and North Carolina.

In short, Grant's drive, calm determination, strategic vision, and restless aggression produced the stillness of Appomattox. Grant's close friend and West Point classmate Rufus Ingalls, brigadier general and army quartermaster, may have put it best. The way Grant broke horses at the Academy, Ingalls recalled, was "not by punishing the animal he had taken in hand, but by patience and tact, and his skill in making the creature know what he wanted to have it do." In much the same way, Grant quietly, but firmly and surely, shaped and directed the U.S. armies into the forces that, together, brought the war to an end.[47]

NOTES

1. Theodore Lyman, *Meade's Headquarters, 1863–1865: Letters of Colonel Theodore Lyman from the Wilderness to Appomattox*, ed. George R. Agassiz (Boston: Atlantic Monthly Press, 1922), 81; Theodore Lyman, *Meade's Army: The Private Notebooks of Lt. Col. Theodore Lyman*, ed. David W. Lowe (Kent, Ohio: Kent State University Press, 2007), 107.

2. Michael Morgan, "From City Point to Appomattox with General Grant," *Journal*

of Military Science Institution 149 (September–October 1907): 230, 234–35. For accounts of Grant's loquaciousness with colleagues and his staff and of his sense of humor, see Horace Porter, *Campaigning with Grant* (New York: Century, 1906), 186, 196, 212–13, 229, 232–33, 250–51, 329–31, 339–40, 354–57; Lyman, *Meade's Army*, 117, 126; and Joseph P. Farley, *Three Rivers: The James, the Potomac, the Hudson* (New York: Neale, 1910), 88.

3. Noah Andre Trudeau, *The Last Citadel: Petersburg, Virginia, June 1864–April 1865* (Boston: Little, Brown, 1991), 418; William Marvel, *Lee's Last Retreat: The Flight to Appomattox* (Chapel Hill: University of North Carolina Press, 2002), 7, 37, 41–43, 60. For a concise summary of the effect of military operations on the U.S. presidential election, see Allan Nevins, *The War for the Union, Volume 4: The Organized War to Victory, 1864–65* (New York: Charles Scribner's Sons, 1971), 117–43; and Brooks D. Simpson, "Facilitating Defeat: The Union High Command and the Collapse of the Confederacy," in *The Collapse of the Confederacy*, ed. Mark Grimsley and Brooks D. Simpson (Lincoln: University of Nebraska Press, 2001), 85, 91–92.

4. Gordon C. Rhea, *The Battle of the Wilderness, May 6, 1864* (Baton Rouge: Louisiana State University Press, 1994), 10–12, 403; Edward Porter Alexander, *Fighting for the Confederacy: The Personal Recollections of General Edward Porter Alexander*, ed. Gary W. Gallagher (Chapel Hill: University of North Carolina Press, 1989), 91–92, 111, 222, 265; Clifford Dowdey, *Lee's Last Campaign: The Story of Lee and His Men against Grant—1864* (Lincoln: University of Nebraska Press, 1993), 43–46; George A. Bruce, "Lee and the Strategy of the Civil War," in *Lee the Soldier*, ed. Gary W. Gallagher (Lincoln: University of Nebraska Press, 1996), 117; Douglas Southall Freeman, *R. E. Lee: A Biography*, 4 vols. (New York: Charles Scribner's Sons, 1934–35), 4:74; Emory M. Thomas, *Robert E. Lee: A Biography* (New York: W. W. Norton, 1995), 140–41, 226.

5. *The Papers of Ulysses S. Grant*, ed. John Y. Simon and others, 32 vols. to date (Carbondale: Southern Illinois University Press, 1967–) 9:145–49, 217–19 (hereafter cited as *PUSG*); Bruce Catton, *Grant Takes Command* (Boston: Little, Brown, 1968), 131. In the letter to Washburne, Grant credits Assistant Secretary of War Charles S. Dana and General-in-Chief Henry W. Halleck with blocking his transfer. *PUSG*, 10:132.

6. Wayne Hsieh, *West Pointers and the Civil War: The Old Army in War and Peace* (Chapel Hill: University of North Carolina Press, 2009), 87; James R. Arnold, *The Armies of U. S. Grant* (London: Arms and Armour, 1995), 157–58, 170–71; Catton, *Grant Takes Command*, 145–49, 165–66; Jeffery D. Wert, *The Sword of Lincoln: The Army of the Potomac* (New York: Simon & Schuster, 2005), 414–15; Stephen R. Taaffe, *Commanding the Army of the Potomac* (Lawrence: University of Kansas Press, 2006), 58–59; Bruce Catton, *Mr. Lincoln's Army* (Garden City, N.J.: Doubleday, 1953), 123, 222, 324–26; Timothy Orr, "'All Manner of Schemes and Rascalities': The Politics of Promotion in the Union Army," in *This Distracted and Anarchical People: New Answers for Old Questions about the Civil War–Era North*, ed. Andrew J. Slap and Michael Thomas Smith (New York: Fordham University Press, 2013), 81–103; Thomas J. Goss, *The War within the Union High Command: Politics and Generalship in the Civil War* (Lawrence: University of Kansas Press, 2003), 117, 154, 168; Michael C. C. Adams, *Fighting for Defeat: Union Military Failure in the East, 1861–65* (Lincoln: University of Nebraska Press, 1992), 100–103; Andrew J. Polsky, "'Mr. Lincoln's Army' Revisited: Partisanship, Institutional Position, and Union Army Command, 1861–1865," *Studies in American Political Development* 16 (Fall 2002): 176–207;

John Gibbon, *Personal Recollections of the Civil War* (New York: G. P. Putnam's Sons, 1928), 26, 107–9, 185–208.

7. Lyman, *Meade's Army*, 100–101; Catton, *Grant Takes Command*, 157, 159–60, 341; Ethan S. Rafuse, "'Wherever Lee Goes . . .': George G. Meade," in *Grant's Lieutenants: From Chattanooga to Appomattox*, ed. Steven E. Woodworth (Lawrence: University of Kansas Press, 2008), 49, 221–22n5; A. Wilson Greene, "Morale, Maneuver, and Mud: The Army of the Potomac, December 16, 1862–January 26, 1863," in *The Fredericksburg Campaign: Decision on the Rappahannock*, ed. Gary W. Gallagher (Chapel Hill: University of North Carolina Press, 2008), 183–89, 207–17; Stephen W. Sears, *Chancellorsville* (New York: Houghton Mifflin, 1996), 1–25; Taaffe, *Commanding the Army of the Potomac*, 73–77, 101–7, 134–38; Goss, *War within the Union High Command*, 130–35; George Meade, *The Life and Letters of George Gordon Meade, Major-General United States Army* (New York: Charles Scribner's Sons, 1913), 2:168–70, 176; Bruce Catton, *The American Heritage Picture History of the Civil War*, (New York: American Heritage, 1960), 2:443.

8. Adam Badeau, *Military History of Ulysses S. Grant*, vol. 2 (New York: D. Appleton, 1881), 29–32; 39–41; *PUSG*, 10:xxi–xxiv.

9. Lyman, *Meade's Headquarters*, 134; Lyman, *Meade's Army*, 91.

10. *Personal Memoirs of U. S. Grant* (1885–86, repr.; New York: Century, 1917), 2:53–63, 72, 74–76, 106, 142; Mark Grimsley, *And Keep Moving On: The Virginia Campaign, May–June 1864* (Lincoln: University of Nebraska Press, 2002), 109–10, 118–20, 122–29; David Work, *Lincoln's Political Generals* (Urbana: University of Illinois Press), 222.

11. John C. Waugh, *Reelecting Lincoln: The Battle for the 1864 Presidency* (New York: Crown, 2001), 296–98; David Herbert Donald, *Lincoln* (New York: Simon and Schuster, 1995), 553; David E. Long, *The Jewel of Liberty: Abraham Lincoln's Re-election and the End of Slavery* (New York: Da Capo, 1997), 208–10, 214.

12. Rafuse, "'Wherever Lee Goes . . . ,'" 55–56; Freeman Cleaves, *Meade of Gettysburg* (Norman: University of Oklahoma Press, 1960), 113–14; Warren W. Hassler Jr., *Commanders of the Army of the Potomac* (Baton Rouge: Louisiana State University Press, 1962), 160–63; Meade, *Life and Letters*, 2:168–83.

13. Bill Hyde, *The Union Generals Speak: The Meade Hearings on the Battle of Gettysburg* (Baton Rouge: Louisiana State University Press, 2003), 161–81; Rafuse, "'Wherever Lee Goes . . . ,'" 54; Gibbon, *Personal Recollections*, 185–208.

14. Cleaves, *Meade of Gettysburg*, 285–86, 313–30; Taaffe, *Commanding the Army of the Potomac*, 185–86; Rafuse, "'Wherever Lee Goes . . . ,'" 70–72; Tom Huntington, *Searching for George Gordon Meade: The Forgotten Victor of Gettysburg* (Mechanicsburg, Pa.: Stackpole Books, 2013), 5, 121, 314, 319–20; Marsena R. Patrick, *Inside Lincoln's Army: The Diary of Marsena Rudolph Patrick, Provost Marshal General, Army of the Potomac*, ed. David S. Sparks (New York: Thomas Yoseloff, 1964), 409–10; Meade, *Life and Letters*, 2:218–21.

15. Grimsley, *And Keep Moving On*, 229–30, italics in original; Taaffe, *Commanding the Army of the Potomac*, 205.

16. *PUSG*, 10:16–17, 35–36, 88; Ezra J. Warner, *Generals in Blue: Lives of the Union Commanders* (Baton Rouge: Louisiana State University Press, 1964), 5, 38, 44–45, 47–48, 54, 89, 92–93, 130–31, 154–55, 164, 231–32, 250, 268, 276, 281, 301, 319–20, 326, 331, 342, 345–

56, 357, 358–59, 370–71, 406, 418–19, 427–28, 448, 467–68, 469, 487, 498–99, 518–19, 522–23, 525–27, 530, 540–41, 545–46, 638; Mark Mayo Boatner and Allen C. Northrop, *The Civil War Dictionary* (New York: D. McKay, 1959), 10, 71, 82, 90, 97–98, 131, 173, 245, 281–82, 319, 413, 462, 472, 474, 485, 525, 534, 543, 552, 584, 616, 617, 653, 702, 711, 727, 761, 791, 816, 831, 856, 881, 891, 899; Steward Sifakis, *Who Was Who in the Union* (New York: Facts on File, 1988), 87, 119, 137, 226, 233, 251, 277–78, 310, 336–37, 383, 398, 408, 426, 427, 443. Grant was apprehensive about leaving Petersburg during the siege, as the second-ranking general in Petersburg was Butler. However, Butler was temporarily in command in New York in the days before and after the election. John H. Eicher and David J. Eicher, *Civil War High Commands* (Stanford: Stanford University Press, 2001, 157.

17. *PUSG*, 10:24, 29, 25–36, 49; Stephen D. Engle, *Yankee Dutchman: The Life of Franz Siegel* (Fayetteville: University of Arkansas Press, 1993), 205–8. For a full examination of the Grant-McClernand relationship, see Terrence J. Minschel, "Fighting Politician: John A. McClernand," in *Grant's Lieutenants: From Cairo to Vicksburg*, ed. Steven E. Woodworth (Lawrence: University Press of Kansas, 2001), 129–50. For a complete examination of the Grant-Rosecrans relationship, see Lesley J. Gordon, "'I Could Not Make Him Do as I Wished': The Failed Relationship of William S. Rosecrans and Grant," in *Grant's Lieutenants: From Cairo to Vicksburg*, ed. Steven E. Woodworth (Lawrence: University Press of Kansas, 2001), 109–27; and Work, *Lincoln's Political Generals*, 216.

18. James G. Hollandsworth Jr., *Pretense of Glory: The Life of General Nathaniel P. Banks* (Baton Rouge: Louisiana State University Press, 1998), 206; Warner, *Generals in Blue*, 67–68; Roy P. Basler, ed., *The Collected Works of Abraham Lincoln* (New Brunswick, N.J.: Rutgers University Press, 1953), 8:131; Peter Cousins, *General John Pope: A Life for the Nation* (Urbana: University of Illinois, 2000), 241–43; *PUSG*, 10:28, 35–36, 78, 192–93. The only City Point staff officer who seemed to notice Pope's presence was Brig. Gen. Marsena R. Patrick, who did not want to cross paths with his former commander. Patrick, *Inside Lincoln's Army*, 445.

19. Albert D. Richardson, *A Personal History of Ulysses S. Grant* (Hartford, Conn.: American Publishing, 1868), 388–89; Brooks D. Simpson, *Ulysses S. Grant: Triumph over Adversity, 1822–1865* (New York: Houghton Mifflin, 2000), 353, 359, 400–401, 408–9, 414; *PUSG*, 10:437–40; Work, *Lincoln's Political Generals*, 222; Waugh, *Reelecting Lincoln*, 270–72; Daniel Ammen, *The Old Navy and the New* (Philadelphia: Lippincott, 1891), 1:533.

20. William B. Feiss, "Grant's Relief Man: Edward O. C. Ord," in *Grant's Lieutenants: From Chattanooga to Appomattox*, ed. Steven E. Woodworth (Lawrence: University of Kansas Press, 2008), 173, 186–194; Bernard Cresap, *Appomattox Commander: The Story of General E. O. C. Ord* (San Diego: A. S. Barnes, 1981), 119; Edward G. Longacre, *Army of Amateurs: General Benjamin F. Butler and the Army of the James, 1863–1865* (Mechanicsburg, Pa.: Stackpole Books, 1997), 269–77; Benjamin F. Butler, *Private and Official Correspondence of Gen. Benjamin F. Butler* (Norwood, Mass.: privately printed, 1917), 5:600–601; *PUSG*, 14:209–10.

21. William Marvel, *Burnside* (Chapel Hill: University of North Carolina Press, 1991), 99, 111, 114, 152, 159, 202, 264, 337, 377, 388, 396, 412, 455n7, 472,; Richard Slotkin, *No Quarter: The Battle of the Crater* (New York: Random House, 2009), 26–29, 322; Jacob D. Cox, *Military Reminiscences of the Civil War* (New York: Charles Scribner's

Sons, 1990), 1:280, 389–90; William B. Styple, *Writing and Fighting the Civil War: Soldier Correspondence to the "New York Sunday Mercury"* (Kearny, N.J.: Belle Grove, 2000), 323; Gibbon, *Personal Recollections*, 252–53; *PUSG*, 14:18, 79, 282, 290.

22. George W. Cullum, *Biographical Register of the Graduates of the U.S. Military Academy at West Point, New York, from Its Establishment* (New York: D. Van Nostrand, 1868), 2:370–71; Patrick, *Inside Lincoln's Army*, 414; Lyman, *Meade's Headquarters*, 212, 246–47; *PUSG*, 14:79, 89, 118; Frederick Steele to Joseph Rowe Smith, March 13, 1865, Gilder-Lehrman Institute of American History, New York, N.Y., http://www.gilder lehrman.org/collections/5f5ddfda-28b5-4d46-93f1-160912332360 (retrieved October 22, 2015); Lyman, *Meade's Army*, 292, 297; Taaffe, *Commanding the Army of the Potomac*, 191–92.

23. Glenn Tucker, *Hancock the Superb* (Indianapolis: Bobbs-Merrill, 1960), 253–61; David M. Jordan, *Winfield Scott Hancock: A Soldier's Life* (Bloomington: Indiana University Press, 1988), 159–64, 169–73; Hampton Newsom, *Richmond Must Fall: The Richmond-Petersburg Campaign, October 1864* (Kent, Ohio: Kent State University Press, 2013), 299; Brooks D. Simpson, "Winfield Scott and the Overland Campaign," in *Corps Commanders in Blue: Union Major Generals in the Civil War*, ed. Ethan S. Rafuse (Baton Rouge: Louisiana State University Press, 2014), 261–63, 276–78; Lawrence A. Kreiser Jr., *Defeating Lee: A History of the Second Corps, Army of the Potomac* (Bloomington: Indiana University Press, 2011), 207–15; Henry H. Humphreys, *Andrew Atkinson Humphreys: A Biography* (Philadelphia: John C. Winston, 1924), 256–59; Thomas L. Livermore, *Days and Events, 1861–1866* (New York: Houghton Mifflin, 1920), 414; Francis A. Walker, *History of the Second Corps in the Army of the Potomac* (New York: Charles Scribner's Sons, 1886), 559.

24. Lyman, *Meade's Army*, 99, 101, 159, 298, 350, 363; U.S. War Department, *The War of the Rebellion: A Compilation of the Official Records of the Union and Confederate Armies*, 127 vols., index, and atlas (Washington, D.C.: Government Printing Office, 1880–1901), ser. 1, 46 (3): 597–98, 1286 (hereafter cited as *OR*; all references are to ser. 1). Why Hays was assigned to command Gibbon's former division in February 1865 is unknown, as he had compiled a spotty record and may have had a drinking problem. Hays was among the few senior officers not awarded brevets after the war, and he never advanced beyond his permanent U.S. Army rank of major. Warner, *Generals in Blue*, 2242–45; *OR* 27 (1): 96–97; Livermore, *Days and Events*, 285.

25. Gibbon, *Personal Recollections*, 26, 209–10, 262; Taaffe, *Commanding the Army of the Potomac*, 124–35, 193–94, 198–99; Lyman, *Meade's Headquarters*, 107; Lyman, *Meade's Army*, 27, 99, 101, 298, 350, 360–66; George B. McClellan, *The Civil War Papers of George B. McClellan: Selected Correspondence, 1860–1865*, ed. Stephen W. Sears (New York: Ticknor and Fields, 1989), 600–601, 613; Hyde, *Union Generals Speak*, 276–77; Meade, *Life and Letters*, 2:153, 209, 256.

26. David M. Jordan, *"Happiness Is Not My Companion": The Life of General G. K. Warren* (Bloomington: Indiana University Press, 2001), 119, 168–69, 211, 225, 237, 315–18; Charles S. Wainwright, *A Diary of Battle: The Personal Journals of Colonel Charles S. Wainwright, 1861–1865*, ed. Allan Nevins (New York: Da Capo, 1998), 378, 387, 404–5, 508–9, 513–14.

27. Donald R. Jermann, *Union General Gouverneur Warren: Hero at Little Round Top*,

Disgrace at Five Forks (Jefferson, N.C.: McFarland, 2015), 41, 44; Simpson, *Ulysses S. Grant*, 423–24; Cleaves, *Meade of Gettysburg*, 314–16; *OR* 36 (2): 654; Jordan, *"Happiness Is Not My Companion,"* 213–14, 225, 232–34; Wainwright, *Diary of Battle*, 513–14; Wert, *Sword of Lincoln*, 401–2; Stephen W. Sears, *Controversies and Commanders: Dispatches from the Army of the Potomac* (Boston: Houghton Mifflin, 1999), 255–82; Huntington, *Searching for George Gordon Meade*, 305; Bruce Catton, "Sheridan at Five Forks," *Journal of Southern History* 21 (1955): 305–15; Bruce Catton, *A Stillness at Appomattox* (Garden City, N.Y.: Doubleday, 1953), 358.

28. Richard Wagner, *For Honor, Flag, and Family: Civil War Major General Samuel W. Crawford, 1827–1892* (Shippensburg, Pa.: White Mane Books, 2005), 236; Taaffe, *Commanding the Army of the Potomac*, 204; Wainwright, *Diary of Battle*, 167, 285, 348; Eric J. Wittenberg, *Little Phil: A Reassessment of the Civil War Leadership of General Philip H. Sheridan* (Dulles, Va.: Brassey's, 2002), 121–29. In selecting Griffin, Sheridan disregarded seniority, usually a key factor in selecting commanders. One firsthand account has Sheridan inquiring of Fifth Corps staff who the senior division commander was and "pooh-poohing" the idea that Brig. Gen. Samuel Crawford would be selected. That Crawford was passed over and that the snub did not engender much comment or even protest from him suggest that his seniority was insufficient to overcome his deficiencies. These deficiencies included poor health and unpopularity with his fellow officers. His lack of a West Point education might have also played a role. Given Sheridan's lack of familiarity with the Fifth Corps, Griffin's promotion could reflect advice he received from headquarters. Wainwright, *Diary of Battle*, 277, 514, 518; Taaffe, *Commanding the Army of the Potomac*, 203; Lyman, *Meade's Army*, 283, 288, 339.

29. William W. Bergen, "The Other Hero of Cedar Creek: The 'Not Specially Ambitious' Horatio G. Wright," in *The Shenandoah Valley Campaign of 1864*, ed. Gary W. Gallagher (Chapel Hill: University of North Carolina Press, 2006), 88–89, 91–96, 98–99, 118–19; Taaffe, *Commanding the Army of the Potomac*, 159–60.

30. Philip H. Sheridan, *Personal Memoirs of P. H. Sheridan, General, United States Army* (1888; repr., New York: Da Capo Press, 1992), 5–7, 100–103; Roy Morris Jr., *Sheridan: The Life and Wars of General Phil Sheridan* (New York: Crown, 1992), 15–23, 27–40, 85–86, 106–12, 136, 144–48; Simpson, *Ulysses S. Grant*, 33–34, 40, 46.

31. Wittenberg, *Little Phil*, 23–25, 50–53, 86, 93–98; Wert, *Sword of Lincoln*, 330, 344; Porter, *Campaigning with Grant*, 84; Waugh, *Reelecting Lincoln*, 297–98.

32. Trudeau, *Last Citadel*, 355–56.

33. Warner, *Generals in Blue*, 171, 176, 183, 190, 202, 240, 316, 430, 437, 462, 541, 575; Taaffe, *Commanding the Army of the Potomac*, 208–18; Bergen, "Other Hero of Cedar Creek," 98–99. Meade was born in Spain but always called Philadelphia home. Sheridan was born in Albany, New York, or in Killinkere, Ireland, but moved to Ohio as an infant (Wittenberg, *Little Phil*, 142–44). Gibbon, though born in Pennsylvania, spent most of his youth in North Carolina and was appointed to the U.S. Military Academy from there. At the time of the Civil War, Gibbon's personal residence was in Philadelphia.

34. Warner, *Generals in Blue*; Eicher and Eicher, *Civil War High Commands*, 253, 264, 269, 309, 384, 409, 559, 588.

35. Simpson, *Ulysses S. Grant*, 393–98; Steven E. Woodworth, "'Old Slow Trot': George H. Thomas," in *Grant's Lieutenants: From Chattanooga to Appomattox*, ed.

Steven E. Woodworth (Lawrence: University of Kansas Press, 2008), 39–43; Catton, *Grant Takes Command*, 395–401.

36. Simpson, *Ulysses S. Grant*, 398–400, 402–3, 408, 409; *PUSG*, 14:19; Morris, *Sheridan*, 231–35; Longacre, *Army of Amateurs*, 245–48.

37. Noah Andre Trudeau, *Out of the Storm: The End of the Civil War, April–June 1865* (Baton Rouge: Louisiana State University Press, 1994), 4–8; *PUSG*, 14:156, 159, 201–2; Grant, *Personal Memoirs*, 2:277–81; Simpson, *Ulysses S. Grant*, 402–3; Trudeau, *Last Citadel*, 266–85; Chris J. Hartley, *Stoneman's Raid, 1865* (Winston-Salem, N.C.: John F. Blair, 2010), 3–4, 16–20, 67–269.

38. Grant, *Personal Memoirs*, 2:291; *PUSG*, 14:19, 159.

39. Elisha Hunt Rhodes, *All for the Union: The Civil War Diary and Letters of Elisha Hunt Rhodes*, ed. Robert Hunt Rhodes (New York: Random House, 1985), 193, 194, 213; Irvin G. Myers, *We Might as Well Die Here: The 53rd Pennsylvania Veteran Volunteer Infantry* (Shippensburg, Pa.: White Mane Books, 2004), 238, 246; J. H. Gilson, *Concise History of the One Hundred and Twenty-Sixth Regiment, Ohio Volunteer Infantry* (Salem, Ohio: Walton, Steam Job and Label Printer, 1883), 108; Robert S. Westbrook, *History of the 49th Pennsylvania Volunteers* (Altoona, Pa.: Altoona Times Print, 1897), 228, 229, 230, 231, 233, 234, 235; Mark Olcott with David Lear, *The Civil War Letters of Lewis Bissell: A Curriculum* (Washington, D.C.: Field School Educational Foundation Press, 1981), 352.

40. *OR* 36 (1): 107–8, 46 (1): 564–66; Frederick H. Dyer, *A Compendium of the War of the Rebellion* (Dayton, Ohio: Broadfoot and Morningside Press, 1994), 1017, 1219–20, 1220, 1253, 1263, 1432, 1433, 1437, 1499–1500, 1585, 1597, 1612; Wert, *Sword of Lincoln*, 380; Richard Moe, *The Last Full Measure: The Life and Death of the First Minnesota Volunteers* (New York: Henry Holt, 1993), 303–5.

41. Longacre, *Army of Amateurs*, xi, 270–71, 273, 274–75, 282–83.

42. Rhodes, *All for the Union*, 198–99; Wert, *Sword of Lincoln*, 396; Styple, *Writing and Fighting the Civil War*, 310–12; Thomas W. Hyde, *Following the Greek Cross; or, Memories of the Sixth Army Corps* (New York: Houghton, Mifflin, 1894), 254–55; Olcott with Lear, *Civil War Letters of Lewis Bissell*, 432.

43. Catton, *Grant Takes Command*, 461.

44. Sheridan, *Personal Memoirs*, 390–92; Elizabeth R. Varon, *Appomattox: Victory, Defeat, and Freedom at the End of the Civil War* (New York: Oxford University Press, 2013), 40–44; Longacre, *Army of Amateurs*, 309.

45. Marvel, *Lee's Last Retreat*, ix, 5–6, 7, 37, 41–42, 60, 201–6; Taaffe, *Commanding the Army of the Potomac*, 205.

46. Taaffe, *Commanding the Army of the Potomac*, 206–7; J. F. C. Fuller, *Grant and Lee: A Study in Personality and Generalship* (Bloomington: Indiana University Press, 1957), 78.

47. Porter, *Campaigning with Grant*, 341.

2

We Can Keep All the Yankees Back That They Can Send

*Morale among Hood's Texas Brigade's Soldiers
and Their Families, 1864–1865*

Susannah J. Ural

James Tiner was a thirty-five-year-old farmer in Concord, Texas, in March 1862 when he accepted a bounty to join Company F of the 1st Texas Infantry. Unlike many younger, unmarried men inspired by patriotism, regional pride, or a desire for adventure to join the Confederate ranks when the war began a year earlier—often summarized as the *rage militaire*—Tiner had stayed home with his wife, Margaret, a thirty-eight-year-old native of Indiana. They owned no land and had only $200 to their names in 1860. With four children under the age of seven and a small farm, the enlistment bounty that Tiner received along with the promise of regular pay was likely a key motivator for his service. He gathered a few belongings and made the thousand-mile journey to Virginia, leaving Margaret to manage their farm and their young children. Tiner was short, coming to most men's shoulders when he stood in the ranks, but the farmer made a good soldier. Or a lucky one. Tiner survived the battles of Gaines's Mill, Second Manassas, and Antietam in 1862 without a wound—which was nothing short of miraculous in a regiment that suffered 83 percent casualties at Antietam—but his luck faltered when Tiner fell wounded at Gettysburg and again at Chickamauga in 1863. He was back in the ranks by January 1864, though, and ready to fight when the campaign season opened that May.[1]

Charles Kingsley also served in the 1st Texas, though in Company L. He was twenty-three years old when he enlisted in 1861, and he received his first combat wound in Miller's cornfield at Antietam in September 1862. He was the third of eight men in the 1st Texas who rushed forward to pick up the colors when they fell that bloody fall day in Maryland. Captured, Kingsley returned to the ranks after he was exchanged in November 1862. Wounded again at Chickamauga in September 1863 after being promoted to first sergeant, Kingsley, like Tiner, rejoined the 1st Texas by January 1864.[2]

Fifth Sgt. Robert Hasson followed a similar pattern as well. Enlisting as a private in Company G of the 4th Texas Infantry, the twenty-eight-year-old Hasson joined the Grimes County Greys in 1861 and slowly climbed his way up the ranks. Federal forces captured Hasson at Cashtown, Pennsylvania, just days after the Texas Brigade's fight at the battle of Gettysburg, and they sent him to the prison at Point Lookout, Maryland, in August 1863. After being exchanged, Hasson rejoined the 4th Texas, like Kingsley and Tiner, in time for the 1864 campaign season. Greenberry McDonald, a private in Company H of the 3rd Arkansas Infantry, had also returned from his wound and capture at Gettysburg, as had Jess Anderson of the 5th Texas. Wounded at Second Manassas and Gettysburg and captured at the latter, Anderson returned to Company C ready for a fresh fight in 1864.[3]

These returning wounded or captured soldiers of Hood's Texas Brigade reflected the hard-fighting reputation their unit had earned by 1864. The men were determined—despite wounds, imprisonment, fracturing supply lines, threats of consolidation, and waning opportunities for furloughs home—to enter the last campaign to secure their independence as they had entered their first campaign: as Hood's Texas Brigade.[4] The men's futures, though, underscore just how devastating 1864's losses would be for the Confederacy. This essay offers a close study of the Texas Brigade—one of the elite units of the war—in the last year of fighting in order to examine the source and significance of this unit's high morale as well as the key role played by junior officers who maintained unit cohesion, bolstered the men's confidence, and adapted to supply challenges at the company and regimental level. The experiences of the Texas Brigade in 1864 and 1865 highlight the power of unit pride and troops' loyalty to the South's most successful commander, Robert E. Lee, and his Army of Northern Virginia. That loyalty sustained the men's and their families' faith in their nation, even as the Confederacy crumbled around them.

In 1864, the Texas Brigade comprised the 1st, 4th, and 5th Texas as well as the 3rd Arkansas Infantry Regiments, and their commanders and peers recognized them as making up one of the best units in the Army of Northern Virginia. In 1862, Confederate major general Thomas Jonathan "Stonewall" Jackson had praised the Texans who helped win the day at the battle of Gaines's Mill, observing that the men "who carried this position were soldiers indeed!" Gen. Robert E. Lee had agreed. After the victory at Gaines's Mill, Confederate postmaster general John Reagan explained, "On different occasions General Lee urged me to aid him in getting a division of Texans for his command, remarking that with such a force he would engage to break any line of battle on earth in an open field."[5] Reagan's loyalty to Texas may have shaped that postwar claim, but after the Texas Brigade's key role in the Confederate victory at Second Manassas and the brigade's sacrifice in Miller's cornfield at Antietam, Lee repeated the request that "every possible exertion" be made in raising more Texas regiments. "I need them much—I rely upon those we have in all tight places and fear I have to call upon them too often—They have fought grandly, nobly, and we must have more of them. . . . With a few more such regiments as those which Hood now has, as an example of daring and bravery I could feel much more confident of the results of the campaign."[6] Lee cheered when the Texas Brigade arrived on the field during the battle of the Wilderness in May 1864 and, once again, helped to secure the Confederate line and push the Federals back. "Texans always move them," Lee observed, as he sent the brigade forward. Though they suffered terrible losses, that moment in the Wilderness solidified Lee's belief that he could rely on the Texas Brigade in any moment of need.[7]

Just before that battle, which marked the opening of the 1864 campaign season in the East, hundreds of men like Tiner, Hasson, and Kingsley had returned to the brigade largely recovered from earlier wounds. Their success in rejoining the unit was essential, because when Brig. Gen. John Gregg arrived to take command of the brigade on March 7, there were only 500 men present for duty.[8] Desertion, never a serious problem for the unit that was as famous for its highly motivated men as for its battlefield successes, had risen to surprising levels during the previous winter. Part of that was caused by a lack of leadership, and First Corps commander Lt. Gen. James Longstreet responded by charging Texas Brigade commander Brig. Gen. Jerome B. Robertson with making complaints about the limited food and clothing, as well as the men's physical condition, that were demoralizing the troops. While Robertson awaited his court-martial, the Texas Brigade was left to the command of 5th Texas colonel King Bryan, a Liberty, Texas, rancher who had been wounded at Second Manassas and Gettysburg but remained with his men. The brigade respected Bryan, but it was an incredibly hard winter, and Robertson was right. The men wanted severely for sufficient food, clothing, and shelter. They had also been detached from their beloved General Lee and the Army of Northern Virginia, sent to East Tennessee in support of Braxton Bragg and later his replacement, Joseph E. Johnston.

That winter of 1863 and 1864 wore the Texas Brigade down to a shell of what it had been. In early February 1864, the brigade could not quite muster 784 officers and men present for duty. When General Gregg arrived to take command of the Texans and Arkansans in March, he confided to a friend that they were nothing more than "a little body of malcontents, some of them deserting every day or two—having, I suppose present for duty about 500 muskets."[9] To be fair, the brigade was not alone in this condition. That February, its division had only 5,931 present for duty with 8,729 men absent. Longstreet's entire corps could muster only 25,514 men, with more absent (27,307) than present.[10]

Many of the absent men were on wound furloughs to nearby family, friends, and hospitals in the Carolinas and Georgia. Some had taken "French leave," sneaking away from camp for weeks or months at a time though with plans to return to the ranks. Others simply deserted their posts. The Texas Brigade maintained a low desertion rate for the entire war compared with other units in the Army of Northern Virginia, averaging about 5 percent of the more than 7,000 men who served in the brigade, while Lee's army averaged nearly three times that rate throughout the war.[11] But of total desertions in the Texas Brigade, 38 percent took place between November 1863 and April 1864.[12]

Thomas Jewett Goree, one of Longstreet's staff officers who had three brothers serving in the 5th Texas, confided in their mother about this situation in February. "The Texas Brigade is not in the condition I would desire to have it," he admitted. "The morale of it is bad. They have got it into their head to go across the Mississippi, and many have gone without leave. I hope, however, soon to see a great improvement." Goree blamed the poor morale more on Robertson than on conditions and supply in Tennessee, and he theorized that the brigade would soon be sent home to rest and recruit more men. "Justice to the men here who have remained at the post of duty demands that this should be done," Goree explained. "Shame upon the men who have gone to Texas for easy service, and have deserted their brave comrades here. I was very much mortified, as well as surprised, to hear that Willie Darby, who had obtained a furlough to go to Alabama, has signified his intention of trying to get to Texas and remaining there. When officers act this way, what must be expected of the privates!"[13]

Despite these setbacks, John Gregg galvanized the efforts of junior officers with astonishing speed. They restored discipline in the ranks, and scores of wounded men returned from hospitals that early summer, as did men on extended leave or through prisoner exchanges. The men received fresh uniforms, shoes, and food, and their optimism soared as they rejoined the Army of Northern Virginia in April. Lee convinced President Jefferson Davis to grant amnesty to all deserters, so long as they rejoined the Army of Northern Virginia in 1864 (just as Lee had done in August 1863).[14]

Fifth Texas lieutenant Dugat Williams noticed the change almost immediately and celebrated the change in the brigade's fortunes, commenting to his fiancée that "the army recruited considerably this winter by the returning furloughed men who were slightly wounded at Chickamauga." So many men returned by May 1864 that Gregg boasted, "At the Wilderness we had 714 muskets. . . . Besides the muskets, there were perhaps officers enough to make the number 800." Of the estimated 1,361 men in the Texas Brigade on the rolls in 1864, 326 of them were returnees from previous wounds, absences with and without leave, prisoner exchanges, or disease. Resupplied with new uniforms and shoes, reunited with their favorite command, and rejoined with absent friends when the First Corps returned to Virginia, the unit, while understrength, was ready and in good spirits for the fight to come: the fight that could end the war and secure Confederate independence.[15]

The problem, though, was that the fighting in Virginia in 1864 would be the bloodiest of the war, and doctors could not keep up with the devastating casualties the men suffered that summer. In May alone, Virginia hospitals treated more than 48,000 soldiers, one-third more than any other month that year. In May, June, and July, doctors treated at least 102,000 soldiers, and, overwhelmed, the medical department began shipping patients to Danville and Farmville, Virginia, while others went to hospitals in North Carolina or Tennessee.[16] Doctors and nurses did impressive work. Of the 1,361 men on the Texas Brigade's rolls in 1864, 307 of those wounded in the Overland campaign or outside Petersburg returned to combat that year. Indeed, 85 of those men were wounded a second time and returned to fight again in 1864. But it would not be enough.

James Tiner fell at the battle of Spotsylvania Court House and remained on a wound furlough through December 1864, physically unable to fight. Sergeant Kingsley was wounded and captured at the battle of the Wilderness; he died a prisoner at Point Lookout, Maryland, in July. Sergeant Hasson was wounded in the hand at the Wilderness but remained in the ranks that summer until he was shot in the leg at Darbytown Road in October—the same battle where Texas Brigade commander John Gregg was killed. Doctors decided that amputating Hasson's leg was the only way to save his life. It did, but Hasson, too, was out of the ranks for the remainder of the war. Jess Anderson suffered a leg wound at Spotsylvania Court House on May 10 but remained with the Texas Brigade. Hit in the leg again at the battle of Chaffin's Farm on September 29, he left Virginia on a wound furlough in October and would not return before the war ended. Of the men who opened this chapter, only Greenberry McDonald remained relatively unscathed by the fighting that summer and fall, though he walked through the 3rd Arkansas lines with a bandaged hand, accidentally shot in the trenches outside Petersburg on June 2.[17] By the fall of 1864, the men worried whether or not there were enough of them to keep the Texas Brigade, as a unit, in the field and began discussing plans to return home as a brigade, rest over the winter, and return to Virginia for the 1865 campaign season with scores of fresh volunteers.

Indeed, despite their losses, morale remained high in the Texas Brigade as the men planned for future victory, not for defeat. Rufus King Felder was an original private of Company E of the 5th Texas Infantry. In the previous three years, he had buried or watched leave camp, permanently disabled, more friends than he cared to count. In 1862, his sister had admitted to Felder that she "hoped the Texians thirst for Yankee blood had been partly quenched." Responding in October, after the bloody fights on the Peninsula, at Second Manassas (where Felder's cousin Miers, serving in the same company, was badly wounded), and Antietam, Rufus Felder promised, "I can speak for the three [Texas] reg. in Va. Their thirst has not only been partially quenched, they have been in so many fights and have suffered so much they would be willing never to go in another fight."[18] But still they fought on.

Nearly two years later, Felder sat in the trenches outside Petersburg to pen yet another letter home. The Texans and Arkansans with him, Felder admitted, were exhausted, but they remained determined to secure Confederate independence. In July 1864 he boasted, "You have, I suppose[,] heard a full account of the recent fights. We have achieved much in deflating the enemy & killing thousands." Despite the fact that the Texas Brigade had "been in the entrenchments six days without relief, sharpshooting with the enemy," he saw the last few months as "very incouraging [sic]. Rebels in two miles of Baltimore. Grant defeated & the Dixie Blues in fine spirits."[19] One month later, Felder admitted to his sister that "we draw nothing here, but corn bread & rancied [sic] bacon. Fruit and vegetables are so high that we can rarely indulge in them." Still, he assured her that "we have had a good time since we have been over here [on the north side of the James River], that is, we have not had any fighting or hard marching." He persevered despite hardships that troubled him, including the death of his brother-in-law, George Elliott, killed in a Texas cavalry regiment. Felder asked, "Oh! When will this dreadful contest end & put a stop to our troubles & suffering[?]"[20]

Susannah J. Ural

Despite his sorrow, Felder was not willing to give up, nor was the rest of the Texas Brigade, and they were counting on the Union forces opposite them to break first. In mid-September, camped near Chaffin's Farm outside Richmond, Felder told his sister that "there is scarcely a day but some of them [African American soldiers] come over & ask to be sent back to their masters. The slaughter pen they were forced into at Petersburg quite demoralized them. They say they don't think they have anything to do with this fuss. This white folks['] fight." Felder saw the surrender of white Union troops as a good sign, as well. "The white soldier[s] are also deserting in large numbers. . . . It is very humiliating to know that we have to fight & expose our lives to this mixed horde of black and white demons."[21]

For the Texas Brigade, their fight continued because it had to. They felt the sorrow of their losses, no doubt. As Felder explained, "Autumn is upon us, but still the campaign goes on, nor do I see any probability of its ever coming to an end until the friendly snows of winter shall come & drop its shroud on the thousand of departed heroes, whose bones & bodys [sic], yet scarced [sic] decayed, are still exposed to the gaze of man & at the sight of which, the very angels weep." Despite this, Felder was determined that the fight had to continue. For families like his, much was at stake.[22]

The Felders moved to Texas in the early 1850s, led by family patriarch Judge Gabriel Felder, who had purchased and cleared 2,500 acres in Washington County in 1851. Rufus Felder and his siblings, along with their widowed mother, followed Gabriel Felder, their grandfather, to Texas in 1854, as had Rufus's cousin Miers a few years earlier. By 1860, the Felders ranked among the wealthiest and largest slave-owning families of one of the wealthiest counties in Texas.[23] As much as practical matters like emancipation threatened the Felders' future, Rufus also remained faithful to the ideals of the Confederacy and shared this with his family. When he witnessed a fellow soldier killed during some sharpshooting in the summer of 1864, Felder marveled that the man "seemed not to think of himself or the agony that he suffered, but prayed to God to spare his life that he may defend his beloved country & avenge himself of the dastard foe." It was a similar devotion to the Confederacy, Felder explained to his sister, that kept him from seeking an officer's commission. "I acknowledge that some positions afford a great many more advantages for ease & pleasure than a private has, but it will be to the private that the honor will be given . . . if our independence is achieved. . . . All that I want on this earth to make me happy is independence & a safe return to our once happy home, but this faint home grows still more glowing."[24] Felder captured the mood that ran throughout Hood's Texas Brigade that late summer of 1864.

All down the line, despite their losses, the men remained determined, if not optimistic.

Not far from Felder, writing in the same heat outside Richmond, Virginia, William Terry shared with his family similar reports of the men's faith in victory. By that point of the war, the twenty-six-year-old lieutenant had been fighting with the Milam County Greys—officially Company G of the 5th Texas Infantry—for three years. His wartime experiences were representative of many of the junior officers throughout the Texas Brigade. Originally a first sergeant, Terry moved up through the ranks partly through talent and partly through his service in the hard-fighting unit. Like Felder, Terry took pride in the praise the Texas Brigade had received in one battle after another since the war's start.

The brigade's fighting reputation, however, came at a heavy cost. As William Terry looked at Company G's position that August, he would have noted that its original company commander, Capt. Jefferson C. Rogers, later promoted to command the regiment, was home on furlough after a wound at Chickamauga caused partial paralysis in his left leg. Lt. John Smith replaced Rogers, but Smith was home on permanent recruiting duty. Second Lt. Sam Streetman died at Chickamauga, and 3rd Lt. Lu Batte had resigned his commission years earlier due to ill health.[25] Company G was a quarter of its original size. The fighting had inured the men to much of the loss, but Terry, like Felder, still counted when each man fell, noting the holes in their ranks and in their friendships. "We lost three men killed dead in our company, [W. W.] Peeks, [D. M.] Sherrill, and Hombleson with several other disabled for life," Terry wrote his mother in mid-August. Three others, "[D. H.] Carson, [R. B.] Henderson, and [S. H.] Walker . . . have died in prison and Ben Green I fear is dead, I have not heard from him in six months." Despite the losses, Terry insisted that "we are fixed here now so that half of our force can hold Richmond against any force they can bring against us. We have the best fortifications in the confederate states and we are satisfied here that the Yankees can do nothing."[26] Terry had made similar claims in a letter to his father a week earlier and boasted that "all of the company that is here is well and in good spirits" and "keeping old Grant back." Terry promised his father, "You need not fear but what we can keep all the Yankees back that they can send."[27]

Even captured Texas Brigade soldiers remained optimistic that fall. Fourth Texas sergeant Sidney E. Moseley, recovering in the prisoners' ward of Hampton Hospital in Hampton, Virginia, had been wounded at Gaines's Mill, the Wilderness, and again at Darbytown Road, where he was finally captured and had a leg amputated by a Union surgeon. Of all men, Moseley certainly had reason to lose faith in the war. But he remained confident of Confederate victory and the justness of his side's cause. That winter, Dr. Alfred Mercer, an English-born abolitionist practicing medicine in Syracuse, New York, had asked a colleague, Dr. John Newel Tilden, "if among your reb prisoners any one is willing to write me I should be glad to hear from him or them, and learn what they expect to gain for liberty or humanity, or what greater worldly prosperity they expect from our division of the Union." Fourth Texan Moseley pledged to "reply with as much brevity as possible" and then went on for over twenty handwritten pages, countering each of Mercer's claims about the nobility of the Union cause with biting sarcasm.[28]

"I am a one legged Confederate Soldier," Moseley began, "having but recently lost my leg in battling against the insolent invader of our country. I am also sorely afflicted with the itch, the sore eye, the Yankees and various other miserable and disagreeable things, too numerous to enumerate." But he took the time to lay out a carefully crafted argument, starting with Mercer's belief that the Union was on the right side of history and that Northerners did not hate Southerners personally but rather "hate the principle of rebellion and the principle of slavery."[29]

After defending state sovereignty and slavery and pointing to Northern "nullification" of the Fugitive Slave Law, Moseley declared, "We glory in the Knowledge that we are eternally and irrevocably separated from all such ranting, fanatical and Puritanical abolitionists as you seem to be. When the war is ended,—which, I think, will soon be,—we will say to you and your meddlesome, prying brethren, as we have been saying since the commencement of the war, 'Go thy way for this time, when I have a more convenient season, I will call thee,' or, in other words, we hope to have nothing more to do with you." Mercer's insistence that he had no animosity toward Confederates only infuriated the Texas sergeant. "And you have no hatred for the rebs! Truly your sense of duty is astoundingly developed. You have no hatred for us, nevertheless you invade and devastate our country, murder our people, burn our houses, barns, mills, and provisions, and our towns and cities, and perform numerous other little delicate, amiable and charitable deeds."[30]

Dr. Mercer had theorized that older Southerners "will most likely die still hating" the Union flag, but he "believe[d] the young and middle aged will yet learn to love it. . . . They may elevate a few to almost Kingly power, but will not the masses be much worse off than the old Union?" Here, again, Moseley fumed from his hospital bed. "The old men of our country will most certainly die, hating the old flag; and can you blame them, when its followers have created so much suffering and misery in our land." The doctor was "entirely wrong when you think the young and middle aged will ever love it. None of us will ever have any reverence or love for it; we may possibly, some day have some respect for it on account of its great power . . . , but no love can we ever have for it; we will concentrate all our love on our own beautiful and blood stained 'Stars and Bars,' we expect to follow our own Banner for all time to come."[31]

The trouble, though, was that the Confederacy was running out of men to wage the battle Moseley continued from his hospital bed. On October 9, two days after the Texans' October fight at Darbytown Road outside Richmond, where they suffered their greatest casualties since the battle of the Wilderness, General Lee issued a circular calling all available men back to the ranks. "With a view to increase effective strength of this army," Lee called on his officers to review their rolls and call back any men on detached duty, any nearly recovered soldier on sick leave, and any man who might possibly perform active service in the army. Lee had "noticed the large number of men (apparently able-bodied soldiers) who frequent the numerous wagon camps and detached encampments to be met with in the rear during an engagement with the enemy and he [did] not think there can be any indispensable service which necessitate[s] the absence of these men from their regiments." Any men incapable of active service, Lee now ordered, were to remain with the army rather than be sent to Richmond or the Carolinas on sick or wound furloughs. They could serve as "Field Hospital attendants, Forage Masters, Couriers," freeing up healthy men currently in those positions. Furthermore, by remaining with the army, even those deemed incapable of field service by a medical review board would be available for just that should the need arise.[32]

In Richmond, the Confederate Congress acted along similar lines and worked to pass a consolidation bill that required understrength companies and regiments to combine and reassign junior officer and staff positions to fill essential holes in the ranks.[33] It was an unpopular move with the army that hurt morale, especially in units that took pride in their long service to the Confederate cause, but General Lee insisted that it was absolutely essential to his army's and the Confederacy's survival.[34]

Lee's First Corps commander, Lt. Gen. James Longstreet, opposed the idea and urged Lee to recognize that "when you break up a regiment you destroy its prestige and its esprit de corps, which are the two most important elements in military organizations."[35] The Texas Brigade was exactly the kind of unit Longstreet described. All fall, the Texans and Arkansans had hoped they would be granted leave to go home for the winter, recruit fresh troops to fill their ranks, and return, strengthened, for the campaign season of 1865.

Col. Frederick S. Bass, commanding the Texas Brigade briefly that winter (and symbolizing the understrength nature of the unit through his rank more officially suited for regimental command), submitted their proposal for leave to Confederate secretary of war James Seddon in December.

The brigade knew the chances of actually receiving leave were not good. Rufus Felder explained to his mother that month that "we have been using every exertion in our power to have the brigade transferred or furloughed to Texas this winter. We have drawn up a memorial to that effect, signed by all the officers & men of the brigade and presented it to the President. Many are confident that we will go home this winter, but I must confess that I think our chances are very slim."[36]

Equally dedicated soldiers like 1st Texan Seaborn Dominey, who had served almost as long as Felder and who would stay with the brigade through its surrender at Appomattox Court House, were also hopeful. But Dominey pushed the issue further. In November he told his wife, Caroline, who had been running their small farm and caring for their young daughter since Dominey left for war almost three years earlier, "There is some talk of consolidating the army this winter. If they do, I don't know what they will do with us as there is not enough for a regiment. The men say if they consolidate them, they will run away to join in the Service in Texas. Some of the best soldiers in the Brigade is using such language."[37] It is significant to note that, even then, the men were not opposed to the war but rather refused to fight with other units that had not, in the Texans' eyes, earned the right to fight with them.

Back in July outside Petersburg, Dominey had been optimistic and sure of victory. "God has certainly helped our cause and arms throughout the Confederacy this year—and especially in Virginia. . . . We have got the best of every fight though out numbered from five to ten to one. General Lee has displayed his great ability by cutting the Yankees all to pieces in every battle and saving his own men. Our army is in good spirits and confident of a final triumph in the end."[38]

By mid-December, though, Dominey had not received a letter from his wife in nearly a year and admitted, "I have become discouraged and can hardly sum up the courage enough to write. I don't think you intend to write any more. It has been so long since I heard from you that I begin to think you have come to the conclusion that three years will divorce you." Smiling at his own humor, he joked, "But I want you to understand that I am not going to give up my claim as easy as that for I am afraid that I may stay four years more and by that time I will begin to look to[o] old to marry as well as I did when I married before." As tired as he was, Dominey promised, "We are all right now. We are in our Quarters. I think the Yankees thought they would slip off from Gen. Longstreet and pitch in on the other wing of Gen. Lee's Army but Old Jim pitched into them and put a stop to their slipping off from him."[39]

Still, the consolidation issue troubled him, as did the chances of getting furloughed to Texas. "I hope we may succeed but I fear we will not get off. If we fail to get off I think that two thirds of the men will come any how. It is not because they are tired of fighting but they know they have not had the chance to visit their homes that other troops have. Some of the best soldiers in the Brigade says they are going to come home but they don't intend to quit the war. The Brigade is too small to enter another campaign as it is. I think something will have to be done with us before Spring."[40]

Six days later he expanded on that issue to his sister-in-law, Eliza Davis. Dominey had just received a letter from her and another from his wife. Eliza praised Dominey's determination, but the private was not feeling as resolute as he had six months or even a week earlier. "You say that you glory in my spunk. I am not so patriotic as I once was and I don't think you will blame me for not being so when you hear my cause." He went on to make his case, and that of the Texas Brigade's, point by point. "First, we are not treated as other soldiers. We are never allowed furloughs like other soldiers. When they pretend to give us furloughs it is only for ten, fifteen or twenty days, and then we are not allowed to go farther west than Mississippi. We are given only one for fifty men & they do visit their homes, while we are to go among Strangers." They could not receive clothing from home, and while Dominey still had several pairs of pants, shirts, and two pairs of shoes, he lacked socks and a blanket, as well as a hat to protect him from the cold and rain. He hoped his family would not think poorly of him for having "picked up stuff often off the Battlefield to supply me." Rations were low, too, he complained, but none of this would matter if they could just get home, even for a short time. Dominey knew his officers were trying to accomplish this, but he feared that if "they don't succeed, I think fully one half will come home without leave & they are all good soldiers, the best we got. They do not want to get out of service but they have been away from their families as long as they are going to [be] without seeing their families & to speak the truth, I don't blame them." Dominey did not want to desert, but he worried about being so far from home for so long. "I will not make any threat or promise," he decided, but he resented the violation of an agreement he believed the men had made with their government. "I think I am as much entitled to visit my family as any man whether he be a Georgian, Virginian or Alabamian. We were promised furloughs, then the Government broke the bargain. I don't think they can expect us to consider them binding," Dominey argued. Still, he clung to dreams of victory and was certain that if defeat came, it would be the fault of an army other than Lee's. "Things look rather gloomy now," he admitted. "It is reported that Gen. Hood has been whipped but I hope it is not true. It has also been reported that Savannah has been captured with a heavy loss to us. I don't think that army worth anything & I believe if we are ever whipped it will be in the fault of that Army but I hope things will come out all right in the end. . . . I will try and take the best side of things."[41]

On January 15, 1865, Secretary of War Seddon responded to the Texas Brigade's furlough request. Rather than try to explain things himself, Seddon opened by quoting their beloved Lee, who noted that with "the opening of the campaign now near at hand, we shall require every man in the Confederacy," and if the Texans went home, they could not return in time. Lee recognized that "no brigade has done nobler service, or gained more credit for its State, than this. Though I should be much gratified at every indulgence shown to this brigade, I cannot recommend" approval of the proposed trip home. Seddon seconded Lee's praise, adding that "the services of the gallant brigade are most highly appreciated," along with his regrets "that the exigency is such as to forbid a compliance with their wishes."[42]

Officially, the men of the Texas Brigade accepted the news and understood the needs that kept them in Virginia. Privately, however, officers worried about the effect that denial of their trip home, combined with consolidation, would have on morale. Men like Seaborn Dominey were veteran fighters. They believed in the Confederate cause and in their commanders. But they were exhausted, and most had not been home since the war had begun, three and a half years earlier.

Texas Brigade quartermaster Maj. J. H. Littlefield confided to his wife in Texas that "we all fear consolidation; do not know what effect that will have." He insisted that, despite an invitation to transfer to Texas to serve on the staff of General Robertson (former commander of the Texas Brigade), Littlefield knew he must remain in Virginia. "I should like to go very much, but will do nothing unworthy of past life, my wife, and my boys, to get home. An honored grave would be a richer legacy to them than a few years in disgrace and remorse." Realizing that such claims did little for his wife's nerves, Littlefield shifted to more positive matters, but his mood swayed between determined optimism and grave concern. "Have no fears; all will be well to those who put their trust in Him," he promised. "Think of our own comparative situation to the poor houseless and homeless wanderers in Georgia. This is a dark hour. All is gloom away from the 'lines around Richmond'; all is confidence here. We have plenty to eat, such as it is. Tomorrow, molasses and sugar will be issued in lieu of meat. Feed us, and this army can never be conquered," though he did not expand on how an army was to fight on a diet that substituted sugars for protein. Littlefield struggled to accept their fate. "I am fearful that consolidation will make many attempt to escape the army," he explained, but knew it was "a great military and financial necessity; to us it will be, seemingly hard, but other States pride themselves on their brigades as much as we do the 'Texas Brigade.'"[43]

It speaks to the dedication of the Texas Brigade that so many men, despite the wealth of setbacks they endured in 1864, remained with the army. Not all of them did, of course. Pvt. Asbury Lawson had joined Company C of the 5th Texas Infantry in the summer of 1861 and was wounded at Gettysburg, exchanged, and returned to the ranks in April 1864. After a brief hospital stay in May, Lawson deserted to Federal forces in September.[44] Others, like Pvt. Edwin Searle, showed signs of trouble from the start. He joined Company C of the 1st Texas Infantry in the summer of 1861 and quickly was promoted to third corporal but reduced back down to private in February 1862. By January 1863, though, he was a second sergeant, and that April the men elected him as their first sergeant. Wounded at Chickamauga, Searle rejoined the Texas Brigade by the end of 1863, only to desert it in January 1864. After being captured and arrested Searle was allowed to return to the ranks to fight, where he deserted again on July 26; this time, he took the Federal Loyalty Oath and joined the 3rd Delaware Infantry.[45] Henry Bradley followed a similar path in late September 1864. An original member of Company F of the 1st Texas, Bradley fought with the Texas Brigade through nearly every major battle until he was wounded at the battle of Chickamauga in September 1863. After returning to the ranks in January 1864, he deserted that fall and took the Federal Loyalty Oath on September 20.[46]

Other deserters like Joseph Chiles and Charles Mixon received pardons by President Davis in the summer of 1864. The men, the *Richmond Daily Dispatch* reported, had been "very despondent, and had little or nothing to say to anybody" while awaiting their fate. Upon receiving their pardons, they "wept for joy" and happily returned to Company D of the 1st Texas Infantry. Reflecting the public's empathy for the desperate men and the public's increasing war weariness, the editor explained that the prison guards "had extended to [Chiles and Mixon] every indulgence in their power during their protracted confinement." Happy with the men's admission of their sin and inspired by their redemption, Richmond readers learned that Mixon and Chiles departed expressing their "determination to be better soldiers in the future," and the *Daily Dispatch* "doubt[ed] not that the resolution will be carried out to the very letter."[47] Perhaps it was, but Chiles was captured at Chaffin's Farm in September, and Mixon was killed the following month at Darbytown Road.[48]

Despite these examples, desertion in the Texas Brigade did not increase due to fears of consolidation or their denied furlough request. Of the more than 1,300 men on the rolls between May and November 1864, only 1 to 2 percent of them deserted the unit.[49] The desertion rate for the rest of Lee's army averaged at about 15 percent throughout the war, though rates spiked in 1864 to 34.5 percent.[50] But desertion was not the key issue for the Texans. These were men who enlisted predominantly in 1861 and 1862, voluntarily joining units they knew would take them more than a thousand miles from their homes. They had been enthusiastic and dedicated Confederates from the start of the war. They were tired and were being wounded and killed too quickly, but the core that remained in December 1864, frustrated though they were, would stay until the end.

That continued determination and ability to fight is particularly noteworthy when Hood's Texans are compared with other strong units in the Army of Northern Virginia. The Stonewall Brigade, for example, enjoyed a similar celebrated status in the Confederacy. Organized in 1861, Virginia's First Brigade had its baptism of fire at the battle of First Manassas. By the following year, the brigade's successes under the leadership of its first commander, Brig. Gen. Thomas J. "Stonewall" Jackson, led to the unit's nickname of "Jackson's Foot Cavalry." By the summer of 1864, however, this brigade had dwindled to fewer than 200 men. Heavy fighting and high casualties led one historian to argue that after the battle of Spotsylvania, "the Stonewall Brigade officially ceased to exist."[51]

Similar comparisons can be made with the Pettigrew-Kirkland-MacRae Brigade. It was not organized until 1862, but it quickly became one of North Carolina's most celebrated units. Despite the Confederates' defeat at the battle of Gettysburg, this unit earned a reputation as one of the hardest fighting brigades in Lee's army for its success against the Union's famous Iron Brigade on July 1 and the North Carolinians' determined if failed efforts during Pickett's Charge on July 3. By the winter of 1864–65, however, desertion, poor health, and demoralization had nearly broken the brigade. In January 1865, fourteen men deserted the ranks, followed by another forty-three men in February. March proved the worst with eighty-nine men deserting the brigade, roughly 13 percent of its total strength.[52]

While a determined core of Tar Heels remained, the North Carolinians' problems with desertion were not seen in the Texas Brigade that winter. Similarly, the Arkansans and Texans did not share the Stonewall Brigade's fate, as the Virginians collapsed due to overwhelming casualties. The Texas Brigade survived as a functioning unit that winter because the men remained confident in a number of strong, respected company and regimental commanders, as well as in their brigade commander. They also benefited from their proximity to Robert E. Lee, who had inspired astonishing levels of loyalty and sacrifice in the Texas Brigade since 1862. After years of desperate fighting, these men returned after wounds, capture, and furloughs, determined that Lee's army and the Texas Brigade held the best hope for their future in an independent Confederacy.[53]

Despite their determination, one major concern plagued them that winter: the question of consolidation, and by extension the loss of their identity and hard-earned fame. As part of the consolidation plan ordered by General Lee that winter, Lt. Col. C. M. Winkler of the 4th Texas, Col. R. C. Taylor of the 3rd Arkansas, and Capt. William T. Hill of the 5th Texas began the task of evaluating company grade officers to be sure they were fit for command. The casualty rates of the previous year had caused rapid turnover and promotion from the ranks. Not all of the men had mastered William J. Hardee's *Infantry Tactics* and the fundamentals of linear tactics that governed Civil War battles and were key to success.[54]

While the officers' examinations took place, the men met and selected Maj. William "Howdy" Martin of the 5th Texas, one of their favorite officers, to go directly to President Davis to make a case that the Texas Brigade, despite its reduced size, should remain an independent unit. Not many units had been consolidated by that point in the war, but some had, including the famous Stonewall Brigade. Unwilling to accept such a fate on top of the denial of their furlough request, the men's selection of Major Martin to make their case was a wise one. With long shaggy hair, bushy brows, and a quick smile, Martin had earned the nickname "Howdy" for his preference for a waved greeting over a snappy salute. Tall and lanky, he was born outside of Texas, like many of the men in camp, and he had enjoyed middle-class success in the years leading up to the war.[55] Educated in Alabama, Martin arrived in Texas in 1850, where he set up a law practice in Athens before winning a seat in the Texas senate, which he held until 1858.

When the war began, Martin recruited ranch hands and farm boys into the Sandy Pointe Mounted Rifles, and he convinced them to stay even when the men discovered they would be foot rather than horse soldiers. A brilliant lawyer known for his ability to move a jury, Martin was self-confident

Maj. William "Howdy" Martin of the 5th Texas was selected by the Texas Brigade to petition President Jefferson Davis to maintain the brigade's independence even as other units were being consolidated in the winter of 1865.
(Courtesy of Martha Hartzog)

without bravado. He was friendly and engaging, known for rowdy "sermons" where, as when they had first marched off to war, he would leap "on an old goods box under a hickory tree . . . long, angular, with a voice like thunder. . . . As he spoke he would shake his long hair and look like he was mad enough to eat a Yankee raw." One contemporary mused that "it seemed he never did anything like other people," and the men loved him for it.[56]

Morale among Hood's Texas Brigade's Soldiers and Their Families

Martin was the personification of a Texas Brigade officer. He led his men in battle and cared for them in camp, often defending those who found themselves in the guardhouse for one offense or another (one account, perhaps apocryphal but it speaks to how the men wanted their commander remembered, insisted that when Martin pleaded before Davis's cabinet that a man's death sentence be commuted, "his words moved the members . . . to tears"). Howdy had not risen through the ranks rapidly. Beloved by his men, Martin was a strict disciplinarian when it came to fighting, but Company K's camp was never the tidiest, and when half of his men failed to appear for drill, Howdy himself would defend their absence. Martin was the 4th Texans' leader, entertainer, adviser, and kindly uncle, a man who inspired and protected lonesome, raucous boys far from home. He was their first choice, the man best able to plead their case to President Davis.[57]

Likely with help from either Postmaster General John Reagan or Texas Confederate senator Louis T. Wigfall, Martin received an appointment to meet with Davis in Richmond, and as fate would have it, General Lee would be in Davis's office that day. Martin's fellow Texans watched him leave camp in "an old blue coat which once belonged to a Union soldier"; the coattails had to be removed to make it a short jacket or roundabout. Despite the modifications, Martin's shirt showed through a split in the back, and "the Howdy Martin hair" poked through a hole in his hat. The major's appearance might not have been to code, but he made his case masterfully when he stood before the president and his commanding general. Holding his weathered hat in his hands, Martin explained that he had "been selected by the Texas soldiers to protest against the order of your Excellency to consolidate the Texas regiments. The fulfillment of the order would break the hearts of our men." For four years they had fought. "The bones of their comrades are bleaching upon many battlefields in the South," Martin reminded the men, and they were still mourned by the soldiers who continued to carry the mantle and by others who "returned to their homes broken down in health forever." All that they asked, Martin explained, was that the Texas Brigade maintain its identity as a separate fighting unit.[58] In the silence that followed Martin's moving plea, General Lee added, "Mr. President, before you pass upon that request, I want to say I never ordered that brigade to hold a place, that they did not hold it." Davis looked at Martin and promised that "as long as there is a man to carry that battle flag, you shall remain a brigade."[59] "Howdy" Martin had saved his boys again.

As an additional response to the consolidation crisis, the Texas Brigade, like other elite units in Lee's Army, drafted a series of resolutions that winter to ensure that their commanding officers, their representatives in Congress, and the families at home understood their determination to win the war. Gathering in late January, the leaders of the group included Lt. Haywood Brahan, Pvt. William H. Burges, and Lt. Col. Clinton M. Winkler, who began the war as a company commander and now found himself commanding the brigade. They came together in Camp Texas outside Richmond, part of the winter entrenchments of Lee's Army of Northern Virginia. All down the line, soldiers hunched in the defenses, coughing and shivering in the frozen ground and "spitting snow" that had given way to "dark, cold, sleety" rain by the end of January 1865. Mother Nature, one soldier declared, had created "too much mud between the two armies for either to make a serious advance," leaving "the troops" with "as much as they can do to keep from freezing."[60]

Despite the miserable weather, the men clustered around Brahan, Burges, and Winkler. Brahan explained that they had gathered to draft resolutions on why this war must continue. For some of them, the approaching spring marked their fourth year of fighting. But they would continue, the men insisted, for a fifth, sixth, or more, if that was what Confederate victory required. They had come together to formally state this as the citizen-soldiers they were, ever aware of their constitutional rights and obligations.

Burges, who served in the same company with Brahan, proposed that they should select five men from each of the four regiments that made up the brigade. These representatives would draft resolutions that expressed the sentiments of their units. Then they would combine these into one clear, bold proclamation that would be submitted to the Confederate Congress, President Davis, and General Lee and for printing in newspapers across the South.

While the selected men departed to draft their resolutions, the rest of the brigade "was agreeably and pleasantly entertained by eloquent and patriotic speeches" by Colonel Winkler and Pvt. T. D. Williams, whose equal billing with Winkler unconsciously symbolized the egalitarian streak that ran through the brigade. When the regimental representatives returned, they tweaked and revised their document until it received unanimous support. "Whereas," it began,

> we have seen with feelings of sadness, the clouds of gloom and despondency that have recently gathered in the sky of our young nation, but which are now happily being dispelled by returning confidence, therefore we, the army, who are the people ... make known to our fellow-soldiers, to our country, the enemy, and to the world, our purpose and determination to maintain, at all hazards, and to

Morale among Hood's Texas Brigade's Soldiers and Their Families   59 the last extremity, the rights and liberties which a merciful God has been pleased to bestow upon us, and even to contend for a perpetual separation from the hated and despised foe, who have murdered our grey-haired fathers, insulted our women and children, and turned out thousands of helpless families to starve — after robbing them and burning their houses — leaving them destitute of all except their honor.[61]

The men of the Texas Brigade, they explained, had "considered well the causes and consequences" of their actions when they went to war in 1861. They had "gone boldly forward, now for nearly four years, and our determination has not abated." Surely, "no one can now be so blind and stupid," they argued, "as not to agree with us, that the warning was the inspiration, and that then was the auspicious time to strike for our rights. . . . We will rid ourselves of the tyranny the enemy would thrust upon us, or die in the attempt."[62]

The Texans clarified their faith in victory, as well as their faith in their leaders. They reminded readers of their numerous battlefield successes and their faith that there were more victories to come. As they awaited the spring campaign season, they mocked the "heterogeneous mass" that was the Union army, "the Babel of modern times, in which is represented the African, shoulder to shoulder with his brother, the Yankee, who sells himself for a bounty and deserts and sells himself again — the man with the brogue so rich — the avaricious Hessian, and the dungeons of Europe." In contrast, the Texans explained, the Confederate army fought "to be free and independent of those who would kill eight millions of whites or enslave them in order to give a pretended freedom to half that number of African negroes." Fear not, they advised their readers, "our final triumph is certain and inevitable, and our subjugation is an impossibility."[63]

The only major problem, they warned, was on the home front. Significantly, of all the resolutions listed, the soldiers' faith in victory and their concern about demoralization at home received the majority of the Texans' and Arkansans' comments. They could not, they explained, "be indifferent lookers on at those in our own country, who would divide and distract the counsels of the nation and tear down the present able and patriotic Administration; and, at the same time, give aid and comfort to the enemy." They warned the "politicians and demagogue newspaper editors, men in and out of positions, croakers, and *those who would fire from the rear*, and those who pull down, whilst we build up," that "there is a point beyond which you cannot go with impunity; that nothing will deter us from the prosecution of our purpose, whether it be

Susannah J. Ural

our open enemies in the front, or the hidden and less respectable enemy in our midst; for the latter of whom, we take this occasion to express our most hearty scorn and contempt."[64]

The men of the Texas Brigade passed their resolutions on January 24, 1865. Their public statement, as they hoped, appeared in newspapers across the South. Other units passed similar resolutions — Humphreys's Mississippi Brigade, the 57th Virginia, the 9th Virginia, five Georgia brigades, and on down to individual companies.[65] While often viewed as a way to measure military morale in early 1865, these resolutions are actually more about home-front morale. The men's statements are too public to fairly gauge their determination or their frustrations. They certainly had complaints of their own. Indeed, only a week earlier, a Texas Brigade soldier's letter revealed some of their frustrations in the *Richmond Examiner* that men like Seaborn Dominey had expressed privately. The man asked, "Why is it that we are not paid our small pittance of wages, four months of which are now due us? We do not want the money for itself, but for the few comforts we could purchase. We were permitted a hundred dollar bond on the first of October. Why hasn't it been paid?" The letter was signed simply, "Texas Brigade."[66]

The resolutions, however, received far more press than a solitary letter to the editor or private letters home might. They served, as their authors intended, like a massive broadside hung in every shop, tavern, or mill that challenged citizens to show the same determination as those who had been risking everything they held dear — their families at home and their lives in battle — for nearly four long years.

One could argue that the problem at home was not one of will or the lack thereof. It was a matter of debilitating inflation, the collapse of the Texas economy, and the inability of middle-class and impoverished Texans to feed their families and themselves. As the conflict dragged on, though, droughts and inflation plagued Texas farmers. Wheat growers boasted an abundant crop in 1862, but their own expenses, they explained, forced them to sell it at exorbitant prices. Editors in Austin frowned at this reasoning and recommended martial law to regulate merchant and farming prices, but poor and middle-class Texans remained pinched between price gouging and inflated Confederate specie. The cattle industry thrived for ranchers supplying the armies' demands, but after the fall of the Confederate stronghold at Vicksburg, Mississippi, in the summer of 1863, even cattlemen began to suffer as their markets dwindled.[67] Texans fared better than other Southern states that both armies had ravaged, but by the middle of 1864, inflation was nearly out of control in the Lone Star State. By late fall, the legislature abandoned efforts to allocate funds to counties to care for the indigent and impoverished soldier families and reverted to barter as they supplied cloth and thread produced at the state penitentiary that county leaders could use to trade for necessary food and supplies.[68]

The soldiers' families were not the only ones who suffered, but they received the most attention because their situation seemed so unjust compared with those with no male family members away at the front. Their suffering revealed a violation of the agreement made between a citizen-soldier and his community. He volunteered to protect the community's larger freedoms with the understanding that his neighbors would, if needed, help support his family in his absence.[69] As one Texas soldier grumbled early in the war upon learning that his wife desperately needed help with the most fundamental tasks, "I think it strange that where there are so many negroes no one can be found that would spare a negro to chop a load of wood for a poor soldier's wife."[70]

Texas, like most Confederate states, responded to these needs. While 1862 had been a year of embarrassment with regard to the care of soldiers' families, 1863 had been a year of riches. For every frustrating case of a veteran on crutches making his way to a county seat for support and then being turned away because he lacked some mundane paperwork, 1863 brought one example after another of everyone from the legislature to the county government to private citizens organizing to support families at home and soldiers at the front. Newspapers were packed with announcements about fund-raiser balls and tableaux. Even the sisters of the Ursuline Convent in Galveston hosted a ball, teasing the local paper as they pointed out, "In making an appeal to the 'Ladies of Texas,' to second you in your charitable designs of relieving the destitution of the 'Texas Brigade' Hospital, in Virginia, you did not, I am certain, think of the Nuns . . . down here in Galveston." The sisters had little personal wealth to share, but they challenged Texas women to model themselves after "the Roman Dames of old" to "part with our most precious jewels to alleviate the intense sufferings of those heroes who have achieved deeds of valor for their country."[71] Not to be outdone, the ladies of Crockett raised $525 in March, and they were matched and surpassed by the women of Seguin, Jefferson, and Livingston and in communities all across the state.[72]

The problem by 1865, though, was that communities were either less willing or unable to give, and rural families had enough to do to simply survive. Their focus on the war was waning. Late in the war, Texas divorcée Ann Raney Coleman admitted that when the women in Lavaca County, Texas, did not receive their rations, they gathered together, walked into the distribution office, "pistol in hand," and just like that "we got our rations, although previously refused." Coleman recalled, too, that when a Baptist church collapsed after a storm hit their community, she and her daughter, whose husband was serving in the Confederate army, went out in the middle of the night to gather the splintered wood for their fires. As the women worked, more arrived to join them in securing firewood. When the guard who had been placed at the church tried to stop the women, "We told him there were enough of us to whip him, so he had as well say nothing. . . . He laughed at us for spunk. We threatened to tie him hand and foot if he should resist us."[73]

Coleman recalled that corn shortages led to similar results. Several of the poor women went to the local miller to request a small portion of what he was preparing for the wealthier families of the county. When he refused, some of the women guarded the man while others filled all of their sacks. They threatened to burn down the entire mill if he tried to stop them. "Be assured," Coleman scowled, "that it was the women that protected themselves in this war and not the men."[74]

Of course, not everyone suffered and not everyone was convinced that the poverty was real. In Walker County, from which 5th Texans William T. Hill, Robert M. Powell, and Mark Smither hailed, an anonymous citizen complained that "the majority of them [soldiers' families], in this portion of the State, at all events, are bountifully supplied with all the necessaries, and to a great extent, with all the luxuries of life at present obtainable in the markets of the country. Several families of soldiers, in this country, within the writer's ken, live better, are better clad, and live in greater idleness than when their 'heads' were at home."[75] Despite his claims, desperation and frustration inspired women in Galveston to march to the headquarters of Confederate general James M. Hawes in June 1864 and demand better rations, asking in particular for flour rations rather than cornmeal. These actions expanded into large-scale seizures of flour and corn across East Texas that year in Grayson, Galveston, Hardin, and Jefferson Counties.[76]

By 1865, things were dire indeed. The entire state had struggled to alleviate the suffering, but nothing seemed to work anymore. Counties distributed cotton and wool cards to aid destitute families with their home production of cloth. This helped, but no matter how much the state produced, it could not keep up with civilian demands, especially when the state also needed to produce for military needs. Before the war, none of the cards were made in the South, so Southerners had played a catch-up game over the last four years to increase card production to increase cloth production to increase uniform and clothing production. As is usually the case, they never quite caught up.

It is significant to note, however, that in the roughly two dozen Texas

Brigade letter collections and diaries that exist for 1864 and 1865, no letter has been found where a family on the home front insisted that their loved one quit the fight.[77] There were complaints, to be sure. But of the wealth of Southern letters from home that encouraged men to desert or begged them to come home to save the farm, none exist for Texas Brigade soldiers. Part of the reason for this may be tied to the fact that Texas Brigade soldiers were exceptionally motivated volunteers who knowingly joined units that would have them fighting far away in Virginia. Their families may have reflected similarly strong ideological motivations that sustained them and their fellow Texas Brigade families, who often lived in the same communities, while their men fought far from home.

In Austin, the state legislature worked desperately to help soldiers' families. Legislators set aside $1 million each for 1864 and 1865 and another $500,000 to be provided each six months to the county courts based on the needs requested in their communities. The money could be used to purchase "necessary supplies" for soldiers' families. It helped a great deal, but, again, Texas could not keep up with its citizens' demands and with inflation. Complaints of women stealing cotton cards, government corn, and other food items, sometimes at gunpoint, surfaced in Galveston, Hardin, and Marion Counties and elsewhere throughout the state in 1864.[78]

Soldiers' complaints poured into the governor's office, too. One of the last of the war came from Calhoun County on April 4, 1865: "At the outbreak of this war," it began, "when the first call for volunteers was made by the Governor of this State, Indianola, then a town of about 900 inhabitants, furnished a company of artillery, 250 strong," for units including Hood's Texas Brigade. "When we enlisted, we were promised that our families never should suffer for want of life's necessary's [sic]; how this promise has been fulfilled the following will show. During the first year of the war, the families received for about 6 months corn and money, when suddenly it stopped altogether until July last year, when they were furnished with cornmeal" that was so fine it hardly baked into anything. The other problem was that the boats the women and townspeople used to gather driftwood for fires were pressed into service by local Confederate forces. Indeed, it seemed that every loose scrap of wood in town—including fences and outbuildings—was burned as civilians and soldiers alike struggled to survive the last winter of the war.[79]

As word of these troubles traveled east, Confederate senator Louis T. Wigfall, on a trip home to Texas, expressed his concerns that such negative accounts were breaking soldiers' morale. He called on women across the state "to refrain from writing their husbands, sons and sweethearts, now in the army, to come home" and to abandon their "doleful accounts of their little troubles at home, which had produced so much uneasiness in the army and caused so much desertion and its consequences." Wigfall asked Texas women to forgo all such talk and instead to "stimulate" their soldiers "in every possible manner to stick to their posts of duty, and either die like heroes or come home at the end of the war covered with glory."[80]

Several women seem to have responded to his appeal. In early February, Robert E. Lee received a package from a "young lady in Texas" that contained stars made of gold "too precious for ordinary use." She asked that they be awarded to the nine bravest soldiers of the Texas Brigade. Senator Wigfall personally delivered the stars to the Texans and Arkansans in camp, then under the command of Col. Frederick Bass. In a fascinating demonstration of democracy, neither Bass, General Lee, nor any commanding officer selected the nine recipients. Rather, the men of the Texas Brigade put it to a vote— two recipients for each regiment except the 4th Texas, which had three. In the 1st Texas the stars went to Pvt. William Durham and Pvt. Josephus Knight. In the 4th Texas, Corp. James Burke, Sgt. James Patterson, and Corp. W. C. May received stars. In the 5th Texas, the recipients were Sgt. C. Welborn and Sgt. Jacob Hemphill. The 3rd Arkansas recognized the bravery of Pvt. J. D. Staples and Pvt. J. W. Cook.[81]

It is significant that four of these men (Durham, Knight, Burke, and Cook) were later enlistees who joined the Texas Brigade in the spring of 1862. By February 1865, it did not seem to matter if a man had volunteered amid the rush to arms following Fort Sumter or remained at home until the following spring. It is also notable that most of these men were not members of the planter elite who led the home communities in which Texas Brigade companies were raised. Instead, the majority of the gold star recipients came from middle-class farming families, some of whom were serving alongside multiple members of their family. In the case of Josephus Knight, he and his three brothers all enlisted in March 1862. Both Andrew and William departed the 1st Texas within about a year due to chronic illness. Brother John had left his twenty-two-year-old wife, Sarah, at home to raise their two sons, both under the age of two, and run their profitable farm with the help of family. Sarah died six months after John enlisted, but still he remained with the Texas Brigade, a twenty-eight-year-old widower who counted on his extended family to care for his children until he felt he could return.[82]

While the identity of the woman who donated the stars was never revealed, several of the Texans later suspected that it was a Miss Fuller of Houston, which means she was likely connected to another key home-front supporter of the Texas Brigade, Maude Jeanne Fuller Young.[83] It might have been Young herself who sent the stars, or perhaps one of her younger sisters. They all lived in their parents' home before, during, and after the war, and their brother, Blucher Pulaski "Pugh" Fuller, had been serving in the Texas Brigade for four years. He was a lawyer before the war and rose from private to second lieutenant in command of Company A of the 5th Texas. Maude Fuller Young's only son was in the unit, too; he joined in 1864 at the age of sixteen. They were all part of the prominent Fuller family of Houston, where Maude's father, Nathan Fuller, earned a fortune before the war as a railroad agent. She had expanded the Fullers' reach in February 1847 when she married Dr. Samuel O. Young of an equally prominent Houston family. They were on the cusp of a bright future together when Samuel died suddenly that November. Seven weeks later their only child was born and named S. O. Young for the father he would never meet. By the final spring of 1865, Maude Young was a widow in her early thirties.[84]

Back in 1862, Maude Young made the 5th Texas's flag, which General Hood had selected as the brigade's official flag at Gettysburg. She also raised $30,000 (about $413,000 in today's economy) to support the construction of the Texas Hospital in Richmond during the war. Few Texans did more to help the Texas Brigade throughout the entire conflict.[85] Late in 1864, the men of the 5th Texas returned the flag to Young because it was so tattered from their many battles. She immediately wrote to them insisting that the day she received their colors would forever be the proudest of her life. She could not look at it, Young said, without thinking of "the weary march, the aching feet and throbbing brow, the cold bivouac, the lonely picket, the pernicious scout, the gloomy hospital, the pride and pomp of battle array, the shock of arms, the victory and Oh! those silent, nameless grass-grown mounds, strewn from Richmond to Gettysburg, from Chickamauga and Knoxville to the Wilderness and Petersburg—mounds whose shadows rest cold and dark upon a thousand hearts and homes."[86]

As honored as Young was that fall, she was worried, too. "You bid me 'hang the flag upon the outer walls' to strike terror to the hearts of the cowards skulking at home. Ah! my noble brothers of the 5th! if the sable-clad forms of mourning women and children, if the numberless maimed soldiers who greet us at every turn," she asked, ". . . if the form of our Confederacy, beleaguered by foes and bleeding at every vein, strike no remorse, and inspire to no patriotic deeds, think you this flag will? They are joined to their idols—money making and selfish ease." But one day, she said, "you shall return and scourge them from the land. If honor or peace or safety were de-

With both a brother and a son in Hood's Brigade, Maude Jeanne Fuller Young
was one of the fiercest supporters of the unit on the home front.
(Courtesy Dolph Briscoe Center for American History, the University of Texas at Austin)

pending upon them, we would long ago have worn the Yankee yoke and ate the bread of slaves."[87]

Though written in November 1864, Young's letter to the 5th Texas was published, at the regiment's request, in the *Richmond Whig* on January 17, 1865. That means it appeared in papers about two or three weeks before the Texas Brigade's and other units' famous resolutions appeared in print. And if inflation and a lack of support, supply, and sustenance were breaking Texans down that final spring, Maude Young was not going to stand by idly.

Members of the Texas Brigade loved Maude Young's loyalty and passion, but even they had their suspicions about victory in 1865. In late February, Rufus Felder's mood fluctuated between determination and doubt. He warned his sister that the reports of Sherman's campaign through South Carolina, where both Felders were born, were true, and he feared that "the insolent foe" had "committed depredations on the property, if not on the persons of our dear, but unfortunate relatives there." Rufus Felder had served more than three years in Company E of the 5th Texas Infantry. "Our cause looks gloomy indeed," he admitted. "We have met with many recent & severe reverses, but I trust that the tide of battle will soon turn." Still, he advised that "you must all prepare your minds to see your negroes freed, at least a portion of them. Congress is preparing a bill to make soldiers of them.... They will have to be freed.... All the soldiers are in favor of it."[88]

Samuel S. Watson of the 1st Texas revealed similar vacillations in his mood that spring. In February, he told a correspondent on the home front, Harriet C. Lewis, that the recent prisoner exchange "will make our Armies considerable stronger." It also meant Lewis's husband was likely on his way home, "if he is Still living." Confederate leaders "are also going to put in two hundred Thousand buck Negros that will also help Sum." Watson had "a notion of applying for a command among them I dont know that I shall but I think of doing so." He thought Confederates could "be able to hold Va." but then added, "I hope so, at least." Indeed, Watson admitted, "I will Say to you that Evry thing looks Sad and gloomy at this time in and a round Richmond, great many people has become dispondant and Sum disertion Sum dissatisfaction in difrant ways Sum for putting in the Negroes ... to fight." Watson wished "they will all stop thare foolishness and let the men go home.... I am not in much of a humer for writing this morning."[89]

William Schadt, also of the 1st Texas, languished as a Confederate prisoner at Point Lookout, Maryland, in the spring of 1865. All winter his sister Caroline, living with friends in Galveston, Texas, read conflicting reports that William had either been left behind with the wounded at Darbytown Road in

Susannah J. Ural

October or had died. In January she learned William was alive, and William himself confirmed that he was all right in February. He had been sent to Richmond and hoped to be exchanged soon. The Schadt siblings were the last surviving members of their families, which may explain why neither pondered the fate of the Confederacy in their final letters. By the end of March, Caroline Schadt focused only on getting William home. She was "made happy" by news that "you were safe. I say happy—yes, happy if I can be happy without my darling Willie. . . . I hear you were wounded. . . . I hope you are in good spirits. Trust in God," Caroline advised. "He knows what is best for us. . . . Brother dear, if the prayers of a loving and affectionate sister are answered you will come home safe." After closing her letter, she scratched once more across the page, "God bless and keep you from harm and let you return home safe." William's safe return was all that concerned Caroline Schadt that spring.[90]

Fifth Texan captain Dugat Williams, like the others, was more steadfast than hopeful. In the opening days of 1865, he "ran the blockade," sneaking into Richmond without a pass. His friend 3rd Lt. R. J. McKinnon had served with Williams since the summer of 1861. Wounded at the Wilderness in May, Chaffin's Farm in September, and Darbytown Road and Williamsburg Road in October, McKinnon had certainly suffered in 1864, and Williams had just received word that McKinnon was fading. The captain snuck into the Confederate capital on January 2, 1865, and managed to say goodbye before McKinnon died the next morning "at half past four." "He was as brave a man as ever faced the enemy," Williams remembered. In the same letter, he also asked his fiancée, Laura Bryan, to welcome 5th Texan Jim Booth should he stop by during his wound furlough home. "He is a good soldier and a brave man. If he should call to see you, which is probably, remember the hardship the members of the Old Texas Brigade have undergone and for my sake please treat him kindly."[91]

Despite the concern sweeping through the ranks, Willis J. Watts of Company G of the 1st Texas Infantry remained unwaveringly and unusually optimistic that spring. His description of his regiment was idyllic; his depiction of camp and morale are among the lengthiest and most detailed of that period of the fighting. He was twenty-three years old when he enlisted in Palestine, Texas, in April 1862. Wounded at Chickamauga and the Wilderness, he had also survived small injuries that did not require care, or at least not official treatment. On March 11, 1865, Watts was "in the enjoyment of excellent health and Spirits." His company, Watts confessed to his cousin, was "very Small out of 150 Men 22 remains, We have about one hundred Men in our Regt about four hundred in the Brigade." Despite all they had suffered, he insisted they were "all in high Spirits, and more determine[d] on gaining our Independance than when we first enterd the army. I hear of no de[s]pondency in the army, but on the other hand they are all determining on our independence." They had "pretty good huts to live in and are always very lively & merry when the weather permits we often Play Town Ball Cat Bull Pin or Something of that Sort." He heard there was some "little despondency" among the Carolinians, Georgians, and Alabamians at home, but Watts insisted that this "all amounts to nothing when the Soldiers are alrigh[t] ." He hoped Texans were "Standing Squair toed to our countrys cause. I have not heard how they Stand on the Subject of reconstruction, but I hope Such a thing has never enterd the minds of our gallent people of Texas."[92]

Despite Willis Watts's determination, General Lee concluded in early April that he would not continue the fight. Doing so would sacrifice his loyal Army of Northern Virginia with no reasonable expectation of victory. On the morning of April 9, 1865, the Texas Brigade occupied a defensive position just southwest of Appomattox Court House, Virginia. Its crescent-shaped line straddled a stagecoach road, defended by breastworks built hastily from any material the men could find. All around them were signs of the heavy marches that both armies had made during those final days. "Cannons, wagons and ambulances in large numbers had been abandoned by the troops ahead of us for lack of teams strong enough to pull them," Capt. William T. Hill recalled. "Horses already dead, and many others fast dying from exhaustion and for lack of feed, lay in the mud, in and by the side of the road."[93] Hill was the original first lieutenant of Company D. He was in his early twenties when the war began, working on his father's plantation in Waverly, Texas, in a family that ranked among the wealthiest planters in Texas.[94] Hill, who received his promotion to captain just before the battle of Second Manassas, was well liked by the men and remembered for the prayer meetings he held throughout the war.[95] Wounded in the foot at Gettysburg, Hill had returned in time for the opening of the 1864 campaign season only to be slightly wounded again, this time in the arm in the Wilderness. He remained with the troops of the 5th Texas through the rest of their fighting that year and was in command of the entire regiment, though only a captain, by the spring of 1865. They numbered just 149 men.[96]

Fighting resumed on April 9 as morning's light revealed their positions, but Hill knew there was little they could do. Our "line of retreat was blocked," he admitted. Then, "suddenly, everything came to a death-like stillness." The men stopped working, "hunger stayed its gnawing, and expectant of evil tidings, but yet unprepared for the worst, faces grew grave and serious, and men

when they talked at all spoke in whispers."[97] That afternoon teamsters walk-
ing into their lines announced that Lee had surrendered the army, but the
Texans refused to believe it and threatened the rumormongers with bodily
harm if they continued to spread nonsense in the ranks.[98] When Lee's farewell address was read to the men the following day, though, Hill knew the
end had come.

Just down the line from William T. Hill stood "Howdy" Martin of the
4th Texas, motionless, trying to comprehend what this meant. Lee had surrendered his army; surrendered them. Like Hill, Martin had commanded,
advised, mourned, and loved the men of Company K since 1861, and he had
helped keep them together, along with the rest of the brigade, even under
the threat of consolidation the previous winter. After a long, stunned stillness as Martin struggled to process what he had just heard, tears began to roll
down his weathered face. Men watching him in camp said the major's head
slumped, shoulders hunched, as sobs shook his entire body.[99]

On the morning of April 12, the regimental officers called the Texans and
Arkansans into formation. On command, the Texans took their place in the
line of Confederates, moving forward in their familiar cadence, rifles rest-
ing on their shoulders. The regiments were small—many had fewer than 200
men—but Maj. Gen. Charles Field's division, in which the Texans served,
remained Lee's largest.[100] As each regiment approached its mark, officers
dressed the lines and the men stacked arms in fours, with the remaining
men likely leaning their rifles on the stack as they went by. Faces gaunt, bel-
lies empty, the men slipped off their belts and dropped their cartridge boxes
in a pile by the weapons.[101] It was, Basil Crow Brashear of the 5th Texas recalled, "the hardest thing I had to do during the whole war." That was a powerful statement from a man who was discharged for chronic rheumatism in
November 1861 but recruited again the following March. Wounded twice at
Gaines's Mill and Darbytown Road, Brashear had buried many friends over
the last four years, including his brother, Charles, who was killed at Gettysburg.[102] But decades later, Appomattox remained his hardest day.

Not far from Brashear, John David Murray felt similar despair as he
moved along with the line of Texans and Arkansans. Murray led Company F
of the 4th Texas Infantry even though he was only a color sergeant. He was
the highest-ranking man left. He was also the last of the Murray brothers in
the Texas Brigade. Four years earlier the Mustang Greys, as Company F was
known, had marched out of Bexar County, sunshine soldiers warmed by the
support of family and friends. John David and his brother, Robert Washington, were with them. Their younger brother, James, joined them as an 1862

recruit the following spring. The Murray boys came from a typical 4th Texas family. Their father had moved the family from North Carolina in the 1850s, trying their luck first in Missouri, before settling in Bexar County by the end of the decade. Owen Murray worked his hog farm in Guadalupe with his wife, Sarah, and two young daughters and awaited the return of their boys from Virginia and their eldest son, Asa, who served with the 8th Texas Infantry. In July 1863, James was killed at Gettysburg, likely by friendly fire from his own company in the chaos of its desperate fight to take Little Round Top. Not quite a year later, Robert fell at the battle of Wilderness. He survived the wound but lost a leg.

By April 1865, John David was the last Murray boy left in Company F. He was one of the last soldiers, period. Of the 120 men who mustered in with the unit in 1861, only 7 remained at the surrender. As he made his way toward the stacked arms and pile of cartridge boxes, it was John's unhappy task to pause, before the entire 4th Texas, and lay their furled battle flag atop the intertwined bayonets. Years later, after a lifetime of hardship, John Murray, much like Basil Crow Brashear, would often return to that somber April day and declare it "the saddest in his life."[103]

The 1st Texans had lost their battle flag to a Federal cavalryman just a few days earlier, and the Texans were never clear on whether they surrendered their colors or not. Most insisted that the tattered flag they returned to its creator, Maude Young, in the fall of 1864 was the last flag they had carried into battle.[104] But the Arkansans had to surrender theirs. Like Murray, the color bearer stepped forward and laid their colors across the stacked arms. As the men marched on, the colors laid there atop the bayonets that rose like fingers. Dangling from the staff was a note, a parting blow. "Mr. Yankee, You will please return this staff and shoulder belt over to the 9th Maine. [It] was captured at [Fort] Gilmore on the 29th October 1864 by the . . . 3rd [Arkansas] Regt. Vols." Below the jab the man had simply signed his name "Big Rebel."[105]

Only 557 men were left in the Texas Brigade that April. More than 7,000 had served in the unit since 1861. Companies A and F of the 1st Texas had only 2 men to surrender. Company B had none. In the 5th Texas, Company D could boast but 9 men. The men of one company after another passed through the surrender point and then made their way quietly back to their encampment and discussed how they would get home.[106] Most of the Arkansans decided to take their own route via Chattanooga and Memphis, while the Texans debated an overland versus a water route to the Lone Star State. Captain Hill and Major Martin offered to lead home whoever wished to follow them. Other men, like A. B. Green of the 5th Texas, chose "to go our own way" along the roads, rivers, and rails to Texas, while Capt. Dugat Williams and a few men from the 5th Texas relied on Williams's prewar familiarity with steamboats and caught a boat with him at West Point, Virginia.[107]

Federal printing presses had worked around the clock for the last two days printing 30,000 parole slips to be distributed to the surrendering Confederates. The parole was their ticket home to Texas and protection from arrest by Union forces along the way. Some of the Virginians or North Carolinians might have lived close enough to walk off without them, but the men of the Texas Brigade needed paroles for their long journey home. By late morning on April 13, all of the paroles had been distributed and the Texas Brigade was on the march within the hour; it seemed the men could not leave Appomattox quickly enough. As they departed the encampment, Robert Lowery of the 3rd Arkansas peered out from the depressive haze that enveloped him. Ever the farmer, he observed that the "trees are budding out." Maybe he could get home in time to plant a crop.[108]

Even after receiving word that her brother and son were among those who had surrendered with Lee at Appomattox Court House, Maude Young continued to rally the troops on the home front. She echoed the Texas Brigade resolutions' damning of the "shameless shirkers" at home, who she, too, suspected were the key to defeat. Hood's Texans may have surrendered, but Confederates out west were not at all sure the war was over. Indeed, many community leaders and military commanders called on Confederates to redouble their efforts, and Maude Young's calls rang loudest and coldest of them all.

Her most powerful editorial that spring appeared in the April 26 issue of the *Houston Tri-Weekly Telegraph* under the byline "A Few Words about Stay-at-homes." Chilling clarity cut through the page. "If there is one thing . . . that marks the degradation that selfish love of ease and shameless shirking of duty will bring men to, it is the way in which some people are now discussing the recent disaster to our army in Virginia," Young insisted. To see Virginia conquered pained her, but not as much as the sight of those so quick to accept defeat. "And now, when the war shout of the tyrant rises, mingled with his wild hallelujahs, over their ruined homes, sacred cities, exiled children, desecrated alters, thy humiliated Lee," Young scowled, "to hear those, who, to their shame and infamy . . . could have helped and did not, to hear them crying out 'all is lost, we are undone, we are conquered,' I can but beg that every true patriot will take the fan in his hand and sweep from the Confederate floor such miserable chaff that is fit only for the burning."

"I tell you, skulkers," Young promised, a "day of wrath, a dreadful day is in store for you. We don't intend to be conquered. We have Right on our side, and God can save by many or by few.... There is no such thing as submission, reconstruction, nothing but freedom for ourselves, and infamy for you. So shoulder your muskets and do your duty at once or leave the country," Young warned.

If this had not yet sent shivers down readers' spines, Young closed with the classical references to which she so often turned. "Dante in his Inferno, tells us of a horrid place that Virgil led him through—a place for the punishment of those who had done nothing either good or bad for Florence." Young reminded her readers that "it was a hell of neutrals,—and the pangs and penalties were more dreadful than even the eloquent Italian could describe. Rejected by Heaven, refused by the abyss below, they wandered in outer darkness and cold; ever for their folly and supineness, shedding tears which congealed as they flowed, into icy masks over their faces, making them unrecognizable even to each other." As Maude Young clarified in a follow-up piece, Texans must be prepared to "make a Thermopylae of Texas" or die.[109]

As word of Gen. Joseph E. Johnston's surrender in North Carolina reached Texas, Maude Young contributed to a broadside, along with Gens. E. Kirby Smith, John Bankhead Magruder, and Joe Shelby, that appealed to the citizens of Texas, New Mexico, and Arizona to continue the fight. Even after Texas surrendered, she kept pushing. Together, she argued, white Southerners could become a giant wave that would "sweep from the face of the earth every Yankee soldier and garrison, from here to the mouth of the Potomac. Be not discouraged," she promised. "God is our father.... We will with His aid make Texas 'a tower of victory' to which every freedom loving soul shall turn like a shrine."[110] Maude Young fought a desperate defensive operation, but the war was over.

A detailed study of the Texas Brigade from late 1864 through the surrender at Appomattox Court House reveals several factors that sustained the men's morale and their determination to win the war. They were highly motivated from the beginning, attracting men who identified quickly with the Confederacy and were willing to fight more than a thousand miles from their families and homes for their new nation's independence. Their success at Gaines's Mill, Second Manassas, Chickamauga, and the Wilderness made the Texas Brigade one of the most elite units in one of the most elite armies of the war, Lee's Army of Northern Virginia. Pride in what they had accomplished helped to sustain the men's morale, as did their faith in their commanders like John Gregg, William T. Hill, and "Howdy" Martin on down to company commanders like Dugat Williams, who led his men home from Appomattox just as he had led them in battle. While there were small desertion spikes and morale issues in the Texas Brigade's record, strong leadership corrected these and kept them from ever being a serious issue, even while they were a key concern in the rest of the Army of Northern Virginia. The Confederacy's improved ability to return wounded and sick men to the Texas Brigade ranks contributed significantly to their ability to make meaningful contributions to Lee's 1864 campaign, especially at the two battles that opened and closed that season and inflicted the most casualties on the Texas Brigade: the Wilderness and Darbytown Road. While their families' overall morale is difficult to judge, the continued efforts by citizens to raise funds for the Texas Brigade hospital and for supplies for the men in camp as late as April 1865, combined with Maude Young's forceful efforts and the lack of letters encouraging men to come home or to desert or questioning the purpose of the war, indicate that Texas Brigade families remained dedicated to the Confederate cause through the end of the war as well.

A close examination of this unit underscores just how late into the war the Confederacy was able to care for and resupply the Army of Northern Virginia. But more specifically, it demonstrates that Texas Brigade officers succeeded in rallying and inspiring their men despite spikes in desertion rates and drops in morale the previous year. In the final year of the war, Hood's Texans and their families continued to find purpose with Lee and his army, which they believed held the key to their future independence.

NOTES

1. U.S. Federal Census, 1860, Concord, Hardin County, Tex. See also Compiled Service Record (hereafter cited as CSR) for James A. Tiner, 1st Texas Infantry Regiment, Company F, M323, National Archive and Record Administration (hereafter cited as NARA). (All CSRs were accessed through Fold3.com, but I have included the NARA microfilm number as well.)

2. CSR for Charles H. Kingsley, 1st Texas Infantry, Company L, M323, NARA.

3. See CSRs for Robert Hasson, 4th Texas, Company G, ibid.; Jess Anderson, 5th Texas, Company C, ibid.; and Greenberry McDonald, 3rd Arkansas, Company H, M317, NARA.

4. Their return rates also reflected improvements that surgeons and General Robert E. Lee had made in the Army of Northern Virginia through better medical care and logistics. The men benefited from the implementation of "Sanitary Camps" or quarantine sections in camp for returning men who still carried contagious diseases. The return rates also reflected the army's increased number of qualified surgeons and the creation of the Reserve Surgical Corps. See Joseph T. Glatthaar, *General Lee's Army: From Victory to Collapse* (New York: Free Press, 2008), 394–96.

5. J. B. Hood, *Advance and Retreat: Personal Experiences in the United States and Confederate States Armies* (Philadelphia: Press of Burk and McFetridge, 1880), 24; John H.

Reagan, *Memoirs, with Special Reference to Secession and the Civil War* (New York: Neale, 1906), 145. For an excellent analysis of Hood's Brigade in the battle of Gaines's Mill, see Robert E. L. Krick, "The Men Who Carried This Position Were Soldiers Indeed: The Decisive Charge of Whiting's Division at Gaines's Mill," in *The Richmond Campaign of 1862: The Peninsula and the Seven Days*, ed. Gary W. Gallagher (Chapel Hill: University of North Carolina Press, 2000), 181–216.

6. R. E. Lee, Genl., Head Quarters, Army Northern Virginia, near Martinsburg, Virginia, to General Louis T. Wigfall, September 21, 1862, Irenus Watson Landingham Collection, RG 552, Auburn University Special Collections and Archives, Auburn University.

7. The incident at the Wilderness has been reported in numerous accounts, sometimes with Lee claiming "Texans always *drive* them," as Texas Brigade commander John Gregg reported it. Brig. Gen. John Gregg to "My dear friend" (possibly Col. Frank B. Sexton), May 25, 1864, "In line on the North Anna," Frank B. Sexton Papers, John W. Thomason Special Collections, Sam Houston State University, Huntsville, Tex. (hereafter cited as SHSU). For the best analysis of Lee and the Texas Brigade at the battle of the Wilderness, see Robert K. Krick, "'Lee to the Rear,' the Texans Cried," in *The Wilderness Campaign*, ed. Gary W. Gallagher (Chapel Hill: University of North Carolina Press, 1997), 160–200.

8. Gregg to "My dear friend," May 25, 1864, SHSU; Harold B. Simpson, *Hood's Texas Brigade: A Compendium* (Hillsboro, Tex.: Hill Junior College Press, 1977), 384–85.

9. Jerome B. Robertson, *Touched with Valour: Civil War Papers and Casualty Reports of Hood's Texas Brigade*, ed. Harold B. Simpson (Hillsboro, Tex.: Hill Junior College Press, 1964), 52–54.

10. U.S. War Department, *The War of the Rebellion: A Compilation of the Official Records of the Union and Confederate Armies*, 127 vols., index, and atlas (Washington: Government Printing Office, 1880–1901), ser. 1, 32 (2): 640–41 (hereafter cited as *OR*).

11. Joseph T. Glatthaar, *Soldiering in the Army of Northern Virginia: A Statistical Portrait of the Troops Who Served under Robert E. Lee* (Chapel Hill: University of North Carolina Press, 2011), 27.

12. These numbers come from a representative sample, about 20 percent, of the more than 7,000 men who served in the Texas Brigade between 1861 and 1865. There are 1,335 men in the sample (1,212 enlisted men, 70 line officers, 31 headquarters officers, 22 headquarters enlisted). The sample was adjusted for the length of time each company and regiment was in the Texas Brigade, pulling more heavily from those units that were in the brigade longer, and it was drawn from Simpson's *Hood's Texas Brigade*, which lists the name, rank, unit, and brief description of service for each man who served in the Texas Brigade between 1861 and 1865. Within the sample, 89 men were listed as deserters, but 20 of them left because their "term of service had ended" or evidence showed that they did not actually desert. Compiled service records and contemporary newspapers, for example, helped eliminate men like Tom Green, Rifles members Thomas E. Cater (listed AWOL in May 1863), E. B. Millican (granted leave to Texas on November 1862 but never returned) and W. B. Burditt (home on wound furlough; listed AWOL in May 1863). When Vicksburg fell and they couldn't get back to the 4th Texas, the men were permitted to raise a cavalry company in Texas, recruiting out of the Avenue Hotel in Austin. All three joined Texas units for the remainder of the war; Burditt was the only one to join

Susannah J. Ural

cavalry. (*Houston Tri-Weekly Gazette*, July 30, 1863.) Of the remaining 69 desertions, 21 of those occurred between January and April 1864 with an additional 5 men abandoning the unit between November and December 1863.

13. Thomas Jewett Goree, Morristown, Tenn., to his mother, Sarah Williams Kittrell Goree, February 8, 1864, in *Longstreet's Aide: The Civil War Letters of Major Thomas J. Goree*, ed. Thomas W. Cutrer (Charlottesville: University Press of Virginia, 1995), 117.

14. Glatthaar, *General Lee's Army*, 448. For discussion of this happening in August 1863, see p. 416.

15. Watson Dugat Williams, Camp 5th Texas near Strawberry Plains [Tenn.], to Laura Bryan, Liberty, Tex., February 20, 1864, Watson Dugat Williams Letters, Historical Research Center, Hill College, Hillsboro, Tex. (repository hereafter cited as HRC); Gregg to "My dear friend," May 25, 1864, SHSU. The number of returnees was compiled from muster roll and compiled service record data shared by Alfred Young, the author of *Lee's Army on the Overland Campaign: A Numerical Study* (Baton Rouge: Louisiana State University Press, 2013). It is significant to note that only four new recruits joined the unit that year. Their growth in numbers is almost entirely due to returnees.

16. Glatthaar, *General Lee's Army*, 394–96.

17. CSRs for James A. Tiner; Charles H. Kingsley; Robert Hasson; Greenberry McDonald; and Jess Anderson.

18. Rufus King Felder to "Dear Sister," Camp near Winchester, [Va.], October 1, 1862, Rufus King Felder Letters (hereafter cited as Felder Letters without reference to repository), Hood's Texas Brigade Letter Collection, HRC.

19. Felder to "Dear Sister," Camp near Petersburg, [Va.], July 14, 1864, ibid.

20. Felder to "Dear Sister," Camp near Chaffins Bluff, [Va.], August 13, 1864, ibid.

21. Felder to "Dear Sister," Camp near Chaffins Bluff, [Va.], September 18, 1864, ibid.

22. Ibid.

23. Stephen Chicoine, ed., ". . . 'Willing Never to Go in Another Fight': The Civil War Correspondence of Rufus King Felder of Chappell Hill," *Southwestern Historical Quarterly* 106 (April 2003): 575. See also the 1860 U.S. Federal Census where Felder's mother is listed as head of household with real estate valued at over $11,000 and personal wealth at over $37,000.

24. Felder to "Dear Sister," Camp near Chaffins Bluff, [Va.], September 18, 1864, Felder Letters.

25. See CSR for each man in Fold3.com along with a brief service record entry for each man in Simpson, *Hood's Texas Brigade*, 167, 218–19.

26. W. J. Terry, Camp near Chaffins Farm, Va., to Mrs. J. S. Terry, August 13, 1864, Terry, William J. and Beal, D. R. Papers 1864, Pearce Civil War Collection, Navarro College, Corsicana, Tex. No soldier by the name of "Hombleson" appears on the roster of Company G, 5th Texas Infantry. It is possible that he joined the company and was killed before his name could be added to company rolls. From the context of the letter, the Terry family would likely have known Hombleson because William Terry mentioned him by his surname, as he does the other men, who do all appear on the company rolls.

27. W. J. Terry, Camp near Chaffins Farm, Va., to J. S. Terry, August 5, 1864, W. J. Terry Letters, Hood's Texas Brigade Collection, HRC.

28. Sidney E. Moseley to Dr. Alfred Mercer, Hampton Hospital Prisoners' War,

Hampton, Va., December 5, 1864, Sidney E. Moseley Letters, Hood's Texas Brigade Letter Collection, HRC. See also Charles D. Grear, ed., "Debating the Rebellion: A Texan and a New Yorker Discuss Secession and the Civil War," *Military History of the West* 39 (December 2009): 41–58.

29. Sidney E. Moseley to Dr. Alfred Mercer, Hampton Hospital Prisoners' War, Hampton, Va., December 5, 1864, Sidney E. Moseley Letters, Hood's Texas Brigade Letter Collection, HRC.

30. Ibid.

31. Ibid.

32. Circular, Headquarters, Army of Northern Virginia, October 9, 1864, folder 18 of the T. L. Clingman Papers, #157, Southern Historical Collection, Wilson Library, University of North Carolina at Chapel Hill. Available online at http://blogs.lib.unc.edu/civilwar/index.php/2014/10/09/9-october-1864/#sthash.nHp5S9s6.dpuf (last accessed December 4, 2015).

33. *A Bill to Be Entitled An Act to Authorize the Consolidation of Companies, Battalions, and Regiments*, November 8, 1864, Confederate States of America (Richmond: CSA, 1864).

34. For discussions of consolidation and morale, see Glatthaar, *General Lee's Army*, 436; and J. Tracy Power, *Lee's Miserables: Life in the Army of Northern Virginia from the Wilderness to Appomattox* (Chapel Hill: University of North Carolina Press, 1998), 239–40.

35. Longstreet to Lee, January 10, 1865, in *OR*, ser. 1, 46 (2): 1033.

36. Rufus King Felder to "Dear Mother," Camp near Richmond, [Va.], December 18, 1864, Felder Letters.

37. Seaborn Dominey to Caroline Dominey, on Charles City Road near Richmond, Va., November 11, 1864, Seaborn Dominey Letters, Hood's Texas Brigade Letter Collection, HRC.

38. Seaborn Dominey to Caroline Dominey, Camp near Petersburg, Va., July 25, 1864, ibid.

39. Seaborn Dominey to Caroline Dominey, on the Charles City Road near Richmond, Va., December 14, 1864, ibid.

40. Ibid.

41. Seaborn Dominey to "Dear Sister" Miss Eliza Davis, Camp near Richmond, Va., December 20, 1864, ibid.

42. Quoted in Angelina V. Winkler, *The Confederate Capitol and Hood's Texas Brigade* (Austin: E. VonBoeckmann, 1894), 207.

43. Littlefield letter dated December 18, 1864, in ibid., 207.

44. CSR for Asbury Lawson, 5th Texas, Company C, M323, NARA.

45. CSR for Edwin B. Searle, 1st Texas, ibid.

46. CSR for Henry F. Bradley, 1st Texas, Company G, ibid.

47. *Richmond (Va.) Daily Dispatch*, July 28, 1864.

48. See CSR for Joseph C. Chiles and C. M. Mixon, 1st Texas Volunteer Infantry Regiment, Company D, M323, NARA.

49. Alfred Young list of the 1,361 on the rolls from *Lee's Army on the Overland Campaign*. Only 17 of the 1,361 officers and men on the Texas Brigade rolls between May

and November 1864 were listed as deserters and cannot be cleared due to an inability to return from wound furloughs in Texas or were actually missing due to wound and capture or wound and recovering in hospital.

50. Glatthaar, *General Lee's Army*, 27.

51. James I Robertson Jr., *The Stonewall Brigade* (1963; repr., Baton Rouge: Louisiana State University Press, 1991), v–vii, 226. See also *OR*, ser. 1, 34 (2): 1001.

52. Earl J. Hess, *Lee's Tar Heels: The Pettigrew-Kirkland-MacRae Brigade* (Chapel Hill: University of North Carolina Press, 2002), xiii–xiv, 286–88.

53. For more on this powerful sense of identity that some white Southerners shared with their new nation as well as with Robert E. Lee and his Army of Northern Virginia, see Gary W. Gallagher, *The Confederate War* (Boston: Harvard University Press, 1997). For more on Confederate nationalism overall, see Anne Sarah Rubin, *A Shattered Nation: The Rise and Fall of the Confederacy, 1861–1868* (Chapel Hill: University of North Carolina Press, 2005). For more on sustained Confederate nationalism within Lee's army, see Lisa Laskin, "'The Army Is Not Near So Much Demoralized as the Country Is': Soldiers in the Army of Northern Virginia and the Confederate Home Front," in *The View from the Ground: Experiences of Civil War Soldiers*, ed. Aaron Sheehan-Dean (Lexington: University Press of Kentucky, 2006), 91–120; and Power, *Lee's Miserables*.

54. Winkler, *Confederate Capitol*, 208. For strong arguments on the effectiveness of linear tactics, see Earl J. Hess, *Civil War Infantry Tactics: Training, Combat, and Small-Unit Effectiveness* (Baton Rouge: Louisiana State University Press, 2015).

55. Martin listed his real estate property at $4,800 and personal property at $600 in the 1860 U.S. Federal Census.

56. Simpson, *Hood's Texas Brigade*, 30. Original in J. J. Faulk, *History of Henderson County* (Athens, Tex.: Athens Review Printing, 1929), 129.

57. Claude H. Hall, "Congressman William H. 'Howdy' Martin," paper presented at the East Texas Historical Association Annual Meeting, Nacogdoches, Tex., October 7, 1967; Mildred Martin Bond and George Doherty Bond, *Alexander Carswell and Isabella Brown: Their Ancestors and Descendants: Genealogy and History of Carswell, Brown, Gordon, Ruthven and the John Martin–Jane Hutchinson Family* (Chipley, Fla.: Carswell Foundation, 1977), 344–46. See also Kenneth W. Howell, *An Antebellum History: Henderson County, Texas, 1846–1861* (Austin: Eakin Press, 1999), 75–76.

58. Martha E. Martin, "Sketch of Major W. H. Martin," *Biographies of Eminent Citizens and Historical Sketches of Henderson County* (Athens, Tex.: Directory of Athens City, 1904), 2:24–25. Martin's widow, Martha E. Gallemore Martin, noted that the physical description of Martin that has been picked up by numerous historians and best captured in art by John W. Thomason Jr., nephew of the Goree brothers of the 5th Texas and Longstreet's staff, came from Judge John Steven's address in Athens about his fellow Texas Brigade veteran.

59. Winkler, *Confederate Capitol*, 108–9. The physical description comes from Martin's CSR, which states that he was forty-one at the end of the war with gray eyes, brown hair, and a florid complexion and was five foot eleven inches tall. CSR, H. William Martin, 4th Texas Infantry, M323, NARA.

60. Robert K. Krick, *Civil War Weather in Virginia* (Tuscaloosa: University of Alabama Press, 2007), 147–49.

61. "Resolutions of the Texas Brigade," January 24, 1865, Confederate Imprints, box 2, C669, Special Collections, McCain Library and Archives, University of Southern Mississippi, University of Southern Mississippi Digital Collections, http://digilib.usm.edu/cdm/ref/collection/rarebook/id/2546 (last accessed March 20, 2016).

62. Ibid.

63. Ibid.

64. Ibid.

65. For a discussion of these resolutions in the spring of 1865, see Jason Phillips, *Diehard Rebels: The Confederate Culture of Invincibility* (Athens: University of Georgia Press, 2007), 7, 22, 161–63.

66. Letter reprinted from the *Richmond Examiner* in the *Houston Tri-Weekly Telegraph*, January 18, 1865, p. 4, col. 4.

67. R. Douglas Hurt, *Agriculture and the Confederacy: Policy, Productivity, and Power in the Civil War South* (Chapel Hill: University of North Carolina Press, 2015), 101–3, 246.

68. Vicki Betts, "'A Sacred Charge upon Our Hands': Assisting the Families of Confederate Soldiers in Texas, 1861–1865," in *The Seventh Star of the Confederacy: Texas during the Civil War*, ed. Kenneth W. Howell (Denton: University of North Texas, 2009), 259.

69. For more on this version of the social contract, see Stephanie McCurry, *Confederate Reckoning: Power and Politics in the Civil War South* (Chapel Hill: University of North Carolina Press, 2011), 198–202.

70. Betts, "'Sacred Charge upon Our Hands,'" 251.

71. *Triweekly News* (Houston, Tex.), February 24, 1863, p. 2, col. 1.

72. This type of response is not unique to Texas. See a discussion of how white women across the Confederacy responded to these appeals in Rubin, *Shattered Nation*, 54–67.

73. Betts, "'Sacred Charge upon Our Hands,'" 258. For the original Coleman quotes, see C. Richard King, ed., *Victorian Lady on the Texas Frontier: The Journal of Ann Raney Coleman* (Norman: University of Oklahoma Press, 1971), 153–55.

74. Betts, "'Sacred Charge upon Our Hands,'" 258.

75. Ibid., 256.

76. Ibid., 257–58.

77. If such letters do exist, they are exceptionally rare when compared with the number of letters calling men home that came in to other Confederate units who lacked the Texas Brigade's unusually strong dedication to the war effort (shown by both the soldiers and their families) from the beginning to the bitter end of the war. For scholarship on fracturing Confederate morale and letters that encouraged men to resign commissions or desert and come home, see Drew Gilpin Faust, *Mothers of Invention: Women of the Slaveholding South in the American Civil War* (Chapel Hill: University of North Carolina Press, 1996), 243; and Faust again in "Altars of Sacrifice: Confederate Women and the Narratives of War," in *Divided Houses: Gender and the Civil War*, ed. Catherine Clinton and Nina Silber (New York: Oxford University Press, 1992), 171–99. For an analysis of Confederates struggling with a desire to secure victory and sacrifice honorably while also desperately wanting the war to end, see Rubin, *Shattered Nation*, 75–79.

78. Betts, "'Sacred Charge upon Our Hands,'" 258–59.

79. Petition from citizens and soldiers in Indianola, Calhoun County, Tex., to Governor

Susannah J. Ural

Pendleton Murrah, April 4, 1865, Governor Pendleton Murrah Records, 1863–1865, box 2014/022–4, folder 112, Texas State Library and Archives, Austin.

80. *Dallas Herald*, September 7, 1864, taken from an August 20, 1864, address by Wigfall in Marshall, Tex.

81. Simpson, *Hood's Texas Brigade*, 451.

82. Details on the Knight brothers can be found in the 1860 U.S. Federal Census, Smith County, Tex., http://search.ancestry.com/cgi-bin/sse.dll?ti=0&indiv=try&db =1860usfedcenancestry&h=35346386 (last accessed March 23, 2016). Sarah Knight's date of death, possibly from childbirth but the record is not clear on that, is found via the FindAGrave website for Sarah Elizabeth Shelton Knight at http://www.findagrave.com /cgi-bin/fg.cgi?page=gr&GRid=37514330&ref=acom (last accessed March 23, 2016).

83. Jacob Hemphill, in his short reminiscence of the war, noted that the stars were sent by "Miss Fuller of Houston, Texas." Jacob Hemphill, "Reminiscences," in *Reminiscences of the Boys in Gray, 1861–1865*, ed. Mamie Yeary (1912; repr., Dayton, Ohio: Morningside Books, 1986), 324.

84. Margaret Swett Henson, "Young, Matilda Jane Fuller," in *Handbook of Texas Online*, http://www.tshaonline.org/handbook/online/articles/fyo10 (last accessed April 3, 2016).

85. See history of 5th Texas Flag at the online exhibit "Historic Flags of the Texas State Library and Archives," https://www.tsl.texas.gov/exhibits/flags/4047FifthTexas.html (last accessed September 12, 2015).

86. *Richmond Whig*, January 17, 1865.

87. Ibid.

88. Rufus King Felder, Camp near Richmond, to "My Dear Sister," February 23, 1865, Felder Letters. The ellipses are due to a tear in the original letter.

89. Samuel S. Watson, "In the trenches North Side of the James," February 1865 (no precise day listed), Samuel S. Watson Letters, HRC. The spelling and punctuation found in the original have been preserved.

90. A. Wakelee, Richmond, Va., to Miss Schadt, January 13, 1865; William Schadt, Richmond Va., to "My dear Sister," February 26, 1865; and Caroline Schadt, Houston, to "My ever dear Brother," March 29, 1865, in Charles Schadt Letters, Rosenberg Library, Galveston, Tex.

91. W. Dugat Williams, Texas Depot, Richmond, Va., to "My Own Dear Lollie" [Laura Bryan], Liberty, Tex., January 3, 1865, Watson Dugat Williams Letters, HRC.

92. W. J. Watts, Army of Northern Va., Camp 1st Texas Regt., to Mr. Philip Gathings "Dear Cousin," March 11, 1865, copy of original letter and transcription shared with the author by descendants of Philip Gathings, HenryEtta Wilson and John Stevens. The spelling and punctuation found in the original have been preserved.

93. Hill's account in Joseph B. Polley, *Hood's Texas Brigade: Its Marches, Its Battles, Its Achievements* (New York: Neale, 1910), 277.

94. The Hills had a combined property and personal wealth of nearly $214,000, which included more than twenty slaves. Hill Family, 1860 Census, http://search.ancestry.com //cgi-bin/sse.dll?db=1860usfedcenancestry&indiv=try&h=35390361.

95. Basil Crow Brashear, Gregory, Tex., to Frank B. Chilton, March 5, 1911, Basil Brashear Papers, HRC.

96. CSR for William T. Hill, 5th Texas Infantry Regiment, M323, NARA. See also Hill in Polley, *Hood's Texas Brigade*, 277.

97. Polley, *Hood's Texas Brigade*, 277.

98. William T. Hill account in Frank B. Chilton, *Unveiling and Dedication of Monument to Hood's Texas Brigade . . .* (Houston: Frank B. Chilton, 1911), 183.

99. Bond and Bond, *Alexander Carswell and Isabella Brown*, 346.

100. William Marvel, *A Place Called Appomattox* (Chapel Hill: University of North Carolina Press, 2000), 227.

101. See diary of A. B. Green that notes, "Stacked arms on the 12th at Appomattox C.H. Started to Texas on the 13th April." A. B. Green's Diary, Company K, 5th Texas Infantry, "The Journey Home: Appomattox to Moscow, TX, April 13–July 11, 1865," privately printed as *A Souvenir of the Hood's Texas Brigade Association, Re-activated June 2015 Tour, 'The Last Trumpet Call.'* See also diary of Robert Lowry, 3rd Arkansas, Company G, that notes, "12th — taken our guns and marched to Appomattox C.H. 4 miles stacked our guns in front of the yankees and marched back to camp. . . . I left my horn with the guns." Robert Lowry Diary, Hood's Texas Brigade Collection, HRC.

102. Brashear to Chilton, March 5, 1911, Basil Brashear Papers, HRC.

103. Thomas Fletcher Harwell, *Eighty Years under the Stars and Bars* (Kyle, Tex.: W. Turner Harwell, 1947), 101, quoted in Robert Maberry, *Texas Flags* (College Station: Texas A&M University Press, 2001), 83.

104. Ibid.

105. Ibid.

106. William T. Hill account in Frank B. Chilton, *Unveiling and Dedication of Monument to Hood's Texas Brigade* (Houston: Frank B. Chilton, 1911), 184.

107. Basil Crow Brashear, Gregory, Tex., to Frank B. Chilton, March 1911, Basil Brashear Papers, HRC. Brashear does not date his second letter to Chilton but comments that he was following up on a letter "I sent you a few days ago." That earlier letter was dated March 5, 1911.

108. "[April] 13th — received our parolls [sic]," Robert Lowery Diary, Robert Lowery Papers, HRC.

109. *Houston Tri-Weekly Telegraph*, April 26, 1865. Young's reference to making a "Thermopylae of Texas" comes from her May 19, 1865, editorial in the *Tri-Weekly Telegraph*.

110. Ibid., May 16, 1865.

A Whole Lot of Blame
to Go Around

The Confederate Collapse at Five Forks

Peter S. Carmichael

While Confederate major general George E. Pickett was finishing his plate of fried fish at a shad bake, Union major general Philip H. Sheridan was devouring Pickett's command at Five Forks. The sounds of the Federal assault were supposedly silenced by abnormal atmospheric conditions called an acoustic shadow. Pickett and his luncheon companions—Maj. Gen. Thomas Rosser and Maj. Gen. Fitzhugh Lee—heard nothing over the sounds of conviviality, but the sudden appearance of a courier alerted the dining party to an alarming reality. This soldier claimed that he was nearly shot out of his saddle by Federal soldiers who were sweeping behind the Confederate infantry. Plates and cups must have dropped to the ground when he pointed to enemy skirmishers advancing just a few hundred yards away. It was abundantly clear to every person at the shad bake, whether the man had imbibed or not, that the enemy was on the verge of enveloping Pickett's entire command.

Such sobering news spurred into action the man who had earned immortality for his failed charge at Gettysburg. Pickett rushed to the front, riding on the right side of his horse as a shield from enemy fire. Everything was in disarray by the time he reached Five Forks. Thousands of men streamed past him, fleeing the field with the single-mindedness of veterans driven by the desire to survive. They showed no regard for their reputations and cared even less for the authority of rank. Their flight cleared the way for the Federals to seize the South Side Railroad, a communication and supply line of immense importance. Union control of these tracks forced Gen. Robert E. Lee to evacuate Petersburg, which in turn meant that Richmond's days as the Confederate capital were numbered. Pickett's debacle at Five Forks, unlike his bloody failure at Gettysburg, could not be redeemed as a grand gesture of romantic heroism. The humiliation of this disaster, however, could be swept under the rug of the Lost Cause, which hid all imperfections by attributing any Confederate setback to Union armies having more troops and resources.

The storyline above encapsulates the standard explanation of Confederate defeat at Five Forks, a crossroads where the White Oak Road, Scott's Road, Ford's Road, and Dinwiddie Court House Road intersected. Without exception, historians have criticized Pickett and Fitz Lee for a dereliction of duty that is virtually unparalleled in the Civil War. Some historians maintain that both officers, even if they had abandoned their men for a fish fry, could have done nothing to check such a powerful Union attack led by Generals Sheridan and Gouverneur K. Warren. Others see Pickett and Fitz Lee as the hapless victims of an acoustic shadow that distorted the soundscape of the battle. How could anyone have expected the Confederate officers to defeat the Yankees when nature itself had turned against them?[1]

The interpretive consensus on Five Forks advances a number of shared conclusions, though not all historians embrace these points with equal conviction. In one explanation Sheridan and Warren remain a virtual sideshow to Pickett and Fitz Lee, whose defeat was of their own making. Union victory, in other words, fell into Sheridan and Warren's lap; the quirky aspects of the battle — the shad bake and acoustic shadow — isolated Pickett and Fitz Lee from their commands and doomed Confederate chances. These arguments, though useful, are almost entirely disconnected from the operational and strategic context of the battle. The result is a lack of historical altitude on Five Forks that keeps Robert E. Lee at a safe distance from one of the greatest calamities that befell his army.

Few generals in military history who were at the helm when their armies collapsed and their cities fell have received less critical scrutiny than Lee. As soon as the war ended, ex-Confederates rallied to their former commander's defense, arguing that he was never outgeneraled or defeated but succumbed to superior numbers and resources in a ruthless war waged by a godless enemy. This idea formed the cornerstone of a Lost Cause explanation of Confederate defeat that continues to raise its ugly head today.[2] The almost militant defense of Lee, however, did not bring unanimity among white Southerners. In 1866, for instance, James D. McCabe Jr. argued in *Life and Campaigns of Robert E. Lee* that the collapse of Confederate forces at Petersburg could have been avoided if Jefferson Davis had relinquished more authority to Lee. The calamity at Five Forks was particularly disturbing to McCabe. He pinned the defeat on Pickett's infantry, whose behavior on April 1, 1865, he

Peter S. Carmichael

condemned as cowardice. McCabe argued that the once proud soldiers of Gettysburg were so weak-minded and demoralized at this late stage of the war that when pressed by the Yankees they "made little to no effort to hold their position." McCabe buttressed his account with some apocryphal stories that were intended to elicit sympathy for the commanding general. According to McCabe, an indignant Lee "had witnessed this disgraceful conduct of his troops, promising those around him that when Pickett's veterans were taken into action again, he would place himself at the head of their charging column. Then turning to a general officer present, Lee ordered 'him sternly and with marked emphasis, to collect and put under guard 'all the stragglers on the field.'" [3] McCabe's Five Forks account was pure fiction. Lee was nowhere close to the Five Forks battlefield, but the reading public would be unaware of such a crucial detail.

The survivors of Five Forks had been shamed, and honor demanded a public response. Walter Harrison, formerly of Pickett's staff, would not allow McCabe's accusations to stand without a challenge. In his 1870 publication, *Pickett's Men: A Fragment of War History*, Harrison tried to restore the tarnished image of the Confederates at Five Forks by discrediting McCabe. He denounced McCabe for his falsification of the past, reminding his readers that "it might not be worth while to notice this foolish and slanderous attack against the 'men of Gettysburg'; upon these veteran soldiers of many battlefields whom Gen. Lee himself 'delighted to honor.'" [4] Yet the dispute between Harrison and McCabe did not erupt into contentious public debate over Five Forks. In fact, the words of Harrison and McCabe were largely forgotten, their writings inconsequential to subsequent debates. The shad bake and the acoustic shadow, which eventually became permanent fixtures in modern studies, were not even mentioned by either author.

The Five Forks debate found new life in 1884 when Confederate cavalryman Tom Rosser revealed the story of the shad bake in the *Philadelphia Weekly Times*. He exposed the embarrassing fact that Pickett and Fitzhugh Lee had absented themselves from their commands for a fish fry. Rosser admitted that he had organized the affair, but he was quick to note that neither Fitz Lee nor Pickett seemed especially concerned about the welfare of the troops or interested in the intentions of the enemy. During the feast, Rosser noted that "couriers came in from" the picket line reporting Federal activity, but their messages failed to convince Pickett and Fitz Lee that the enemy was on the move. They trusted their ears over the eyes of their subordinates. As long as the popping sounds of picket fire did not escalate into sustained cannonades and musketry, they saw no reason to stop eating. Not until a

Maj. Gen. George E. Pickett, renowned for his failed charge at Gettysburg,
blamed subordinates and superiors alike for his debacle at Five Forks.
(Library of Congress Prints and Photographs Division,
reproduction number LC-USZ6-284)

courier reported that he had been fired upon did the party break up. After so
many years, Rosser still could not understand Pickett's behavior. "It seems to
have been a surprise to General Pickett, yet one would have supposed that
he would have been on the alert in the presence of an enemy he had so recently been fighting, but from all I could see on the occasion I am satisfied
that all the generalship and management was on the Federal side."[5] For the

Peter S. Carmichael

man who was behind the fish fry and apparently enjoyed the food and drink as much as any other officer there, it took some nerve for Rosser to single out Pickett for negligence.

Although Rosser had an unquenchable passion for disparaging his fellow officers, there are no outlandish claims in the *Philadelphia Weekly Times*—as one would have expected from the Virginia cavalryman. Historians have largely accepted Rosser's conclusion that Five Forks was lost at the shad bake, where Pickett and Fitz Lee unknowingly sat in a soundproof vault of nature's own creation. The echoes of battle that reverberated across the gloomy pine flats surrounding Five Forks never reached the two most important Confederate officers on the field. No historian has done more to popularize this interpretation than Douglas Southall Freeman, whose four-volume Pulitzer Prize biography of Lee, *R. E. Lee: A Biography*, and three-volume history of the Army of Northern Virginia, *Lee's Lieutenants: A Study in Command*, established him as one of the most influential of all Civil War historians of his generation. In both works, Freeman, who was never shy about his Confederate sympathies, does not go easy on Pickett and Fitz Lee. He blames both men for attending a shad bake rather than tending to their troops. This lapse of judgment, he insists, turned an inevitable defeat into a rout. In the end, Freeman articulated the interpretation that has become the widely accepted historical interpretation: the position at the Forks was indefensible, Sheridan's force was too strong, and in the face of such extreme odds no act of generalship could have rescued Pickett's small command. Freeman offers a well-reasoned and researched explanation for the Confederate collapse at Five Forks, but when the author turns to Lee, he loses his critical perspective. As was typical of Freeman, he always went out of his way to dust off Lee's fingerprints from any reverse. The calamity at Five Forks was no exception.

Lee stands behind a Lost Cause barricade, shielded from criticism about April 1, 1865, at the expense of his subordinates, who are left without cover and easily targeted for the operational and tactical mistakes made by the Army of Northern Virginia on that day. In *R. E. Lee*, Freeman removes the general from the Five Forks debacle without exploring all that Lee could have done to protect the South Side Railroad. To identify such possibilities would have challenged the inevitability of Confederate defeat, a point that Freeman treasured. Instead, he checked the standard interpretive boxes: too many enemy soldiers, too few resources, and a lack of subordinates who could carry out Lee's brilliant designs. With his typical seductive eloquence, Freeman wrote of Five Forks, "Thus in two calamitous hours, the mobile force that Lee had established to protect his right flank was swept away and virtually ceased to be." Although the general was physically present on the extreme western edge of the Petersburg lines, Freeman insisted that "his [Lee's] most strategic position had been lost. Fought in accordance with the plans made by two subordinates, and without Lee's participation or knowledge of what was happening, Five Forks was only one scene removed from the dread denouement."[6]

If one accepts Freeman's assessment of Five Forks, then one must also excuse Lee for not participating in or knowing anything about a situation that the general himself deemed a threat to the very existence of his army and nation. It is unfortunate that Freeman distanced Lee from the battlefield at Five Forks, but this was in keeping with his belief that Lee's generalship was beyond reproach. Freeman needed to strike a better balance between criticism and empathy. If he had done so, his analysis would have been more incisive and his interpretation more enduring. A more critical approach, however, does not mean entertaining the what-ifs that plague much of the anti-Lee scholarship.[7] Any suggestion that the general could have saved his army with an offensive maneuver reminiscent of Second Manassas or Chancellorsville is pure fantasy. The Army of Northern Virginia had long passed its zenith of power, and the grind of siege warfare had reduced the fighting spirit and strength of the rank and file. In the spring of 1865, Lee only had 31,400 men to cover twenty-seven-and-a-half miles of trench line that stretched from the Richmond defenses just north of the James River to the western outskirts of Petersburg. On the ground it came to 1,140 men per mile, or one man every yard and a half.[8]

Lee's veteran soldiers were hanging on by a gossamer thread. Quite simply, Petersburg was a fiendish place. Clean water was difficult to find, and rations were inadequate and insufficient in nutrients. Weakened bodies living in filth and mud were vulnerable to diarrhea and dysentery. The physical decline of the troops decimated morale. It was no surprise that desertion surged among Confederates who had neither the will nor the physical energy to continue the fight. Confederate lieutenant general Richard Anderson admitted as much in his official report of the Petersburg campaign to Lee: "Our army (from what causes it is useless to inquire) had received no accession of strength and was in all points weaker than when it had marched the year before to the battle of the Wilderness." "That of the enemy," he added, "was much more powerful than it had been and his number, his equipage, his transportation and his ammunition were ostensibly exhibited to our half starved, poorly equipped and depleted ranks, and disheartened and discouraged they entered upon the campaign of 1865 with but little of the spirit of former days."[9]

The Army of Northern Virginia was falling apart because of Lt. Gen. Ulysses S. Grant's calculated strategy to deprive Lee of the means to wage war in the early spring of 1865. The Army of the Potomac extended its tentacles westward beyond Petersburg, choking off all but two of the Confederates' important links to the outside world—the South Side and Richmond & Danville Railroads. In so doing, Grant locked Lee's army in place while damaging valuable railroads leading to Petersburg from the south and west. Lee attempted to break the Army of the Potomac's chokehold by attacking Fort Stedman on March 25. Lee had committed to evacuating Richmond and Petersburg prior to his attack against Fort Stedman, which was designed as a means to that end, not as the catalyst for it. Initially the Confederates punched a hole in the enemy lines, but the Federals regrouped and restored their broken lines. The defeat helped convince Lee that the fall of Richmond was unavoidable. He started to outline contingency plans to evacuate both cities, assuring civil authorities that abandoning the nation's capital would not be akin to throwing away the cause. He wrote to the secretary of war that "if the army can be maintained in an efficient condition, I do not regard the abandonment of our present position as necessarily fatal to our success."[10] But a controlled and methodical evacuation could occur only if Lee withdrew on his timetable—not the enemy's.

There was no reprieve for the Army of Northern Virginia after Fort Stedman. Within days of the failed assault, Grant sent some 13,000 of Philip Sheridan's troopers on an expedition to end the siege. They were to head west and sweep around the Confederate flank by moving toward Dinwiddie Court House. From there, Sheridan could head north, using his mobility and firepower to get astride the South Side Railroad. Communications would be severed and supplies would be shut off, leaving Petersburg and Richmond untenable.

To protect the Confederate right flank from Sheridan's slashing offensive, Lee organized a task force of 5,500 horsemen under Fitzhugh Lee and 6,000 infantry under George Pickett. The shifting of troops to Petersburg was no easy matter. The situation on the Confederate left flank above the James River was also vulnerable. Stripping troops from that area worried Lt. Gen. James Longstreet, who was uncertain of the enemy's intentions on his own front. Lee warned Longstreet that he might need to lead a division in person. In the meantime, he called on three brigades of Pickett's division, the closest thing that Lee had to a reserve force.[11] These troops were north of the James River and close to Richmond in order to await a possible raid by Sheridan. When the attack never materialized and Sheridan's movements toward Petersburg were detected, Pickett's men boarded trains for Petersburg on March 29. During the movement they tried to conceal themselves from the enemy until they reached Sutherland Station, some ten miles beyond the western edge of the Petersburg trenches.

Once they disembarked, Pickett received orders to move to Hatcher's Run and report to Fourth Corps commander Richard Anderson near Burgess Mill. It was a wicked march in a fierce night rain. Swollen streams and mud nearly derailed the operation. The misery did not end until the troops reached their destination early on the morning of March 30. Escaping the shackles of trench warfare was supposed to rejuvenate weary veterans, but Pickett's men were reminded that campaigning in the field had its own way of oppressing body and mind.[12]

Shortly after the troops arrived, Pickett headed to an important meeting with Robert E. Lee and Maj. Gen. Henry Heth. Both officers had just finished a morning reconnaissance. A Virginia artillerist watched the pair ride by, recording the moment in his diary. He noted that Lee did not appear to be in "a good humour."[13] It is easy to imagine why; nothing in his reconnaissance with Heth offered much cause for hope. Wherever he looked, Lee saw trenches sparsely held. What could be done to meet a situation that was turning into a full-blown crisis when there were so few soldiers? The previous day the Confederates had been unable to hold the Boydton Plank Road for a lack of manpower in a sharp little fight known as Lewis Farm House or Quaker Road. The loss of this important roadway, coupled with the news that Sheridan's troops were massing around Dinwiddie Court House, demonstrated Grant's intentions. The entire Confederate right flank—and not just the South Side Railroad—was imperiled. To meet this Federal offensive, the Confederate commander had no choice but to lengthen his lines to the west along the White Oak Road. This would extend his position past the Claiborne Road and toward Five Forks.[14]

It was midmorning when Lee and Heth met Pickett and Anderson at the Turnbull House. A staff officer described this gathering as "a considerable *pow-wow* . . . among the chiefs."[15] It appears that everyone agreed that a purely defensive posture would play into the hands of Grant and Sheridan. Heth opened the conversation with the suggestion that his division, supported by Pickett, would strike the Federals near Burgess Mill. If successful, Grant would have to contract his lines and regroup, thus buying Lee more time to shift forces to his distressed flank. The proposed movement, however, would have done nothing to blunt Sheridan's inevitable advance from Dinwiddie Court House. Lee's reservations about Heth's proposal were not recorded, but his alternative plan of sending Pickett and Fitz Lee as a strike force outside the main Confederate line was consistent with his belief in a defensive-offensive philosophy. This had guided his operations from the beginning of the siege.

To suggest that the general should have stayed in his formidable trenches to simply preserve his manpower overlooks the inescapable political imperatives that forced Lee's hand. Unless he took offensive action, he would be relinquishing Petersburg without any resistance. The Confederacy could not handle another Joseph E. Johnston. From the start of the siege in June 1864, Lee had wanted his counterstrokes to drive the Army of the Potomac from the besieged city, but it quickly became apparent that Grant, no matter how serious the battlefield setback, was not going to budge. All Lee could do was frustrate his adversary's operations. He did so in a series of offensive forays throughout the summer and fall of 1864. The Army of the Potomac staggered back from the Confederates' well-directed counterpunches, but without sufficient reserves, Lee lacked the offensive muscle to deliver a knockout blow. And yet the Confederates had still managed to achieve tactical success at Jerusalem Plank Road (June 22–24), Weldon Railroad (August 18–21), Ream's Station (August 25), Peebles Farm (September 30–October 2), Boydton Plank Road (October 27), and Hatcher Run (February 5–7, 1865).[16]

With the opening of the spring campaign in early 1865, Grant was eager to resume the familiar dance of trying to sidestep the enemy. Union forces would push to the west, extending their reach around Petersburg, and the Confederates would respond by coming out of their trenches to resist the advance. As this pattern of operations had already revealed, Federal troops were often dispersed, isolated, and vulnerable to attack. At the same time, Grant had induced Lee to move his troops outside of his powerful fortifications. This must have pleased the Union commander, but Lee had history on his side. Since the beginning of the siege, his troops had been outmanned, but they had never been outfought. Lee had good reason to believe that a mobile Confederate force would disrupt and embarrass the Federal advance, especially in the open field. Lee had said as much to his cavalry subordinate and nephew Fitz Lee—and most likely to Heth, Pickett, and Anderson as well. According to Fitz Lee, the general had stated, "We could attack that force (Sheridan), and had better attack it as the best way to break it up and prevent any movement upon their part."[17]

As grim as things were in late March 1865 for the Army of Northern Virginia, Lee knew that Federals operating south of Petersburg were vulnerable to a Confederate counterstroke. A static defense of Five Forks and the Burgess Mill area would have rendered Pickett's situation hopeless. Lee clearly expected Pickett and Fitz Lee to keep the enemy off-balance through creative maneuvering and aggressive fighting. Pickett and Fitz Lee proved that they were not up to the task at hand, but reading backward from their breathtaking failure on April 1 obscures how Lee thought at the time. He constantly looked to create possibilities for his army, particularly at those times when others had turned to despair and fatalism. Recent history at Petersburg had taught him that his troops were always ready to exploit any misstep by the enemy. In the end, Pickett's expedition to Five Forks and Dinwiddie Court House was not a desperate gamble on Lee's part but a sound decision rendered during desperate times. In fact, it was entirely consistent with his operational strategy throughout the campaign against Grant's flanks. The only departure from Lee's pattern on March 31 was his decision to attack Sheridan's exposed flank rather than to slice between Sheridan and the permanent Union works. The presence of the Union Fifth Corps in that "gap" dictated the course of Lee's counterpunch.

When the meeting closed at the Turnbull House between Lee and his chief subordinates, Pickett received his marching orders. He would have five brigades of infantry under his command; three came from his own division and two drew from the ranks of Maj. Gen. Bushrod Johnson. The gap that the brigades left in place along Burgess Mill was filled by Maj. Gen. Cadmus M. Wilcox's soldiers. Pickett's amalgamated force amounted to some 6,000 foot soldiers. He also carried six pieces of artillery under the direct supervision of the renowned cannoneer William R. J. Pegram. His task force marched to join Fitz Lee's three cavalry divisions at Five Forks. From there, Pickett would assume command of all the forces in a coordinated movement against Sheridan to drive him away from Dinwiddie Court House. Tactical arrangements were clearly left to the discretion of Pickett and Fitz Lee, but what operational issues extended beyond their immediate authority? To what degree did Lee expect Pickett to cooperate with Richard Anderson's forces at the intersection of the White Oak and Claiborne Roads? What about the reserve troops at Burgess Mill? Had anyone outlined contingency plans if Pickett met with a reverse? Could he count on any reserves? It is impossible to reach any firm answers to these crucial questions. In fact, it is quite likely that Lee's officers would have struggled to offer consistent answers to these questions. The army's meltdown at Five Forks was not entirely the fault of Pickett and Fitz Lee, though they certainly bear much of the blame. Some of the communication difficulties originated at headquarters, where Robert E. Lee lost

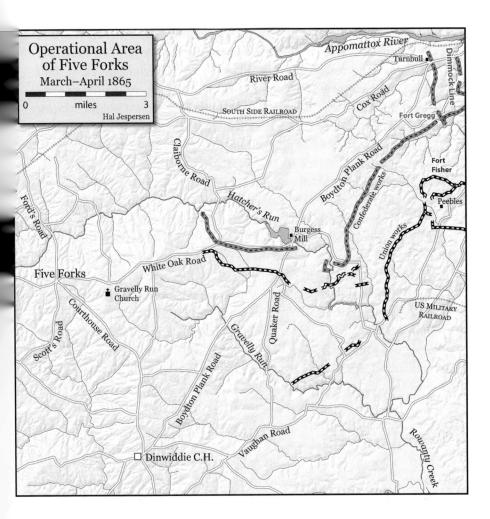

Operational Area
of Five Forks
March–April 1865

0   miles   3

Hal Jespersen

operational control of the all-important right flank of his army before the battle even started.

Evidence of Lee's deep concern for the safety of his right flank was on display on March 31 when he rode to the White Oak and Claiborne Roads. This intersection marked the western outpost of the Confederate line. From there, Lee spotted the flank of the Union Fifth Corps hanging in the air. To keep the Federals from breaking through Anderson's position along the White Oak Road or turning on Pickett at Dinwiddie Court House, Lee personally directed an attack against Gouverneur Warren's unprepared men, who were sent reeling backward. A few undersized Confederate brigades almost wrecked Warren's Fifth Corps, whose retreat nearly turned into a rout until one division rallied and counterattacked. With great reluctance, Lee pulled his forces back to the original trenches along the White Oak Road. But the commanding general found no solace in nearly wrecking the entire Fifth Corps, since Warren's infantry stopped the Southern advance within a stone's throw of the Confederate line. What a reversal of fortune it was for Warren, whose men were poised to take the vital White Oak Road on April 1.[18]

Lee received more bad news during the early morning hours of April 1, when a messenger relayed Pickett's decision to withdraw from Dinwiddie Court House. This must have caught Lee off guard, since the reports throughout March 31 had been so encouraging. Sheridan's troopers were unable to hold their own against the combined strength of Pickett and Fitz Lee. They had been driven eight miles south of the Forks, spared humiliation only by the darkness that brought a close to the fighting.[19] March 31 had started out just as Lee had envisioned, but unfortunately it had not ended as he had hoped. Pickett and Fitz Lee, operating outside of the main fortifications, looked like the second coming of William Mahone and Wade Hampton. They had whipped Sheridan, who had cried out to Grant for reinforcements. Success, though, was a mirage. Pickett saw through it, but Robert E. Lee did not. The commanding general expected Pickett to hold his advanced position at Dinwiddie Court House, but the whereabouts and the intentions of Warren's Fifth Corps were relatively unknown. Pickett had good reason to be concerned, particularly when captured Union prisoners revealed that Union infantry lurked behind his lines. The Confederate position was untenable, and Pickett had no choice but to retire. At two o'clock in the morning of April 1, word quietly passed along the line to retreat. The men extricated themselves with little difficulty and without alerting Sheridan to their movements. They crossed over the ground gained the previous day, stumbling through the blackness of night, to arrive at the Forks just as dawn was breaking. Pickett's men were wet, exhausted, and famished. For three days they had had little rest, little food, and too much rain.

There was still no time for weary men to rest. Out of habit the troops immediately started throwing up earthworks that stretched along the northern side of the White Oak Road. Brig. Gen. Matt W. Ransom's North Carolina infantry and Virginian Col. Thomas T. Munford's dismounted cavalry anchored the far left flank of Pickett's position, which rested 0.7 miles to the east of the Forks and roughly 3.6 miles to the west of the main Confederate fortifications at the intersection of the White Oak and Claiborne Roads. (This was the area where Robert E. Lee had clashed with Warren on March 31.) This 3.6 miles amounted to a dangerous gap between the Confederate position at the

White Oak and Claiborne Roads and the Confederate left, which was held by Ransom and Munford. Only a thin picket line of a few hundred North Carolina troopers had the task of covering this vital line of communication along the White Oak Road between Pickett and Anderson's forces at Burgess Mill.

The Confederate right flank was one mile to the west of the Forks. Maj. Gen. William "Rooney" Lee's cavalry had the assignment to defend this area with infantry support and three of William Pegram's guns, which unlimbered across from the Gilliam field. Pickett had instructed Pegram to place his three other pieces at the Forks, a dismal place for artillery. They were in the midst of a thick woods, the ground was low, and the position commanded nothing, except the intersecting roads at the junction. Pegram's adjutant, Lt. William Gordon McCabe, protested the order, pleading with Pegram to make a direct appeal to Pickett. Pegram flatly refused, rebuking his good friend for suggesting that he violate orders. Later that day Pegram would fall with a mortal wound to his left side. The loss of his dear comrade embittered McCabe, who never forgave Pickett for his placement of the guns. Writing after the war, McCabe charged that Pickett "knew far more about brands of whisky than he did about the uses of artillery."[20] There were also four guns of William Morrell McGregor's horse artillery positioned on the far left flank and under the authority of General Ransom, but the boggy landscape curtailed mobility, keeping McGregor from using his guns as "flying artillery."[21]

Pickett felt as if he had little choice but to align his forces along the White Oak Road, even though there were large swaths around the Forks that proved impassable for artillery, cavalry, and even infantry. One Confederate officer observed that "It is generally a boggy country, and the most indifferent land for cavalry to move in, and in those low points you could not move many infantry. Our horse artillery, which generally went everywhere with us, we did not dare carry in there, simply because they would have been stuck there."[22] It is important to note that this was not the ground of Pickett's choosing but of his commander's. Lee, upon learning of his subordinate's forced withdrawal from Dinwiddie Court House, had issued a directive to Pickett that left no room for interpretation: *Hold Five Forks at all hazards.* Protect road to Ford's Depot and prevent Union forces from striking the South-Side Railroad. Regret exceedingly your forced withdrawal, and your inability to hold the advantage you had gained."[23]

In all of Lee's written orders to his subordinates, his dispatch to Pickett stands out as truly exceptional. It was customary for Lee to give his officers wide latitude to make decisions in the field as they saw fit. This generally worked to Lee's advantage, but a Second Corps staff officer complained after the war about the vagueness of Lee's orders. "I have frequently noticed before & have also since this occasion [referring to the Wilderness] that Gen. Lee's instructions to his Corps Comrs are of a very comprehensive & general description & frequently admit of several interpretations—in fact will allow them to do almost anything, provided only it be a *success*. They caution them particularly against failure & very frequently wind up with the injunction to 'attack whenever or wherever it can be done to advantage.'"[24] Whether this officer was correct in his assessment or not is not at issue. His words are more valuable in understanding how Lee typically communicated his expectations to his subordinates. In Pickett's case, he certainly broke from customary practice. There was no room for interpretation, no allowances made for changing circumstances, and no discretion to move away from Five Forks—a place that Lee had never seen with his own eyes.

The directness of Lee's order does not necessarily suggest a lack of faith in Pickett; rather, it speaks to how desperate the situation had become in Lee's mind. It is understandable why he demanded that Pickett hold his ground at all costs because of the South Side Railroad, but the commanding general had essentially fixed his subordinate to a static defense of an indefensible position along the White Oak Road. Pickett made this very complaint in his May 1865 report. The modest bluffs of Hatcher's Run, located just 1.5 miles north of Five Forks, would have been more suitable for a Confederate last stand. Lee's order, above all else, reveals an imperfect understanding of the operational situation on April 1. To criticize Pickett for his forced withdrawal is incomprehensible; Lee knew that Pickett had no choice but to retreat. It is possible that Lee thought the Fifth Corps was still lodged at the White Oak Road, but Pickett's dispatches alerted Lee to the movements of the Federal infantry. There could very well have been other dispatches, messages, or oral communications in which Lee accounted for Warren's troops, but they do not survive. Nonetheless, Lee should have spelled out contingency plans for his subordinate, especially since the odds were so steep—as Lee himself had discovered the previous day at the White Oak Road. The most astonishing oversight of the "Hold Five Forks at all hazards" order is the lack of guidance in coordinating Pickett with Anderson's troops at the White Oak and Claiborne Roads. Only by uniting Anderson and Pickett could Lee have forestalled a disaster at the Forks. Lee's flawed order is not responsible for the debacle at Five Forks, but its inflexibility conveyed language that can only be read as a reprimand that did not allow for the creativity that Lee so prized in his subordinates.

Peter S. Carmichael

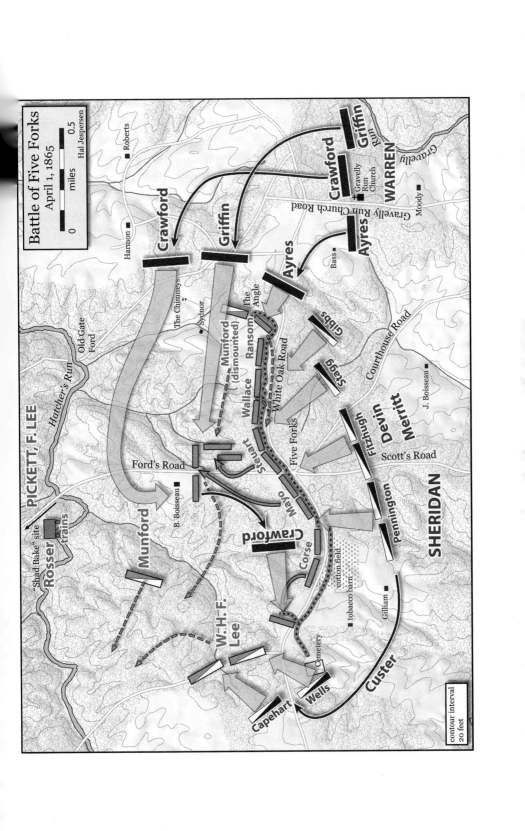

Battle of Five Forks
April 1, 1865

0   miles   0.5

Hal Jespersen

contour interval
20 feet

Pickett and Fitz Lee should have overcome Lee's poorly worded orders, but a combination of factors clouded their judgment and kept them from acting with the vigilance expected of senior officers. The popular perception of Pickett and Fitz Lee sacrificing their army so that they might enjoy some shad and whiskey is an oversimplification. A more nuanced and complicated picture emerges when one consults the underutilized *Proceedings, Findings, and Opinions of the Court of Inquiry in the Case of Gouverneur K. Warren.* A number of ex-Confederates, including Fitz Lee and Thomas Munford, were subpoenaed to the 1879 court of inquiry into Sheridan's unjust dismissal of Warren at the close of the fighting on April 1. Unfortunately, Robert E. Lee and Pickett had passed away by the time the court convened, but there were a number of front-line Confederate officers who offered important insight into the many facets behind the Confederate collapse at Five Forks.

On the whole, the testimony counters the simplistic idea that Pickett and Fitz Lee were more interested in eating fish and drinking whiskey than looking after their troops. Witnesses attest to the fact that both officers personally placed their soldiers along the White Oak Road throughout the morning of April 1. They remained at the front until going to Hatcher's Run (which they probably did around 2:00 P.M.) A little after noon, Col. Joseph Mayo Jr. of the 3rd Virginia Infantry remembered that "General Pickett called us together at Five Forks in the rear of those guns, pulled out a map showed us where we were, then gave directions to strengthen our position as well as we could; and he rode of[f] with General Fitz Lee down this Ford road to the north. We went immediately to execute that order."[25] From Mayo's testimony and that of others, it is clear that Confederate officers knew the location of Pickett and Fitz Lee's headquarters north of Hatcher's Run, where Rosser was guarding the army's wagons. The idea that Fitz Lee and Pickett simply disappeared without telling anyone is misleading. Couriers had no problem in finding both men throughout the day. The challenge for the couriers was getting Pickett and Fitz Lee to believe there was a crisis brewing in front of the Confederate left flank. It also appears that Pickett had not left explicit instructions with the ranking officer on the line, Maj. Gen. Rooney Lee, who himself was not in position to react to an emergency. Rooney was on the far right of the line when the Union attack commenced and was completely unaware that he was the ranking officer responsible for giving commands until Pickett or Fitz returned. Such negligence on Pickett's part was absolutely indefensible.

Why did Pickett and Fitz Lee dismiss even the mere suggestion of an enemy attack? Victory at Dinwiddie Court House had deceived them into believing that Sheridan needed time to regroup. They must have also assumed

Peter S. Carmichael

that Warren's Fifth Corps could not pressure them without support from Sheridan's troopers. But the outcome at Dinwiddie Court House should not have kept Pickett and Fitz Lee from scouting the enemy's movements. Both officers neglected the spadework of army command, which was elemental to success and something that their commanding general valued above all else.[26] One would have thought that curiosity alone should have prompted both men to locate the Fifth Corps, but Pickett and Fitz Lee acted as if Warren's men had vanished into thin air. Sheridan could appear out of nowhere, but Pickett and Lee, having never encountered the fiery Union cavalryman on the battlefield, grossly underestimated the tenacity of their adversary. "I considered that the movement [Sheridan's] had been broken up," Fitz Lee admitted at the Warren trial, and "hearing nothing more of the infantry's move which we had heard of the night before, I thought that the movements just there, for the time being, were suspended, and we were not expecting any attack that afternoon, so far as I know."[27] To trust their ears rather than seeking hard intelligence through the eyes of their cavalry was an egregious and indefensible mistake that left Pickett's men isolated from the rest of the Army of Northern Virginia.

If Fitz Lee and Pickett had monitored Sheridan and Warren's movements with a modicum of attentiveness, they would have kept a closer eye on their exposed left flank. This point, called the "return line" because the trench line extended to the north, or perpendicular to the White Oak Road, was almost entirely exposed to an enemy attack. Only a few hundred North Carolina troopers extended beyond the return line and covered the 3.6 miles to Anderson's troops at the White Oak and Claiborne Road intersection. This was not an adequate force to maintain a secure line of communication. Throughout the afternoon the North Carolinians sparred with Sheridan's troopers, and control of the White Oak Road, as a result, was in flux. It is a mystery why Anderson and Pickett did not cooperate on April 1. They might as well have been in two distant theaters of war. The best chance of seizing the initiative and catching Sheridan and Warren off guard depended upon Pickett and Anderson coordinating their movements. It appears that they failed to communicate or to discuss any contingency plans if the Confederate defense unraveled. Even if Pickett and Anderson had been in communication, it is hard to imagine what could have been accomplished in closing the gap between them. The moment of truth had arrived for Lee, whose troops were finally stretched to the breaking point. Weakening his lines to the east even more (considering that Scales's and McGowan's brigades had been withdrawn) would have been an act of desperation that could have had ruinous results, given that the Union Second Corps troops could have attacked. It is easy to understand why Lee could not live up to his reputation as audacity personified.

Shortly after 3:00 P.M., Munford's cavalry along the White Oak Road detected the Fifth Corps massing for an attack near the Confederate left flank. Munford went in person to Fitz Lee, who was incredulous about the report. He instructed Munford to return to the front and make a personal reconnaissance. Munford hurried back to his picket line along the White Oak Road, dismounted, and took cover in the woods. He caught a glimpse of Warren's 12,000 men taking position in a deep and expansive swale surrounding the Gravelly Run Church. The enemy was a little more than a quarter of a mile from Ransom's left flank. "As soon as I got there," Munford recalled, "I found that the Fifth Corps were out there."[28]

Again and again Munford sent couriers to Pickett and Fitz Lee to warn them of the impending attack. He waited for a response, but none came. "I was very anxious to see General Pickett," Munford later told the Warren court. "I had sent three or four staff officers to him, advising him of the condition of things, but had no reply." Munford did not panic. He quickly extended the Confederate left flank to the east, ordering his dismounted troopers to throw up some rails directly north of the Fifth Corps staging area. But this obstruction, Munford realized, would do little to impede Warren's formations once they got moving.[29]

The failure of Fitz Lee and Pickett to respond to Munford's pleas for help caused an irretrievable breakdown in command and control that eventually trickled down the Confederate line from Ransom's position to the far right flank. To the Warren court, Munford captured the feeling of doom that was settling over his isolated command. "I felt alarmed about the condition of things because there did not seem to be any general officer there who was controlling the infantry movements. . . . The Fifth Corps was on our flank, moving, and there was no support for Fitz Lee's division of cavalry."[30] Not hearing from Fitz Lee or Pickett, Munford turned to General Ransom for help, but the infantry officer refused any request without Pickett's approval. "I had asked General Ransom for his artillery and he would not let me have it. . . . I urged him to open on the Fifth Corps. He said that Pickett was in command. *Pickett was not in command, in person.* Ransom told me that himself, that Pickett was in command, and that he [Ransom] would not come out, nor would he let me have the artillery."[31]

Without the assistance of Ransom, Munford was essentially reduced to being a spectator to the advance of the Fifth Corps. Thanks to a faulty map

Peter S. Carmichael

sketched by Sheridan's troopers, one division of Warren's corps overshot its target — Ransom's return line — and headed due north, nearly marching off the battlefield. Fortuitously, this brought much of Warren's infantry behind Pickett's White Oak Road line. It was not so easy for Warren to capitalize upon this brilliant but accidental flanking maneuver. The ground was marshy, small tributaries had turned into nasty creeks, and much of the area was covered with dense vegetation. No body of troops could possibly move quickly across such a hostile landscape. Munford's dismounted Confederate troops, some 1,000 men in total, were able to slow down the Federal advance. They used the cover of the ground to get off a few shots before retiring to another favorable position, but they could not stop the Federals from getting squarely behind the Confederate infantry on the White Oak Road. The loose skirmish formations diluted Confederate fire, and the Federals apparently did not respond for twenty minutes as they wheeled into position. Once the maneuver was complete, they began their westward advance toward the Ford's Road. Munford's men retreated in a methodical fashion, firing randomly. They did not unleash massed volleys as a collective unit.

About the time that elements of Warren's command neared the Ford's Road, other portions of his corps had located the return line. Ransom's men did not offer much resistance; the vast majority abandoned their position without firing a shot. "Our infantry were not doing much," recalled Munford, who never forgave Ransom for his passivity. "There was no artillery fire of any consequence, and there was a good deal of cheering. It looked very singular to me, without knowing what was the cause. There was some sharpshooting but there was not a heavy engagement going on anywhere."[32] Other witnesses backed Munford's significant observation: there was no massive eruption of musketry or artillery that announced the Fifth Corps attack. All afternoon the fire along Pickett's front was described as desultory, erratic, or light. An occasional cannon shot could be heard from Pegram's guns on the Confederate right flank. It appears that when Warren launched his attack, the clash with Pickett's left flank did not result in a substantial increase in the volume of the battle. There was no great escalation in noise that one would have associated with a general engagement. It is no wonder that Pickett, Fitzhugh Lee, and Rosser were stunned to hear of the battle from the lips of a courier who had just dodged enemy bullets at Hatcher's Run.

The men of Brig. Gen. George H. Steuart's Virginia brigade, positioned just to the right or west of Ransom and Wallace's brigades, were as unaware of the attack as Pickett and Fitz Lee. The heavy woods not only restricted lines of sight but also muffled gunfire. Lt. Col. William Walter White of the

14th Virginia Infantry saw an old friend in Munford's cavalry who alerted him to the shocking fact that Federal infantry was in their rear. At that same moment, White looked down the White Oak Road and saw Ransom and Wallace's brigade coming toward him. To his surprise, they "were in order," White told the Warren court, "and in such good order that I thought they were marching under command." He realized that something was amiss when he saw General Ransom riding on horseback, clearly agitated and yelling at White that "his men were retreating against orders." White called on his soldiers to stop the fugitives and to bring them into line.[33] Roughly a third of Ransom and Wallace's brigades escaped, but White's regiment and the rest of Steuart's Virginians managed to form a new line perpendicular to the White Oak Road and facing to the east. They could handle any Union attack that came directly from the direction of the return line, but their left flank was exposed to Warren's men to the north and Sheridan's troopers to the south. They could not hold out for long.

In spite of Pickett and Fitz Lee's negligence, their subordinates managed to patch together a temporary line of defense that staved off an immediate rout. The assault had been underway for at least forty-five minutes, but it appears that only the desultory sounds of picket fire wafted across Hatcher's Run. The lack of auditory intelligence was the cornerstone of Fitz Lee's defense at the Warren court, but neither he nor Pickett had said anything about the deceptive soundscape of Five Forks or the shad bake in their official reports or in their personal correspondence spanning the five years following Appomattox.[34] A sheepish Fitzhugh Lee did not mention the shad bake to the Warren court. He looked to the environment for exoneration. An acoustic shadow, he maintained, had muted the sounds of battle along Hatcher's Run. "My experience is that in certain conditions of the atmosphere," he explained to the court, "it is very difficult to hear the firing of infantry. You can only hear the firing of infantry at a short distance where the undergrowth is thick." The court pressed Lee on this matter, and he insisted that "I did not hear any." In fact, he added that "General Pickett, who was closer than I, for he was just along the run, evidently did not hear it either, for he only got across this ford just about the time the Federal infantry got possession of the road."[35] He told the court that he had been at the front until noon and then had retired to Hatcher's Run. He did admit to hearing a little skirmishing before going among the wagons to see Rosser for "ammunition and rations." There was no mention if there was a special ration on the menu for pescatarians. Claiming that he had heard nothing from Munford, which certainly was not true, Fitz Lee told the court that he was surprised when a courier reported the Union attack. "As soon as I got information of the attack on the left," he stated, "I immediately mounted my horse, and before I could get to where the road crosses Hatcher's Run, . . . I found that road in possession of the enemy."[36]

From the banks of Hatcher's Run, Fitz Lee pulled back on the reins of his horse, deciding that he would not risk a Yankee bullet to rejoin Munford's cavalry. Instead, he watched Pickett gallop down the Ford's Road with his body angling off his saddle, his horse shielding him from enemy fire. He managed to ride the mile and a half to the woods just north of the Forks. There Pickett met a furious Munford, who apparently dressed down his superior. The Warren court asked Munford, "If you had any conversation with General Pickett, when you met him at the Ford road, you may repeat it, unless you prefer not." Munford replied, "If you don't want me to say it, I prefer not." The court did not press the issue, telling Munford, "Well, we do not ask for it then."[37]

Unlike Munford, who was somewhat guarded before the court, former colonel Joseph Mayo Jr. of the 3rd Virginia Infantry showed no restraint. He condemned Pickett for vanishing from the field and leaving his subordinates to find their own way out of chaos. At a time when decisiveness was needed, Pickett's subordinates became unusually tentative, hesitant to take any action that might violate a chain of command that was essentially headless. Mayo recalled a revealing conversation that he had with General Steuart. "Colonel [Mayo]," began Steuart, "I have just received an important message from Ransom to bring my brigade to his support." "Of course I cannot do that," Steuart continued, "I do not like that firing there. We cannot leave here. I will send him two regiments if you will send him one." Mayo explained to the court that "I told him I did not like to take that responsibility, and asked him where General Pickett was. He said he did not know; he had not seen him. I saw something had to be done. Affairs were growing worse and worse. Then, at that interval of time, the enemy had got so far to our rear that the balls came continually across over our heads, and then in front, too."[38]

By the time Pickett finally reached Munford on the Ford's Road, a hot converging fire on the Forks came from three directions. Even a man who had as sluggish a military mind as Pickett knew that the situation was on the precipice of a catastrophe, that something dramatic had to be done, or the Confederate infantry on the White Oak Road risked capture. Pickett had one of Mayo's regiments about-face and move just 200 yards north of the Forks to strike the Union infantry commanding the Ford's Road. From the edge of the woods, Colonel Mayo encountered Pickett, who pointed to the Union forces and said, "Colonel, the enemy are in our rear, and if we do not drive them out we are gone." Testifying before the court, Mayo recalled that "I said that was perfectly apparent to everybody." It also became apparent that a token Confederate advance could not withstand the overwhelming pressure from the front and flank. Pickett quickly rescinded his order without knowing what to do next. He bluntly told Mayo that "we cannot stay here: get out the best way you can."[39]

When Mayo reached the Forks he found panicked men in broken formations, and he knew that he had to get them out of this predicament. Mayo headed west, trying to keep his men in order, but Union volleys into the rear and flank of the fleeing Confederates turned the retreat into a rout. At the far right flank, far removed from the Union assault, Brig. Gen. Montgomery D. Corse had refused his left flank with his intact Virginia brigade so that his men were perpendicular to the White Oak Road. Pickett instructed them to cover the retreat. Any soldier who was not part of Corse's brigade and who had managed to escape should "get back to the railroad."[40] Pickett's instruction made no attempt to bring order out of his scattered and demoralized mass of troops who were rolling down the White Oak Road toward a setting sun. There was no chance they would rally around Pickett, who was hardly a paragon of inspiring leadership. As men were streaming by him, Pickett ordered his cavalry officer Rooney Lee "to throw a mounted regiment" to "stop the flight of the infantry."[41] Pickett then vanished from the field, ending the battle just as he had started it.

From his headquarters in Petersburg, Robert E. Lee was also wondering about Pickett's whereabouts. He had received a detailed dispatch, likely a telegram from Fitzhugh Lee that outlined with remarkable specificity the disposition of Confederate troops and their collapse at Five Forks. He forwarded this information to Secretary of War John C. Breckinridge in Richmond, but he acknowledged that General Pickett's "present position" was unknown.[42] He also informed Breckinridge that "a large force of infantry, believed to be the 5th Corps with other troops, turned Genl Picket's left" and that it "is supposed" that the same body of infantry that had engaged Anderson on March 31 was also part of the operations on April 1. The lack of certainty in Lee's message is telling, and it points to an intelligence and communication breakdown between Anderson and Pickett that the commanding general could have prevented.

Only the commanding general could have ensured that Pickett and Anderson worked in harmony. What exactly Lee had asked of his two subordinates is impossible to determine. There are no surviving written orders or verbal instructions recorded. Yet, both Pickett and Fitzhugh Lee, in separate statements, criticized Anderson for failing to provide direct support to the Confederates at the Forks (Anderson, in fact, had a long history of failing to cooperate with his other officers). Fitz Lee, in a report to Robert E. Lee dated April 22, 1865, does not name names but makes it clear that he and Pickett were dangling from a hook. "Should their Infantry [Fifth Corps] be withdrawn from the position of their lines contiguous to our operations, a corresponding force of our own would have been thus made available, and would be used to restore the status or numerical balance between the two sides."[43] Even if the expectation of supporting Pickett had not been clearly articulated to Anderson, he and his subordinate Bushrod Johnson showed a breathtaking lack of initiative on April 1. By 11:00 A.M., the Confederates at the White Oak and Claiborne Roads reported the retreat of the Fifth Corps. For the rest of the day, Anderson's men, who were under the direct command of Johnson, did nothing—no reconnaissance of note and no attempt to communicate developments on their front to Pickett. Both Anderson's and Johnson's official reports are somewhat incriminating.[44] They reveal an almost disinterest in the enemy's whereabouts, particularly Maj. Gen. Andrew Humphrey's Second Corps.

To be sure, Pickett and Fitz Lee were just as culpable as Anderson and Johnson. The former never monitored the thin line of communication held by Brig. Gen. William P. Roberts's brigade of North Carolina cavalry. Not a single piece of information was transmitted between the two commands until the very end of the day, when all was lost. It was true that Roberts's troopers were under duress from Sheridan's slashing attacks, but this, if anything, should have spurred a closer investigation of this vulnerable portion of the line, ensuring communication between Pickett and Anderson. A coordinated attack against Warren at the staging area around the Gravelly Run Church was not beyond the realm of possibility, and it would have been disastrous for the Federals.

Operational oversight from Lee's headquarters could have brought attention to this issue and likely averted disaster, though not defeat. If the commanding general had a chief of army operations who had been at Pickett's or Anderson's side, a more harmonious and effective partnership could have been forged between his subordinates. Grant had such a position in the Army of the Potomac, and Andrew Humphreys was incredibly effective at the post. In no way should Lee shoulder all the blame for the disaster at Five Forks. Sheridan's aggressiveness and the Federal firepower were insurmountable. In fact, Lee had resigned himself to the inevitable loss of the South Side and Richmond & Danville Railroads. On April 1 he bluntly informed President

Davis of "the necessity of evacuating our position on James River at once."[45] It is important to note that Lee wired this telegram on April 1, before he even knew of Pickett's defeat at Five Forks.

It is tempting to see Lee's expedition against Sheridan as a fool's errand, but it was not, as Pickett and Fitz Lee had demonstrated by driving Sheridan back on March 31 at Dinwiddie Court House. Possibilities still existed after their impressive victory to slow down the Federals, but Pickett and Fitz Lee squandered them by underestimating Sheridan's resolve and losing track of Warren's troops. There was no recovering from these monumental mistakes, especially on ground that was so poor for a defensive stand. Fitz Lee and Pickett compounded their errors by dismissing intelligence reports received from the front. Their isolation from their troops — due to both the shad bake and the atmospheric conditions — was a misunderstanding on the part of officers who thought they knew better than their subordinates. They were, at the most fundamental level, ridiculously careless, something for which Pickett was notorious. When the Union attack came, Confederate infantry and cavalry officers could not adjust without violating military protocol. Under the circumstances, Pickett's command fought as well as men could fight when enemy bullets were crisscrossing over their heads. The sudden collapse of Ransom's and Wallace's brigades did not occur with the other Confederate brigades, but it underscores the fragility of Pickett's entire force at this late stage of the war.

The suggestion that Lee could have rescued Pickett at Five Forks if he had exerted stronger operational control over his subordinates is highly debatable. The discussion is necessary only for the simple fact that commanding generals are responsible for positioning their subordinates for tactical success. Lee's role in the battle, however, did not enter the private and public conversations among Pickett, Fitz Lee, Harrison, and Rosser. Their analysis of the battle, as a result, was too narrow and lacked a broad perspective. They focused on isolated incidents and personality issues in their writings, and this partially explains why they had such a difficult time reaching a consensus about the battle. The controversies that emerged about Five Forks have inspired "what-if" questions that remain popular among students of the war today. Counterfactual scenarios are often viewed as harmless, if not pointless, inquiries into the past. Robert E. Lee knew better. He understood that what-if questions kept the political questions about the war alive and that the battlefield was not just a chessboard of tactics. On August 1, 1865, Lee wrote to the celebrated cavalry officer Wade Hampton, expressing his regret that the South Carolinian had been absent at Five Forks. "If you had been there with all of your cavalry, the result at Five Forks would have been different, but how long the contest would have been prolonged it is difficult to say." But, he concluded about the war: "It is over."[46]

The war kept living for Lee's subordinates, who fought among themselves for decades after 1865 over who was to blame for the fiasco at Five Forks. Ironically, the general's subordinates had little choice but to turn on each other, since criticizing Lee was unthinkable. Even in a world ruled by Lost Cause doctrine, where Lee was deified and every Confederate veteran enshrined, it was impossible to forge perfect solidarity among former soldiers who defended their public reputations at all hazards.

NOTES

I am indebted to the kind assistance of A. Wilson Greene, Robert E. L. Krick, and Keith Bohannon, who took time from their demanding schedules to read this essay, and I am also grateful for the editorial suggestions of Elizabeth Getz Carmichael and the research assistance from Petersburg National Battlefield's Tracy Chernault and Gettysburg College's Kaylyn Sawyer.

1. The modern historiography on Five Forks begins with Douglas Southall Freeman, *Lee's Lieutenants: A Study in Command* (New York: Charles Scribner's Sons, 1944), 3:662–74. Scholars have largely adopted Freeman's description and analysis of the Confederate side of the battle; see for example Ed Bearss and Chris Calkins, *The Battle of Five Forks* (Lynchburg, Va.: H. E. Howard, 1985), esp. chap. 5; J. Tracy Power, *Lee's Miserables: Life in the Army of Northern Virginia from the Wilderness to Appomattox* (Chapel Hill: University of North Carolina Press, 1998), 272; Lesley J. Gordon, *General George E. Pickett in Life and Legend* (Chapel Hill: University of North Carolina Press, 1998), 146–53; A. Wilson Greene: *The Final Battles of the Petersburg Campaign*, 2nd ed. (Knoxville: University of Tennessee Press, 2008), 186; and Joseph T. Glatthaar, *General Lee's Army: From Victory to Collapse* (New York: Free Press, 2008), 458–59.

2. On Robert E. Lee's place in the Lost Cause, see Alan T. Nolan, *Lee Considered: General Robert E. Lee and Civil War History* (Chapel Hill: University of North Carolina Press, 1991).

3. James D. McCabe Jr., *Life and Campaigns of Robert E. Lee* (Atlanta: National Publishing Company, 1866), 603.

4. Walter Harrison, *Pickett's Men: A Fragment of War History* (New York: D. Van Nostrand, 1870), 133–34.

5. Thomas Rosser, "Annals of the War: Chapters of Unwritten History, Rosser and His Men," *Philadelphia Weekly Times*, April 5, 1884.

6. Douglas Southall Freeman, *R. E. Lee: A Biography*, 4 vols. (New York: Charles Scribner's Sons, 1934–35), 4:40, see especially n. 79.

7. For a response to the revisionist critics of Lee, see Gary W. Gallagher, "'The Idol of His Soldiers and the Hope of His Country: Lee and the Confederate People," in *Lee and His Generals in War and Memory*, ed. Gary W. Gallagher (Baton Rouge: Louisiana State University Press, 1998), 3–20.

8. Earl J. Hess, *In the Trenches at Petersburg: Field Fortifications and Confederate Defeat* (Chapel Hill: University of North Carolina Press, 2009), 354.

9. "Richard Anderson's Report," June 15, 1866, in *Supplement to the Official Records of the Union and Confederate Armies*, ed. Janet B. Hewett and others, 95 vols. and 5-vol. index (Wilmington, N.C.: Broadfoot, 1994–2001), pt. 1, 7:819–20 (hereafter cited as *ORS*; all references are to pt. 1).

10. Robert E. Lee to John C. Breckinridge, March 9, 1865, in *The Wartime Papers of R. E. Lee*, ed. Clifford Dowdey and Louis H. Manarin (Boston: Little, Brown, 1961), 913.

11. Bearss and Calkins, *Battle of Five Forks*, 8–13.

12. Harrison, *Pickett's Men*, 135–36.

13. Armistead C. Gordon, ed., *Memories and Memorials of William Gordon McCabe* (Richmond, Va.: Old Dominion Press, 1925), 1:163.

14. Bearss and Calkins, *Battle of Five Forks*, 21, 30.

15. Harrison, *Pickett's Men*, 135.

16. We still lack a comprehensive treatment of the Petersburg campaign. A. Wilson Greene's forthcoming trilogy on the siege will fill this void. In the meantime, readers should begin with a fine overview of the campaign by Noah Andre Trudeau titled *The Siege of Petersburg*, part of the National Parks Civil War Series published by Eastern National in 1995. Those who seek more details should consult Richard J. Sommers, *Richmond Redeemed: The Siege at Petersburg* (New York: Doubleday, 1981); John Horn, *The Destruction of the Weldon Railroad: Deep Bottom, Globe Tavern, and Ream's Station, August 14–25, 1864* (Lynchburg, Va.: H. E. Howard, 1991); and Greene, *Final Battles of the Petersburg Campaign.*

17. Fitzhugh Lee testimony in U.S. Army Adjutant General's Office, *Proceedings, Findings, and Opinions of the Court of Inquiry in the Case of Gouverneur K. Warren* (Washington D.C.: Government Printing Office, 1883), 2:481 (hereafter cited as *WCI*; all references are to vol. 2).

18. Freeman, *R. E. Lee*, 4:33–35.

19. For the best treatment of Five Forks, see Bearss and Calkins, *Battle of Five Forks.*

20. Thomas T. Munford's Narrative on Five Forks with Marginalia: Notes by W. Gordon McCabe, miscellany, box 2, Munford-Ellis Family Papers, William R. Perkins Library, Duke University.

21. Thomas T. Munford testimony, *WCI*, 447.

22. Ibid.

23. Lee's original order to Pickett has never surfaced in an archive or private papers. The first version appears in Walter Harrison's 1870 publication, *Pickett's Men*. This was followed by the release of a similar dispatch by the general's widow, LaSalle Corbell Pickett, in her *Pickett and His Men* (1899). She unquestionably altered or fabricated some of her husband's correspondence, but in this instance her reprinted dispatch appears to be authentic. It contains some of the wording from the Harrison version, and the military language departs from LaSalle's excessively romantic prose. On LaSalle as the gatekeeper of her husband's legacy, see Gordon, *General George E. Pickett in Life and Legend*, and Gary W. Gallagher, "A Widow and Her Soldier: LaSalle Corbell Pickett as the Author of George E. Pickett's Civil War Letters," in *Lee and His Generals*, 227–42.

Peter S. Carmichael

24. Campbell Brown, *Campbell Brown's Civil War: With Ewell and the Army of Northern Virginia*, ed. Terry L. Jones (Baton Rouge: Louisiana State University Press, 2001), 248.

25. Joseph Mayo testimony, *WCI*, 498.

26. On Lee's belief in "spade work," see Elizabeth Brown Pryor, *Reading the Man: Portrait of Robert E. Lee through His Private Letters* (New York: Viking, 2007), esp. chap. 10.

27. Fitzhugh Lee testimony, *WCI*, 481.

28. Thomas T. Munford testimony, ibid., 442.

29. Ibid., 447.

30. Ibid.

31. Ibid., 442.

32. Ibid., 454.

33. William Walter White testimony, ibid., 486–87.

34. George Pickett to Fitzhugh Lee, May 24, 1870, and Thomas T. Munford to H. C. Lee, August 2, 1870, in Fitzhugh Lee Papers, box 2, Albert and Shirley Small Special Collections Library, University of Virginia, Charlottesville; "George Pickett official report," May 1, 1865, in *ORS*, 7:778–85; "Report of Richard Anderson," June 15, 1866, in *ORS*, 7:817–22.

35. Fitzhugh Lee testimony, *WCI*, 471–72.

36. Ibid., 471.

37. Thomas T. Munford testimony, ibid., 448.

38. Joseph Mayo testimony, ibid., 499.

39. Ibid., 499, 500.

40. Ibid., 501.

41. R. M. T. Beale testimony, ibid., 617.

42. R. E. Lee to Breckinridge, April 1, 1865, in *Wartime Papers of R. E. Lee*, 923.

43. Fitzhugh Lee to R. E. Lee April 22, 1865, box 2, Fitzhugh Lee Papers.

44. "Journal of Bushrod Rust Johnson, March 15–April 16, 1865," in *ORS*, 7:746; report of Richard Anderson, June 15, 1866, in ibid., 7:817–22.

45. Robert E. Lee to Jefferson Davis, April 1, 1865, in *Wartime Papers of R. E. Lee*, 922.

46. Robert E. Lee to Wade Hampton, August 1, 1865, reprinted in Thomas T. Munford, "Narrative of the Battle of Five Forks, April 1, 1865," Munford-Ellis Papers.

Lucky Inspiration

Philip Sheridan's Uncertain Road to Triumph
with the Cavalry of the Army of the Potomac

Wayne Wei-Siang Hsieh

A deceptive anticlimax enshrouds the Appomattox campaign. While it resulted in the final defeat of Robert E. Lee's Army of Northern Virginia, we
might easily forgive historians for glancing over the operational details of the
last spring campaign in Virginia. Even historians such as James McPherson
who emphasize the war's contingent outcome cite the fall of Atlanta, long
before the spring of 1865, as the last turning point in the war. And those historians who see the war's outcome as driven by more structural factors would
obviously be disinclined to focus on the uncertain elements of the Virginia
theater's final campaign. Indeed, scholars such as Joseph Glatthaar have well
chronicled the decrepit state of Lee's forces, worn down by continuous combat in the Richmond and Petersburg siege lines while subsisting on increasingly meager rations. Even if the Army of Northern Virginia had somehow
achieved a concentration with Joseph E. Johnston's forces, it is hardly believ-
able that such would have changed the larger war's outcome. Nevertheless,
the Appomattox campaign showed that Lee was neither a Gideon Pillow nor
a John C. Pemberton, Ulysses S. Grant's previous adversaries who either surrendered their armies after feeble breakout attempts or allowed their forces
to be completely besieged.

Instead, one of Grant's most talented subordinates, Philip H. Sheridan,
would have to bring the Army of Northern Virginia to heel. Sheridan imbued
the Union cavalry arm in the East with his aggressive command style. Over
the course of the war, the eastern cavalry had surmounted systemic problems
in its leadership and organization introduced during George B. McClellan's
command tenure, while Sheridan himself had grown into an effective army

commander capable of leading both cavalry and infantry during the Shenandoah Valley campaign of the fall of 1864. He thus oversaw a cavalry arm by the time of Appomattox that served as a mobile shock force capable of fighting with both the state-of-the-art Spencer repeater and the hoary saber of Napoleonic warfare. In doing so, he restored a measure of fluidity to military operations in Virginia that had evaporated by the close of the Overland campaign. Moreover, the Cavalry Corps's evolution required such a varied constellation of factors involving institutions, technological advances, and the peculiar quirks of personal leadership that it belies any notion that the course and outcome of the Appomattox campaign was foreordained.

The importance of Sheridan's cavalry in ending the war in Virginia when it did had larger repercussions. By the spring of 1865, it was clear that barring a literal act of God, the Confederacy would not win its independence. What was not so clear, however, was when and how exactly the war would end. Grant's ability to compel Lee to surrender both himself and most of his army (the former was really the most important element, considering the immense importance of Lee's own personage) depended on Sheridan's driving presence. Especially in light of the disorderly circumstances surrounding Lincoln's assassination, the orderly surrender of Lee's army at Appomattox under legal auspices fully approved by the Union's civilian and military leaders set important legal and political precedents for the demobilization of Confederate armies, which needed to precede Reconstruction. The conflict and disarray among Northern leaders surrounding William Tecumseh Sherman's terms for Johnston's army highlighted the importance of the precedent Grant established. The absence of both a competent Federal cavalry arm and as tenacious a commander as Sheridan might very well have allowed Lee to escape and fight another day. That would not have led to an eventual Confederate victory, but it could very well have had significant effects on the coming course of Reconstruction.

Napoleon, whose legacy loomed large over both the Union and Confederate armies and their Old Army antecedent, had utilized cavalry as an offensively oriented corps of shock troops that could at a decisive moment deal a crushing blow to enemy troops, mounted or dismounted, but the European model of saber-armed cavalry trained to use shock tactics had no practical precedent in American history. For a variety of reasons, most Union and Confederate cavalry forces focused on raiding, reconnaissance, and screening operations instead. Heavy cavalry using shock tactics required intensive training for both troopers and horses, and the frontier army had little use and less funding for such measures while pursuing Indians on the frontier. The absence of antebellum institutions to build upon and the pressures of mass war-time mobilization presented insurmountable impediments to the creation of Napoleonic-style heavy cavalry at the start of the Civil War.

Worse yet, antebellum cavalry officers, despite their practical experience to the contrary, remained imprisoned to some degree by Napoleonic models. For example, Philip St. George Cooke (a future senior cavalry commander in McClellan's Army of the Potomac and the father-in-law of Confederate cavalry general J. E. B. Stuart) introduced a new set of cavalry tactics into the U.S. Army in 1861, which promulgated a one-rank tactical system to re-place the two-rank system previously used by the antebellum U.S. Army. In the same way that William J. Hardee's tactical reforms had reduced an in-fantry line of battle from three ranks of soldiers to two, Cooke thinned cav-alry lines of battle from two ranks of troopers to one. Cooke argued that his one-rank system "greatly simplified all cavalry movements," which "would go far toward lessening the difficulties, by many considered insuperable, of the efficient instruction of volunteer cavalry in a period of actual war." Yet he also remained wedded to the idea that "the charge is the decisive action of cavalry."[1] Cooke still conceived of the charge as a decisive stroke to be made by heavy cavalry armed with sabers, or perhaps in skirmishes with Indi-ans on the frontier, as opposed to the more complex arrangements of Sheri-dan's cavalry corps where individual brigades or regiments would dismount some units to fight on foot, while others remained mounted. While the saber charge certainly did not vanish during the Civil War, it required particular cir-cumstances, such as an opportune tactical situation, to be effective. Only tal-ented and experienced commanders could make such judgments, which fre-quently involved assessments of the psychological state of one's foes — what one writer has described as "the golden moment of the *wavering* . . . which side shall run?"[2] Furthermore, for cavalry to have the opportunity to use the charge to effect, it would also need more firepower to cope with veteran in-fantry and cavalry so that it could even be available on the field for opportu-nities to mount a charge.

The introduction of the Spencer repeating carbine into the Union cav-alry arm, which saw limited but significant action in combat at Gettysburg among select units fortunate enough to have received the weapon,[3] gave cav-alry that staying power, and it helped transform the Union trooper into a sort of super-dragoon who moved swiftly by hoof and could fight both on foot and in the saddle. The Spencer's swift rate of fire more than compen-sated for the one-in-four drain on the firing line imposed by the need to detail horse-holders while engaged in battle dismounted, and the cavalry's horses gave it an operational flexibility that infantry did not possess. McClellan himself, a prewar authority on cavalry whose last commission in the antebellum army had been as a horse soldier, had earlier recognized the value of the "true dragoon," who could fight both mounted and dismounted. Experienced Union cavalry officers would agree with McClellan that to be most effective, cavalrymen must be able to fight in the saddle and could not simply be mounted infantry. In his antebellum report on the Crimean War, McClellan argued that only Russia possessed such true dragoons. Nevertheless, in McClellan's conception, even these dragoons were "principally employed in covering retreats, occupying isolated posts, making sudden attacks upon villages, &c.,"[4] as opposed to the more decisive role the Union cavalry played in both Sheridan's Shenandoah Valley campaign and the final engagements leading up to Lee's surrender at Appomattox. It would be later officers such as Sheridan who "clearly perceived, what few other commanders appear to have comprehended, that cavalry which could use breech-loading arms with effect dismounted, and at the same time preserve its ability to make successful charges with the sabre mounted, was capable, with the assistance of artillery, of undertaking any operations within the power of the three arms of the service combined; its celerity of movement giving it an immense advantage over infantry."[5] Or, as James Harrison Wilson put it more succinctly, "The best cavalry is the best infantry, mounted."[6]

Despite McClellan's understanding of some of the theoretical issues involved, he proved a poor organizer of cavalry during his time in command of the Army of the Potomac—with far-reaching consequences that persisted long after his departure from field command. To the misfortune of the Union war effort, McClellan's main contribution to the mounted service was his design for a saddle that remained in use until the end of horse cavalry as an organized institution in the U.S. Army.[7] McClellan's deep knowledge of European cavalry services may have made him too pessimistic about the prospects for the American arm. Indeed, he himself had argued in his Delafield Commission report that due to frontier conditions and the persistent Indian threat, only light cavalry should be established in the antebellum army and heavy cavalry dispensed with entirely.[8] Finally, McClellan's early aim was to equip his cavalry to fight primarily in the saddle, as he prioritized equipping *all* cavalry troopers with sabers and revolvers, but he required only two squadrons in each regiment to possess the carbines necessary for dismounted fighting.[9]

Perhaps because of the belief that even the vaunted Russian dragoons he so admired could focus only on screening, raiding, and reconnaissance, McClellan proceeded to disperse most of his cavalry regiments almost willy-nilly during the crucial organizational phase of the Army of the Potomac in the fall and winter of 1861. He attached individual regiments to infantry divisions, and after corps organizations were instituted in March 1862, each corps received two to five regiments of cavalry organized as individual units, as opposed to consolidated brigades. Without a coherent and separate organization, infantry and division commanders tended to disperse their troopers as hangers-on for generals and "to provide orderlies for dashing young staff officers and strikers for headquarters," as opposed to a purposeful military organization.[10] McClellan organized a cavalry division in July 1862, but even that organization saw its two brigades dispersed to different wings of the Army of the Potomac. By the time of Antietam, additional brigades joined this organization, in addition to four batteries of regular artillery, but about one-sixth of the squadrons were detached from their home regiments to various miscellaneous duties attached to corps and infantry divisions.[11] McClellan recognized the flaws of this arrangement. In his official report he claimed that "circumstances beyond my control, rendered it impossible to carry out" his hope of forming a sufficiently large cavalry reserve, "and the cavalry force, serving with the army in the field, was never as large as it ought have been."[12]

Even when he was able to concentrate a small force of cavalry, McClellan used it ineffectively. At Antietam, he ordered Alfred Pleasonton's cavalry division to while away in the Union center while Little Mac contemplated a cavalry charge, which Pleasonton refused to embark on. Standing fast there, it failed to watch the Army of the Potomac's flanks and to detect or delay the arrival of A. P. Hill's Light Division in time to save the Confederate position at the close of the day.[13] McClellan fully understood in theoretical terms the dilemma of balancing the different duties of reconnaissance and screening versus staying ready in reserve as a shock force for decisive offensive action. Indeed, as an observer in the Crimea, he had praised the Cossacks for relieving regular cavalry of burdensome duties of "advanced posts, patrols, reconnaissances, escorting trains, carrying despatches, acting as orderlies, &c."[14] But he never resolved this problem in his own command.

Furthermore, McClellan's cavalry struggled with logistical problems, although over time, some of these problems would be sorted out with experience and the weeding out of weak officers. The care of horses, both in camp and on the march—their feeding, shodding, and general upkeep—presented a real challenge to the Army of the Potomac's green cavalry regiments. It did not help matters that as government property, troopers tended to neglect the proper care of their mounts in the absence of strong-willed regimental leadership.[15] As one cavalry officer put it, "An officer of cavalry needs to be more horse-doctor than soldier. . . . You are a slave to your horses, you work like a dog yourself, and you exact the most extreme care from your Sergeants, and you see diseases creeping on you day by day and your horses breaking down under your eyes."[16] Until the Army of the Potomac's troopers acquired these basic skills of horse management, all the Spencers and Sheridans in the world would have little or no effect on a cavalry organization bereft of healthy mounts.

Joseph Hooker would correct many of the organizational defects Mc-Clellan institutionalized when he took command of the Army of the Potomac in early 1863, but reforming the cavalry arm with superior mobility and fire-power did not alone lead to a decisive victory for the Union army at Appomattox. Sheridan still needed the support of infantry corps to strike killing blows, and his controversial relief of Fifth Corps commander Gouverneur Warren at Five Forks stemmed from his belief that Warren had not cooperated as fully as he should have with Sheridan's own efforts. We should not, then, see Appomattox as in large part the triumph of a single elite branch of the Union army, equipped with a state-of-the-art weapon. Instead, it was the fruit of finally coordinating cavalry and infantry in battle, as opposed to relegating troopers to screening and reconnaissance functions separate and apart from pitched battle. Oddly enough, early in his tenure as a cavalry corps commander Sheridan had failed to accomplish even these scouting functions, much less arrive at the lethal combination of infantry and cavalry he achieved during the Appomattox campaign.

McClellan, whatever his faults as an army commander, put it well when he described cavalry as "the antennæ of an army. It scouts all the roads in front, on the flanks, and in rear of the advancing columns, and constantly feels the enemy."[17] For all his merits as a commander, Sheridan proved unsuccessful at fulfilling these important cavalry responsibilities during the Overland campaign. Instead, Sheridan was overly fixated on defeating the Confederate cavalry, and he failed to balance these competing priorities. He allowed his most inexperienced division commander, James Harrison Wilson (who would later grow into his position but performed poorly early in the Wilderness campaign), to expose himself to serious peril while failing to properly screen Grant's advance. His corps acquired little useful information for Grant and George Gordon Meade to guide Union operations. Meade and Sheridan had clashed before the campaign had even started, and matters boiled over on May 8, 1864, in the aftermath of the bloody fighting in the Wilderness. Sheridan demanded the freedom to go pursue Stuart, and Grant acceded to his request, with decidedly mixed results.[18]

Sheridan's famous confrontation with Meade not only exemplified Sheridan's difficult relationship with the Army of the Potomac's command echelon but also led to his diversion on a raid of dubious operational and strategic significance. Resisting the siren song of raiding was an important part of exploiting the full potential of the Union army's cavalry arm in Virginia. Ever since Stuart's famed raid around McClellan's army in 1862, both the Union and Confederate cavalry arms found it difficult to counter the allure of raids that only sometimes corresponded with the larger operational needs of their respective field armies. While Stuart's ride around McClellan's army had provided useful intelligence on the Army of the Potomac's positions, his excursion at the opening of the Gettysburg campaign would famously leave Lee virtually blind at a key moment during that campaign. Stuart's vaunted cavalry served at its best when it focused on its screening and reconnaissance functions, and it never acquired the potent mix of firepower and shock that Sheridan's cavalry achieved by the time of the Appomattox campaign.

While raids could wreak havoc on extended lines of communication, the relatively constrained confines of the Overland campaign reduced the potential benefits of cavalry raids aimed at logistical infrastructure, as compared with the Western Theater. In those wider expanses it was possible to derail an entire campaign with a raid, as had occurred at Holly Springs during the Vicksburg campaign. In Sheridan's defense, his victory at Yellow Tavern on May 11 where Stuart perished boosted morale in the Cavalry Corps and sealed the somewhat uncertain command relationship between himself and his troopers,[19] but the cavalry's various raids during the Overland campaign achieved little.

Grant's dispatch of Sheridan to the Shenandoah Valley to resolve once and for all the Confederate threat coming from that vexatious subordinate theater would finally free all parties concerned from the false hopes of raiding while elevating cavalry to its fullest offensive potential. In addition to providing a solution to the immediate problem of Jubal A. Early's corps wreaking havoc on Union arms in the Valley and sowing panic in Washington, it also separated Sheridan from the Army of the Potomac command structure, with which he frequently clashed. Furthermore, it made possible Sheridan's emergence not just as a cavalry commander but also as something akin to the competent army commanders who served Sherman in the Atlanta campaign. In the West, by the time of the Chattanooga campaign, Grant was not just an army commander but an army group commander, with both George Thomas commanding the Army of the Cumberland and Sherman at the head of Grant's old Army of the Tennessee capable of either independent or coordinated operations. Grant found no such equivalents in Virginia when he arrived. The rough Napoleonic rule of thumb was that a corps needed enough forces and a competent enough commander to survive on its own for a day's worth of fighting, with reinforcements no more distant than a day's march away. In contrast, a commander such as Sheridan in the Shenandoah Valley campaign of 1864 would need far more independence than a corps commander fighting under the direct supervision of Grant or Lee in a confined theater such as northern Virginia.

The Confederacy had always benefited from having corps commanders capable of this next level of responsibility conducting its operations in the Shenandoah Valley, whether it was Thomas J. "Stonewall" Jackson in 1862, John C. Breckinridge afterward, or Early wreaking havoc all the way to the outskirts of Washington in 1864. Sheridan's arrival at the head of a unified Valley command for the Union would finally rectify this problem in Virginia. In the Western Theater Grant had both inherited and cultivated a crop of subordinate commanders capable of executing such responsibilities. Sherman would go on to great achievements at Atlanta and beyond, and even if one takes the least charitable view of Thomas's performance during the Nashville campaign, he remained a competent commander of troops even in the absence of direct supervision. In contrast, Grant arrived in a Virginia where supporting armies were commanded by the likes of Franz Sigel and Benjamin F. Butler. The shift of the Army of the Potomac's front to Petersburg would help resolve the problem of the underperforming Army of the James by placing it under Grant's direct supervision (the long-term solution would be Butler's replacement by Edward O. C. Ord), but the Valley would require a commander with enough drive and initiative to battle the capable Early.

Highlighting the anything but preordained nature of the Appomattox campaign's course and outcome, Sheridan had not been Grant's first, or even second, choice to take over a unified Federal military command in the Valley. If Sheridan and his troopers had not acquired the invaluable experience and confidence that they gained in the Valley, it is uncertain that they would have played the same decisive role that they did in the spring of 1865. Indeed, Grant had even considered taking the Valley command himself, but he discarded the idea out of fear that it would only exaggerate the significance of Early's raid in the minds of Northern voters and also place Butler in command around Petersburg due to the latter's seniority.[20] Maj. Gen. Horatio Wright, commander of the Sixth Corps, which Grant had dispatched to the Valley, had acted too sluggishly during his initial operations against Early to justify such a promotion to the Valley command. Grant proposed

William B. Franklin, but his close association with McClellan and poor performance at Fredericksburg made him politically unacceptable. As is covered by William W. Bergen's essay in this collection, Grant also proposed Meade as the new Union commander for the Valley.

Lincoln resisted Meade's appointment for political reasons, and Grant in consultation with Lincoln eventually decided on Sheridan as the new Union commander in the field to restore order to the Valley. Indeed, as one perceptive officer later put it, without knowing all the tortured details of the decision, "It was a lucky inspiration of Grant's or Lincoln's to make a Middle Military Division and put [Sheridan] in command of it."[21] Even now, there was still some uncertainty in assignments, and Grant's initial instructions still left Maj. Gen. David Hunter in overall command. Furthermore, Grant originally ordered only one division of cavalry to accompany Sheridan.[22] Shortly after his arrival, Sheridan through Henry Halleck also made the case "that for operations in the open country of Penn. Md & northern Va, cavalry is much better than infantry and that the cavalry arm can be much more effective there than about Richmond or south."[23] Grant then sent another division of cavalry to join Sheridan, and after some further wrangling over who really held overall command in the Shenandoah Valley, Grant finally relieved Hunter at his own request in favor of Sheridan to resolve lingering command ambiguities.[24]

Perhaps frustrated with all the indecisiveness and confusion, Grant also empowered Sheridan "to give commands to officers in who you repose confidence without regard to claims of others on account of rank. . . . What we want is prompt and active movements after the enemy in accordance with the instructions you already have." Finally, Grant gave Sheridan a final expression of confidence, which his subordinate would ultimately justify—"I feel every confidence that you will do for the very best and will leave you as far as possible to act on your own judgement and not embarrass you with orders and instructions."[25] One newly appointed brigade commander wrote shortly afterward that "everything is chaos here, but under Sheridan is rapidly assuming shape. . . . It is *exhilarating* to see so many cavalry about and to see things going *right* again."[26]

Sheridan thus arrived in the Valley with a large cavalry force working in tandem with two corps of infantry already in theater, in terrain more suitable for cavalry operations than the Petersburg front. In contrast, Meade, the other most capable candidate for command, possessed a far less promising background. Although the victor at Gettysburg was obviously a competent army commander, his prior service in the Army of the Potomac made him

Wayne Wei-Siang Hsieh

much less receptive to Sheridan's innovative use of cavalry both in the Valley and during the Appomattox campaign. Unlike Sheridan, who had headed a cavalry regiment and then a cavalry brigade in William Rosecrans's command in the West, Meade had no direct experience leading cavalry prior to rising to division command. Before the war, he had served in the artillery and topographical engineers, and his whole wartime career had been with infantry units in the Army of the Potomac, whose cavalry problems dated back to McClellan's tenure as its commander. That earlier service may very well have colored his view of the mounted arm; indeed, in November 1862 he reassured his wife that because his son had joined the cavalry, "he will have a comparatively pleasant time . . . we have not lost over a dozen cavalry officers since the war began."[27] At Gettysburg, Meade also had his disagreements with Alfred Pleasonton's management of the Cavalry Corps, which probably did not help improve his impression of the army's horse soldiers.[28] Like his predecessor McClellan, Meade tended to see cavalry as properly limited to a screening and reconnaissance role, and while he had had the better part of the argument with Sheridan regarding the cavalry's proper functions at the opening of the Overland campaign,[29] there is no evidence he would have used cavalry as the powerful offensive arm Sheridan led during the decisive Appomattox campaign.

To his credit, Meade had not scrapped the cavalry reforms instituted by his predecessor, but like Hooker, he inherited many of the mediocre cavalry commanders McClellan had installed in 1861. Nevertheless, Hooker had finally taken the crucial step of consolidating the Army of the Potomac's cavalry into one organization, as had always been the case with its Confederate foes, helping lay the institutional foundation for the unit Sheridan would mold into such an effective strike force. Instead of being split up in dribs and drabs among infantry units, unified regimental organizations could enforce higher standards of discipline, and cavalry commanders could ensure that horse soldiers were properly used on the battlefield. In February 1863, Hooker had thus created a cavalry corps under George Stoneman comprising three divisions, commanded by Pleasonton, William W. Averell, and David McMurtrie Gregg. In addition to a brigade of horse artillery, an independent brigade of regular cavalry under John Buford was attached to this corps. Unfortunately for the Union army, not only would Stoneman prove to be a weak cavalry commander, but Buford would be relegated to a brigade command despite being the better horse soldier than any of the three division commanders. Nevertheless, consolidation into a single corps represented a significant organizational advance for the cavalry in the Army of the Potomac.[30]

Each of the other army corps would now be limited to only one squadron of cavalry for miscellaneous duties, with no more than three squadrons detached from any one of the three divisions.[31]

Unfortunately, defects in leadership would defer any immediate benefits from this important cavalry reorganization, and that leadership deficit would persist (uncorrected by Meade) until Sheridan's arrival. Stoneman's shortcomings as a commander would shortly manifest themselves in his poor handling of the cavalry raid against Lee's communications, ordered by Hooker at the start of the Chancellorsville campaign. Here, it is sufficient to say that Stoneman's sluggish conduct of his command did not match his superior's injunction "that celerity, audacity, and resolution are everything in war."[32] Hooker allowed Stoneman to take a medical leave of absence shortly after the battle, which may very well have been a mutual solution to his untenable position under Hooker.[33] His career in the West would prove him hardly a loss to the Army of the Potomac. When assigned to Sherman's armies, his troopers would nickname him "Dyspepsia," and he would be ignominiously captured after a failed attempt to liberate the Union prisoners at Andersonville.[34]

On paper, at least, Stoneman should have been a good candidate to lead the new Cavalry Corps, and like Sheridan, he would eventually gain experience leading large infantry formations. Unlike Sheridan, however, he could not combine paper credentials with effective battlefield leadership. McClellan had appointed Stoneman, who had served in either the dragoons or the cavalry after graduating from West Point in 1846, to the administrative post of chief of cavalry in August 1861. He had then commanded various ad hoc cavalry operations during the Peninsula Campaign. The aforementioned Cooke, arguably the most experienced cavalry officer of the Old Army and commander of the Cavalry Reserve brigade, might have plausibly served as the commander of the Cavalry Division first organized by McClellan in July 1862, but a misbegotten charge at Gaines's Mill led to his relief. Stoneman then took command of the division but moved to command of an infantry division in the Third Corps shortly before the battle of Antietam (although Stoneman's unit was not on the field). After Ambrose Burnside reorganized the Army of the Potomac, Stoneman took command of a reconstituted Third Corps, which he led until being selected by Hooker to command the new Cavalry Corps.

Stoneman's prior wartime record had shown little inspiration, but neither did it bear the burden of spectacular failure. While posted on the Upper Potomac, he failed to interdict another one of Stuart's specular raids

Wayne Wei-Siang Hsieh

in October 1862, which penetrated as far as Chambersburg, Pennsylvania.[35] At Fredericksburg, Stoneman's superiors had placed him in an awkward position in that his three divisions were assigned to different parts of the battle-field, with his own division in action, David Birney's, essentially assigned to John Reynolds's First Corps, leaving Stoneman without an actual command. Stoneman accompanied Birney, however, and saw fit to move units on the field, contributing to a generally confused chain of command. This in turn contributed to Birney's unwillingness to provide desperately needed reinforcements to Meade's division in Reynolds's corps, which had just scored a tactical breakthrough against A. P. Hill that would never be properly exploited.[36] Stoneman hardly carried the majority of blame for this missed opportunity, but the poor results matched his generally middling service record. In sum, while Stoneman possessed, like Sheridan, a wide breadth of administrative and operational experience in both the cavalry and the infantry (indeed, Sheridan had only commanded a division beforehand while Stoneman had led a whole corps), the former officer did not possess that important but less tangible aggressiveness and decisiveness needed for battlefield victories.

Stoneman's division commanders also displayed mixed records throughout the war, but their seniority meant that they would long have influence on the Army of the Potomac's cavalry. Pleasonton had graduated from West Point in 1844 and had also served as a horse soldier in the Old Army. After winning a brevet promotion for gallantry during the Mexican War, he spent the remainder of the antebellum years in a wide variety of assignments on the frontier, including extensive experience fighting various Indian tribes. He commanded one of the brigades in the First Cavalry Division organized by McClellan and took over the division after Stoneman's transfer to the infantry. But on occasion Pleasonton had inspired animosity, even hatred, from his fellow officers.[37] Charles Francis Adams described him after Chancellorsville as the "*bête noire* of all cavalry officers. . . . To us who have served under him and seen him under fire he is notorious as a bully and toady. He does nothing save with a view to a newspaper paragraph."[38] Hooker may have preferred Buford to be his new cavalry commander after Stoneman's relief, but Pleasonton's commission antedated that more worthy officer in an army bound by iron laws of seniority.[39] Grant recognized the flaws of relying too heavily on seniority in selecting commanders (without fully escaping the system), which helped make possible both Sheridan's own appointment and the relative freedom Sheridan then enjoyed in selecting his own subordinates.

Despite his flaws, however, Pleasonton was by no means a disaster as the commander of the cavalry. He also led the Army of the Potomac's cavalry at its first major victory, the engagement at Brandy Station on June 9, 1863, which is commonly seen by both historians and participants as a crucial pivot point in the Cavalry Corps's escape from a debilitating sense of inferiority vis-à-vis Lee's horsemen—another prerequisite for its eventual evolution into Sheridan's decisive combat arm. While Pleasonton missed an opportunity for scoring an even larger victory, his Cavalry Corps would also go on to do good service during the Gettysburg campaign.[40] Like the Army of the Potomac's other senior cavalry leaders at this point, he lacked the killer instinct of a Sheridan, but the cavalry continued to grow in confidence and capability during his command. Nevertheless, his poor reputation among his brother officers would contribute to his replacement by Sheridan after Grant's arrival in the East.

Another one of Stoneman's division commanders, William Averell, also had a record of middling competence. He graduated from West Point in 1855 and saw a great deal of action fighting Indians in New Mexico. Like the other division commanders, he had spent the whole war in the Army of the Potomac's Cavalry Corps, and thus benefited from the seniority in rank that came with such prior service. At the engagement of Kelly's Ford on March 17, 1863, his forces scored a striking victory over Fitzhugh Lee. One staff officer described it as "a brilliant and splendid fight—the best cavalry fight of the war—lasting five hours, charging and recharging on both sides, our men using their sabers handsomely and with effect, driving the enemy 3 miles into cover of earthworks and heavy guns."[41] Like Pleasonton at Brandy Station, however, Averell remained unable to close in for the kill, and he had outnumbered Lee more than two-to-one.[42] More seriously, during the Chancellorsville campaign, Averell would prove himself an officer with little initiative, especially in the absence of clear orders, and an infuriated Hooker would relieve him of his division command.[43] As Hooker put it, "In detaching him from this army my object has been to prevent an active and powerful column from being paralyzed in its future operations by his presence."[44] Exiled to West Virginia, Averell would do good service in that relative backwater while displaying some of the personal cantankerousness that would help lead to his eventual undoing. After Sheridan's arrival in the Shenandoah Valley in 1864, Averell's division of cavalry would be attached to Sheridan's new command. Sheridan, even more of a fighting general than Hooker, would relieve him again for his dilatory pursuit of Confederate forces after the battle of Fisher's Hill on September 22, 1864. Like his later relief of Gouverneur Warren, one can reasonably criticize Sheridan's actions as excessive and unfair to his subordinate, but Averell had indeed been sluggish, and his bad-temper earned him no favors from his superior.[45] Both Averell and Warren had essentially grown up in the Army of the Potomac, both mixed middling competence with argumentative personalities, and both would run afoul of Sheridan. Full harmony between Sheridan and much of the Army of the Potomac's high command never seemed possible, and it was fortunate Sheridan was detached to the Valley at a critical moment.

Gregg, the last of Stoneman's first division commanders, was also the strongest. A classmate of Averell, he had fought Indians as a horse soldier in the Pacific Northwest. James Wilson, no partisan of the Army of the Potomac, praised him to the skies, but he also remarked that Gregg was "somewhat lacking in enthusiasm and possibly in aggressive temper, he was a man of unusual modesty, but of far more than usual capacity."[46] When Sheridan moved to the Valley with two divisions, it was Gregg's division that stayed with the Army of the Potomac. Perhaps Sheridan or Grant believed Gregg lacked the aggressiveness for offensive operations in the Valley, or perhaps Gregg's solid service was simply too valuable to the Army of the Potomac's siege operations. Furthermore, Gregg had served the whole war in the Army of the Potomac's cavalry, unlike Wilson and Alfred T. A. Torbert, relative outsiders who had been inserted into the cavalry's senior echelons by Sheridan and Grant. After all the bad blood between Meade and Sheridan, it might have been wise to allow an Army of the Potomac man to stay behind in Petersburg to manage its important screening and scouting duties.

As Kelly's Ford, Brandy Station, and Gettysburg would show, however, Sheridan would inherit a cavalry organization with quality troopers led by able regimental and brigade commanders. For example, by the time he arrived east, both Wesley Merritt and George Custer had risen to brigade commands. Both were young West Pointers (classes of 1860 and 1861, respectively) who had first served as staff officers with the Army of the Potomac. Merritt had been aide-to-camp to Cooke and then Stoneman, eventually commanding the reserve brigade of Stoneman's raid during the Chancellorsville campaign. Custer had been an aide to both McClellan and Pleasonton, impressing his superiors so much that he was given a Michigan brigade of cavalry shortly before Gettysburg. Both would justify their youthful commissions as brigadiers. Merritt would be promoted to brigade command when Torbert took over the Cavalry Corps in the Valley, and Custer would gain his own division shortly before the opening of the Appomattox campaign.

Custer would quickly win fame at Gettysburg, along with the finest cavalry officer produced by the Army of the Potomac, John Buford. After Stoneman's and Averell's departures, Buford finally would receive the overdue division command he deserved. His troopers fought a tenacious delaying action against Confederate infantry on the first day of Gettysburg, where they used breech-loading carbines to great effect—a small proportion of Buford's troops were fortunate enough to be equipped with Spencer repeaters, while the remainder fought with single-shot Sharps carbines. The episode remains one of the stock stories of valor to come out of the battle. Custer's cavalry action at Gettysburg on July 3 has attracted less attention, but in guarding the Federal rear against an assault by Stuart, Custer's men also used repeaters to great effect. Despite his fondness for the romantic cavalry charge—he personally led one charge himself at the battle—Custer fully respected the firepower of the Spencer.[47] Indeed, his Michigan brigade's organization revealed the hybrid nature of the Union cavalry, with two Spencer-armed regiments specializing in fighting dismounted, while three focused on mounted charges with the saber. Nevertheless, as one of its veterans remarked, "it often happened . . . that the entire brigade fought dismounted at the same time; and sometimes, though not often, all would charge together mounted."[48] Once again, the best cavalry units could fight both mounted and dismounted, with either the repeater fired on foot or the saber swung from the saddle.

Sheridan obviously did not see Buford's and Custer's dismounted troops in action, but he had personally commanded repeater-armed troops during his own short but significant time as a cavalry commander. Historians have tended to skim over this brief period of Sheridan's career, but one finds some significant premonitions of the future during Sheridan's time as a regimental and later a brigade commander of cavalry.[49] During his first operation as a commander of the 2nd Michigan Cavalry in the West in 1862, Sheridan saw some of his troopers repel a Confederate cavalry charge while fighting dismounted with Colt repeating rifles.[50] Sheridan's troopers, however, by no means fought exclusively on foot. Later, during the Union army's pursuit of Confederate troops under Pierre G. T. Beauregard retreating from Corinth, Sheridan ordered a saber charge to be supported by troopers armed with repeaters to try to cut off and capture some Confederate pickets.[51] On another occasion, this time when he commanded a brigade, Sheridan repelled a major assault by Confederate cavalry by ordering saber-armed troopers to attack the rear of the Confederates via a back road in support of dismounted troopers fighting on foot with the aforementioned Colt repeaters.[52] Sheridan had not been in command of the regiment when it acquired the repeaters, but he clearly recognized the potential of using such weapons and the benefits of troopers being able to fight both mounted and dismounted.

Moreover, during the haphazard pursuit of Beauregard after the Confed-

Wayne Wei-Siang Hsieh

erate evacuation of Corinth, Sheridan saw firsthand how *not* to handle a campaign against a retreating enemy. As he later put it in his memoirs,

> The enemy was considerably demoralized. Under such circumstances, an energetic and skillfully directed pursuit might not have made certain the enemy's destruction, but it would largely have aided in disintegrating his forces, and I never could quite understand why it was not ordered. The desultory affairs between rear and advance guards seemed as a general thing to have no particular purpose in view beyond finding out where the enemy was, and when he was found, since no supporting columns were at hand and no one in supreme control was present to give directions, our skirmishing was of little avail and brought but small reward.[53]

While Sheridan's recollection probably was colored by his presence at Appomattox, the general comparison between the two campaigns remains trenchant and significant.

In sum, none of the Army of the Potomac's cavalry officers with enough seniority to take command of the Cavalry Corps in 1864 possessed the same breadth of experience as did Sheridan, with his wartime career as first a quartermaster, then a brigade commander of cavalry, and after that a division commander of infantry. Even Buford did not enjoy the infantry experience possessed by Sheridan, although his superb record in the cavalry might have made that irrelevant. Unfortunately for the Union, Buford perished from typhoid fever in December 1863. Even more important, with Buford's death, none of the Army of the Potomac's senior cavalry officers could match Sheridan's ability to inspire troops to victory by sheer force of will. That determination, especially in the Shenandoah Valley campaign, would build a confidence and esprit de corps in the Cavalry Corps that later served as an indispensable part of the Union cavalry's success during the climactic campaigns of 1865.

As one officer put it, Sheridan "was the only commander I have ever met whose personal appearance in the field was an immediate and positive stimulus to battle—a stimulus strong enough to turn beaten and disorganized masses into a victorious army. . . . [His soldiers] simply believed he was going to win, and every man apparently was determined to be on hand and see him do it."[54] Furthermore, despite Sheridan's famed propensity for towering rages, there was a steady, almost workmanlike quality to him, which was needed for the administrative duties associated with army command. As another cavalry officer put it, "Whether he succeeds or fails, [Sheridan] is the first General I have seen who puts as much heart and time and thought into his work as if he were doing it for his own exclusive profit. He works like a mill-owner or an iron-master, *not* like a soldier, — never sleeps, never worries, is never cross, but isn't afraid to come down on the man who deserves it."[55]

Sheridan provided the Army of the Potomac's cavalry with crucial advantages in leadership, but that does not mean every decision he made was flawless. Shortly after arriving in the East, he elevated two outsiders to division command in his Cavalry Corps, the aforementioned James Harrison Wilson and Alfred T. A. Torbert. Wilson had graduated from West Point in 1860 as an engineer. He had served first on McClellan's staff and then had moved west where he became a senior officer on Grant's staff in the Army of the Tennessee. He did fine service before taking over his division as head of the Cavalry Bureau, where he reformed government purchasing procedures for horses and officially made the Spencer repeater the standard arm of the Union cavalry — two important administrative reforms for Union troopers. However, he had no experience in leading troops, and while he would eventually become an exemplary field commander (including an independent command in the West that captured Selma in 1865), he would show some of his inexperience during the Overland campaign. He would be suitably seasoned by field service by the time he arrived in the Shenandoah Valley, however, and would do good service there. Torbert was a West Point classmate of Sheridan's but a curious choice for division command in the cavalry as he had been a brigade commander of infantry in the Sixth Corps. He would be elevated to command of the Cavalry Corps in Sheridan's Valley command but would disappoint his chief. He would eventually be left behind with a small garrison when Sheridan rejoined Grant for the Army of the Potomac's final campaign.

Before Sheridan could triumphantly return to Grant's army, however, he had to first deal with Early in the Valley. After some desultory maneuvering, Sheridan decided to make his move and advance against Early near Winchester. Sheridan used his three infantry corps in conjunction with the cavalry, and the foot soldiers' frontal attack on September 19 pinned and battered the Confederate infantry as the Union cavalry made its way around the Confederate flank and into the rear.[56] One Union cavalryman after the war described Winchester as "the first time that proper use of [cavalry] had been made in a great battle during the war. [Sheridan] was the only general of that war who knew how to make cavalry and infantry supplement each other in battle."[57] Even Wilson, that stout defender of the cavalry's prerogatives, acknowledged the importance of cooperation between different arms both at the battle of Winchester and in general, although he also pointedly referred to cavalry as having "played the decisive part."[58] Furthermore, as we have seen, Wilson saw no contradiction in highlighting the virtues of the Spencer repeater and the efficacy of mounted charges, of which Winchester proves a spectacular example. Indeed, the battle even witnessed the deployment of Confederate infantry under Breckinridge into a square to resist Union cavalry charges.[59] Emory Upton, one of Wilson's future cavalry division commanders during the Selma campaign, also commanded an infantry division at Winchester, and he asked afterward for a transfer to the cavalry. Upton was perhaps the army's most innovative infantry tactician, and he seems to have recognized early on the innovative significance of Spencer-armed cavalry.[60]

Sheridan continued to batter Early's army. He scored another victory at Fisher's Hill on September 22, 1864, which resulted in Averell's aforementioned relief and Torbert's eventual exile from Sheridan's command (the latter had also been tardy). Sheridan's cavalry would score another crushing victory over Early's battered cavalry force at Tom's Brook on October 9, 1864.[61] Early had one last card to play, however, and he would score quick success with a surprise attack on the Union forces at Cedar Creek on October 19, while Sheridan attended a conference in Washington with senior Union leaders. Sheridan had already been traveling back to his command, and he made haste as he heard sounds of fighting in the morning. He rallied stragglers he met as he approached the battlefield and then organized a crushing counterattack that for all intents and purposes ruined the prospect of Early ever seriously threatening Washington again and put an end to Confederate military power in general in the Valley. Sheridan and his troopers departed the Valley like triumphant conquerors, leaving behind a wake of destruction of its economic resources. As one of his aides put it, the cavalry's success in 1864 had taught them "that their duty was to fight the enemy wherever found; that if the rebellion was not to be ridden down, it must be trampled under foot; and the cavalry, with patience, gallantry, and devotion, followed this teaching, and rendered themselves capable of profiting by the glorious opportunities which later campaigns afforded."[62] Unlike the hard-luck Army of the Potomac bogged down in its siege lines, with its string of failures and missed opportunities, the morale of Sheridan's troopers benefited from their string of victories while waging aggressive, offensive operations in the Valley.

After Early's defeat, Grant originally intended for Sheridan to destroy the Virginia Central Railroad and the James River canal and then move south to join Sherman in North Carolina. Sheridan, however, sensed that blood was in the water regarding the Army of Northern Virginia, and he conducted his operations in such a manner as to make his return to Grant's position at Petersburg a fait accompli. From a strict understanding of military obe-

Maj. Gen. Philip H. Sheridan and his staff in January 1865.
Left to right: Sheridan, Col. James Forsyth, Chief of Staff Wesley Merritt,
Brig. Gen. Thomas C. Devin, and Bvt. Maj. Gen. George A. Custer.
(Library of Congress Prints and Photographs Division,
reproduction number LC-DIG-cwpbh-03133)

dience, Sheridan had defied his chief's intent and orders, but Grant rightly gave Sheridan discretion as an army commander. When Sheridan rejoined Grant, he returned to commanding only cavalry forces, but he retained his independence as an army commander and reported directly to Grant, bypassing Meade.

In the prelude to the opening of the Appomattox campaign, Grant ordered Sheridan on March 29 to turn the Confederate right; Sheridan put his forces in motion toward Dinwiddie Court House, a strategic road intersection.[63] Grant smelled blood, and he informed Sheridan that he "intended to close the war right here."[64] As the campaign developed, Grant offered Sheridan control of the Fifth Corps on March 30 if "you can turn the enemys' right with the assistance of a corps of Infantry entirely detached from the balence [sic] of the army."[65] Sheridan asked for the Sixth Corps instead, but Grant refused, since it was too far out of position to reinforce Sheridan.[66] Lee responded to the threat to his right by concentrating three divisions of cavalry under Fitzhugh Lee and five brigades of infantry under George Pickett, all understrength, at Five Forks. Lee intended for this risky concentration of combat power to strike at Sheridan's position at Dinwiddie Court House. Despite the relative strength of Pickett's forces (roughly 11,500 total men versus approximately 5,700 troopers under Sheridan),[67] Sheridan was able to hold on at Dinwiddie Court House. After his repulse, Pickett saw no choice but to withdraw to a fortified line at Five Forks.

In his initial report to Grant on the action, Sheridan noted that "our fighting to-day was all dismounted,"[68] as his troopers focused on holding their position against furious assaults by both Confederate cavalry and infantry. Moreover, as Wesley Merritt (Sheridan's senior cavalry general) reported, "The ground on which the fighting took place was very heavy, and for the most part densely wooded; when it was open, it was impossible for a single horseman to cross, owing to the nature of the soil and the heavy rains which had just fallen."[69] The battle showed that cavalry could take advantage of offensive opportunities only if it could survive sharp engagements such as this battle on terrain unsuitable for mounted operations — a task for which the firepower of the Spencer proved invaluable.[70]

Shortly after the battle, despite "one of the liveliest days in his experience," Sheridan saw more opportunities than risks in his position. He told Horace Porter, one of Grant's staff officers, that "we at last have drawn the enemy's infantry out of its fortifications, and this is our chance to attack it." He once again pleaded for Wright's Sixth Corps, "because it had been under his command in the valley of Virginia, and was familiar with his way of fighting."[71] Grant once again rebuffed the request, but Sheridan's persistent requests for Wright as opposed to Warren show how large his experiences in the Shenandoah Valley loomed over his conduct during the Virginia theater's decisive campaign. It also revealed that even at this point, Sheridan's relations to much of the Army of the Potomac's high command remained tense. In retrospect, Wright's Sixth Corps should have remained with Sheridan in the first place as a combined arms task force, but institutional inertia had overridden the success of the command arrangements used in the Valley, much to the coming discomfort of both Sheridan and the ill-starred Warren.

Sheridan's plan to storm the Confederate position at Five Forks was to pin Pickett's infantry in its works with dismounted troopers fighting with carbines, while part of Custer's division would launch a mounted attack as a diversion. The primary attack would be made by Warren's Fifth Corps of infantry at a vulnerable point in the Confederate line. When Warren's three infantry divisions engaged the enemy, Thomas C. Devin's reinforced cavalry division would also join the assault.[72] Sheridan, who had started the Overland campaign demanding complete independence for his cavalry, supervised the infantry assault and at one point grabbed his own battle flag to rally wavering foot soldiers. Porter recounted one episode when, after a mortally wounded skirmisher fell to the ground, Sheridan's exhortations were so "electric" that "the poor fellow snatched up his musket, and rushed forward a dozen paces before he fell, never to rise again."[73] Sheridan scored a huge victory, and the Army of Northern Virginia suffered irreplaceable losses, including almost 6,000 captured infantry.[74]

Unlike at Dinwiddie Court House, Sheridan's troopers fought both in and out of the saddle. In the broken terrain, such as the area west of the Dinwiddie road, dismounted fighting was unavoidable,[75] but when possible, Sheridan's subordinates used both mounted and dismounted forces. For example, when Devin assaulted across Chamberlain's swamp, he ordered Charles L. Fitzhugh's brigade to make the water crossing on foot. Once it established a lodgment, Peter Stagg's mounted troops crossed the swamp, and both mounted and dismounted troops charged the Confederate position in the woods in front of Five Forks. Devin's men made progress, but a strong line of Confederate ranks manned by infantry eventually stalled their progress. For the general assault later made in coordination with the Fifth Corps infantry, Devin dismounted all his men but ordered one regiment of regulars to remain "mounted and in readiness to charge should the enemy's line be broken." When such a contingency became real, the regulars made a mounted charge, "clearing the breast-works at a bound, and charging far in

Wayne Wei-Siang Hsieh

advance of the division."[76] Merritt also ordered Custer to keep a whole brigade mounted "to make the most of a pursuit when the enemy was dislodged
from his works."[77] Custer, presumably on his own discretion and due to the
nature of the terrain, elected to mount two of his brigades instead of one, and
while the prompt response of Rooney Lee's Confederate cavalry prevented
him from completely enveloping the Confederate right flank, Sheridan still
inflicted grievous losses on his foes.[78] Lee now had no choice but to denude
his thin trench lines defending Petersburg even further to save what was left
of Pickett's command.

Recognizing the gravity of Lee's losses, Grant then ordered a general assault on the Petersburg defenses, and the Sixth Corps that had fought so well
with Sheridan in the Valley scored a breakthrough in the Confederate lines
on April 2. Lee then ordered an evacuation of Richmond and Petersburg,
in the hope of escaping eventually to Danville and, after that, uniting with
Johnston in North Carolina. Sheridan anticipated the move and positioned
his forces accordingly. What followed was a cat-and-mouse game as Sheridan's cavalry relentlessly pursued Lee in an effort to not just nip at the heels
of the retreating Army of Northern Virginia but to overtake it and cut off all
avenues of escape. The perspicacious Edward Porter Alexander, in analyzing
the war in Virginia's final campaign, described Sheridan as Grant's "best general" whose "presence & personality changed incipient disaster into victory."
Moreover, Alexander praised Grant for having kept the cavalry near him for
that final clash of armies, as opposed to strategically barren raiding — in striking contrast to Lee's management of his own cavalry at Gettysburg.[79]

Sheridan recognized the importance of infantry supports for his
mounted troops and controlled both the Second and Fifth Corps at the outset of the Appomattox campaign, but it was the horse soldiers who provided
the flexibility and mobility crucial to the capture of Lee's army. For example,
cavalry troopers were the first to reach the critical hamlet of Jetersville in
the late afternoon on April 4, which blocked Lee's most direct route to Danville. While Fifth Corps infantry began to arrive shortly afterward, it was
mostly horse soldiers who faced a possible attack by Longstreet's corps on
the fourth, before the arrival of another two corps of Federal infantry on the
fifth. Lee elected not to attack on the fourth with so much of his army scattered across the countryside, but as a consequence he ceded to Grant control
of the Army of Northern Virginia's most direct escape route.[80] Alexander succinctly described the Confederates' subsequently grim position in recounting
his first exposure to a map three days later during a meeting with Lee — "The
most direct & shortest road to Lynchburg from Farmville did not cross the

river as we had done, but kept up the south side near the railroad. The road we were on bent up & then back, & was evidently longer, finally recrossing the headwaters of the river & rejoining the straighter road at Appomattox Court House."[81]

If Lee had decided to hazard an attack on the Federal position at Jetersville on April 4, the potency of Sheridan's Spencer-armed troopers would have made even a determined assault by Longstreet's veterans a hazardous undertaking, to say the least. Even more important than the Federals' technological advantage was the high morale and aggressiveness that further enhanced the military effectiveness of Sheridan's troopers. These self-confident veterans of Sheridan's Valley campaign were by no means invincible, but even when not concentrated at crucial points such as Jetersville, their continual harassment of Lee's forces further wore down a Confederate army already mauled by a winter's worth of siege warfare, while hindering the concentration and reorganization of his battered army. Indeed, it was Sheridan's troopers on April 3 who caught wind of Lee's intended concentration at Amelia Court House and subsequently captured roughly 1,200 Confederates. Moreover, Richard Anderson's corps could not have provided assistance to Longstreet for a possible attack on the Federals at Jetersville on the fourth, because it remained preoccupied with Thomas Devin's cavalry division.[82]

This continual harassment by Sheridan's troopers only depleted Lee's forces further as they desperately sought an alternate escape route to Danville. On April 5, while the main body of Lee's forces escaped Amelia Court House to fight another day, a brigade of Union cavalry captured or destroyed valuable ordnance and supplies carried by Lee's exposed supply trains, along with another 300 prisoners. Just as they had in the Shenandoah Valley the previous fall, both Union cavalry and infantry forces, including foot soldiers not under Sheridan's direct command, worked together to obtain the larger Federal triumph at Sailor's Creek on April 6, capturing thousands of Confederate troops, much of Lee's depleted baggage train, and eight general officers. Indeed, while Sheridan by no means deserved sole credit for the triumph, the engagement did see the Sixth Corps returned to his direct control.[83] Sheridan's success on April 6 prompted him to declare to Grant, "If the thing is pressed I think Lee will surrender."[84]

The boldness of the Union cavalry also allowed it to better exploit the excellent intelligence produced by its own scouts, including a daring group who operated far in advance of Federal forces wearing Confederate uniforms. It was one of those scouts who learned on April 8 that four railroad trains with valuable supplies awaited Lee at Appomattox Station. Custer's swift-hooved division captured the trains on April 8 and were the first Federal forces to establish yet another blocking position astride Lee's new intended avenue of escape. On April 9, Lee attempted one final attack to open yet another road south, but Sheridan and his cavalry once again played an important role in trapping the Confederates—with important contributions from Ord's Army of the James and Meade's Army of the Potomac. As hard-marching infantry-men arrived on the battlefield, sensing the war's coming conclusion, Sheridan sought to insert them into the Federal lines in the place of his cavalrymen, whom he then ordered to extend the Federal right in order to envelop the Confederate left.[85] Reflecting the tactical flexibility the Union cavalry now possessed and his own earlier experience as a cavalry commander, Sheridan later wrote in his report that he initially ordered his cavalry troops to fight dis-mounted to slow the Confederate attack "so as to give time for the infantry to form its lines and march to the attack, and when this was done to move off to the right flank and mount."[86]

As Bergen's essay in this volume points out, the Union infantry had by this point obtained commanders in the aggressive style embodied by Grant, and after Herculean forced marches, they arrived in time to force even Lee to accept surrender as his only remaining option. But the mobility of Sheridan's troopers combined with his hard-won experience coordinating large units of both cavalry and infantry on the same battlefield had played a crucial role in the campaign's victorious conclusion. Frederick C. Newhall's comments on the cavalry's role at Sailor's Creek in relation to infantry forces could be ex-tended to the whole campaign—that "if at the close of the game the cavalry seemed to play the winning card by throwing brilliantly upon the cloth their unexpected and resistless trump . . . nobody could deny that the partner had played good cards boldly and well."[87]

Looking at the Civil War as a whole, the British military writer G. F. R. Henderson later characterized American cavalry as able to "charge infantry when surprised or demoralized; that they fought well on foot, but were not equal to well-trained infantry; and that, as cavalry, they were deficient in ma-nœuvring power and in cohesion."[88] As a general statement, this is a reason-able one, and while the Federal cavalry retained the ability to make cavalry charges, they probably did not match the precision of European troopers. Nevertheless, the firepower of the Spencer put Union troopers on firmer footing when confronted with infantry[89] and in large part compensated for its lower proficiency in shock tactics. Writing in January 1865, with experience in both the Eastern and Western Theaters at the head of Spencer-equipped cavalrymen, James Harrison Wilson declared that "there is no doubt that

Spencer carbine is the best fire-arm yet put into the hands of the soldier. . . .
Our best officers estimate one man armed with it equivalent to three with
any other arm. I have never seen anything else like the confidence inspired
by it in the regiments or brigades which have it. A common belief amongst
them is if their flanks are covered they can go anywhere. I have seen a large
number of dismounted charges made with them against cavalry, infantry, and
breast-works, and never knew one to fail."[90] Wilson overstated the case, but
the Spencer did indeed give the Union cavalry a real advantage.

As Sheridan's Valley campaign and Appomattox showed, even with the
additional firepower of the Spencer, the cavalry could not reach its full potential without large supporting infantry formations — in both cases, at least one
whole corps's worth. Moreover, the Spencers would not have had such a telling effect if the Army of the Potomac had not instituted important institutional reforms to its reorganization — the most significant being Hooker's
consolidation of the cavalry into a corps under the command of a cavalry general. Finally, even Spencer-equipped troopers working within a competent
administrative and organizational apparatus still needed effective battlefield
leadership, and in this case, the Union found just such a leader in Sheridan.
Not only did Sheridan possess the requisite aggressiveness and killer extinct,
but his earlier wartime service prepared him well for the complex task of coordinating cavalry and infantry together for maximum effect at Five Forks. "A
lucky inspiration" for the Union, indeed.

NOTES

1. Philip St. George Cooke, *Cavalry Tactics, or, Regulations for the Instruction, Formations,
and Movements of the Cavalry of the Army and Volunteers of the United States* (Washington:
Government Printing Office, 1861), 1:1, 2:60. On antebellum Civil War cavalry tactics
more generally, see Edward Hagerman, *The American Civil War and the Origins of Modern
Warfare: Ideas, Organization, and Field Command* (Bloomington: Indiana University
Press, 1988), 21; and Perry D. Jamieson and Grady McWhiney, *Attack and Die: Civil War
Military Tactics and the Southern Heritage* (Tuscaloosa: University of Alabama Press,
1982), 63–66.

2. Edward Waldo Emerson, *Life and Letters of Charles Russell Lowell, Captain Sixth
United States Cavalry, Colonel Second Massachusetts Cavalry, Brigadier-General United
States Volunteers* (Boston: Houghton, Mifflin, 1907), 60.

3. Stephen Z. Starr, *From Fort Sumter to Gettysburg, 1861–1863*, vol. 1 of *The Union
Cavalry in the Civil War* (Baton Rouge: Louisiana State University Press, 1979), 438.

4. George B. McClellan, *Report of the Secretary of War, Communicating the Report of
Captain George B. McClellan, (First Regiment United States Cavalry,) One of the Officers Sent
to the Seat of War in Europe, in 1855 and 1856* (Washington: A. O. P Nicolson, 1857), 125.

Wayne Wei-Siang Hsieh

5. Moses Harris, "The Union Cavalry," in *War Papers Being Papers Read before the Commandery of the State of Wisconsin*, repr., vol. 1, Military Order of the Loyal Legion of the United States 46 (Wilmington, N.C.: Broadfoot, 1993), 371–72.

6. James Harrison Wilson, *Under the Old Flag; Recollections of Military Operations in the War for the Union, the Spanish War, the Boxer Rebellion, Etc.* (New York: D. Appleton, 1912), 2:172.

7. Starr, *From Fort Sumter to Gettysburg*, 50.

8. McClellan, *Report of the Secretary of War*, 277.

9. George B. McClellan, *Report on the Organization of Campaigns of the Army of the Potomac* (New York: Sheldon & Co., 1864), 54.

10. Starr, *From Fort Sumter to Gettysburg*, 235–37; quote in Harris, "Union Cavalry," 351.

11. Frank J. Welcher, *The Eastern Theater*, vol. 1 of *The Union Army, 1861–1865: Organization and Operations* (Bloomington: Indiana University Press, 1989), 512–13.

12. McClellan, *Report on the Organization and Campaigns of the Army of the Potomac*, 54. After the war, McClellan cited the general shortage of cavalry regiments as preventing him from consolidating troopers into one brigade for each corps, along with a general reserve for the whole army. George B. McClellan, *McClellan's Own Story: The War for the Union, the Soldiers Who Fought It, the Civilians Who Directed It and His Relations to It and to Them* (New York: Charles L. Webster, 1887), 118–19.

13. Stephen W. Sears, *Landscape Turned Red: The Battle of Antietam* (New Haven: Ticknor and Fields, 1983), 270–71, 276.

14. McClellan, *Report of the Secretary of War*, 125.

15. Starr, *From Fort Sumter to Gettysburg*, 370.

16. Worthington Chauncey Ford, ed., *A Cycle of Adams Letters, 1861–1865* (Boston: Houghton Mifflin, 1920), 2:3–4.

17. McClellan, *Report on the Organization and Campaigns of the Army of the Potomac*, 422.

18. Gordon C. Rhea, "Union Cavalry in the Wilderness: The Education of Philip H. Sheridan and James H. Wilson," in *The Wilderness Campaign*, ed. Gary W. Gallagher (Chapel Hill: University of North Carolina Press, 1997), 111, 124–28, 130.

19. Stephen Z. Starr, *The War in the East: From Gettysburg to Appomattox, 1863–1865*, vol. 2 of *The Union Cavalry in the Civil War* (Baton Rouge: Louisiana State University Press, 1981), 106–7.

20. Joseph T. Glatthaar, "U.S. Grant and the Union High Command during the 1864 Valley Campaign," in *The Shenandoah Valley Campaign of 1864*, ed. Gary W. Gallagher (Chapel Hill: University of North Carolina Press, 2006), 41.

21. Emerson, *Life and Letters of Charles Russell Lowell*, 322.

22. *The Papers of Ulysses S. Grant*, ed. John Y. Simon and others, 32 vols. to date (Carbondale: Southern Illinois University Press, 1967–) (hereafter cited as *PUSG*), 11:354.

23. Ibid., 11:359.

24. Glatthaar, "Grant and the Union High Command," 50.

25. *PUSG*, 11:379–80.

26. Emerson, *Life and Letters of Charles Russell Lowell*, 322.

27. George Gordon Meade, *The Life and Letters of George Gordon Meade, Major-General United States Army*, 2 vols. (New York: Scribner's, 1913), 1:325.

28. Ibid., 2:71. Also see the postwar dispute between the two, pp. 404–6.

29. Rhea, "Union Cavalry in the Wilderness," 111.

30. Starr, *From Fort Sumter to Gettysburg*, 339; Welcher, *The Eastern Theater* 515–16. The service biographies for the Army of the Potomac's cavalry generals can be found in George W. Cullum, *Biographical Register of the Officers and Graduates of the U.S. Military Academy at West Point, N.Y.*, 8 vols. (Boston: Houghton Mifflin, 1891), and Welcher, *The Eastern Theater*.

31. U. S. War Department, *The War of the Rebellion: A Compilation of the Official Records of the Union and Confederate Armies*, 127 vols., index, and atlas (Washington: Government Printing Office, 1880–1901), ser. 1, 25 (2): 72 (hereafter cited as *OR*; all references are to ser. 1).

32. Ibid., 25 (1): 1067.

33. Starr, *From Fort Sumter to Gettysburg*, 367–68.

34. David Evans, *Sherman's Horsemen: Union Cavalry Operations in the Atlanta Campaign* (Bloomington: Indiana University Press, 1996), 50.

35. Welcher, *The Eastern Theater*, 346; Sears, *Landscape Turned Red*, 327–28.

36. Francis Augustín O'Reilly, *The Fredericksburg Campaign: Winter on the Rappahannock* (Baton Rouge: Louisiana State University Press, 2006), 198–201.

37. Starr, *From Fort Sumter to Gettysburg*, 213–14.

38. Ford, *Cycle of Adams Letters*, 2:8.

39. Starr, *From Fort Sumter to Gettysburg*, 368n6.

40. Ibid., 391–92, 395.

41. *OR* 25 (2): 147.

42. Starr, *From Fort Sumter to Gettysburg*, 347–49.

43. Ibid., 362–63.

44. *OR* 25 (1): 1073.

45. Starr, *From Fort Sumter to Gettysburg*, 281, 284–85.

46. Wilson, *Under the Old Flag*, 1:364.

47. Starr, *From Fort Sumter to Gettysburg*, 435, 439.

48. James Harvey Kidd, *Personal Recollections of a Cavalryman with Custer's Michigan Cavalry Brigade in the Civil War* (Ionia, Mich.: Sentinel, 1908), 282.

49. See, for example, Paul Andrew Hutton, *Phil Sheridan and His Army* (Lincoln: University of Nebraska Press, 1985). Starr devotes only a few pages to this early episode in his magisterial study of the Union cavalry. Stephen Z. Starr, *The War in the West, 1861–1865*, vol. 3 of *The Union Cavalry in the Civil War* (Baton Rouge: Louisiana State University Press, 1985), 65–67. Also see ibid., 2:72.

50. Philip Sheridan, *Personal Memoirs of P. H. Sheridan*, 2 vols. (New York: Charles L. Webster, 1888), 1:147–48.

51. Ibid., 151.

52. Ibid., 158–64.

53. Ibid., 152–53.

54. E. R. Hagemann, ed., *Fighting Rebels and Redskins: Experiences in Army Life of Colonel George B. Sanford, 1861–1892* (Norman: University of Oklahoma Press, 1969), 222–24.

55. Emerson, *Life and Letters of Charles Russell Lowell*, 336.

56. Starr, *War in the East*, 276.

57. Kidd, *Personal Recollections of a Cavalryman*, 393–94.

58. Wilson, *Under the Old Flag*, 1:557.

59. Starr, *War in the East*, 276.

60. Peter S. Michie, *The Life and Letters of Emory Upton, Colonel of the Fourth Regiment of Artillery, and Brevet Major-General, U.S. Army* (New York: D. Appleton, 1885), 189–90.

61. William J. Miller, "Never Has There Been a More Complete Victory: The Cavalry Engagement at Tom's Brook, October 9, 1864," in *The Shenandoah Valley Campaign of 1864*, ed. Gary W. Gallagher (Chapel Hill: University of North Carolina Press, 2006), 134–60.

62. Frederick C. Newhall, *With Sheridan in the Final Campaign against Lee*, ed. Eric J Wittenberg (Baton Rouge: Louisiana State University Press, 2002), 24.

63. *OR* 46 (3): 234–35.

64. *PUSG*, 14:244.

65. Ibid., 270.

66. *OR* 46 (3): 380.

67. Ed Bearss and Chris Calkins, *The Battle of Five Forks* (Lynchburg, Va.: H. E. Howard, 1985), 124; William Marvel, *Lee's Last Retreat: The Flight to Appomattox* (Chapel Hill: University of North Carolina Press, 2002), 7.

68. *OR* 46 (3): 381.

69. Ibid., 46 (1): 1117.

70. On the potency of the Spencer, see, for example, Bearss and Calkins, *Battle of Five Forks*, 37, 91.

71. Horace Porter, *Campaigning with Grant* (New York: Century, 1897), 431–32.

72. Bearss and Calkins, *Battle of Five Forks*, 86.

73. Porter, *Campaigning with Grant*, 437.

74. Starr, *War in the East*, 448–50.

75. Bearss and Calkins, *Battle of Five Forks*, 83.

76. *OR* 46 (1): 1123–24.

77. Ibid., 1118.

78. Ibid., 1130; Bearss and Calkins, *Battle of Five Forks*, 108.

79. Edward Porter Alexander, *Fighting for the Confederacy: The Personal Recollections of General Edward Porter Alexander*, ed. Gary W. Gallagher (Chapel Hill: University of North Carolina Press, 1989), 512.

80. Marvel, *Lee's Last Retreat*, 37, 47–49.

81. Alexander, *Fighting for the Confederacy*, 525.

82. Marvel, *Lee's Last Retreat*, 31, 47, 50.

83. Ibid., 56–58, 83.

84. *OR* 46 (3): 610.

85. Marvel, *Lee's Last Retreat*, 142, 147, 170.

86. *OR* 46 (1): 1109.

87. Newhall, *With Sheridan in the Final Campaign against Lee*, 98.

88. G. F. R. Henderson, *The Science of War — A Collection of Essays and Lectures, 1892–1903* (London: Longmans, Green, 1905), 275.

89. Henderson himself acknowledges the importance of the Spencer; see ibid., 267–68.

90. *OR* 45 (2): 488.

5

Lee, Breckinridge, and Campbell

The Confederate Peacemakers of 1865

William C. Davis

The Confederate surrenders came entirely on terms dictated by the victors. Generous though their provisions were in the circumstances, some Confederate leaders had hoped for more. A small group of them led by the legendary Gen. Robert E. Lee, the immensely popular Secretary of War John C. Breckinridge, and Assistant Secretary of War John A. Campbell plotted behind the scenes for months beforehand, often in opposition to their congress and president, hoping to negotiate something better, a reunion short of the humiliation of absolute surrender. None of these peacemakers had espoused secession in 1861, yet they all fought hard for the Confederacy, and never more than now as they struggled to influence the manner of its demise. They would actually achieve a fleeting "victory" in one of the April 1865 capitulations, but it lasted just hours. Had they succeeded, they would have left a large mark on the war's ending and the peace that followed, a potentially lasting impact and a tantalizing "might-have-been" that could have made all their efforts worthwhile. We know most of these men well, but these particular efforts of theirs are all but forgotten now. Yet for a few months in 1865 they struggled to recast the postwar course of America.

General Lee avoided involvement with politics and politicians whenever possible, beyond that necessary to sustain his army and do his job. Politicians, he quipped during the secession crisis, were "the most difficult to cure of all insane people."[1] By the early weeks of 1865 his patience with them was about exhausted, and that included President Jefferson Davis. That winter, when Senator Benjamin Hill of Georgia asked Lee for his opinion on shifting the capital to a safer place than Richmond, Lee declined comment, mindful that anything he said might be used as ammunition in some political squabble. Hill did not give up, however, pressing him that it was Lee's business, since if the Confederacy lasted long enough for Davis's six-year term as president to expire, then the people would undoubtedly turn to Lee as his successor. Lee reacted vehemently. "Never!" he shot back. "I think the military and civil talents are distinct, if not different, and full duty in either sphere is about as much as one man can qualify himself to perform." He would do the people a great "injustice" if he sought or accepted political office.[2] Of course a posited future presidential election was more than three years off, and most of the people were quite happy with Lee where he was. What little speculation circulated about the next president focused chiefly on Virginia senator Robert M. T. Hunter and even more on Maj. Gen. John C. Breckinridge, then commanding in southwest Virginia.

That suited Lee, who was weary of presidents by that time. Thanks chiefly to his own patience and diplomacy in dealing with Davis, Lee enjoyed almost model relations with the president, but still there were strains. Events left him little alternative, however, but to meet and cooperate with some political leaders in his effort to awaken Richmond to the dire condition of the armies. At the same time, he also met and made plans with one group of appointed and elected officials whose stated objective was seemingly unthinkable, an end to the war that would most likely also include the death of the Confederacy.

Lee knew that by all reason and logic the war was lost now. He was never one of those who regarded Southern victory and independence as inevitable outcomes. Indeed, the possible eventuality of defeat was the warning he consistently employed in trying to get the government to provide more manpower and matériel. The previous June, as he faced the possibility of being hemmed into the earthworks and forts protecting Richmond and Petersburg, he had told Lt. Gen. Jubal A. Early that if the enemy managed to tie him up in his defenses in a siege, "then it will be a mere question of time."[3] It did become a siege, and then Abraham Lincoln's November reelection dashed the Confederacy's last hope of outlasting Northern commitment.

If that did not convince Lee the cause was lost, events in Richmond must have. The political opposition to Davis had been noisy, to be sure, but essentially a toothless tiger, more nuisance than anything. By January 1865, however, his opponents and the newspaper press supporting them called for Davis's impeachment, and there were scattered demands that Congress leave him in office as a figurehead and install Lee as commander in chief, "the military head of the Government."[4] Rumors of a movement to make Lee dictator had been rising to the surface for fully a year by that time.[5] Recently Davis's most virulent critic, the fire-eating South Carolinian Robert Barnwell Rhett, had told Vice President Alexander H. Stephens that Congress must remove Davis at once without the delay of the lengthy impeachment process and that Stephens should forgo succeeding to the presidency in order to allow Lee's installation as dictator.[6] The whisperings in Richmond grew loud enough that Davis's own minister believed "the idea of a military dictator in the person of General Lee seems to be predominating."[7]

Like most people, Stephens wisely ignored Rhett, and Lee would never have countenanced such a scheme in any case. Nevertheless, by the end of 1864 he had to know at least something of the dissidents' scheming, with half of the capital press then openly calling for his installation as some kind of supreme leader. It spoke volumes about the crumbling prestige and effectiveness of Confederate civil authority. On January 17, "rumors of revolution" and deposing Davis to install Lee swept through the War Department, just a day after the Senate, in a direct strike at Davis's power, passed a bill creating the office of "general in chief of the armies," and no one had any doubt as to whom they expected the president to appoint.[8]

Meanwhile Lincoln made indirect peace feelers, all of them inconclusive. His volunteer emissary Francis Preston Blair Sr. arrived in Richmond on January 12 to consult with Davis on a possible basis of discussion, but Lincoln's insistence on reunion and Davis's on independence were mutually exclusive. No sooner did Blair leave than on January 17 Lincoln's friend James W. Singleton of Illinois appeared in the Confederate capital with a pass through the lines.[9] Ostensibly he came to buy Southern produce for shipment north under a trade cartel, but his real mission was to sound particular Confederate leaders on the possibility of acceptable terms for reunion. It was no secret that some senior elected and appointed officials virtually acknowledged that the war was lost, though that did not necessarily mean that they regarded all possibility of an ultimate Confederate independence as ended. Vice President Stephens had long been a member of the opposition to Davis, as was the president pro tempore Hunter of the Senate. The assistant secretary of war, Virginian John A. Campbell, and one or two of the bureau chiefs in his department also admitted in private that military defeat was all but inevitable.

Singleton met with them—or soon claimed that he did—and heard Stephens, Hunter, and Campbell tell him that lieutenant generals James Longstreet and Richard S. Ewell of Lee's Army of Northern Virginia agreed with them and that Lee himself felt their fortunes were beyond recovery. The recent Senate resolution creating the office of general in chief suggested to

Singleton that Lee—the obvious and only choice to fill the office—would soon have the power to make a virtual peace if by his new authority he ordered all Confederate land forces under his command to lay down their arms.[10]

Coincidentally, the same day that Singleton arrived in Richmond, so did Breckinridge. As a sop to opposition clamor for the removal of all of Davis's cabinet, the president made one change by removing his unpopular secretary of war James A. Seddon, widely regarded as a failure in an admittedly almost impossible portfolio. Rumor said that Davis had offered the post to Breckinridge. Vice president of the United States under President James Buchanan, Breckinridge had been the reluctant presidential candidate of the more conservative wing of the Democratic Party in 1860 and carried all of the soon-to-be-Confederate states but three. Though he opposed secession, when it came he went with the Confederacy with equal reluctance, only to become a generally successful medium-grade division and corps commander and one who, moreover, negotiated the notoriously poisonous political command culture of the Army of Tennessee unscathed. In 1864 he came to Virginia and won laurels protecting Lee's flank and rear in the Shenandoah Valley and southwest Virginia. A cause by now desperate for living heroes, with so many killed in battle, hailed him as the new "Stonewall" Jackson. At the rumor of his becoming secretary of war, John B. Jones, the chief clerk of the War Department's Passport Office, concluded that "every effort will be made to popularize the cause again," while a woman in Richmond added that "from the character of the new Secretary, the people were induced to hope."[11] Jones saw confirmation of that when he learned that on arriving, Breckinridge became a guest at the home of influential attorney Gustavus A. Myers, observing that "Myers has a keen scent for the sources of power and patronage."[12] Arguably the new secretary was the only man in Richmond besides Lee with the prestige to challenge Davis if necessary.

As it happened, Singleton and Breckinridge knew each other before the war, and Singleton called on him at Myers's, yet more evidence of the rumored new secretary's influence. Revealing his secret agendum, Singleton got Breckinridge's promise to arrange a meeting with Lee. On January 19—Lee's birthday, as it happened—they met at army headquarters. Lee did not disagree when Singleton said continuing the war only postponed the inevitable, responding only that the outcome was "in the hands of Providence" and that as a man of peace he wanted to stop the carnage. A few days later Singleton recalled Lee going on to say that he "would go as far as any man in the Confederacy in his efforts to do so." Duty required him to fight on if necessary, but he would welcome a permanent peace that could spare him that.

After being appointed Confederate secretary of war in 1865, former major general John C. Breckinridge hoped to negotiate an end of the war short of absolute surrender. (Library of Congress Prints and Photographs Division, reproduction number LC-DIG-cwpb-04791)

As Singleton reported it, Lee said he believed that a sixty-day armistice could lead to a negotiated reunion on liberal terms and that the South would forfeit slavery at once if promised fair monetary compensation and constitutional amendments to protect its other rights of person and property. Lee went on to say that he would gladly meet with Lt. Gen. Ulysses S. Grant to construct between them a basis for an armistice.[13]

Singleton left Richmond convinced that Lee was "the man with whom to treat." Others wanting to end the war, even if it meant reunion, realized that as well.[14] One of them was Breckinridge, who walked through four inches of fresh snow to assume his new office on February 7. He had for some time believed that the war was lost and that reunion in some form was now inevitable. Fresh support for his conviction arrived in the capital on February 5 when Stephens, Hunter, and Campbell returned from a meeting with Lincoln and Secretary of State William H. Seward on Lincoln's steamer at Fort Monroe. Davis had authorized the three to seek a meeting with Lincoln to determine upon what terms he would be willing to discuss ending the war. The Union president had but three: the Confederates must first acknowledge the full national authority of the Union; there would be no discussion of retreating one atom from the Emancipation Proclamation or his plans for a Thirteenth Amendment abolishing slavery; and he would not cease hostilities until the Confederacy agreed to abandon the war and disbanded its armies. Once those conditions were settled, he told them, virtually anything else they wanted to discuss was on the table, and he would be liberal in his terms. Stephens told Lincoln that they sought "a just and honorable peace" when they met with him for several hours on February 3, but the Confederates did not enunciate any specific terms by which they would agree to reunion.[15]

What they wanted was postponement of that question. Whether or not the trio had consulted with Lee beforehand, it is evident that as of early February virtually all of the would-be Confederate peacemakers regarded armistice—a simple ceasefire—as their preferred first step. Their thinking was simple and seemingly reasonable. Throughout history when armies stopped fighting under an armistice agreement, they could not move from their positions while negotiations ensued. It was also widely recognized that once the guns went silent, it became increasingly difficult to get them started again, and especially to marshal home-front support for renewed hostilities. The result was often less than defeat but also less than victory for either side. Rather than restart the bloodshed, Washington and Richmond might agree to end the war with slavery forever dead but the Confederacy still alive, and the two independent nations might then entangle themselves in military and commercial alliances to protect their continent and encourage their economies, meanwhile building a tradition of cooperation on mutual objectives that in time could overcome the animosities raised by the war itself. Hunter in particular raised the issue of an alliance during that ceasefire in order to cooperate in driving an army of French interlopers out of Mexico in defense of the Monroe Doctrine. Another of the Confederate commissioners joined him in speculating that such joint action might also lead to later reunion, but Lincoln rejected that as nothing more than an indefinite postponement of the question.

After the commissioners returned to Richmond on February 5, all of the documents supporting the history of their mission appeared in the press four days later.[16] Lincoln's insistence on reunion seemed to close the door to ending the war without the eclipse of the Confederacy. Despite Lincoln's reading of the armistice suggestion as an obvious attempt to avoid reunion, perhaps indefinitely, Hunter somehow came away thinking that the proposed Mexican venture might lead eventually to Southern independence based on a close military alliance with Washington and a settlement of all their outstanding issues on commerce and intercourse.[17] Three days after the commissioners' return, Campbell and Stephens spent several hours conferring behind locked doors. The result was the decision for Campbell to draft an armistice document that he believed could be "a plan by which a settlement could be initiated."[18] A ceasefire was still their top priority.

Breckinridge took office just the day before Campbell and Stephens met. Whether or not Breckinridge and Campbell deliberated what the assistant secretary would discuss with the vice president, the two men were of like mind: the war was lost and reunion virtually inevitable. In one of their very first meetings, Campbell showed his new superior the draft armistice plan, hoping that Breckinridge might take some action, presumably advocating it before the president. Breckinridge did nothing to promote the document, however, most likely because he knew that armistice was never on the negotiating table so far as Lincoln was concerned.[19]

Campbell put his finger on another major impediment to a peaceful settlement with Lincoln. The Confederacy had no "competent party" with the authority, the power of prestige, or the will sufficient to act. The president's position against any negotiation involving reunion was that "he could not commit a suicide" and that only the states that had created the Confederacy could dissolve it in their separate state conventions. Meanwhile the Senate would not initiate any steps toward peace in its advisory and foreign affairs capacity, though it was generally known that several senators from the

William C. Davis

Upper South border states felt amenable to accepting reconstruction of the Union in return for peace.[20]

Breckinridge's arrival and Lee's recent expressions to Singleton appeared to offer a change in the dynamic. The Senate confirmed Davis's nomination of Lee for general in chief on February 1.[21] Lee actually assumed the command on February 9.[22] Though he might not be the dictator some had wanted, he now had power to act for all Confederate land forces everywhere. That made him the one and only general who could make a peace. Of course he could not do so by his own fiat, for President Davis as commander in chief could override any order. What Lee could do, however, was take advantage of his preeminent popularity and prestige with soldiers and civilians alike and issue his own declaration that they were beaten and should sue for terms. Jefferson Davis was no fool. He could feud with and even fire any other general, but by this time the soldiery and citizens almost universally regarded Robert E. Lee as the Confederacy and the cause they fought for.[23] That made him virtually untouchable, punctuating Singleton's perception that Lee was the man to deal with.

The day after Lee assumed his new duty, the new secretary of war did something none of his predecessors had done: he called on the heads of the several bureaus of his department to submit reports of their means and resources for maintaining their armies in the field for the coming season. Of course a new secretary needed to be apprised of matters in a hurry, but he had another motive. Breckinridge had been a field general for more than three years and commanded an important military department for the immediate year just passed. He knew as well as any other senior officer the deplorable state of Confederate manpower, communications, and supply. So did President Davis, to whom the forthcoming reports, no matter how gloomy, would be nothing new. But the people were another matter. If they were fully and frankly informed of the desperation of the case and able to read for themselves the War Department officials' gloomy forecasts in the press, then public opinion could overrule Davis and demand that he sue for peace; otherwise, individual states might call conventions to initiate their own separate state action. Already there were rumblings that powerful leaders in North Carolina considered doing so.

To make the public aware, however, Breckinridge and Campbell—the two largely acted as one in the following days, making it sometimes difficult to determine which originated specific ideas and policy—needed to get those reports before the public. As appointed officials of an executive department, they served at the president's pleasure. They might want to end to the war, even if by reunion, but they were also firm democrats determined to act within the framework of their constitution if at all possible. Hence they could not directly release harmful confidential reports to the public press, and they hardly expected Davis to allow them to do so if asked. Congress had a right to see such reports, however, and should they become the subject of debate on the House and Senate floors, then they must inevitably become public knowledge, thereby accomplishing Breckinridge and Campbell's aim.

It seems no coincidence that Breckinridge immediately began hosting a number of members of Congress in his office each morning, particularly senators, since under article 2, section 2, paragraph 2 of the Confederate constitution the Senate was to be consulted on all treaties and ambassadorial appointments. By logical extension that body had a right to see any reports that might portend the need for negotiations with Lincoln or for the creation of commissioners to do so. Thus the Senate would be Breckinridge and Campbell's forum to bring the dire state of the armies to public notice. Though the discussions in the secretary's office remained confidential, certainly much centered on the Confederacy's ability to continue resistance and what to do if it could not, as Breckinridge felt out just which members might be most useful.[24]

Soon he identified at least six as possible allies, beginning with Henry C. Burnett from Kentucky. Burnett had been an ardent secessionist before the war and was known as one of Davis's staunchest allies, yet he faced their situation frankly now. Like Kentucky, Missouri never formally seceded, but it also had its star on the Confederate flag and two senators in Richmond. The senior was Waldo P. Johnson, a Virginian by birth who fought with the 4th Missouri Infantry at the battle of Pea Ridge in 1862, and despite his personal friendship with Davis he had been an outspoken critic of some of the president's cabinet. Most recently he worked with the group who all but forced Davis to make Lee general in chief and replace Seddon, as had his junior colleague George G. Vest, a Kentucky native who may have known Breckinridge before moving to Missouri. A strong secessionist, Vest served in the Confederacy's original Provisional Congress and since had been a strong supporter of the administration, but he, too, was disillusioned with Davis now.

Potentially more influential were the Virginia senators. Allen T. Caperton originally opposed his state's secession. In the Senate he was a consistent critic of Davis's policies, and he had worked with the others who pressured the president to change his cabinet. Then there was his colleague, who initially stood with the president's most faithful friends but was by now firmly in the anti-Davis camp. The anomaly added to this quintet of border state men was Louis T. Wigfall, a South Carolina–born fire-eating secessionist who represented Texas. Once a close friend and aide to the president, Wigfall was now perhaps Davis's bitterest and most outspoken enemy. He largely fathered the bill that made Lee general in chief and openly and intemperately blamed the president for all the Confederacy's ills.

Possible allies with the group, though not consistently with them, included Burnett's colleague William E. Simms, who had been at Transylvania University with Breckinridge and later served with him in the Kentucky legislature. An even more radical secessionist than Burnett, Simms faithfully supported the president but by now felt almost ready to give up. John C. Watson of Mississippi came reluctantly to secession and now heartily favored negotiating for peace, while Gustavus A. Henry of Tennessee supported the president and the war wholeheartedly until 1865, when he, too, joined in the move to give Lee his new position.

In the primary bloc of six senators, at least five had sought to curtail Davis's powers, as had Henry, and all but Wigfall were at least willing to consider options leading to peace that included reunion, though Hunter still cherished his unrealistic dreams of some kind of national identity for the Confederacy following peace. They were a diverse group, but one thing they all shared was a race with the calendar. The date of Congress's adjournment was critical to their several hopes, for the Senate was the only body that could constitutionally push the president to negotiations on Lincoln's terms. In the last extremity, should Davis remain defiant, the House could impeach him and the Senate would try the case. To achieve anything toward peace, Congress had to remain in session. It had sporadically discussed dates for adjournment since late December, when the House proposed January 24, 1865, which was tabled.[25] Wigfall wanted it to sit permanently to keep the Confederacy alive and continue his vendetta against the president. The rest surely knew it could take some time to get the War Department reports onto the floor of the Senate and into public awareness, and any adjournment now would delay that until a time when it might be too late to accomplish their purpose.

On February 10, the same day that Breckinridge called for the bureau reports, a resolution proposing adjournment in ten days came to the floor, and Wigfall moved to postpone that until February 28. He had several motives, including wanting time to defeat legislation designed to enlist black men in the Confederate armies. Then he came closer to speaking for the bloc when he added in a barb aimed at Davis that in recent days there had been much talk of predicted successes and that the Union would be ready to give up by summer. Those were "delusive hopes," he charged, "not only silly, but criminal." They must be honest with the people that much suffering and disaster lay ahead, even if somehow they won, and he was not about to "palm off a fraud upon the people." In this crisis it would be a "stupendous evil" for Congress to adjourn. When the question came to a vote after long discussion, a tie vote and the vice president's absence, by Senate rules, defeated the resolution, all of the bloc but Johnson voting against a February 20 adjournment.[26]

Meanwhile Breckinridge and Lee met frequently on matters of supply and defense. Then in late February, Longstreet came forward with a surprising proposal. During a meeting under flag of truce to discuss prisoner issues with Union major general Edward O. C. Ord, one of them changed the subject to how Grant and Lee themselves might bring about an end to the war. Ord suggested that he was sure Grant would agree to meet with Lee to discuss the matter. Of course President Davis would have to approve any such meeting, and so Lee went to Richmond to confer with the president on February 26 about the issue, which in the end went nowhere.

Lee had other reasons for the visit. His relations with Davis were at their lowest ebb of the war. He was weary of being summoned to the capital on minor matters by a president who as much as anything just wanted to talk to a friendly ear, and Lee often returned to the army in an irritable mood. On February 25, when Davis sent yet another request for a needless visit, Lee replied that he was too busy. That set off Davis, who responded coolly, "Your counsels are no longer wanted in this matter." Seeing no choice, Lee went to try to mollify the president, though their correspondence would be a bit chilly for a time thereafter.[27] He needed the president to be receptive to the Longstreet-Ord suggestion for it to have any chance of success. Even though just three weeks earlier Lee had averred publicly that no "compromise or negotiation" could yield any of their claimed rights without surrendering "liberties we derived from our ancestors," now he endorsed such a meeting.[28] Conferring privately with Davis and Breckinridge, he said he hoped for peace without defeat if he and Grant could agree on an armistice and then negotiate the points at issue and submit recommendations to a military convention.[29]

Davis dismissed the idea that anything productive would come of such a discussion, just as he had with the Hampton Roads conference, but he was always ready to use negotiations to buy time. Lee told Davis he doubted that the Confederate people would accept reunion "yet awhile," but that "yet" implied his belief that reunion was all but inevitable now.[30] With Davis's permission, Lee wrote to Grant on March 2 to ask for a meeting, even though he feared that Grant, like Lincoln, would make agreement on reunion prerequisite to discussion of anything else. In fact, Grant responded that he could not even go that far. His authority allowed him only to meet with Lee to deal with military issues, not political.[31]

The day that Lee received Grant's response, he met with Breckinridge and the quartermaster general and commissary of subsistence at the War Department to discuss the prospect for sustaining his army in the field that spring, and it was gloomy. Then they turned their conversation to peace. Breckinridge believed that a strong and determined push from the Senate could force the president to address the issue, and Lee said he knew Hunter well enough to approach him about assuming the lead in that chamber. When they met, Lee suggested to Hunter that he introduce in the Senate a resolution calling on Davis to commence discussions with Lincoln looking toward an honorable surrender. Lee's own role, he told the senator, would be publicly to recommend opening negotiations, which he believed the armies and the people would regard as "almost equivalent to surrender." A later visit to Hunter from Breckinridge emphasized the power of the general's personal prestige. This was no palace coup but rather a design by constitutional means to nudge Davis to action.[32]

At about the same time, the secretary and the general took a suggestion from Campbell, who agreed with them that any peace would inevitably come on terms of reunion and emancipation. Campbell seemingly never stopped working on one scheme or another for an end to the war. He was already wooing Senator William A. Graham of North Carolina, a stern opponent of the president's and a budding leader in the peace faction, telling him that though Lincoln would not make a treaty with the Confederacy—since that would tacitly acknowledge its existence as a legitimate political entity—he would agree to meet with any individuals from states resisting national authority and give them his terms for peace.[33] By implication, Lincoln encouraged separate state action, and Campbell secured Graham's promise to advise Davis to send his Hampton Roads commissioners north again, to Washington this time to meet Lincoln and agree to his terms. Should Davis refuse, then Graham would advise leaders in North Carolina to pursue a separate state peace.[34]

Breckinridge and Lee met yet again on March 4, and their discussions may have had something to do with a letter Campbell addressed to the secretary of war the following day, suggesting that he ask Lee to present a full and frank statement of his opinion of the ability to continue to prosecute the war with any expectation of success.[35] Campbell later called the letter his "last of several efforts to promote a negotiation for peace." He showed a draft to Lee, whose role was to produce a report sufficiently pessimistic that when

As assistant secretary of war, former U.S. Supreme Court justice John A. Campbell worked with Breckinridge to try to orchestrate peace throughout the spring of 1865. (Library of Congress Prints and Photographs Division, reproduction number LC-DIG-cwpbh-04017)

the people read it in the press, public opinion would force Davis to acquiesce. Campbell also showed the draft to William C. Rives of Virginia, a haltingly committed peace advocate who had resigned his House seat a few days earlier.[36] After securing approval of his letter, Campbell then asked Rives to draft a resolution to be introduced in the Senate advising the president to propose that Lee request an armistice as a "preliminary to the re-establishment of peace and union." When that was done Rives gave it to Campbell, who asked Graham to introduce it on the floor, but Graham unaccountably declined, an unfortunate but hardly fatal setback.[37]

When Breckinridge received Campbell's lengthy letter, he and Lee met again on March 6 or 7 to discuss it and ensure that each knew his role. They agreed that Breckinridge would formally call on Lee for such a report, and the next day he did so. If Lee publicly declared that further resistance was futile, then surely the president must yield. At once, pending receipt of Lee's report and the ensuing public reaction to it, the question of adjournment became vital. Apparently Breckinridge or Campbell or both asked the bloc to try to forestall an early adjournment to allow time to get Lee's report in hand and then get it onto the Senate floor, where debate should result in resolutions calling on Davis to approach Lincoln for negotiations based on that president's stipulations at Hampton Roads. In the current climate, should Davis defy the Senate as it performed its mandated "advice and consent" role, the president risked impeachment and removal, while Vice President Stephens, who would constitutionally succeed him, was already in the Reconstruction camp. While the bloc sometimes divided on issues like slave enlistments, in the main they voted together with no more than one breaking ranks.[38] On this most vital issue, however, they stood steadfastly unanimous, determined not to see the Senate adjourn before it had an opportunity to take action.

Two days earlier, the Missourian Vest had moved in the Senate that a House resolution setting March 8 for adjournment be postponed indefinitely. On March 8, three from the bloc stood to make the case against a new House resolution calling for adjournment on March 11. Doing so now, said Vest, "would have a disastrous effect," without saying why he thought so. Then, as if to mitigate any speculation about the bloc's ultimate goal, Johnson rose to say that he opposed "everything looking to reconstruction." Wigfall seconded that, proclaiming that "Congress should stand by the ship, and let its fate be theirs."[39] In a cryptic remark that most if not all in the chamber had to understand, Burnett hinted at their real purpose when he declared that "exigencies might arise any day which should require the presence of the Senate," adding what amounted to a verbal nudge and wink by concluding that "senators would understand him."[40] When the resolution passed despite their oppo-sition, Burnett called for the yeas and nays to be written down in the body's journal, and Vest added that he wanted to ensure that the record showed that he and Johnson had opposed the action.[41]

Fortunately, the next day President Davis made a gift to the bloc when he sent a message to Congress advising that he very soon expected to be send-ing both houses a communication that might require their deliberation and action and thus asked that they postpone adjournment a few days. The House immediately changed its date for adjournment to two o'clock on March 14 and sent notification to the Senate.[42] Davis did not further explain his impor-tant "communication," but Lee's delivery of his report that same day removed any mystery. Dutifully, Breckinridge had forwarded a copy to Davis. But even before doing so, the secretary and Campbell knew there was more work to be done and more time needed. Probably that same evening, March 9, Burnett summoned his associates to meet in his room at the Spotswood Hotel.[43] Vest arrived last to find awaiting him his colleague Johnson, their host Burnett, Wigfall, Caperton, Hunter, and the secretary of war.

It seems clear that Breckinridge requested the meeting and the timing was critical, with at that moment fewer than four full days before adjourn-ment. While all of them no doubt spoke up, the secretary of war dominated the meeting. He frankly described the Confederate cause as "hopeless," its existence now numbered in just "a very few days." He had two reasons now for calling them together. "I have wished for some time to confer with the members of the confederate Senate, and especially with those from Ken-tucky and Missouri," he said, "as to the effect of the final collapse upon the confederate soldiers from those states." If the Confederacy simply "goes to pieces" and their armies disbanded without any formal action on the part of their government, he expected that the soldiers from the cotton states and any territory not yet occupied by the enemy would be able to go home with-out fear of molestation.[44]

"But what will become of the Kentuckians and Missourians who have fol-lowed us into the war, and who are disbanded far from home, without means, and with no certainty of a friendly reception, even if they should return to their own states?" he asked. Those two states occupied an uncomfortably anomalous position. They were represented in both governments and both armies, but unlike the rest of the Confederacy, neither Missouri nor Ken-tucky seceded by a representative-elected convention. He feared that Union-ists in them might exact reprisals against returning Confederates, whom they could accuse of treason. "Our first duty, gentlemen, is to the soldiers who have been influenced by our arguments and example," said Breckinridge, "and we should make any and every sacrifice to protect them."

Then he moved beyond the two states to the Confederacy itself. As Senator Vest later remembered his words, Breckinridge told them, "What I propose is this: That the confederacy should not be captured in fragments, that we should not disband like banditti, but that we should surrender as a government, and we will thus maintain the dignity of our cause, and secure the respect of our enemies, and the best terms for our soldiers." He had no illusions. "I may be, for reasons well known to us all, more obnoxious to the North than many others, but I am willing to assume the risk, and to surrender as secretary of war." It was a subtle but significant distinction, for if he gave himself up as a general he would be subject to the terms of any military convention like any other officer, but as secretary of war he was a civil official of a government regarded as treasonous, and already there were indictments for treason awaiting him back in Washington and in Union-held Kentucky. When one of the senators asked what would happen to President Davis, Breckinridge admitted, "That gives me more concern than anything connected with the plan I have stated." Davis was in greater danger of retribution than anyone else, yet he believed that the president would not consent to any settlement that excluded him from sharing the same peril awaiting Breckinridge.

Much else must have been discussed, and it is probable that Breckinridge revealed to the bloc the unexpected problems with the report just received from Lee, making it all the more imperative that there be no adjournment on March 14. As events demonstrated, Burnett and the others must have promised to do their best to buy him time. Then the meeting broke up, but not before Breckinridge said one thing more that Vest for one never forgot. "This has been a magnificent epic," said the secretary of war. "In God's name let it not terminate in a farce."

While the bloc resolved to try for more time, Breckinridge and Campbell addressed Lee's report. Confessing that their case was "full of peril"; that Confederate forces were ill equipped, ill fed, and outnumbered everywhere; and that he entertained little hope of standing up to the foe in the coming spring, Lee went on to add that "it is not worse than the superior numbers and resources of the enemy justified us in expecting from the beginning." The Confederacy had already held out "longer than we had reason to anticipate," he added, but then he temporized. The fall of Richmond and Petersburg would be a blow but not necessarily fatal if the army in the field could be sustained. In fact, he did not say that their case was hopeless, and he did not mention opening surrender negotiations. Instead he said that everything depended on how much more sacrifice the elected representatives believed the people could sustain, the closest he came to a hint that Congress might conceivably act in the matter.[45] For reasons still murky, Lee fatally compromised the purpose of his report. Either he recoiled in the end from working with the politicians — some of them the same men whose failures had brought on the war — or his loyalty to Davis and his duty trumped his conviction of inevitable defeat, which remained unchanged.

Observers in the War Department and close to Davis detected an uncharacteristic caution in Lee's words, while Campbell finally concluded that Lee "declined to do more than perform his military duty and would not assume to counsel much less to act upon the question of peace."[46] Then another problem arose. Hunter balked at getting even this watered-down report onto the Senate floor. The problem for Hunter was the conflict between his clear appreciation of the situation and his own ambition. In mid-January a rumor circulated in government circles that he was a "submissionist," willing to accept defeat and reunion. On January 23, he forwarded to the War Department a letter from a Virginia regiment deploring the demoralization and disintegration in the army and calling for negotiations to get "the best possible terms without delay." Hunter strengthened such rumors by endorsing the letter: "I fear there is too much truth in it."[47]

According to the later recollections of longtime friend Littleton Q. Washington, Hunter's former secretary when he was secretary of state in 1861–62, Hunter fully realized that the cause was hopeless and wished he could do something to save the South from absolute military subjugation and "a conquest without any terms of peace."[48] Moreover, Hunter was known to dream of succeeding Jefferson Davis in the presidency. From the day of Breckinridge's arrival in Richmond, it was noticeable that Hunter avoided calling on the new secretary, whom war clerk Jones perceived as "a formidable rival for the *succession* — if there should be such a thing." Hunter apparently believed that a "succession" was just possible, based on his notion of a military alliance of North and South against the French in Mexico paving a path for Lincoln to allow the Confederacy to coexist with the Union on the basis of commercial reciprocity.[49] That meant continuation of a Confederate presidency. Hunter had regarded Breckinridge as a potential Democratic presidential rival back in 1860.[50] Now as president pro tempore of the Senate, he would play an important role in any trial of Davis should there be an impeachment, and though Stephens as vice president ought constitutionally to succeed a deposed Davis, the diminutive Georgian's health and his own conviction that defeat was inevitable might impel him to step aside. That could leave Hunter the senior serving elected official in the government and a natural choice for the presidency.

Being perceived as a follower of Breckinridge's or enjoying too close an association with men seeking peace at the price of surrender, however, would open no doors to the executive mansion. Almost a daily visitor at the War Department before, the Virginia senator all but stopped coming by after Breckinridge took office.[51] Hunter's explanation for neglecting to execute his role was that his well-known controversy with Davis would prompt his enemies to claim that he had been motivated by personal spite.[52] Now Hunter joined Lee in failure to carry out their previously agreed-upon assignments.

While awaiting Lee's report, on March 14 the bloc got two additional senators to vote with them to defeat a resolution setting a new deadline at three o'clock on March 17. They wanted even more time.[53] On March 16, all six opposed a new resolution, and four others joined them to defeat it. Later that same day the author of the resolution brought it up again for reconsideration. Even though two of the bloc's allies went over to the other side, it still ended in a tie vote, which by the body's rules meant defeat. Still later that day, when the resolution's author managed to get it on the floor yet again, setting noon on March 18 for adjournment, only one of the bloc's allies stood with the senators, and the measure finally passed by that single vote.[54] On the appointed day, Hunter, the president pro tempore, selected delegates to join with counterparts from the House as a committee to inform the president that Congress was ready to adjourn if he had no more business for them. Perhaps significantly, Hunter selected not one member from the bloc as he continued to distance himself from the alliance.[55] Bloc members had delayed adjournment for more than a week at Breckinridge's behest to buy time for Lee's report, but in the end Davis outmaneuvered them. He released a watered-down version to the Senate on March 13 that omitted what little force there was in Lee's account. Even then an injunction of secrecy kept the report out of circulation as late as March 20, after Congress had adjourned and no longer presented a threat.[56]

Soon after adjournment, the bloc began to break up. Wigfall left in late March, and Hunter distanced himself even more by publishing a notice in the local press denying rumors that he favored reconstruction of the Union.[57] Breckinridge meanwhile rode on adjournment day to Lee's headquarters to spend the next three days in private conference.[58] Stymied by Congress and president, the bloc still had a potent bargaining chip in Lee's army. There was a suggestion of uniting the Army of Northern Virginia with the one in North Carolina and another in Alabama and of Lee then leading them north across the Ohio, but Lee dismissed that as an impractical dream. Even if it was possible to effect the concentration, he doubted they would reach the Ohio in any condition to invade the North and thereby force Yankee armies to abandon Confederate territory to go after them.[59] Lee thought his better course would be to tie Grant down at Richmond long enough for Lee to leave a decoy holding force while he got most of his army away intact to merge with General Joseph E. Johnston's forces then being pushed back in North Carolina by Maj. Gen. William T. Sherman. Together they might defeat Sherman before Grant caught up and then turn to meet him, a desperate, even delusional idea at this point in the war if proposed by any but Lee.

To do even that, Lee had to first break out from Grant's near-encirclement. On March 25, Lee launched a surprisingly potent strike on the right end of the Federal siege line that he had hoped might force open a door elsewhere to allow him to get much of his army out of its trenches and in the field again. The attack's failure left Lee with no alternative but to hold on as long as he could and then evacuate the whole army before the enemy closed off all avenues of escape. One week later that moment came, and on April 2 Lee notified Breckinridge that he must evacuate his lines that evening and the government should immediately prepare to depart Richmond. Thanks to Breckinridge's and Campbell's conviction that defeat was inevitable, the War Department was entirely ready to go, the only executive branch so prepared.[60]

Breckinridge himself was the last government official to ride out of the capital. But before departing he met one last time with Campbell, who had determined to remain in hope of securing an interview with Union authorities when they occupied the city, and perhaps even with Lincoln himself. He asked Breckinridge for authorization to "confer at large upon public affairs," which the Kentuckian declined to give since only the president had constitutional authority to appoint what amounted to a diplomatic envoy. At the same time, however, Breckinridge did not prohibit Campbell from having any discussions with anyone, and he had to know perfectly well Campbell's purpose.[61] There could be several avenues to peace, and Davis himself had argued that any reunion could be accomplished only by the individual states. Fortuitously Lincoln himself came to the captured capital on April 4, and Campbell secured an interview that afternoon and again the next day. Once again Lincoln stated his terms for peace, emphasizing that he would be liberal in granting other requests and adding that he would release confiscated property back to the individual states that agreed to his terms now but would exact more confiscations on any that continued resistance and sell the property to defray the expense of continuing the war. There could be no pardon for Jefferson Davis, he said, but he went on, gesturing with his hands for emphasis, that with that single exception, "most anybody could have anything of that kind by the asking for it."[62] Campbell commented that now more than ever, with Congress adjourned and the president and cabinet on the run, there was no "competent party" with the authority or the power of prestige to agree to a settlement. Lee certainly had the latter but had been to date unwilling either to speak out or act. Privy as he was to the latest information on the condition of Lee's army, Campbell went on to say that he believed its condition was such that an armistice of even a few days "would bring a peace," and he handed Lincoln a copy of his February armistice plan as an example.[63]

There had always been multiple paths to peace. So long as Confederate armies remained intact as viable — if not mortal — threats to Yankee success, there was the faintest of possibilities that even Hunter's notion of an eventual independence might somehow miraculously emerge. Breckinridge and Campbell seem never to have regarded that as realistic, but they were not done yet. Now Lee's freedom from protecting Richmond and his return to the open field changed the dynamics of the situation. Perhaps no one but the president really expected Lee to get away from Grant's massive pursuing army with its better equipment, transportation, and morale. If — far more likely when — Grant cornered Lee somewhere, the option would be to stand and fight one last hopeless battle or enter into negotiations looking to the surrender of the Army of Northern Virginia. Ever since the failure of their efforts in March, Breckinridge and others were turning their thinking toward a fallback scenario. By this time if not before, Postmaster General John H. Reagan joined them. He was with the secretary of war late into the night of April 1 and again the next day when Lee's dispatch arrived announcing that he must evacuate.[64] Together, and perhaps with Campbell as well, they were evolving a new peace strategy to fit the new situation at hand. With a universal surrender brokered by Congress a dead issue now, there still might be meaningful concessions to salvage from the ruins, and once again there might be a critical role for Lee to play, if he was willing.

Lee's hope at the moment was to outrun the Federals, fill his empty haversacks from depots at Lynchburg, and then make a junction with Johnston's army a hundred miles distant in North Carolina. It was an unlikely scenario conceived in desperation but all that was left to him. By April 4, as his army reached Amelia Court House, it became even more unrealistic when the trainload of rations he expected to find was not there. The hungry Confederates had no choice but to move on the next day. Breckinridge appeared that morning to confer with Lee, and then the two met again on April 6 when

Lee halted the remnants of his army at Farmville after a disaster at Sailor's Creek cut off a third of his army that was soon captured by the Federals. Lee had barely 25,000 in the ranks that night, and the chimera of catastrophe loomed before him.

Lee and Breckinridge met again the next morning, April 7. Most likely they discussed the necessity of avoiding battle and getting the remnant of the army away quickly to meet Johnston if possible. Yet it seems apparent from subsequent events that they also discussed, at least in outline, an approach Lee might take should he be forced to deal with Grant on surrender terms. Taking the same approach as Campbell back in Richmond, Lee could press first for something short of outright surrender, the armistice the Confederate Reconstructionists first put on the table with Lincoln three months earlier at Hampton Roads. The conviction still remained that once there was a ceasefire and the carnage stopped, neither side would have the stomach to start it again, and that any subsequent negotiated peace could gain the Confederates more than they might expect if they surrendered outright. So long as they had armies in the field, depleted though they were, they still had the power to force the Union to expend more blood and treasure in defeating them. They could save the North that additional cost if offered terms attractive enough. Lee could make that case to Grant if events gave him no choice, and especially if the reward were not just the Army of Northern Virginia but all remaining Confederate land forces everywhere. If Lee and Grant did open communication, Lee could stall for as much time as possible, try for an armistice if he could, and hold out the lure of his authority as general in chief to end all military resistance at a word. Then Breckinridge left Lee to ride on in search of the fleeing government.

Lee was on his own. This moment must have been on his mind for months. Now if a peace was to be made, at least in Virginia, he was to be the peacemaker. As a practical matter, only he could approve any terms, since each passing day put Davis and what remained of the Confederate government ever more distant and beyond communication. He might yet have an opportunity to argue for at least some elements of the Breckinridge-Campbell reconstruction. Coincidentally, just hours later Grant sent a note by truce flag suggesting that it was surely useless to resist further and thereby produce only more needless bloodletting. He proposed that Lee surrender. Lee bought almost a full day's time by not replying until April 8. He denied that his condition was that critical, but then he asked what terms Grant proposed before he would consider any call for capitulation. It sounded almost like a rhetorical question, but Grant seized on the apparent opening to respond that, *"peace being my great* desire," he made only one condition: Lee's soldiers should go home on their parole, not to raise arms against the government again unless and until properly exchanged, an eventuality both generals knew was extremely unlikely.

Lee continued to stall. "I did not intend to propose the surrender of the Army of Northern Virginia," he replied. Nevertheless, he went on to add that "the restoration of peace should be the sole object of all" and that he wanted to meet with Grant in person to discuss just how any proposed terms "may affect the C. S. forces under my command, & tend to the restoration of peace." Hidden within Lee's note was more meaning than his words literally conveyed. Did he mean he declined to discuss the surrender of his Army of Northern Virginia, or did he hint that he did not want to *limit* surrender inquiry to *only that army*? He told Grant he was prepared to talk about matters affecting "the C. S. forces under my command, & tend to the restoration of peace." As general in chief, the "C. S. forces" under his command were all soldiers everywhere, the entire Confederate army. Moreover, when he spoke of "the restoration of peace," he said nothing to imply that he meant only a local peace between his army and the one facing him. His choice of words implied the universal, an end to hostilities everywhere.[65] Lee finally attempted now what Breckinridge and Campbell hoped he would do a month earlier, only now, with the president beyond reach and Congress adjourned, Lee perhaps felt more comfortable. Besides, if he got Grant to agree to a local armistice, or better yet an all-encompassing ceasefire, he might buy even more time while waiting for Davis to be found and notified and brought into actual surrender negotiations. Like Campbell and perhaps all of the rest except Breckinridge, Lee believed that time might work to the advantage of the Confederates and that the North would make significant concessions — though perhaps not actual independence — rather than charge its guns again.

Lee's note said nothing of reunion or emancipation. All of the Reconstructionists accepted those as facts of life in any postwar America. That still left other significant considerations facing Southerners, however. What rights of person and property would their officers and men have in a new Union? Would Davis and other leaders face trial for treason or be left alone? Would Confederates face further confiscation of their real property as punitive damages to redeem the North's war debt? Would Washington assume Confederate debts and thereby preserve the honor of the Confederacy in death? Were their governors and legislatures to continue in office, and could they once more send representatives to Congress with full rights? What was to be the relation of the states to the federal government now, and were they hereafter to be subordinate to the central authority?

Lee hoped that Grant would agree to an armistice followed by a voluntary disbanding of Confederate forces. It would be not so much a defeat as a "withdrawal" from the war with honor, a semantic fine point, perhaps, but an important one to a proud people who had suffered unimaginable loss. As a lure, Lee could point to as many as 150,000 or more Confederate soldiers still under his orders from Farmville to Texas. If forced to, they could still exact a dear price from the North for a complete military victory and subjugation of resistance. No doubt Lee had discussed that with Breckinridge and perhaps Campbell, concluding that they had something of value to offer in return for some concessions and a death for the Confederacy short of humiliating surrender. For Davis, who Lee now knew was trying to plant his standard in a new capital at Danville, independence was always the sine qua non in any discussion about possible negotiations with the Union. It was not for Lee. With the Confederacy already dead in all but name, he could propose euthanizing it if its states and people came away with something in return. That was a lot to read into those few words in his reply to Grant, but it was all there.[66]

Certainly Grant saw it there and quickly cut Lee off by replying the next morning, April 9, that he had "no authority to treat on the subject of peace." He would not talk about armistices and ceasefires, nor would he discuss anything relating to armies other than Lee's; hence he declined a proposed meeting as pointless. In his unique and isolated position Lee might undertake considerable latitude in negotiations, but not Grant. Less than a fortnight before, Lincoln had specifically given Grant the limits of what he could negotiate with Lee, and it did not include matters political or social or anything beyond Lee's own army. The Campbell-Breckinridge-Lee peace plan was always a fleeting hope, and now that was dead so far as this army was concerned. Grant's reply told Lee that, and now all his other options evaporated. When he read Grant's note that morning, he knew there was nothing left to him but to reply requesting that they meet to discuss surrender.[67]

Lee did, in fact, secure a few modest concessions when he met Grant in a parlor at Appomattox Court House later that day, but they were the sort granted out of grace and generosity, for Lee had nothing to offer in return, or at least not then and there. The next day, however, he learned that Grant wanted to see him again. Each rode to a spot between their now-silent lines and spoke from the saddle as Grant stated his reason for wanting to see Lee. They had brought peace to most of Virginia at least. Could they not extend that beyond the Old Dominion? Clearly Grant understood Lee's cryptic reference to the extent of his command and, while he had heretofore avoided that subject in order to get the surrender of the Army of Northern Virginia accomplished and out of the way, now he could address the further-reaching ramifications of what they did the day before. In turn, Lee obviously understood exactly what Grant was proposing and that now, for a change, it was he who had some power, albeit fleeting, to direct events.

That part of the Confederacy not yet occupied by the Federals was still vast, he told Grant. Scattered, ill equipped, and undermanned as they were, remaining Southern armies could not hope to postpone indefinitely an ultimate Union victory. But Lincoln's divisions would have to crisscross that wide expanse several times before they cleared out all resistance, and at what further cost in human suffering? Lee wanted to avoid further bloodshed, but he could not foretell the ultimate cost should some Confederates turn to irregular warfare. The war had already shown how difficult it was to root out partisans and guerrillas. Even though Lee himself firmly opposed that resort, he had no problem implying to Grant that it might happen once he had no further control. Even if he actually said nothing at all about armistice and negotiations, his hint was unmistakable that a universal ceasefire might yield great results if Confederates were offered—through him—some guarantees of civil and property rights. He was still trying for an armistice in the hope that it would lead to reunion with the least cost and the most honor.

Grant forthrightly replied that they could avoid further fighting and losses on both sides if General in Chief Lee would "advise" remaining Confederates to surrender. Lee's response seemingly implied willingness to consider such a course, but then he told Grant that he would have to consult his president first. That would take time, for within hours Davis and his cabinet would be on the move again into North Carolina, and it seems implicit that Lee assumed there would be a ceasefire with the armies of both sides remaining in place until they could know Davis's response. Grant did not come there to sell time, however. Neither he nor Lincoln recognized the existence of a legitimate government or president in the Confederacy, hence Davis's acceptance or rejection of any terms was relevant to them only insomuch as Southern people and soldiers felt bound by his assent. Lee had what Grant wanted, but Grant could not meet Lee's conditions, so they parted and rode back each to his own lines.[68]

Early on the morning of April 12, Lee left to ride back to Richmond, with one last duty to perform. He had to submit a report to President Davis, whereabouts then unknown, detailing the causes leading up to his surrender. In fact, he finally wrote the letter that Breckinridge and Campbell wanted from him back in March. He regarded their cause as irretrievably lost, and their only remaining alternative was for their armies to disband and withdraw into the hills and mountains to continue resistance as partisans by raiding and sniping on occupying Union troops, a mode of warfare that could go on for years with promise of nothing but suffering to no end. "I see no prospect of achieving a separate independence," he concluded and called on the president to suspend hostilities immediately, by an armistice if possible or surrender if he must.[69] He clearly still hoped there might be some gain in negotiation if the Yankees would talk with them.

"As to my own fate, I know not what is in store for me," he told callers. For several weeks he remained almost a recluse in his house considering what to do next. Meanwhile he could not avoid hearing the sounds from Franklin Street outside as regiment after regiment of Union troops passed through on their way to Washington and the close of their war service. Lee's house became a noted curiosity to the victors. Now and then as they marched past, one of them looking up at it to see a shadowy movement at one of the windows where Lee, veiled by a curtain, watched them.[70]

Lee may never have sent that letter to Davis, for the president was a moving target and there was no way to get it to him. Soon there was no point. On April 26, General Johnston surrendered his army to Sherman on terms similar to those given Lee, but not before the last of the Confederate peacemakers made one more try. When Sherman and Johnston agreed to meet to discuss an armistice and possible terms on April 18, Johnston consulted Davis and the president agreed to a ceasefire to buy time but sent Postmaster Reagan and the recently arrived secretary of war to be his representatives. What emerged from the discussion with Sherman was almost everything Breckinridge, Campbell, the Senate bloc, and others had hoped for since February. Persuaded by his own feelings and the influence of what the three Confederates, especially Breckinridge, had to say, Sherman drafted a set of terms that were startling. All Confederate armies, not just Johnston's, were to disband, not surrender, and go home under discipline of their own officers and under arms, there to hand over their weapons to their state arsenals or presumably employ them as peacekeepers since civil order had largely broken down and would take time to reestablish. In return they had only to acknowledge the authority of the U.S. constitution. When a state's governor and legislature did the same, they were to be recognized as legitimate and allowed to continue their civil administration without losing time in electing new ones. Cases of legitimacy such as the Confederate legislatures of Missouri and Kentucky should be referred to the Supreme Court. The people of the former Confederacy were to enjoy all of their prewar rights without molestation from Washington, and Sherman even added a general amnesty for all with no exceptions, not even Jefferson Davis. It was almost in every detail what Campbell had proposed to Lincoln in Richmond on April 4–5.

A shocked Washington rejected Sherman's terms and required him to treat only for the surrender of Johnston's army and nothing more. Accordingly, on April 26 Johnston surrendered. Two weeks later the Confederate army in Alabama gave up. Meanwhile, Federal cavalry had captured Davis and his entourage on May 10 in Georgia, and all of the rest of the top elected or appointed officials of the Confederacy were under arrest or had fled—all but one, that is. On May 7 in Georgia, after dispersing the remains of the Confederate treasury as payment to the soldiers accompanying the fleeing government, the secretary of war set out to lead a decoy company of cavalry in hopes that it would lure pursuing Federal horsemen away from the president's route of flight.

Before leaving, Breckinridge wrote a note for his son to take home to Kentucky. Without specifically mentioning his work with Campbell and Lee and the others for a negotiated peace, he hinted at it when he wrote that "should my friends ever know my part in the occurrences of the last three months, I venture to think it will give me an increased claim on their confidence and regard."[71] Upon learning of Davis's capture, Breckinridge and a small party headed south into Florida, not to escape but to find a boat to get him to Cuba. So far as he knew, the Army of the Trans-Mississippi, the last real Confederate army left, was still in the field in Texas. He was now the only officer of the Confederate government still at large.[72] If he could get to Texas he might hope to surrender that last army on favorable terms, with perhaps even a few of the concessions he had gotten from Sherman. When he reached Cuba on June 11, however, he learned that the Trans-Mississippi army had surrendered on May 26 and it was all but over.

Still, there remained scattered pockets of units not covered by the surrenders to date, and a few determined to hold out or even cross into Mexico rather than yield. In the last official act of any Confederate "government" still at large, Breckinridge asked Havana correspondents from Northern newspapers to publish his call for all remaining Confederates under arms to cease resistance and apply for pardon and clemency.[73] Then this last of the peacemakers left for Europe and exile.

They had all failed. None of the surrender documents of April and May 1865 contained any provisions revealing the influence of the plans made in Richmond between January and March. Neither does it appear that there might have been other circumstances under which the peacemakers could have realized any meaningful gains. Lincoln's resolution on recognition of the national authority of the Union was an immutable prerequisite, as was Davis's insistence on Confederate independence. There was no room for middle ground between those two fixed and immovable points. Lincoln and Grant were wise enough to avoid armistices. With the Union in firm control of the war and victory in sight, armistice offered the Yankees nothing. Only if Washington had accepted the Sherman-Johnston agreement would the peacemakers have influenced the end.

The peacemakers themselves went on to a variety of fates. Henry C. Burnett survived the war by just eighteen months; he was only forty years old when he died at his Kentucky home. Waldo P. Johnson went into self-imposed exile in Canada for a year after the surrenders and then went home to Missouri to end his days as an attorney. George G. Vest was one of only two from the bloc to return to politics after the war. In 1879 Missouri elected him to a seat in the U.S. Senate, where he served for the next quarter-century. Allen T. Caperton became an industrialist in the new state of West Virginia, and he, too, won election to a Senate seat representing the state spawned by the Civil War. Robert M. T. Hunter spent several months in prison after the war and held a couple of minor offices for a time, meanwhile renewing his acrimonious feud with Jefferson Davis. Louis T. Wigfall fled to England at the collapse but returned to the United States six years later and finally relocated to Galveston, only to die soon afterward.

John A. Campbell also spent several months in the same prison with Hunter, which may have been a bit uncomfortable given the way Hunter failed to honor his commitments to the peacemakers, and after release went to Louisiana, where he fought against Reconstruction and became an attorney of national note.

John C. Breckinridge left Cuba in the summer of 1865 to spend the next three and a half years in exile in England, mainland Europe, and finally Canada before President Andrew Johnson's universal amnesty of December 1868 allowed him to return to Kentucky. There he eschewed politics entirely, in spite of which he wielded considerable influence that he lent to oppose the Ku Klux Klan, to support constitutional rights for the freed slaves, and to discourage acrimony among his former Confederate associates, especially the feuding fueled by Jubal Early. When he died in Lexington in May 1875, aged only fifty-four, he was being considered as a keynote speaker for Philadelphia's 1876 Centennial celebration.

Robert E. Lee returned to Richmond from Appomattox almost penniless. Dozens of railroads and insurance companies wanted him to serve as titular chief executive in return for a handsome stipend, but he refused all, wanting to stay quiet, to rebuild his and his family's fortunes, and to help Southerners rebuild their lives. Avoiding all controversy, he accepted the presidency of struggling Washington College in Lexington, Virginia, and in the five years before his death in 1870, he had transformed it into what later became Washington and Lee University. Lee acquiesced in the result of the war, but he never really assimilated back into the Union, which he now regarded as held together solely by armed force.

Breckinridge gave one of his very few postwar public speeches when Lee died, a brief eulogy in Louisville. "Success often gilds the shallow man, but it is disaster alone that reveals the qualities of true greatness," he said of Lee. The Virginian had faced the ultimate disaster with "valor, moderation and courage, with all their associate virtues," and in the outpouring of sympathy and respect all across the reunited nation, Breckinridge saw hope and promise for the future as rancor and bitterness made way for the North and South to mourn in unison at a great man's passing.[74] Just under five years later Breckinridge joined Lee in death, and while the eulogies and encomia were many, none were as eloquent as a few words Lee himself had said in May 1868 when talking with one of his Washington College professors. Despite some prewar acquaintance with Breckinridge, "I did not *know* him till he was secretary of War, and he is a lofty, pure, strong man," said Lee. "He is a great man."[75]

Not one of the three had supported secession in 1860–61. Not one of them wanted the war that followed, and each was in his way almost forced to become a Confederate by circumstances outside his control. In 1865 Campbell, Breckinridge, and Lee had taken the lead in trying to save the South from even greater trauma and loss than was already inevitable, both during the last months of the war and in the months and years of readjustment to follow. That they failed ultimately takes nothing away from their courage and determination in the effort.

NOTES

1. "Thoughts on Politicians," n.d., Robert E. Lee Headquarters Papers, 1850–1876, Virginia Historical Society, Richmond.

2. Speech of Benjamin Hill given on February 18, 1874, *Daily Chronicle and Sentinel* (Augusta, Ga.), March 11, 1874.

3. J. William Jones, *Personal Reminiscences, Anecdotes and Letters of Gen. Robert E. Lee* (New York: D. Appleton, 1875), 40, quoting Early's January 19, 1872, address at Washington University.

4. Alfred P. Aldrich to Lewis M. Ayer, January 9, 1865, Lewis M. Ayer Papers, South

Caroliniana Library, University of South Carolina, Columbia; John B. Jones, *A Rebel War Clerk's Diary at the Confederate States Capital*, vol. 2, ed. James I. Robertson Jr. (1866; Lawrence: University Press of Kansas, 2015), 352 (diary entry for January 17, 1865).

5. *Raleigh (N.C.) Progress*, n.d., in *Hartford (Conn.) Daily Courant*, January 14, 1864; *Worcester (Mass.) National Aegis*, January 30, 1864; *New York Herald*, December 30, 1864.

6. William C. Davis, ed., *A Fire-Eater Remembers: The Confederate Memoir of Robert Barnwell Rhett* (Columbia: University of South Carolina Press, 2000), 80–81. Rhett does not date the sending of the Stephens letter, though the context would suggest that it was in the summer of 1863. However, Rhett's chronology in his fragmentary memoir is often off, and late 1864 or early 1865 seems more probable.

7. Charles Minnegerode to Mary Carter Minnegerode, November 17, 1864, Charles Minnegerode Letters, copies on file at Richmond National Battlefield Park.

8. Jones, *War Clerk's Diary*, 352 (diary entry for January 17, 1865).

9. *Richmond Sentinel*, January 16, 1865; *Baltimore Sun*, January 21, 1865.

10. *Boston American Traveller*, July 8, 1865; *Norwich (Conn.) Aurora*, February 11, 1865.

11. Jones, *War Clerk's Diary*, 371 (diary entry for February 6, 1865); "A Richmond Lady" [Sallie B. Putnam], *Richmond during the War* (New York: G. W. Carleton, 1867), 356.

12. Jones, *War Clerk's Diary*, 352–53 (diary entry for January 17, 1865).

13. *Boston American Traveller*, July 8, 1865; *Norwich Aurora*, February 11, 1865. Some of Singleton's claims are more than suspect, especially the involvement of Grant, who scarcely knew Singleton and regarded him as just another speculator trying to profit from the war. In a few weeks, in fact, Grant would revoke Singleton's pass to go through the lines. Still, it was common rumor in the army and in the North that the Illinoisan was on some kind of peace mission. Grant to Edwin McM. Stanton, March 8, 1865, in *The Papers of Ulysses S. Grant*, ed. John Y. Simon and others, 32 vols. to date (Carbondale: Southern Illinois University Press, 1967–) (hereafter cited as *PUSG*), 13:283n, 14:113–15n. Even in Richmond his mission was no secret, as one paper commented on his arrival that the city was experiencing "a Perfect Diarrhoea of Peace Commissioners" (*Richmond Whig*, January 16, 1865). Yet elements of his story are corroborated. He and Breckinridge did arrive in Richmond on the same day. Stephens, Campbell, Commissioner for Prisoner Exchange Robert Ould, and Hunter were among the men then seeking a means to peace, even at the price of reunion, and so were Longstreet and Ewell, and perhaps even Lee.

14. *Boston American Traveller*, July 8, 1865.

15. *New York Times*, Feb. 11, 1865.

16. See, for instance, *Richmond Examiner*, February 9, 1865.

17. John A. Campbell to Joshua Speed, August 31, 1865, "Papers of Hon. John A. Campbell—1861–1865," in *Southern Historical Society Papers*, ed. J. William Jones and others, 52 vols. (1876–1959; repr., with 3-vol. index, Wilmington, N.C.: Broadfoot, 1990–92), 42:45–46, 51.

18. Jones, *War Clerk's Diary*, 374 (diary entry for February 8, 1865).

19. Campbell to Speed, August 31, 1865, "Papers of Hon. John A. Campbell," 69.

20. Ibid.

21. U.S. Congress, *Journal of the Congress of the Confederate States of America, 1861–1865*, vol. 4 (Washington, D.C.: Government Printing Office, 1904–5), 456–58, 510–11 (hereafter cited as *Journal*).

22. Robert E. Lee to James A. Seddon, February 4, 1865, in *The Wartime Papers of R. E. Lee*, ed. Clifford Dowdey and Louis H. Manarin (Boston: Little, Brown, 1961), 888–89, 891.

23. For a development of this idea of Lee as symbol, see Gary W. Gallagher, *The Confederate War: How Popular Will, Nationalism, and Military Strategy Could Not Stave Off Defeat* (Cambridge, Mass.: Harvard University Press, 1997).

24. Jones, *War Clerk's Diary*, 376, 385 (diary entries for February 10 and 19, 1865).

25. *Richmond Examiner*, January 4, 1865.

26. Ibid., February 14, 1865; Frank E. Vandiver, ed., "Proceedings of the Second Confederate Congress, Second Session in Part," *Southern Historical Society Papers*, 52: 322–23; *Journal*, 541.

27. U.S. War Department, *The War of the Rebellion: A Compilation of the Official Records of the Union and Confederate Armies*, 127 vols., index, and atlas (Washington, D.C.: Government Printing Office, 1880–1901), ser. 1, 46 (2): 1256 (hereafter cited as *OR*); Charles S. Venable to Walter H. Taylor, March 29, 1878, Walter Herron Taylor Papers, Jesse Ball DuPont Library, Stratford Hall, Stratford, Va.; R. Lockwood Tower, ed., *Lee's Adjutant: The Wartime Letters of Colonel Walter Herron Taylor* (Columbia: University of South Carolina Press, 1995), 228.

28. Lee to Henry A. Wise, February 4, 1865, printed in *Richmond Daily Dispatch*, February 17, 1865.

29. James Longstreet, *From Manassas to Appomattox: Memoirs of the Civil War in America* (Philadelphia: Lippincott, 1896), 584.

30. Lee to Davis, March 2, 1865, and Lee to Grant, March 2, 1865, in *Wartime Papers of R. E. Lee*, 911–12.

31. Grant to Lee, March 4, 1865, in *PUSG*, 14:98–99n; Grant to Stanton, March 4, 1865, ibid., 14:100.

32. R. M. T. Hunter to William Jones, n.d. [November 1877], in *Jefferson Davis, Constitutionalist: His Letters, Papers, and Speeches*, ed. Dunbar Rowland, 10 vols. (Jackson: Mississippi Department of Archives and History, 1923), 7:576–77.

33. Campbell to William A. Graham, February 24, 1865, "Papers of Hon. John A. Campbell," 58–60.

34. Campbell to Horace Greeley, April 26, 1865, ibid., 64.

35. Jones, *War Clerk's Diary*, 398 (diary entry for March 4, 1865).

36. Ibid., 396 (diary entry for March 2, 1865).

37. Campbell to John C. Breckinridge, March 5, 1865, "Papers of Hon. John A. Campbell," 52–56; "The Resolution of Mr. Wm. C. Rives, of Virginia," *Southern Historical Society Papers*, 42:57–58.

38. *Journal*, 4:617–18, 663, 670–71, 711.

39. Vandiver, "Proceedings," 52:464–65.

40. *Richmond Examiner*, March 9, 1865.

41. *Journal*, 4:668–69; Vandiver, "Proceedings," 52:465.

42. Jefferson Davis to the Senate and House of Representatives, March 9, 1865, *Journal*, 7:735; *Richmond Examiner*, March 7, 1865; *Richmond Whig*, March 14, 1865.

43. The date and location of the meeting in Burnett's hotel room are uncertain. In 1862 Burnett stayed at the Spotswood Hotel, but of course he could have been elsewhere in 1865. Vest's account makes it clear only that the meeting took place "in the spring of

1865" after the failed Hampton Roads Peace Conference and Lee's submission of his March 9, 1865, report on the condition of his army. The latest possible date is set by Wigfall's absence in North Carolina at least as early as March 26. Given the clear hope of the Reconstructionists to get the Senate to take some action on the matter at hand, however, the meeting must have occurred prior to the Senate's adjournment on March 18. Samuel T. Moore, *Moore's Complete Civil War Guide to Richmond* (Richmond: privately published, 1978), 73; Alvy L. King, *Louis T. Wigfall, Southern Fire-Eater* (Baton Rouge: Louisiana State University Press, 1970), 218.

44. This account of the meeting by Vest first appeared in an unknown issue of the *Sedalia (Mo.) Democrat* in early June 1875, two weeks after Breckinridge's death on May 17. The earliest located reprinting is in the *Louisville Courier-Journal*, June 8, 1875, and thereafter it appeared in varying forms in the *Cairo (Ill.) Bulletin* June 10, 1875; the *Pittsburgh Daily Post*, June 11, 1875; the *Springfield (Mo.) Republican*, June 14, 1875; the *Macon (Ga.) Weekly Telegraph*, June 15, 1875; and no doubt others. None of the other participants appears to have left an account of the meeting.

45. Lee to Breckinridge, March 9, 1865, in *Wartime Papers of R. E. Lee*, 912–13.

46. Edward Younger, ed., *Inside the Confederate Government: The Diary of Robert Garlick Hill Kean* (New York: Oxford University Press, 1957), 203; Burton Harrison to Davis, May 24, 1877, in *Jefferson Davis, Constitutionalist*, 7:551; John A. Campbell to Joshua Speed, August 31, 1865, "Papers of Hon. John A. Campbell," 69.

47. Jones, *War Clerk's Diary*, 353, 358 (diary entries for January 17 and 23, 1865).

48. L. Quinton Washington address, n.d. (1897), in Martha T. Hunter, *A Memoir of Robert M. T. Hunter* (Washington, D.C.: Neale, 1903), 160.

49. Campbell to Speed, August 31, 1865, "Papers of Hon. John A. Campbell," 45–46, 51.

50. *Cleveland Daily Leader*, February 27, 1859; *Louisville Courier-Journal*, November 17, 1887.

51. Jones, *War Clerk's Diary*, 384 (diary entry for February 17, 1865).

52. R. M. T. Hunter to William Jones, n.d. (November 1877), in *Jefferson Davis, Constitutionalist*, 7:576–77.

53. *Journal*, 4:710.

54. Ibid., 723–25.

55. Ibid., 741–42.

56. Jones, *War Clerk's Diary*, 411 (diary entry for March 20, 1865).

57. *Richmond Sentinel*, March 31, 1865; *Richmond Daily Dispatch*, March 21, 1865; Jones, *War Clerk's Diary*, 411 (diary entry for March 20, 1865).

58. Jones, *War Clerk's Diary*, 411 (diary entries for March 18–20, 1865); Nelson D. Lankford, ed., *An Irishman in Dixie: Thomas Conolly's Diary of the Fall of the Confederacy* (Columbia: University of South Carolina Press, 1988), 60–61.

59. Lee endorsement of John Bell Hood, March 23, 1865, "Notes on the Spring Campaign of 1865" addressed to Davis, n.d., Civil War Collection, Huntington Library, San Marino, Calif.

60. Venable to Taylor, March 29, 1878, Taylor Papers.

61. Campbell to Greeley, April 26, 1865, "Papers of Hon. John A. Campbell," 61.

62. Ibid., 63. In August, Campbell reported Lincoln's statement as "most anyone can have most anything of the kind for the asking (Campbell to Speed, ibid., 68).

63. Campbell to Speed, ibid., 67–69.

64. John H. Reagan, *Memoirs with Special Reference to Secession and the Civil War* (New York: Neale, 1906), 196. Reagan is frustratingly silent as to just when he concluded defeat was inevitable and got involved with the peacemakers.

65. The correspondence between Grant and Lee will be found in *PUSG*, 14:361–73, and *Wartime Papers of R. E. Lee*, 931–34.

66. This theme is developed in Elizabeth R. Varon, *Appomattox: Victory, Defeat, and Freedom at the End of the Civil War* (New York: Oxford University Press, 2013), 35–37.

67. The April 7–9, 1865, correspondence between Lee and Grant has been widely published. Definitive transcriptions will be found in *Wartime Papers of R. E. Lee*, 931–34, and *PUSG*, 14:361, 367, 371–73.

68. *Personal Memoirs of U. S. Grant*, 2 vols. (New York: Charles L. Webster, 1885–86), 2:497. Unfortunately, this is the only account by one of the two participants. Lee left nothing behind about the conversation. Grant spoke of the meeting that evening with his staff, and two decades later Horace Porter wrote his recollections of what Grant said that night, his account agreeing with Grant's in his memoirs, adding only that Lee supposedly said that emancipation would not be an obstacle to reunion. Horace Porter, "The Surrender at Appomattox Courthouse," in *Battles and Leaders of the Civil War*, ed. Robert Underwood Johnson and Clarence Clough Buel (New York: Century, 1887–88), 4:745–46.

69. Lee to Davis, April 20, 1865, in *Wartime Papers of R. E. Lee*, 938–39.

70. *Pickens (S.C.) Keowee Courier*, June 2, 1866.

71. Breckinridge to unknown, n.d. (May 7, 1865), *OR*, ser. 1, 49 (2): 719.

72. Modeled on the U.S. Constitution, the Confederate constitution did not specify a line of succession beyond the vice president in the event of the president's death or incapacity. The Presidential Succession Act of 1792 was in effect in the Union, however, providing that if the vice president could not succeed to the presidency, then the Speaker of the House was to do so, and in his absence the president pro tempore of the Senate should assume the office. Presumably the Confederate government would have followed that line on an ad hoc basis, as Union authorities certainly assumed it would (*Washington (D.C.) Daily National Intelligencer*, May 24, 1865). The point was moot in any case since, by late May, Vice President Stephens and the president pro tempore Hunter were prisoners and Speaker of the House Thomas Bocock was at large and unmolested but behind Federal lines in occupied Richmond. The Confederate Congress was out of session with nowhere to convene to elect new leaders, while all of the cabinet members except Breckinridge were either prisoners, in hiding, or on the run, leaving Breckinridge as the only functioning member of the executive branch.

73. *Daily National Intelligencer*, June 29, 1865; *New York Herald*, June 29, 1865.

74. *Louisville Courier-Journal*, October 16, 1870.

75. William Preston Johnston, "Memoranda of Conversations with General R. E. Lee," in *Lee the Soldier*, ed. Gary W. Gallagher (Lincoln: University of Nebraska Press, 1996), 30.

Many Valuable Records and Documents Were Lost to History

The Destruction of Confederate Military Records during the Appomattox Campaign

Keith Bohannon

On the morning of April 7, 1865, during the Appomattox campaign, Union colonel Theodore Lyman of Maj. Gen. George Meade's staff rode through the wreckage of a collapsing Confederate army. The road followed by Lyman's party, which included Meade, was "completely strewed with tents, ammunition, officers' baggage, and, above all, little Dutch ovens" that the rebels used for baking hoecakes. Upon reaching a point where Sailor's Creek passed between steep hills, Lyman saw many wagons abandoned the day before by Confederates after a fierce rearguard action. "Waggons, ambulances, cannon filled the hollow near the bridge" over the creek, Lyman noted, while the hillside "was white with Adjutant-General's papers scattered from several wagons of that department."[1]

The paperwork Lyman saw on the hills bordering Sailor's Creek dramatically illustrated the destruction of Confederate army records that began with Richmond's evacuation and ended with Gen. Robert E. Lee's surrender on April 9, 1865. During the Appomattox campaign, Lee and his generals were primarily concerned with keeping their army intact. Wagons filled with papers and personal baggage were less important than those carrying ammunition and rations.

Union military authorities in occupied Richmond did little for several weeks to collect and preserve captured Confederate records, despite U.S. War Department orders to forward such papers to Washington, D.C. The destruction of Lee's army was the main goal of Lt. Gen. Ulysses S. Grant and his subordinates during the Appomattox campaign, and they took no substantive steps to preserve Confederate army paperwork. Instead, Union officers allowed their men to plunder captured headquarters wagons and then often burned the vehicles and their contents to prevent possible recapture. When the Army of Northern Virginia surrendered, securing captured arms and paroling prisoners took precedence over the seizure of army records. The fate of Confederates States records held by Lee's army at Appomattox is unclear, as no concrete evidence suggests that they ended up in Washington.

Even before the Appomattox campaign, Army of Northern Virginia inspection reports from late 1864 and early 1865 reveal the difficulties of creating and preserving records. In several brigades of Maj. Gen. Charles Field's division, inspectors found that company and regimental record books, as well as other required paperwork, were incomplete. Many records had been lost for want of sufficient transportation. A report of Brig. Gen. Goode Bryan's brigade explained that the command's limited number of wagons forced staff officers to deposit books and papers at depots, where they were subsequently lost.[2]

Inspection reports from Brig. Gen. William Terry's brigade revealed company and regimental record books in "a very disordered and incomplete state" in late November 1864 owing to "unavoidable circumstances," resulting in officers having to rely on memory for statements of facts. A month later, the records remained incomplete due to a "great scarcity of stationery." The absence of officers from their shattered regiments because of wounds, disease, or other factors also prevented records from being kept. By the end of February 1865, an inspector noted that the "entire absence of company and regimental records" in Terry's regiments made it impossible to furnish correct reports.[3]

The same week that the inspector of Terry's brigade lamented the incomplete records of that command, General Robert E. Lee informed Confederate secretary of war John C. Breckinridge that the dire situation facing the besieged Army of Northern Virginia might necessitate the abandonment of the Confederate capital. On February 22, Lee said that "everything of value should be removed from Richmond." Three days later, in a confidential circular to bureau chiefs within the War Department, Breckinridge instructed that all records not "requisite to the current operations of the Department" be "removed without unnecessary delay to Danville, Va., or points on the railroad beyond Danville, from which they may be readily collected together." Stores capable of being moved by wagon could be sent from Danville to Lynchburg and intermediate points at the discretion of the bureau chiefs.[4]

Diaries of two War Department employees in Richmond reveal efforts to pack up records beginning in the first week of March 1865. War Office clerk

John B. Jones wrote on March 6 that it was unclear whether records in the War Department building, located in the brick Mechanic's Institute on Ninth Street, would go to Danville or to Lynchburg. Three days later Henri Garidel in the Ordnance Bureau heard that "all the government offices were going to be moved out of Richmond next week." At least some of the archives, including the principal records of the Quartermaster's Department in 128 boxes, ended up in Lynchburg.[5]

The packing of War Office records continued on April 1, when a visitor to the War Department witnessed Breckinridge assisting clerks in placing "most of the valuable records of his office" into boxes and nailing them shut. The pace of work undoubtedly increased on April 2, when around 9:00 A.M. a messenger brought a telegram from Lee announcing that his lines had broken and it was unlikely that they could be reestablished. Two hours later a second telegram from Lee said that Richmond must be evacuated that night. By 6:00 P.M., the head of the Bureau of War, Robert G. H. Kean, noted that War Department records had arrived at the Richmond & Danville Railroad depot.

Eighty boxes of War Department records, enough to fill almost two boxcars, left the Confederate capital at 11:00 P.M. on April 2, reaching Danville the following afternoon. By April 21, the records were in Charlotte, North Carolina, where a few days later Confederate adjutant and inspector general Samuel Cooper turned them over to General Joseph E. Johnston. Johnston subsequently surrendered the records in early May 1865 to Union major general John Schofield, who had the boxes shipped to Washington under orders from U.S. secretary of war Edwin Stanton.[6]

Confederate War Department clerks could not save everything in their offices, and the destruction of remaining records commenced during the evening and night of April 2 as the Confederate army and government evacuated the capital. Virginia Military Institute cadet Thomas Hughes wrote how "great piles of official documents and papers of all sorts were brought out . . . piled in the centre of the streets in separate piles at short distances apart and then set on fire to be destroyed." Hughes observed how some piles burned entirely, others only smoldered, and some failed to burn at all. The result, he guessed, "seemed to depend on the quality of the paper and the density of the bundles." When Col. Alexander R. Boteler passed through the same area after 2:00 A.M. on the morning of April 3, he saw several men burning piles of paper in the street, replenishing the blazes with baskets brought out of the War Department, which itself burned the following day.[7]

Many Confederate army records stored in buildings outside of the War Department remained in Richmond at the time of the city's evacuation on

Ruins of Confederate War Department, 1865, located in the Mechanic's
Institute on Ninth Street, by William Ludwell Sheppard.
(From Alexander W. Weddell, *Richmond, Virginia, in Old Prints, 1737–1887*
[Richmond, 1932], 169; photograph courtesy of the Library of Virginia)

the night of April 2. Lt. Col. Osmun Latrobe of Lt. Gen. James Longstreet's
staff had sent the "great bulk" of the First Corps records to Richmond for
storage in the spring of 1865, retaining with the army "only such books as
were necessary in an active campaign." The subsequent fires that destroyed
parts of Richmond charred these First Corps records and undoubtedly those
of other commands.[8]

Some records left with Richmond civilians likely suffered the fate of those of Pickett's division. On the day of the Confederate capital's evacuation, Maj. Charles F. Pickett left the records of his brother, Maj. Gen. George Pickett, with family members. An elderly uncle, fearful that the Yankees might search the house and implicate the family, burned them.[9]

On April 4, the day after Union troops entered Richmond, Secretary Stanton telegraphed Maj. Gen. Godfrey Weitzel, commanding the city's garrison, to forward immediately to Washington all papers found in Richmond. Two days later, U.S. assistant secretary of war Charles Dana reported that he had been unable to find much of value in Richmond, important records having been removed by the Confederates. Federal officials in Richmond expended little effort to collect records for a number of days, even when the U.S. adjutant general's office issued General Orders No. 60 on April 7, directing commanding officers in the field to forward to Washington all captured Confederate military records "which may be of public use or interest."[10]

The indifference of Richmond's Union garrison to preserving Confederate archives is illustrated in the observations of Northern newspaper reporters and Southern civilians. New York Tribune reporter Charles A. Page wrote of "acres of ground, and all the streets," being "thick with paper — flying with the wind, picked up by the curious, gathered in baskets by negroes . . . papers and letters everywhere." George Shepley claimed that "our horses sank fetlock-deep in . . . documents of every kind, which covered the ground for acres." Emma Mordecai, who lived just north of Richmond, wrote in her diary on either April 5 or 6 that the street immediately north of the ruins of the War Department was ankle-deep from curb to curb "with fragments of Confederate printed blanks & other papers, while burnt piles of the same were seen in many places."[11]

Abraham Lincoln's assassination on April 14 furnished a powerful impulse to seize Confederate records in hopes of finding evidence that Southern leaders had been complicit in the plot to kill the president. When Maj. Gen. Henry Halleck assumed command at Richmond of a newly created department a week after Lincoln's death, the former chief of staff directed the city's military governor to take care of records pending the arrival of Col. Richard D. Cutts, who would take charge of them. On April 25, Cutts received an appointment as "keeper of the public archives," and by the end of May he had sent "347 boxes, barrels, and hogsheads of Confederate materials to Washington."[12]

While an exact inventory of the Confederate War Department records destroyed in Richmond is impossible to determine, archivist Dallas Irvine concluded in 1939 after an intensive study that it "greatly impresses one with the way in which the [Confederate] government was able to remove its important archives," but he also described what had been lost. Irvine stated that the records of the surgeon general, commissary general, Signal Office, and Army Intelligence Office had definitely been destroyed. The principal records of other offices, including the Engineer Bureau, Ordnance Bureau, Niter and Mining Bureau, Office of Foreign Supplies, and Bureau of Indian Affairs, were also likely largely destroyed. Confederate officials had turned over some records to the occupying Federals, but they were not extensive in scope; these included those of the Exchange Bureau, two boxes of Engineer Bureau records, and a few boxes of papers from the offices of the chief paymaster.[13]

When the Army of Northern Virginia evacuated Richmond and Petersburg on April 2, 1865, a train of approximately 1,400 wagons accompanied Lee's troops. According to the army's chief of transportation, Maj. James L. Corley, approximately 300 vehicles were ambulances, while most other wagons carried ordnance, commissary, and quartermaster stores. Some 200 or 300 wagons were assigned to army, corps, division, brigade, and regimental headquarters carrying records needed in the field.[14]

These trains encountered problems as the army moved westward. North Carolinian T. J. Watkins explained that the army's horses, "like ourselves[,] had been on short rations all the winter, were poor and weak, and with scarc[e]ly time to eat what little was given them on the march; could scarcely drag themselves along, many falling in harness" and having to "be cut loose and dragged out of the way." The collapse of horses and mules caused serious delays "whenever the trains reached a steep hill or muddy lane," wrote Second Corps staff officer Lt. Thomas G. Jones. He likewise described wretched road conditions along the retreat route of Lt. Gen. Richard S. Ewell's corps to and beyond Amelia Court House. Immense wagon caravans converted narrow roads, softened by heavy spring rains, into "a perfect sea of mud" through which the trains struggled to reach dry land.[15]

Last, Lee's teamsters dealt with problems that plagued all wagon trains accompanying Civil War armies. Confederate surgeon John H. Claiborne wrote how "only those who have followed a large army can know how slowly and with how many halts a wagon train can move." Claiborne, whose ambulance was in one of these trains during the Appomattox campaign, explained how "a broken axle or a balky horse can detain the whole line, as there is rarely afforded an opportunity for one wagon to turn out and pass another."[16]

The first major destruction of slow-moving Southern wagons took place

Capture of guns and destruction of a Confederate wagon train
at Paineville by Union cavalry on the morning of April 5, 1865.
(Robert Underwood Johnson and Clarence Clough Buel, eds.,
Battles and Leaders of the Civil War, 4 vols.
[New York: Century, 1887], 4:719)

near Paineville on the morning of April 5 at the hands of Union cavalrymen. Federal troopers from Brig. Gen. Henry Davies Jr.'s brigade struck two columns of rebel wagons, one from Ewell's command moving south and another moving in the opposite direction from Amelia Court House. Davies's men cut large numbers of mules and horses from their traces, drove off panicked teamsters, and captured dozens of vehicles, including the headquarters wagons of Maj. Gen. Fitzhugh Lee, commander of the Confederate army's Cavalry Corps.

After plundering Lee's vehicles of "quite a variety of loot," the Federals burned them along with many other wagons. Lee's troopers eventually drove the enemy away, but not before the Yankees had destroyed much of the Confederate army's reserve ordnance and medical supplies. Confederate lieutenant Moses Handy, encountering the wreckage that day, was surprised that "so much property had been destroyed in so short a space of time. Scores of broken-down and wrecked wagons and ambulances were overturned and abandoned, their contents being strewed over the road . . . while quartermasters' papers were scattered in every direction."[17]

Around 9:00 A.M. the following day, Federal cavalrymen began launching attacks from the south against Confederate wagon trains traveling west between Deatonville and Rice's Station. A member of the 16th Pennsylvania Cavalry described in his diary one such movement when his regiment charged but fell back, then dismounted and advanced again, firing their carbines at the enemy. Once the Federals were close enough, they began using pistols, driving off the wagon guard and seizing between twenty and thirty vehicles. After burning the wagons, the Federals sent the mules they had captured to the rear.[18]

Confederate lieutenant Joseph Packard recalled that during these attacks, "the wagons of our own and other trains would dash across an exposed portion of the road and turn out into fields which were more sheltered." In this way, Packard explained, the train "soon broke up into fragments." During one of these Federal forays, the clerks in charge of Robert E. Lee's headquarters wagon, fearing imminent capture, "burned the chest containing the headquarter archives, including order books, letter-copying books and other valuable documents." Lt. Col. Walter Taylor of Lee's staff later claimed that the "irreparable loss" had been unnecessary, as the wagon was eventually saved.[19]

When the Confederate wagon train reached Holt's Corner, Union major general George Crook sent two of his cavalry brigades to attack the vehicles. An initial Federal charge reached the column of vehicles, burning a few of them, before the Southerners rallied and drove the horsemen back down the Pride's Church Road. A second Union cavalry brigade advanced, but as a Maine trooper remembered, "The nature of the ground . . . was such as to render success impossible. The horses sunk to their knees at every step. And so dense were the woods and thickets, that at only two points were they penetrated at all." While the Confederates repelled the Union attacks, the halt at Holt's Corner disrupted the Southerners' line of march, leaving a gap between most of Longstreet's command, which had continued its march westward, and the divisions of Maj. Gen. Bushrod Johnson and Maj. Gen. George Pickett.[20]

Marching south from Holt's Corner, Johnson's and Pickett's commands reached the vicinity of Marshall's Crossroads, where they prepared to fend off mounted and dismounted attacks from three divisions of Union cavalry under the overall command of Union major general Wesley Merritt. While Pickett's division formed the left of the Confederate line, Johnson's men threw up works along the Rice Station–Deatonville Road, protecting a long wagon train in their rear. Although an initial Federal attack against Johnson's position failed, the Yankees eventually enveloped both flanks of the Confederate line, causing Pickett's and Johnson's infantrymen to scatter and expose their wagon train.

Realizing the impossibility of saving the wagons, Confederates began burning many of them. A Maine cavalryman recalled a "long line of burning wagons, like a serpent of fire, stretched in graceful curves along the road." In other instances, Union horsemen overtook and burned fleeing wagons, some of them undoubtedly carrying headquarters papers. J. E. Whitehorne of the 12th Virginia noted that the vehicles lost by Johnson's division included all the Third Corps wagons and ambulances. A New York cavalryman claimed that the captured train consisted primarily of "ammunition, commissary and quartermasters' stores, general merchandise, and plunder from Richmond."[21]

To the north and east of Holt's Corner, the Confederate rear guard consisting of Maj. Gen. John B. Gordon's Second Corps spent the morning of April 6 taking up defensive positions to slow the pursuit of the Union Second Corps. Gordon's old division, commanded by Brig. Gen. Clement Evans, and Southern cavalry initially delayed the Union advance until the ponderous rebel wagon train moved out of danger. Gordon's three divisions subsequently formed successive lines to slow the Federals. The withdrawal continued for several miles before the wagon trains' slow movement and Federal pressure forced the Confederates to deploy along a range of hills in the vicinity of Deatonville. This line held until the road in Gordon's rear had been cleared for more than a mile.

Around 3:00 P.M. on April 6, the "deep and almost impassable stream" of Sailor's Creek delayed the continued withdrawal of Confederate wagons. The main roadblock was a location known locally as the double bridges, where two "rickety" wooden spans crossed Big and Little Sailor's Creeks near their confluence. Confederate engineer troops under Col. Thomas M. R. Talcott labored that day to provide additional crossings of the stream, which, according to Talcott, relieved the congestion to some extent. To protect the wagons until they crossed the streams, two of Gordon's understrength divisions, commanded by Brig. Gen. Bryan Grimes and Brig. Gen. James Walker, deployed on high ground surrounding the James Lockett house along with a small number of artillery batteries.[22]

Gordon's men repulsed an initial Federal attack, but by 5:00 P.M. the situation was desperate. Gordon sent a message at that time to Robert E. Lee, fearing "that a portion of the train will be lost as my force is quite reduced and insufficient for its protection." Without assistance, Gordon predicted that he could "scarcely hope" to protect the wagons much longer.[23]

Two Union Second Corps divisions launched a final attack against the front and flanks of Gordon's attenuated line around 6:00 P.M., resulting in the Confederates being driven in disorder from the field. The scene among the wagons, wrote a Southern ordnance officer, was "one of pell-mell confusion. They were driving in lines, eight or ten abreast, across the field" toward the bridges over Sailor's Creek. Maj. Giles Cooke of Robert E. Lee's staff had been getting wagons across the bridges when the rebel infantry line broke. "Drivers of ambulances and wagons were screaming and shouting," Cooke wrote in his diary, "and making desperate efforts to get their teams across the one small bridge that spanned the stream. It was dreadful to see how frantic horses and mules and men became on the occasion." When it became clear that the wagons could not get across the bridges or navigate down and up the creeks' steep banks, many teamsters unhitched horses, abandoned their wagons, and attempted to ford the stream.[24]

Some Confederate teamsters and infantrymen refused to run as the Federals closed on the wagons, and for a brief time fighting took place at close quarters. A member of the 2nd New York Heavy Artillery recalled that Confederates stood behind some wagons with combatants firing at each other through the vehicles. Yankee Charles Mattocks of the 17th Maine wrote with disgust in his diary how many Confederates "would crouch behind fences and other hiding-places and continue to fire upon our men until with[in] ten or twenty feet, and then throw up their hands as a signal of surrender." While Mattocks opined that the rebels "did not deserve to be taken prisoner," they were nonetheless "taken and treated kindly." Another Maine soldier thought the teamsters were fools to fight for "goods which they had not one cent of interest; everything in these wagons belonged to the aristocracy."

Confederate lieutenant colonel William W. Blackford and his engineer troops watched from some distance away as the Federals plundered the vehicles. "Wagon sheets were torn off," Blackford wrote, "and there was a perfect fountain of things rising in the air as the men threw out what was of no value to them, in search of trunks and private baggage." The officers' baggage wagons, including Blackford's, provided a "heap" of plunder for the exultant Federals. While most Union soldiers sought uniforms, spurs, swords, shotguns, bridles, surgical instruments, and other trophies, some took army records or the personal papers of general officers. One New Yorker secured Maj. Gen. William Mahone's grip with his commission as major general and other papers in it while also dressing up in the Virginia officer's coat and sash. Charles Mattocks seized General Longstreet's general order book.[25]

Maj. Gen. Andrew A. Humphreys, commander of the Union Second Corps at Sailor's Creek, claimed that his men captured more than 200 wagons on April 6, while between 30 and 50 wagons had been seized or destroyed earlier in the day. Responsibility for guarding the captured trains on the evening of April 6 belonged to Lt. Col. James J. Smith of the 69th New York. The next morning, Smith received word that he would be relieved of guard duty shortly, but no one reported for such duty for some time. When Smith explained his situation to Col. Richard N. Batchelder, chief quartermaster of the Army of the Potomac, Batchelder said he would speak to the army's commander, General Meade.

When Batchelder returned, he instructed Smith to "remove ammunition from the wagons, harness up the mules to ambulances, and send as many as possible of them to the front and turn them over to the Second Corps." Once Federal troops and trains had passed Smith's captured vehicles, the lieutenant colonel was to "burn all the wagons, ambulances, caissons, limbers, &c," to prevent their being recaptured by the enemy. No orders were provided for the preservation of papers remaining in wagons or littering the hillsides along Sailor's Creek. Although a captain from the 66th New York arrived to relieve Smith, the lieutenant colonel from the Irish Brigade felt it his duty to carry out Meade's orders and burned the train, which included by Smith's count 203 army wagons.[26]

Keith Bohannon

The destruction of dozens of captured headquarters wagons at Sailor's Creek took place despite instructions telegraphed from Secretary of War Stanton to Grant on April 5 that it was "desirable that all letters, papers, and correspondence, private or public, found at Richmond, in the post-office or elsewhere, should be immediately sent to Mr. Seward by special messenger." Grant may have read this telegram to apply primarily to Confederate government documents in Richmond rather than to army records captured in the field. Regardless of how Grant interpreted Stanton's telegram, the seizure of military paperwork from Lee's disintegrating army was understandably not a priority for the Federal high command. As Grant stated to Meade on April 5, "Lee's Army is the objective point and to capture that is all we want."[27]

On the morning of April 7, Confederate wagon trains crossed the Appomattox River at Farmville. Some officers may have emulated Lt. Col. Briscoe Baldwin, Lee's chief of ordnance, who decided while in Farmville "to deposit the most important records of my office in safe hands until I could have the opportunity of regaining them." In other instances, poor road conditions and the complete exhaustion of mule teams resulted that day in the destruction of additional headquarters wagons and their contents. Upon reaching the hills north of the Appomattox River, surgeon John H. Claiborne encountered clerks "lightening the loads of headquarters wagons by destroying letters and papers in them." Osmun Latrobe of Longstreet's staff jotted in his diary for April 7, "Begun to destroy our wagons," while another Longstreet staff member, Capt. Frank Potts, recalled that the staff "abandoned all baggage which we could not carry on our horses." Brig. Gen. Walter H. Stevens, the army's chief engineer, said only that "a reduction [was] made."[28]

The large-scale destruction of Confederate wagons on April 7 is revealed in Union Sixth Corps accounts of the following day. After crossing the Appomattox on the morning of the eighth, these Federals continued their pursuit of the Confederates. Along several stretches of road, Union troops encountered abandoned and burned wagons, the number of destroyed vehicles ranging from a low of 150 to inflated estimates of 300 to 400. While waiting for rations, Judson Andrews of the 2nd Connecticut Heavy Artillery examined a scorched rebel wagon train, observing that the debris included "blanks of all kinds, official papers, [and] officers['] baggage." Men of the 15th New Jersey described a partly burned train with "adjutants' desks, and company books . . . scattered along the road."[29]

While Union infantry columns followed the beleaguered Confederates on April 8, Maj. Gen. Philip H. Sheridan's cavalry reached Appomattox Station that evening, capturing several locomotive trains filled with rations and uniforms for Lee's army. Near dusk, Federal troopers moving north from the station encountered Confederate artillery batteries under Brig. Gen. Lindsay Walker. Although the Union advance caught many of the Confederates by surprise and caused some panic, more resolute cannoneers moved their batteries into a semicircular line and soon had every gun "pouring canister into the ranks of the enemy, who had advanced to the edge of a woods, less than two hundred yards distant." The fighting continued after dark, with multiple Union cavalry charges eventually forcing a Confederate withdrawal.

When the Federal horsemen reached the Lynchburg Road, they encountered a "mass of guns, caissons, and baggage-trains ... in ... inextricable confusion, some headed one way and some another." An ordnance sergeant in the 12th Virginia Artillery Battalion recorded in his diary that the Union troopers seized at least 108 wagons, while Federal sources place the number of captured wagons at between 150 and 200 vehicles.[30]

The vehicles captured at Appomattox Station by Bvt. Maj. Gen. George Custer's troopers included headquarters wagons belonging to Lee's artillery arm. Third Corps artillerist Lt. William G. McCabe recorded in his diary that his headquarters wagon had been captured on April 8 "and in it the few things I had saved, leaving me not even a change of clothing." Another Third Corps artillery officer, Lt. Ham Chamberlayne, wrote his sister on April 12 that his commissions had been "burnt up in my wagon along with all my clothes."[31]

Many Confederate officers received orders on the evening of April 8 to reduce their trains even further. Giles Cooke of Robert E. Lee's staff noted how the general "directed his staff to dispose of everything that was not necessary, as he intended (so it was believed by us) to cut his way out with the invincible remnant of the grand old army." Capt. Oscar Hinrichs, a Second Corps engineer officer, recorded similar instructions that night, saying that the officers were "to organize the largest train and destroy all unnecessary wagons." Maj. Erasmus Taylor of Longstreet's staff remembered orders to destroy all wagons "except those carrying ammunition and foodstuffs."[32]

Following an unsuccessful attempt by Confederate infantry on April 9 to break through the encircling Union lines, Robert E. Lee met with Grant at the McLean residence at Appomattox Court House and surrendered the Army of Northern Virginia. The terms of surrender allowed Southern officers to keep private baggage, but on April 10, the Confederates received instructions from a surrender commission composed of three Union and three Confederate generals that "public horses and public property of all kinds" must be turned over to Federal staff officers. Unfortunately, the terms of surrender made no specific reference to the disposition of Confederate army records.[33]

The absence of documentation regarding the fate of Confederate records at Appomattox is puzzling given the issuance of a general order from the U.S. War Department on April 7, 1865, directing commanders in the field to send captured Confederate records to Washington, D.C. Despite this general order, securing the records of Lee's army was clearly not a priority for Grant or his lieutenants at Appomattox. Instead, the Federal high command focused on the formal surrender process, including paroling Confederate soldiers and securing captured arms and military stores.[34]

Accounts suggest varied fates for the records still held by Lee's army at Appomattox. When news of Lee's surrender reached the command of South Carolina brigadier general John Bratton encamped at Appomattox, the general's brother and assistant adjutant general requested permission "to go to our wagon & destroy his papers as he did not wish them to fall into the hands of the Yankees." General Bratton, thinking his brother meant his private papers, granted the request. "It was not until too late," wrote the general, "that I learned that he meant the Brigade papers & had fired the Brigade Desk & its contents—which was a complete record of the Brigade from its organization in 61 . . . up to the surrender." Lt. William Fulton of the 5th Alabama Battalion took the official papers of his company home with him. And some documents were undoubtedly taken from wagons by Yankee souvenir hunters, as suggested by a June 12, 1864, letter written by Maj. Gen. William Mahone to Lt. Gen. A. P. Hill that contains a notation at the bottom that it was "captured in Gen. Hill's HeadQuarters wagon at the surrender of Gen. Lee April 9, 1865."[35]

On April 10, 1865, Lee requested his subordinates to submit reports of their operations from March 29, 1865, "to the present time" and to include statements giving the strength of their commands as of April 8. Responses reveal the widespread destruction of records during the Appomattox campaign. Maj. Gen. Henry Heth said it was "utterly impossible" to make such a report, explaining that "all company and Regimental records & papers have been lost or destroyed." A field return of Maj. Gen. Charles Field's division completed at Appomattox explained that all "the books and papers of the several Brigades" in the division had been "destroyed on the late march and the aggregate present last Field Return cannot be obtained." Other commands submitted strength reports for April 8, but whether they had saved their books or papers is unknown.[36]

While it is impossible to state the number of Confederate headquarters wagons destroyed in the Appomattox campaign, an April 15, 1865, return submitted to Lee by his chief of transportation estimated that the army had lost a total of 300 wagons since the evacuation of Richmond. At Appomattox, Maj. Corley turned over 480 four-horse wagons and 160 ambulances to the Federal quartermaster. Corley also indicated that he had loaned to paroled officers and men of Lee's army 73 four-horse wagons and teams and 31 ambulances for the transportation of baggage.[37]

The loss of one wagon particularly upset Robert E. Lee. In several post-bellum letters, Lee deplored that the clerks in charge of his headquarters wagon had "needlessly destroyed" its contents shortly before the army's surrender. Lee's desire to obtain copies of these records resulted in a July 31, 1865, circular letter sent to former general officers stating that he was anxious to obtain information for a history of his army's campaigns. While Lee had his battle reports for 1862 and 1863, he asked for reports covering 1864 and 1865. Campaign reports for the war's final year that had been sent to Lee's headquarters, along with "all the records, returns, maps, plans" and the commanding general's public and private letter books, had been destroyed during the Appomattox campaign. Regular reports and returns transmitted to the Confederate adjutant general at Richmond had been burned or lost.[38]

The slow pace with which former subordinates responded to Lee's request for reports likely frustrated the former Confederate chieftain. On November 2, 1865, Lee wrote Walter Taylor that he had made little progress in collecting information, supposing that his subordinates had been "embarrassed by the loss of papers" and the "necessary devotion" to business. The following month, Lee told Charles Marshall that he had "not yet received a single memoir from any of the officers to whom I had written."[39]

Lee followed up the July 1865 circular with some later letters. In January 1867, Lee wrote John B. Gordon, mentioning the 1865 circular. "Not having heard from you on the subject," Lee continued, "I fear my letter did not reach you, and therefore take the liberty of repeating my wishes." Gordon responded many months later by sending his report of the battle of Monocacy to Lee but stated that he had been unable to obtain his reports of later 1864 Shenandoah Valley campaign engagements.[40]

Lee did have some limited success in obtaining records, as he wrote George A. Barksdale in April 1866 of recovering "one of the Rebel books of the telegrams issued from 1st May to 1st of October '64 which ought to contain all of my dispatches to the Sec. of War." Lee had also learned that "some of my returns were among the captured documents, & are now in the bureau of Rebel papers in Washington, but I have not been able to get hold of them." The bureau to which Lee referred was the Archive Office of the U.S. War Department under Dr. Francis Lieber. Lieber's superior, Secretary of War Edwin

Stanton, rarely gave anyone outside of the federal government permission to access Confederate records, even with Lieber's recommendation. Lee may have made an attempt, perhaps through an intermediary, to get permission to copy records from the Archive Office but without any success.[41]

Many publishers contacted Lee wanting to print his book on the campaigns of the Army of Northern Virginia. The publisher with whom Lee corresponded the most, C. B. Richardson of the University Publishing Company of New York, forwarded material to the former Confederate general, including books, reports, and addresses of former ex-Confederate generals. In March 1866, Richardson succeeded in obtaining condensed monthly returns of the Army of Northern Virginia that had been captured by the Federals and repeatedly urged Lee to write Grant to request copies of additional captured material, but as of July 1868 Lee had not done so.[42]

According to biographer Douglas Southall Freeman, Lee "never wholly abandoned his project" to write a history of his army, but after 1866 he accumulated few reports and returns and made no start at composition. In a conversation held in the last year of his life with a Washington College professor, the ailing Lee claimed that he was "hardly calculated for a historian," saying that he was "too much interested and might be biassed." Former staff officer A. L. Long noted that Lee relinquished work on a book with little reluctance "because he felt that its truths and indispensable facts must expose certain persons to severe censure." These factors, along with failing health and a heavy workload as president of Washington College, contributed to Lee's failure to write a history of his army. At the same time, his inability to acquire official reports and returns discouraged him. Four months before his death, Lee wrote his cousin Cassius Lee that while he had collected some material for a work on the campaigns in Virginia, he lacked "so much that I wish to obtain that I have not commenced the narrative."[43]

The paucity of surviving Confederate army records frustrated others who hoped to chronicle the campaigns of Lee's army. Brig. Gen. Edward Porter Alexander collected material for some years after the war with plans to write a history of the First Corps of the Army of Northern Virginia, but in 1876 he wrote that he "could not procure all I required & was unwilling to proceed with less." Instead, Alexander donated his papers to the Southern Historical Society in Richmond, which subsequently published some of them. Charles Marshall of Lee's staff told a crowd at a Confederate reunion in 1875 that he had been denied requests to "examine the captured records of the Confederate government," a factor that undoubtedly weighed into his decision to postpone for several decades writing a book.[44]

Efforts to publish official records of the Civil War by the U.S. War Department's Archive Office, known as the War Records Office beginning around 1878, also faltered due to difficulties securing Confederate records. Fortunately for the compilers, former Confederate general Marcus J. Wright offered to assist in locating Confederate documents. While Wright initially volunteered his time, in 1878 he received an appointment as official agent of the War Department to secure privately owned Confederate records. Wright worked with former Union army officer Robert N. Scott, director of the project to publish war records, to copy Confederate material in possession of the Southern Historical Society. Wright's subsequent labors proved invaluable in securing Confederate documents from across the South to include in the *War of the Rebellion: A Compilation of the Official Records of the Union and Confederate Armies*, the publication of which began in 1881 and ended almost exactly twenty years later.[45]

Despite the efforts of Wright, Scott, and others to obtain Confederate documents for the *Official Records*, the sections of volumes devoted to Confederate army correspondence and battle reports covering the final campaigns in Virginia are very thin. The paucity of material is due in part to the destruction of records during the Appomattox campaign, as the officers in charge of the War Records Office suggested in a conversation with ex-Confederate officer Frederick Colston. The burning of Lee's headquarters wagon, the War Records officers told Colston, "was much deplored."[46]

The incomplete record keeping in Lee's army during the final year of the Civil War, combined with the extensive loss of records in the Appomattox campaign, has not prevented historians in recent decades from producing excellent studies of the Civil War's final battles in Virginia. These works compensate for the dearth of official military correspondence and reports by drawing on large numbers of published and unpublished letters, diaries, and memoirs; wartime and postbellum newspapers; and Broadfoot Publishing Company's *Supplement to the Official Records*. Unofficial sources can reveal only so much, however, and many Confederate command decisions and details of troop deployments can never be recovered or fully understood. The destruction of muster rolls and regimental records likewise makes it impossible to reconstruct fully the wartime service of many Confederate soldiers. Historians today must acknowledge that the campaign that ended the Civil War in Virginia also resulted in many valuable records and documents being "lost to history."

My thanks go to the following individuals for their assistance with this essay: Chris Calkins, Gary W. Gallagher, A. Wilson Greene, Noel Harrison, Caroline E. Janney, Robert E. L. Krick, Robert K. Krick, William Marvel, Eric Mink, Michael Musick, James Ogden III, Trevor Plante, Patrick Schroeder, Brooks Simpson, and Larry Stephens.

1. Lyman observed unit identifications of various brigades on the captured wagons but doesn't identify the commands. In his personal notebooks, Lyman wrote that the papers scattered on the hillsides at Sailor's Creek came from "some office boxes that had been broken open." Theodore Lyman, *Meade's Headquarters 1863–1865: Letters of Colonel Theodore Lyman*, ed. George R. Agassiz (Boston: The Atlantic Monthly Press, 1922), 351–52; Theodore Lyman, *Meade's Army: The Private Notebooks of Lt. Col. Theodore Lyman*, ed. David W. Lowe (Kent, Ohio: Kent State University Press, 2007), 364–65.

2. Inspection Reports dated October 29 and December 27, 1864, for Law's Alabama and the Texas Brigades, 11-P-42, 5-P-31, M 935, Inspection Reports . . . Received by the Inspection Branch in the Confederate Adjutant and Inspector General's Office, National Archives, Washington, D.C. (repository hereafter cited as NA).

3. Inspection Reports dated August 19, November 29, and December 29, 1864, and January 28 and February 27, 1865, for Terry's and York's Brigades, 9-P-17, 38-P-37, 19-P-42, 23-P-51, 13-P-52, M 935, ibid. Extensive marching in the summer and fall of 1864 done by the Second Corps, which included Terry's Brigade, added to the difficulty of maintaining records. York's Louisiana Brigade, for example, had left all of its records "far in the rear" at the time of an August 1864 inspection.

4. U.S. War Department, *The War of the Rebellion: A Compilation of the Official Records of the Union and Confederate Armies*, 127 vols., index, and atlas (Washington, D.C.: Government Printing Office, 1880–1901), ser. 1, 46 (2): 1247, 1257 (hereafter cited as *OR*; all references unless otherwise stated are to ser. 1).

5. John B. Jones, *A Rebel War Clerk's Diary at the Confederate States Capital*, 2 vols. (Philadelphia: Lippincott, 1866), 2:437, 441, 443, 455; Michael Bedout Chesson and Leslie Jean Roberts, eds., *Exile in Richmond, The Confederate Journal of Henri Garidel* (Charlottesville: University of Virginia Press, 2001), 343; Dallas D. Irvine, "The Fate of the Confederate Archives: Executive Office," *American Historical Review* 44 (July 1939): 829–39.

6. Nelson Lankford, *Richmond Burning* (New York: Viking Press, 2002), 35–36; W. H. Swallow, "Retreat of the Confederate Government from Richmond to the Gulf," *Magazine of American History* 15 (1886): 596–97; Irvine, "Fate of the Confederate Archives," 828–39; Edward Younger, ed., *Inside the Confederate Government: The Diary of Robert Garlick Hill Kean* (New York: Oxford University Press, 1957), 205–7. For details of the disposition of the War Department records in Charlotte, see Mark L. Bradley, *This Astounding Close: The Road to Bennett Place* (Chapel Hill: University of North Carolina Press, 2000), 243–44, 356–57.

7. Thomas Hughes, *A Boy's Experience in the Civil War, 1860–1865* (n.p., 1904), 30; Peter Cozzens and Robert Girardi, eds., *The New Annals of the Civil War* (Mechanicsburg, Pa.: Stackpole Books, 2004), 571.

8. Osmun Latrobe to Edward P. Alexander, September 22, 1866, Edward Porter Alexander Papers, Southern Historical Collection, Wilson Library, University of North Carolina, Chapel Hill, N.C. (collection hereafter cited as SHC without reference to repository).

9. Charles F. Pickett to James Longstreet, October 12, 1892, James Longstreet Papers, SHC.

10. Dallas D. Irvine, "The Archives Office of the War Department, Repository of Captured Confederate Archives, 1865–1881," *Military Affairs* 10 (Spring 1946): 93–96; OR 46 (3): 573; ser. 3, 4:1258–59.

11. Charles A. Page, *Letters of a War Correspondent* (Boston: L. C. Page, 1899), 323; George Shepley, "Incidents of the Capture of Richmond," *Atlantic Monthly* 46 (1880): 24; Emma Mordecai Diary, entry for either April 5 or 6, 1865, SHC.

12. Irvine, "Archives Office," 93–96.

13. Irvine, "Fate of the Confederate Archives," 829–30. On the destruction of records of the Confederate adjutant general's office, see Susan L. Blackford, ed., *Letters from Lee's Army* (New York: Charles Scribner's Sons, 1947), 291.

14. James L. Corley to Robert E. Lee, April 15, 1865, item 514, Robert E. Lee Headquarters Papers, Mss3 L515a, Virginia Historical Society, Richmond (repository hereafter cited as VHS). The estimated number of headquarters wagons comes from General Orders No. 27, Head Quarters, Army of Northern Virginia, April 5, 1864, which lists the number of wagons allowed to the various headquarters throughout the army. A February 28, 1865, inspection report for Rodes's division suggests that General Orders No. 27 was still in effect at that time. General Orders No. 27, Head Quarters, Army of Northern Virginia, Orders and Circulars Issued by the Army of the Potomac and the Army and Dept. of Northern Virginia, M 921, NA; Inspection Report dated February 28, 1865, for Rodes's division, 2-P-62, Inspection Reports . . . Received by the Inspection Branch in the Confederate Adjutant and Inspector General's Office, NA.

15. T. J. Watkins Memoir, Bound Volume 85, Fredericksburg and Spotsylvania National Military Park, Fredericksburg, Va. (repository hereafter cited as FRSP); Thomas G. Jones, *Last Days of the Army of Northern Virginia: An Address Delivered by Governor Thomas G. Jones* (Richmond, 1893), 24.

16. George S. Bernard, *War Talks of the Confederate Veterans* (Petersburg, Va.: Fenn and Owen, 1892), 244.

17. *Supplement to the Official Records of the Union and Confederate Armies*, ed. Janet B. Hewett and others, 95 vols. and 5-vol index, (Wilmington, N.C.: Broadfoot, 1994–2001), pt. 1, 7:767 (hereafter cited as ORS; all references are to pt. 1); Thomas A. Snyder Memoir, Bound Volume 42, FRSP; Moses Handy, "A Courier's Experience during the Great Retreat. From His Journal. No. V.," undated newspaper clipping from *The Watchman* (1866), Moses Handy Papers, Duke University Special Collections. Fitzhugh Lee's official report of the Appomattox campaign states that his destroyed headquarters wagon contained "all my retained reports, records, and data of every kind." OR 46 (1): 1301, 1304.

18. James C. Mohr, ed., *The Cormany Diaries: A Northern Family in the Civil War* (Pittsburgh: University of Pittsburgh Press, 1982), 533.

19. Joseph Packard, "Ordnance Matters at the Close," *Confederate Veteran* 16 (1908):

Keith Bohannon

228; Frederick M. Colston, "Recollections of the Last Months in the Army of Northern Virginia," in *Southern Historical Society Papers* (hereafter cited as *SHSP*), ed. J. William Jones and others, 52 vols. (1876–1959; repr., with 3-vol. index, Wilmington, N.C.: Broadfoot, 1990–92), 38:9; William Marvel, *Lee's Last Retreat: The Flight to Appomattox* (Chapel Hill: University of North Carolina Press, 2002), 21. Lee undoubtedly lost papers on April 2, 1865, during the hasty departure from his headquarters in the Turnbull House, as Federals noticed large amounts of paperwork in the yard of the building's smoldering ruins. *ORS*, 7:767.

20. Chris Calkins, "From Sailor's Creek to Cumberland Church, April 6–7, 1865," *Blue and Gray* 31 (2015): 20; Marvel, *Lee's Last Retreat*, 78; Samuel H. Merrill, *The Campaigns of the First Maine and First District of Columbia Cavalry* (Portland, Maine: Bailey and Noyes, 1866), 347.

21. Calkins, "From Sailor's Creek to Cumberland Church," 28; Merrill, *Campaigns of the First Maine*, 350; J. E. Whitehorne, "Seven Days of Sunset," *Military Engineer* 31 (1939): 184; N. D. Preston, *History of the Tenth Regiment of Cavalry New York State Volunteers* (New York: D. Appleton, 1892), 250, 540.

22. *ORS*, 7:797, 798; Thomas M. R. Talcott, "From Petersburg to Appomattox," in *SHSP* 32:67; Colston, "Recollections of the Last Months," *SHSP* 38:10.

23. John B. Gordon to Robert E. Lee, April 6, 1865, item 448, Lee Headquarters Papers, VHS.

24. Packard, "Ordnance Matters at the Close," 228; Giles B. Cooke Diary, entry for April 6, 1865, Giles B. Cooke Collection, M5:1C7745, VHS. Randolph Barton claimed that a broken-down caisson or wagon on one of the bridges caused the crowding. Randolph Barton, *Recollections, 1861–1865* (Baltimore: Thomas and Evans, 1913), 81–82.

25. William W. Blackford, *War Years with Jeb Stuart* (New York: Charles Scribner's Sons, 1945), 284; Delavan S. Miller, *Drum Taps in Dixie: Memories of a Drummer Boy, 1861–1865* (Watertown, N.Y.: Hungerford-Holbrook, 1905), 166; John W. Haley, *The Rebel Yell and the Yankee Hurrah: The Civil War Journal of a Maine Volunteer*, ed. Ruth L. Silliker (Camden, Maine: Down East Books, 1985), 261; Thomas D. Marbaker, *History of the Eleventh New Jersey Volunteers* (Trenton, N.J.: MacCrellish and Quigley, 1898), 294; Philip N. Racine, ed., *"Unspoiled Heart": The Journal of Charles Mattocks of the 17th Maine* (Knoxville: University of Tennessee Press, 1994), 267.

26. *OR* 46 (1): 682, 730.

27. *The Papers of Ulysses S. Grant*, ed. John Y. Simon and others, 32 vols. to date (Carbondale: Southern Illinois University Press, 1967–), 14:348–50.

28. Bernard, *War Talks of the Confederate Veterans*, 255; Osmun Latrobe Diary, April 8, 1865, Mss 5:1L3543:1, VHS; Frank Potts, *The Death of the Confederacy* (Richmond, Va.: privately printed for Allen Potts of Happy Creek, 1928), 11; *ORS* 7:767, 774.

29. Judson Andrews Diary, entry for April 8, 1865, Bound Volume 214, FRSP; Alanson A. Haines, *History of the Fifteenth Regiment New Jersey Volunteers* (New York: Jenkins and Thomas, 1883), 305; *OR* 46 (3): 687.

30. Michael Marshall, *Gallant Creoles: A History of the Donaldsonville Cannoneers* (Lafayette: University of Louisiana at Lafayette Press, 2013), 339–41; James W. Albright Diary, entry for April 8, 1865, SHC; Newel Cheney, *History of the Ninth Regiment New York Cavalry* (Jamestown, N.Y.: Martin Merz and Sons, 1901), 269; Chris Calkins, *The*

Battles of Appomattox Station and Appomattox Court House, April 8–9, 1865 (Lynchburg, Va.: H. E. Howard, 1987), 37–38.

31. Armistead C. Gordon, *Memories and Memorials of William Gordon McCabe*, 2 vols. (Richmond, Va.: Old Dominion Press, 1925), 1:291; John H. Chamberlayne and C. G. Chamberlayne, *Ham Chamberlayne, Virginian: Letters and Papers of an Artillery Officer in the War for Southern Independence, 1861–1865* (Richmond, Va.: Dietz Print. Co., 1932), 321.

32. Giles B. Cooke, "Just before and after Lee Surrendered to Grant," undated typescripts, in Giles B. Cooke Collection, Mss1C77526, VHS; Richard B. Williams, ed., *Stonewall's Prussian Mapmaker* (Chapel Hill: University of North Carolina Press, 2014), 266; Erasmus Taylor Memoir, Mss5:1T2135:1, VHS.

33. *OR* 46 (3): 665, 685.

34. Sources consulted for evidence that the high command of the Army of the Potomac seized records at Appomattox include the *OR*; the *ORS*; RG 393, Correspondence and Issuances, Headquarters of the Army of the Potomac, 1861–65, General Orders Issued, vol. 7 (1865), M 2096, NA; Fifth Corps, Army of the Potomac Order Book, RG 393, entry 226, vol. 7, stack area 10W2, row 14, compartment 4, NA; Second Corps, Army of the Potomac Order Book, RG 393, stack area 10W2, row 13, compartment 14, shelf 1, pt. 2, entry 47, NA; Report of Francis Lieber, Chief of the Archive Office, January 18, 1866, RG 109, entry 436, box 1, NA.

35. John Bratton to Ezra Carman, May 15, 1876, box 1, "Correspondence, 1875," Ezra Carman Papers, New York Public Library; William F. Fulton II, *The War Reminiscences of William Frierson Fulton II, 5th Alabama Battalion* (repr.; Gaithersburg, Md.: Butternut Press, 1986), 118; William Mahone to A. P. Hill, June 12, 1864, item 119, Historical Collectible Auctions Catalog for March 24, 2005, 30, in author's personal collection; James L. Morrison Jr., *The Memoirs of Henry Heth* (Westport, Conn.: Greenwood Press, 1974), 197. Members of Grant's staff allowed Maj. Gen. Henry Heth to take his "effects" home in a C. S. ambulance attached to Heth's division.

36. Douglas Southall Freeman, *R. E. Lee: A Biography*, 4 vols. (New York: Charles Scribner's Sons, 1934–35), 4:149; HdQrs Heth's Div, April 11, 1865, item 464, Field Return of Field's Division April 1865, item 481, Head Quarters Early's Division 8th April 1865, item 484, Effective Strength of Gordon's Division on the night of the 8th instant, item 485, Lee Headquarters Papers, VHS. On April 12, Assistant Secretary of War Charles Dana told Secretary of War Edwin Stanton that the surrender of Lee's forces had not been completed since "all their company rolls" had been lost in flight but "would be replaced in a day or two." *OR* 46 (3): 716.

37. James L. Corley to Robert E. Lee, April 15, 1865, item 514, Lee Headquarters Papers, VHS. For criticism of the poor management of Lee's wagon trains during the Appomattox campaign, see Robert J. Driver Jr., *First and Second Maryland Infantry, C.S.A.* (Bowie, Md.: Heritage Books, 2003), 339; Pulaski Cowper, comp., *Extracts of Letters of Major-General Bryan Grimes, to His Wife* (repr.; Wilmington, N.C.: Broadfoot, 1986), 110; McHenry Howard, "Closing Scenes of the War about Richmond," in *SHSP* 31:137–38. See Marvel, *Lee's Last Retreat*, 259n54, for an estimate of the number of Confederate wagons destroyed at various points during the campaign.

38. Lee claimed in July 1865 that the records in his headquarters wagon had been destroyed "the day before the army reached Appomattox C.H." It seems more likely that

the wagon burned on the morning of April 6, as related by Lee's staff officer Walter Taylor to Fred Colston. Allen W. Moger, "General Lee's Unwritten 'History of the Army of Northern Virginia,'" *Virginia Magazine of History and Biography* 71 (July 1963): 343, 345; Colston, "Recollections of the Last Months," *SHSP* 38:9.

39. Walter H. Taylor, *Four Years with General Lee* (repr.; Bloomington: Indiana University Press, 1996), 156; Robert E. Lee to Charles Marshall, December 4, 1865, Alexander Autographs (Stamford, Conn.) Auction Catalog, April 29, 2008.

40. Robert E. Lee to John B. Gordon, January 8, 1867, and John B. Gordon to Robert E. Lee, February 2, 1868, folder 4, box 5, John B. Gordon Papers, University of Georgia Special Collections, Athens.

41. Robert E. Lee to George A. Barksdale, April 30, 1866, typescript in possession of Robert K. Krick, Fredericksburg, Va.; Robert E. Lee to Charles S. Venable, March 8, 1866, MSS 5660, Minor-Venable Papers, University of Virginia Special Collections, Charlottesville; Carl L. Lokke, "The Captured Confederate Records under Francis Lieber," *American Archivist* 9 (October 1946): 308; Armistead L. Long, *Memoirs of Robert E. Lee* (New York.: J. M. Stoddart, 1886), 442; J. William Jones, *Personal Reminiscences of General Robert E. Lee* (1875, repr.; Baton Rouge: Louisiana State University Press, 1989), 181–82, 268; Gary W. Gallagher, ed., *Lee the Soldier* (Lincoln: University of Nebraska Press, 1996), 32.

42. Moger, "General Lee's Unwritten 'History,'" 346–47, 350, 358–59.

43. Freeman, *R. E. Lee*, 4:419; Moger, "General Lee's Unwritten 'History,'" 346–48, 359; Long, *Memoirs of Robert E. Lee*, 442; Gallagher, *Lee the Soldier*, 32; Robert E. Lee to Cassius F. Lee, June 6, 1870, http://leefamilyarchive.org/9-family-papers/114-robert-e-lee-to-cassius-f-lee-1870-june-6.

44. David L. Ladd and Audrey J. Ladd, eds., *The Bachelder Papers*, 3 vols. (Dayton, Ohio: Morningside Press, 1994), 1:483; J. William Jones, *Personal Reminiscences*, v. Walter Taylor of Lee's staff expressed "considerable misgiving" in 1877 at approaching the U.S. War Department in 1877 for permission to look at captured records, being aware of several unsuccessful attempts to do so. Taylor did receive permission to examine the records. Walter H. Taylor, *Four Years with General Lee* (repr.; Bloomington: Indiana University Press, 1996), 162–63.

45. Irvine, "Archive Office," 105–7; Harold E. Mahan, "The Arsenal of History: The Official Records of the War of the Rebellion," *Civil War History* 29 (March 1983): 14–16.

46. Colston, "Recollections of the Last Months," *SHSP* 38:10–11.

We Were Not Paroled

The Surrenders of Lee's Men beyond Appomattox Court House

Caroline E. Janney

When Lt. N. B. Bowyer of Company G, 10th Virginia Cavalry, learned that Gen. Robert E. Lee had ordered his men to cease firing on the morning of April 9, 1865, in order to surrender to Lt. Gen. Ulysses S. Grant, he quit the war. "I took the battle flag of the old regiment from the color-bearer, cut it from the staff, placed it across my saddle in front of me, and in company with two others, left the field," he recalled. Along with several of his men, Bowyer headed for the James River, believing that his ability to elude capture by Union forces depended on fording the river as quickly as possible. Crossing near New Market, the men made their way north into Nelson and Albemarle Counties, where they rested for a few days. "I bade my two friends farewell," he later remembered; "I then left for my old home in the Kanawha Valley."[1] Rather than surrendering at Appomattox, he simply headed home.

Bowyer was not the only one of Lee's men who refused to surrender that day. "My first inclination was to stay with my command and share their fate," South Carolinian David McIntosh wrote of his artillery battalion. "Reflection convinced me that my first and only duty was to my country," he continued, "and that as long as I could be of service to her I should avoid surrender." Unable to witness the "spectacle of surrender," he and seven others selected a ravine protected by woods for their escape. Ripping off their badges of rank and disguising their uniforms as much as possible, they cut through a swamp, leading their horses on foot for several miles before forcing a black man to guide them southwest toward Pamplin's Station.[2] Among those escaping with McIntosh was Lt. John Hampden "Ham" Chamberlayne, an artillery captain from Virginia. "I am by no means conquered yet," Chamberlayne wrote his siblings on April 12 from Halifax County. "We refused to take part in the funeral at Appomattox C.H. & cut or crept our way out," he defiantly explained. He was bound for Joseph E. Johnston's army in North Carolina, but if "they can do nothing there" he would head for Texas, as he had "no notion of laying down my arms." "Farewell to Virginia and to you both," he closed.[3]

The end of the war for Bowyer, McIntosh, and Chamberlayne proved to be far different from the way most have understood the final days of Lee's army. In the years since 1865, Appomattox has become shorthand for the swift closing of the Civil War based on Grant's generous terms under which Confederate soldiers would turn in their arms and go home on parole to be left undisturbed so long as they abided by the law.[4] But as Maj. Gen. George H. Sharpe, head of the U.S. Bureau of Military Information and assistant provost marshal, observed only a month after the surrender, "A large number of Lee's army were not paroled at Appomattox."[5]

Of the approximately 60,000 men available to Lee after the evacuation of Petersburg and Richmond on April 2 (which included those in the trenches surrounding Petersburg along with the various units from the Richmond defenses), only 26,000 to 28,000 were formally paroled between April 9 and 12 at Appomattox. Accounting for the approximately 11,530 casualties sustained between April 2 and 8, a conservative estimate suggests that at least 20,000 of Lee's men failed to surrender at the famed site.[6] Their reasons were as varied as the men themselves. Many had been footsore and starving stragglers unable to keep up with the relentless pace of Lee's army as it pushed west. Others believed that there was little use resisting any further and elected to go home before ever reaching Appomattox. A good many cavalry troopers and artillerists escaped the Union cordon on April 9. And some simply hoped to forgo the humiliation of surrendering, slipping from the lines that day and refusing to acquiesce or be conquered. Appomattox thus presents a great irony: it was—and continues to be—seen as the end of Lee's army and by extension the war, but a significant portion of the Army of Northern Virginia did not surrender in the small village.

Yet in the days and weeks that followed, thousands of Lee's men decided it was in their best interest to turn themselves in to Union provost marshals throughout the region in order to receive paroles. Some did so in order to obtain rations or transportation from the Union armies. Others found themselves hunted down by the U.S. cavalry. Regardless of Confederates' reasons in seeking or accepting paroles in the weeks after April 9, their ability to do so reflected both the inclusiveness and flexibility of Grant's surrender terms. But it was not mere magnanimity that motivated Grant. Instead, it reflected his desire to bring a swift and clear end to Lee's army and thus the war.

Desertions from Lee's army had run rampant throughout the winter of 1865, with an average of 120 men abandoning the trenches at Petersburg each day during February and March.[7] But even after evacuating the siege lines on April 2, hundreds more dropped out of the ranks or hid when their comrades departed. Near Namozine Church on April 3, Maj. Gen. Philip H. Sheridan informed Grant that his troopers had captured approximately 1,200 prisoners, adding, "All accounts report the woods filled with deserters and stragglers."[8] Members of a Pennsylvania unit likewise could not help but observe that the once seemingly invincible Army of Northern Virginia was withering before their eyes. As the regiment pursued Lee's men westward, the men encountered "thousands who deserted the failing cause at every by-road leading to their homes, and filled every wood and thicket between Richmond and Lynchburg."[9]

An officer with the 7th U.S. Colored Troops noted that the proximity to home seemed to induce Virginia Confederates to give up the fight sooner than their comrades from farther south. "The Rebel Soldiers whose homes are here in Virginia are leaving the Rebel service and returning to their homes and they say that the whole Rebel forces that belong in Virginia will desert Lee as soon as he leaves for North Carolina," he informed his wife on April 8. Historian William Marvel concurs, estimating that "Virginia units lost an average of 75.4 percent of their aggregate present from March 1 until the last volley at Appomattox."[10] Benjamin Sims of the 17th Virginia was one such soldier. A conscript from Louisa County who had enlisted in 1863, Sims fled along with much of his regiment at Five Forks on April 1. "We take to the woods, every man for himself," he scribbled in his journal, adding that he had joined up with two of his company about a mile from the field. Unable to find a spot to cross the Appomattox River on April 2, he and his comrade Robert Old "conclude[d] to go home."[11]

But even those from farther afield elected to abandon their units. On the same day that Sims decided to quit the army, William Andrew Mauney of the 28th North Carolina found himself in a harrowing fight at Petersburg. But the next morning he too slipped from the lines, heading first toward Amelia Court House. Learning that Union troops occupied Farmville, he detoured north before making his way to Charlotte County and caught a train bound for Greensboro, where he hoped to offer his services to Johnston's Army of Tennessee in North Carolina.[12] After rearguard action at Sailor's Creek on

April 6, Maj. Joseph G. Blount of Georgia likewise left with two guns from the Macon Light Artillery. The remainder of the battalion surrendered at Appomattox, but Blount's detachment headed west toward Lynchburg, where the soldiers destroyed the guns and disbanded. Writing to his wife on the tenth, Blount informed her that he had sent his men home and would now attempt to join Johnston.[13]

Countless men no doubt failed to keep up with their units due to broken-down bodies and exhaustion, but others simply gave up the fight. Attributing the attrition to cowardice rather than to fatigue, Lt. William Gordon McCabe arrested scores of stragglers between April 6 and 9. "But still they came by in an unceasing flow," he wrote his future wife. "The capitulation of the Army was brought about entirely by cursed straggling of the men and some cowardly infantry officers," he declared after the surrender.[14]

If thousands of soldiers dropped out of the ranks during the first week of April, thousands more refused to surrender themselves at Appomattox. Some did so as part of the battle plan, as proved the case for much of the Cavalry Corps. At a council of war on the evening of April 8, Cavalry Corps commander Fitzhugh Lee had informed his uncle Robert E. Lee that he would "try to extricate the cavalry" if surrender seemed imminent.[15] At dawn the next morning, the Confederate horsemen in support of John Gordon's Second Corps had prepared to advance against what they thought was only Sheridan's troopers when they discovered infantry from the Army of the James massed in their front.[16] Hope for breaking free from the Union lines was quickly dissipating. But Fitzhugh Lee discovered that two of his three divisions had already passed the Union flank, and the road to Lynchburg lay open. Recognizing that his uncle had been forced to capitulate, Fitz Lee consulted Maj. Gen. Thomas L. Rosser and Col. Thomas T. Munford only to learn that they were adamant in their refusal to surrender. Instead, along with 1,500 to 2,400 of their troopers, they rode west.[17]

Among them was Pvt. William L. Wilson of the 12th Virginia Cavalry. Heading toward Lynchburg twenty miles distant, he rode with "officers and men of different regts jammed up together, always in a trot sometimes in a gallop." Nearing the city, they discovered Maj. Gen. Lunsford L. Lomax's division of cavalry had arrived from the Shenandoah Valley, and together what remained of Lee's cavalry rode into Lynchburg at sundown. In his diary Wilson noted that the entire command remained in a state of confusion. After much squabbling, officers moved to the north side of the river and made camp. "Here Col Ball and Col White made speeches," Wilson wrote, "the former advising the men to retain their formation and seek to join the Southern Army announcing on Genl Rosser's authority that Gordon had simply surrendered 8000 men while Gen Lee had escaped. The latter advised them to go to their homes in the Valley and recruit their horses, when, should a Southern Army really exist, he would lead them to it." "This speech decided the men," Wilson concluded, noting that many elected to strike for their homes the following morning.[18]

Other cavalrymen apparently never made it to Lynchburg, including Pvt. Hiram W. Harding of Company D, 9th Virginia Cavalry. In his diary the evening of April 9, he noted that the "noble army of Northern Virginia was surrendered to day at ten Oclock & the Cavalry ordered to Buckingham courthouse there to be disbanded." Having heard the news, Harding headed home. "I made my way out," he wrote, and "crossed the James at Hardwicksville ferry came down the river & stop[p]ed for the night at Mr. Lewis in Albemarle county." From there he headed east, through Fluvanna, Caroline, and Richmond Counties, before reaching his home near Heathesville on the Chesapeake Bay the following Sunday.[19]

Hundreds of artillerists and infantryman likewise fled the field during the ceasefire.[20] "A great many save themselves the humiliation by escaping as best they may," scribbled a signalman in his diary, adding, "Some Genls tell their men to save themselves if they can."[21] Several artillery batteries escaped as units. Capt. John J. Shoemaker, Lt. Charles R. Phelps, and Lt. Marcellus N. Moorman, along with many of the men of Shoemaker's Battery, abandoned their guns before heading to Lynchburg, where the officers likewise disbanded the battery on April 9 before venturing south to join Joseph E. Johnston's army in North Carolina.[22] Just west of Appomattox Court House, Col. C. E. Lightfoot informed the remaining men of the Surry Light Artillery Battery that he was not going to surrender his command but disband them, leaving them all to their own devices. But first, he ordered each of his drivers to take his best horse and give the other to a cannoneer so that the men might have some way to travel home. Pulling his cap over his eyes, he silently extended his hand in good-bye. The men then saddled their mounts and headed north toward the James River in small groups.[23]

Those who had remained at Appomattox almost immediately began to take stock of the numbers—of those there and not there. By the ninth, Confederates speculated that there were only 8,000 to 10,000 infantry with arms. "Hungry, sick, weak men have dropped out by the thousands," a member of the 12th Virginia noted in his diary.[24] In the 23rd South Carolina, Corp. John Forrest Robertson estimated that only 17 men with guns remained in his regiment on April 9. "The second day Grant had issued to us nine biscuits and pieces of beef each," he wrote. "When the dinner bell rang, two hundred and fifty reported without arms. In the meantime, they had managed to keep out of the way of Yankees and bullets." Who knows what a man like Robertson who had not fled to the woods thought in 1865, but years later he was sympathetic. "All without doubt did the best they could, so charity covers the doings of the weaker ones," he observed.[25]

Not all felt so generous. Speaking to his men on the evening of April 9, Brig. Gen. James A. Walker rebuked those who had fled earlier that day only to return once the fighting had ceased. "This morning I led into battle seven hundred good and true men," he began. "This afternoon, my muster rolls showed me fifteen hundred." Where had these men been during the battle? he demanded. Mincing no words, he condemned those who had taken to the woods as "sulking cowards!" To the 700 who had stood in ranks that morning, he echoed Lee's farewell to his troops, imploring them to go home with a clear conscience, knowing that the cause had failed through no fault of theirs. But he warned them to be wary of their comrades who had not shown such devotion. "You well know those who were not with you," he continued. "If you meet them in the social circle, avoid them, if on the walks of business, distrust them, and if at the altar of your God, turn from them."[26] Capt. Frank Potts of Lt. Gen. James Longstreet's staff likewise offered a stinging indictment of the stragglers. "We have proven ourselves unworthy of independence," he wrote his brother only days after the surrender. "The great mass of people sighed for the fleshpots of Yankeedom, and deserted the leader of whom they were not worthy."[27] Jedediah Hotchkiss (who had not been with Lee's army on April 9) likewise quipped that "skulkers and deserters are coming out of their holes."[28] It was one thing to have escaped on April 9, quite another to have abandoned the ranks before surrender was imminent.

At least a handful of officers who had escaped the Union lines believed it in their best interests to return. After ordering his command to disperse and go home, Fitz Lee and five of his staff officers had ridden to Farmville and surrendered to Maj. Gen. George Meade on April 11. Meade promptly sent them to Appomattox, where they reported to Maj. Gen. John Gibbon the next day.[29] Upon receiving orders on April 9 to withdraw from the field, Brig. Gen. W. P. Roberts had likewise ordered his brigade, which included the 4th North Carolina Cavalry, the 16th North Carolina Battalion, a "remnant" of Barringer's North Carolina Cavalry, and part of the 8th Georgia Cavalry, to disband and directed his men to head toward their homes. "Shortly thereafter I traveled South, accompanied by one of my men," he later wrote, "but upon reflection I felt it my duty to return to Appomattox, which I did, and surrendered to the officer in command, General Gibbon."[30] Both Fitz Lee and Roberts were included in the Appomattox parole lists along with at least twelve other officers who reported themselves for parole after the departure of their commands.[31]

The offer of paroles to these officers provides evidence of the flexibility of Grant's surrender terms — something that we should be careful not to take for granted. On the afternoon of April 10, U.S. secretary of war Edwin Stanton had written Grant inquiring as to whether the cavalry troops in Loudoun County or those operating in Western Virginia would be included in the surrender "or only those under Lee's immediate personal command." Were the terms to include those men who had fled the lines in the days leading up to April 9? "The surrender was only of the men left with the pursued army at the time of surrender," Grant replied, noting that "those who had escaped and were detached at the time are not included." Nevertheless, he believed that the same terms should be offered to "all the fragments of the Army of Northern Virginia" so that they might voluntarily surrender.[32] Ending the war as quickly as possible was Grant's objective, and key to that would be extending paroles to all of Lee's men, even if they had not surrendered with their commander on April 9.

After receiving a telegram from Secretary Stanton affirming Grant's decision, Maj. Gen. Winfield Scott Hancock announced the terms of Lee's surrender from the headquarters of the Middle Military Division in Winchester.[33] In newspaper columns and circulars posted throughout the area, he noted that all "detachments and stragglers from the Army of Northern Virginia," with the exception of "the guerrilla chief Mosby" and his rangers would be paroled under the same conditions as those at Appomattox and allowed to return peacefully to their homes. "Every military restraint shall be removed that is not absolutely essential," he promised, "and your sons, your husbands, and your brothers shall remain with you unmolested." Those who failed to do so, however, would be captured and treated as prisoners of war. He added one more word of caution especially to those who had harbored marauding bands: "Every outrage committed by them will be followed by the severest infliction." "It is for you to determine the amount of freedom you are to enjoy," he declared.[34]

Although Stanton had initially instructed Hancock that Col. John Singleton Mosby and his 43rd Virginia Battalion were exceptions to the surrender terms, by the evening of April 10 Grant indicated that he was willing to extend the same conditions even to the famed guerrilla. Earlier that day Union officials reported rumors that some of Mosby's men had crossed the Blue Ridge

Caroline E. Janney

with intentions of capturing and plundering Hancock's trains south of Winchester, that others had been sent to Maryland on a raid, while yet another unnamed group of partisans had attempted to steal U.S. horses and mules in Fairfax County. This continued threat necessitated that Mosby and his men be brought in as quickly as possible. On April 11, Hancock forwarded Mosby copies of the exchange between Grant and Lee and offered the same terms conferred upon those at Appomattox to the colonel and his rangers.[35] Grant would be extraordinarily generous and inclusive if it meant thoroughly ending the rebellion.

As news of Lee's capitulation—and, perhaps more important, Grant's liberal terms—reached men who had abandoned the ranks in the previous days and weeks, thousands began to seek out U.S. forces in the surrounding vicinity. On April 11, the day prior to the surrender ceremony at Appomattox Court House, Union provost marshals began issuing paroles thirty miles to the southeast in Farmville. During the next ten days, no fewer than 2,231 Confederates received parole papers in the town. To be fair, nearly 600 of these men had not absconded from the ranks but had been patients in the town's hospitals—some admitted only days earlier.[36] Pvt. John N. Barnett of the 18th South Carolina had arrived on April 3 at the CSA General Hospital in Farmville, where surgeons amputated his right leg. After receiving his parole, he was sent to a Federal hospital in Burkeville for further recovery.[37] Brig. Gen. W. G. Lewis entered the Confederate hospital on or prior to April 10 with a gunshot wound. By the thirteenth, he too had been paroled and transferred to a U.S. hospital.[38] Others proved to be hospital workers—doctors, nurses, and clerks—as was the case with S. S. Keeling, who had spent much of the war as a clerk and later a steward in Richmond-area hospitals.[39]

The vast majority of parolees, however, appear to have been able-bodied men whose units had been present at Appomattox on April 9. Men from the ranks that hailed from Virginia, North Carolina, South Carolina, Georgia, Maryland, and Tennessee arrived in the Prince Edward County town where they signed paroles that provided the same conditions as those given to their comrades who had remained in the ranks.[40] Such was the case for Pvt. Bradford Ivy of the 16th Georgia, who had enlisted in July 1861 and served as a teamster for much of the war.[41] Pvt. J. B. O'Neal of the 27th North Carolina and Pvt. T. J. Howell of the 44th Virginia likewise turned themselves in at Farmville, while the remainder of their units surrendered at Appomattox.[42] Whether they had been stragglers hoping to find some extra provisions after the escape from Petersburg, had intended to abandon the army for good given its dismal prospects, or had fled along with much of the cavalry and artillery, at least 1,742 men who should have been at Appomattox made their way to Farmville.[43]

To the west in Lynchburg, the key railroad junction Lee had been trying desperately to reach, thousands more Confederates offered themselves up to the Federal provost marshal. Between April 12 and 16, U.S. authorities issued approximately 5,000 paroles in the city.[44] Again, the lists included men from the numerous hospitals and various invalid corps, but most were soldiers whose units had either disbanded or surrendered at Appomattox. Unlike at Farmville, where men had tended to come in as individuals, most of those who arrived in Lynchburg did so as part of a unit.[45] While thirty members of the Louisiana-based Washington Artillery had surrendered at Appomattox, at least forty-two men from the battalion arrived on April 13 to sign paroles. Sixty members of Lynchburg's own Otey's Battery, twenty-one from the 2nd Maryland Battery (Baltimore Light Artillery), and fourteen of the 2nd Virginia Cavalry—all units that had been present on the morning of April 9—likewise presented themselves for parole. In the days that followed, groups of men from Shoemaker's Battery, the 3rd Virginia Reserves, and the 17th Tennessee, among others, drifted into the city, where the provost marshal compiled their names in lists, just as Confederate regimental and company officers had done at Appomattox.[46]

Even as thousands of Lee's men poured into Federal posts in the counties surrounding Appomattox, General Rosser headed south to Danville to consult with Confederate secretary of war John C. Breckinridge after temporarily disbanding his cavalry division at Lynchburg on April 9. The secretary instructed Rosser to return to central Virginia and round up all of his troopers who had not yet been paroled. Under these instructions, Rosser rode to Staunton, where he issued a proclamation on April 12 from what he deemed the headquarters of the Army of Northern Virginia. Promoting himself to lieutenant general, he called upon his men to shoulder their muskets once more "and return to the field to meet the arrogant invader who had insulted you, robbed you, murdered your dearest friends and relatives, outraged your fair women, despoiled your homes, and dishonored all that is most dear and sacred." He would lead the men against this dastardly foe, he promised, and would never surrender "until the purple current ceases to flow from my heart, or until you are a free, independent and happy people!" "Rise like men and come to me," he commanded, instructing companies and regiments to assemble at Charlottesville, Staunton, or Lynchburg "without delay."[47]

Although Lee's army had served as the centerpiece of Confederate nationalism since 1862, even its demise could not sway some of his men from

Caroline E. Janney

Maj. Gen. Thomas L. Rosser, who, along with much of the Army of
Northern Virginia's cavalry, escaped the Union cordon at Appomattox on
April 9. On April 12, Rosser issued a proclamation from Staunton calling on
those who had evaded surrender to join him in sustaining the fight.
(F. Trevelyan Miller, ed., *The Photographic History of the Civil War*,
10 vols. [New York: Review of Reviews, 1911], 4:75)

their ardent belief in the viability of the cause.[48] Among those who remained committed to continue fighting was cavalry major Thomas J. Rowland. On April 12 he wrote to his mother from Pittsylvania County, Virginia, informing her that he was not yet subjugated. He expected to remain in Virginia for another month and then to head south, perhaps to Texas. "I will follow the fortunes of the Confederacy as long as there is any hope of retrieving our fallen fortunes," he explained. "If all our efforts to achieve independence fail, I shall leave the country & find a home for you in some other land. We will carry our household goods to some new Virginia," he promised, adding in closing, "I can not believe that our cause will ultimately fail." More than two weeks later he wrote again from the mountains of Rockbridge County. He still planned to start soon for Texas but had hoped to visit her before departing. In order to do so, however, he would have to go to Richmond, surrender himself, and seek a parole. "But even my duty to my mother would not justify me in surrendering my person or my principles to the enemies of my country," he informed her. "I embraced the cause of the South when it was prosperous & triumphant; I will not desert it now that it is downfallen & perhaps hopeless, & if I can do nothing more for it here, rather than make terms with the conquerors of my country, I will exile myself to some foreign land."[49]

Avoiding Union troops was imperative for those rebels who refused to surrender themselves, whether cavalry, artillery, or infantry.[50] "As we have no parole pass we are uncertain what would be our fate in the event of our capture," a Confederate signalman scribbled in his diary on April 12; "consequently we avoid the Yanks as we would a pestilence."[51] The same held true for Benjamin Jones and seven of his comrades from the Surry Light Artillery Battery as they headed toward their home in Virginia's Tidewater. Rather than taking the more direct route due east, the men set off on a circuitous route that led them northwest through Nelson County before turning east through Albemarle and Fluvanna Counties. On the north side of the James River by April 16, they proceeded around Richmond, "passing Mechanicsville in time to escape a train-load of Federals." Discovering a canoe on the Chickahominy, two of the boys, George C. Holmes and Thomas Williams, attempted to travel downriver to procure a larger boat upon which they might all travel. But choked with fallen timber, the river proved impassable, and the two men quickly became separated from their small party.[52] Their separation proved disastrous. Unable to find a way down the clogged river, Holmes and Williams gave up and proceeded to Richmond, where they were arrested as prisoners on April 18 and sent to Point Lookout, Maryland.[53]

A similar fate awaited several other members of the Surry Light Artillery Battery. When three men departed on horseback from the small group with whom they had been traveling and rode into Richmond, they too were taken as prisoners of war and sent to Newport News, where they remained until July. Others found themselves detained for only a few days. Twenty-year-old Charles C. Richardson and six of his traveling companions had managed to cross the James River at Scottsville on their way home to Sussex County. But upon reaching Chesterfield County, they had seen bluecoats on the other side of the Appomattox River who offered a canoe to carry them to the southern shore. Whether it was hunger or another reason that compelled them to agree is unknown, but Richardson and his fellow artillerists — none of whom had parole passes — quickly found themselves confined to a tobacco barn in Dinwiddie County. Here they were kept for two nights and a day before being transported under guard by railcar to Petersburg, where they were again imprisoned. Finally, on the morning of April 19 the men were paroled and allowed to continue on their way home.[54]

Federal soldiers most likely detained these Confederates in accordance with a policy stipulating that all "deserters and stragglers of Lee's army must be brought in as prisoners of war unless specially paroled."[55] These men could be paroled on the same conditions as Lee's army, but if they refused they were to be arrested and held. Such proved the case for Holmes, who was held as a prisoner at Point Lookout until July 1.[56]

Holmes's comrades in the Surry Light Artillery Battery had no idea what had befallen him and Williams, but they remained vigilant as they tramped toward their Tidewater homes. Managing to find a small boat of their own, the remaining men had slowly made their way to the confluence of the Chickahominy and James where they discovered gunboats stationed every mile or so guarding the stream. Only three miles from home, they determined to wait for darkness. That night, they wrapped their oars to prevent making any sound and set off silently across the James. "At last," Benjamin Jones recounted, "our little craft grated upon the sands of old Surry shore!" On Tuesday the eighteenth, the men reached their home in Charles City County, where they finally learned the fate of their comrades who had remained at Appomattox. "All of them have surrendered," Jones reported. Some were on their way home; others had been sent to Point Lookout or detained at Fort Monroe. "It was this that we feared and that made us so resolved to thread our way homeward without falling into the hands of the foe, and thus of being delayed indefinitely, until it might suit the convenience of the Federals to permit us to proceed onward," he noted.[57] For Jones and his comrades, the surrender terms offered little solace — and little incentive to seek paroles.

Hoping to provide themselves some sort of protection without the humiliation of surrender, some men forged paroles. John Kerr Oakes of the 38th Virginia had been absent on furlough since at least January 1, 1865. But upon hearing the news of Lee's surrender, he hid in a stable for three days near Farmville before forging a pass so that he might make his way back home to Pittsylvania County.[58] Unlike cavalry general Joseph Wheeler of Johnston's army, who was captured in early May with "a forged parole on his person," Oakes apparently made it home unscathed.[59]

Despite the defiance of such men, not all who had fled Appomattox remained determined to continue resisting. Caldwell Calhoun Buckner of the 17th Virginia Cavalry had escaped with Rosser on April 9. Accompanying the general as far as the Staunton River, on April 11 Buckner determined "to return and start back" toward central Virginia, where he joined Mosby for an evening. Two days later he finally heard word that Lee had indeed surrendered his entire command. After another week of visiting friends in the area and purchasing a wagon, he arrived at his Orange County farm, "Island View," where he immediately set about clearing the peach orchard and plowing fields. Perhaps he had never been as devoted to the cause as some of his comrades. The thirty-six-year-old had at best been a reluctant Confederate. During the spring of 1861, he "did all in his power to prevent the secession of his native state," and while his fellow Virginians marched off to war he remained at home raising his thoroughbred stock until conscripted in January 1864. Having escaped with much of the cavalry at Appomattox, by late April he was thoroughly involved in harrowing and cleaning weeds, planting his fields, and rebuilding fences.[60]

Throughout the remainder of April, thousands of Lee's men—both those who had eluded Union forces at Appomattox and those who had dropped out of Confederate lines prior to April 9—continued to surrender. At Burkeville, a key junction of the Richmond & Danville Railroad and South Side Railroad, the provost marshal recorded 1,614 names in a three-day stretch from April 14 to April 17.[61] While the number of paroles issued at Burkeville failed to match those at Lynchburg, it no doubt proved a popular site because it provided access to a rail line that ran to Petersburg. It seems likely that many Confederates who had escaped—or otherwise failed to arrive at—Appomattox would make their way to this key railroad junction in order to get papers that allowed them to board the trains and receive rations. If remnants of Lee's army streamed into federal posts in small towns throughout the Virginia countryside, they gushed into Richmond. A report of paroles through April 18 observed that except in the cases of men who had been attached to hospitals, the great bulk of the rolls included "stragglers from the Army of Northern Virginia."[62]

Surprisingly, the assassination of President Abraham Lincoln on April 14 did not curtail but encouraged U.S. authorities to seek out the remnants of Lee's army. The issuance of parole passes thus continued to radiate out from Appomattox.[63] Recognizing that hundreds if not thousands of Lee's men continued to congregate in the Shenandoah Valley without paroles, Hancock did not simply wait for Lee's soldiers to come to him. Instead, he authorized expeditions to hunt down those rebels who had not yet signed paroles. From his home in Staunton, the as-yet-unparoled mapmaker Jedediah Hotchkiss noted on April 17, "Many are disposed to go and seek this parole."[64]

Among those who availed themselves of the opportunity to sign paroles were many cavalrymen—troopers who had escaped with Munford and Rosser. Whether they had not yet heard Rosser's proclamation calling for them to reassemble or whether they simply decided to call it quits remains unclear. But on April 18, at least forty-six members of Company D, 12th Virginia Cavalry, presented themselves to the provost marshal in Mount Jackson. For more than a week the men had stayed together as a unit, led by Capt. Henry Walper Kearney. The following day at least seventy-three men from the 1st Maryland Cavalry (CSA) gathered seven miles to the south, where they signed paroles in New Market.[65] Unlike so many of Lee's men who were daily arriving at Federal posts throughout Virginia, these were not local men who had already returned to their homes. Instead, many in Company D, 12th Virginia Cavalry, hailed from Shepherdstown, a town in Jefferson County claimed by both Virginia and West Virginia in 1865, while companies of the 1st Maryland Cavalry had been organized at Baltimore and Williamsport, Maryland; Pittsburgh, Pennsylvania; and Washington, D.C.[66] In other words, these Confederates were either reluctant to return to their homes in the loyal states or had not the resources to do so.

While negotiations between Hancock's and Mosby's subordinates continued, men from Mosby's 43rd Virginia Battalion began to file into provost marshal offices. As early as April 17, individuals such as thirty-five-year-old William Skinner had elected to leave the rangers and head to Winchester to seek their paroles. On April 21, the same day Mosby officially disbanded the 43rd Battalion at Salem, at least forty-seven arrived in Winchester to surrender themselves. The next evening, Hancock reported to Stanton that "nearly all of Mosby's command has surrendered, including nearly or quite all of the officers except Mosby himself, who has probably fled. His next in rank, Lieutenant Colonel Chapman, surrendered with the command." Mosby had refused to acquiesce, despite a bounty of $2,000 (later raised to $5,000) on his head, but Hancock estimated that nearly 380 of his men had been paroled.[67] Grant's efforts to convince the guerrillas to lay down their weapons without penalty appeared to be working.

Even as Mosby disbanded his rangers, Colonel Munford, who had escaped with his cavalry division at Appomattox, remained determined to continue the struggle. Claiming the rank of brigadier general, on April 21 he issued a stirring special order intended to rally his men.[68] "Our cause is not dead," he intoned. In language that sounded much like Rosser's April 12 proclamation, he reminded his men of the atrocities committed by the Union, of the "devastated fields, our burned homesteads, our violated daughters, and our murdered thousands." "Their present pretend policy of conciliation is but the cunning desire of the Yankee to lull us to sleep, while they rivet the chains . . . which they will surely make *us* wear *forever*," he warned.

Underscoring the limited impact of April 9, Munford informed his old brigade that "there are more men at home today, belonging to the army of Northern Virginia, than were surrendered at Appomattox." "You have never been surrendered!" he added. Having cut their way out before the surrender was completed, "you, together with the majority of the cavalry are free to follow your country's flag." He beseeched them to rally once more. And in language that must have inflamed Unionists only a week after Lincoln's assassination, he employed the Virginia motto — the same words reportedly shouted by John Wilkes Booth: "Virginia, our beloved old Commonwealth[,] shall yet stand triumphant and defiant, with her foot upon her tyrants prostrate, and her proud old banner, never yet sullied, with its 'Sic Semper Tyrannis' streaming over her." He commanded the men to be ready to assemble at a time and place to be disclosed.[69]

Despite Munford's appeal, members of Company F, 18th Virginia Cavalry, John D. Imboden's brigade, which had been on detached duty in the Shenandoah Valley, decided to seek paroles as a unit on April 22. "We met at Back Creek Tollgate and footed to Winchester," wrote I. Norval Baker. "The people along the road told us where we would find their outpost, so we all gathered up in marching order before we got in sight of the post. The guard saw us coming and it raised quite a commotion in their little camp and long before we got there, all the guard was across the road in line of battle. We marched by twos and kept step in fine order when about twenty-five yards from them, they ordered us to stop," he recalled. An unnamed Union officer then escorted the men under guard to the provost marshal's office in Win-

Caroline E. Janney

chester where one by one they signed paroles. "We wrote our names and they gave us free papers to walk out with and take in the town."[70]

It is unclear whether Baker's choice of the term "free papers" to describe his parole was meant to be ironic. Was he suggesting that the subjugated Confederates were no better off than slaves? This would not be a stretch, considering much of the language and rhetoric employed by Confederates both prior to and during the war to describe what they saw as the Union's attempt to enslave them by stripping their constitutionally protected rights. Or perhaps Baker merely used the phrase to point out that he and his comrades no longer had to move in the shadows, evading U.S. soldiers. Regardless of his intention, it is hard to escape noting that former Confederate soldiers now *did* have to carry passes, just as slaves moving beyond their owners' property or free African Americans at all times had been forced to do. The paroles became proof of white men's status, just as the pass had been proof of the black man's.

Some 200 miles to the southeast, more of Lee's men sought paroles in Norfolk. On April 21 and 22, in excess of 500 men surrendered themselves at the headquarters of the District of Eastern Virginia. Most belonged to the 5th and 13th Virginia Cavalry, units organized in the surrounding Princess Anne, Accomack, Norfolk, and Nansemond Counties as well as in Norfolk City. On the very day that Munford issued his stirring call to arms, men like W. C. Taylor, George Brown, William S. Hancock, and L. D. Robinson who had returned to their homes after their units disbanded now believed it was in their best interest to secure whatever protection the paroles might bring.[71] Infantrymen and artillerists likewise sought out provost marshals. On April 27, Benjamin Sims, who had quit the war after Five Forks, traveled from his home in Louisa County to obtain a parole outside of Richmond at Ashland.[72] Along the Northern Neck and the Eastern Shore, on the Peninsula, in Richmond, at Farmville and Lynchburg, and throughout the Shenandoah Valley, Lee's soldiers trickled in, sometimes as individuals but more often in groups, to secure their paroles.[73]

As thousands of Lee's men turned themselves in on paroles, others who had eluded Union troops at Appomattox attempted to join Joseph E. Johnston's army in North Carolina. On the morning of April 9, the same William Gordon McCabe who had sought out stragglers during the preceding days, along with Capt. Richard Walke and Maj. Joseph McGraw of Pegram's Battery, rode west through a drenching rain toward Lynchburg. Stopping occasionally to rest, without blankets or oilcloths, they were nearly delirious for want of sleep as they pushed south toward Johnston's lines. "After a ride of nearly two hundred and thirty miles on horseback we reached the advance of the Army of Tennessee [on April 17], and at once reported for duty," McCabe informed his future wife, Jane Harrison. It quickly became apparent, however, that their trip had been in vain. "We could get literally nothing to do, and furthermore were considerably disgusted to find many officer of rank very badly whipped." Moreover, Johnston and Maj. Gen. William T. Sherman had just agreed to, in McCabe's words, a "cursed Truce." But even with the future of Johnston's army seemingly doomed, McCabe refused to acquiesce just yet. "There are a great many Va. officers here, who are forming themselves into a Battalion, — a sort of *Corps d'Elite*," he told Jane. "Where we are going, of course, I do not know; to Trans-Miss., I suppose, if we can elude Sherman."[74]

While Lee's men, paroled and unparoled, brought news of the Army of Northern Virginia's surrender to Johnston's troops, those who had hoped to continue the fight soon found out that their efforts had been futile.[75] Several artillerists from Shoemaker's Battery, for example, returned to Lynchburg by April 20 having learned that Johnston "could not receive them as Genl Lee had surrendered his whole army whether present or not."[76] Others found that they would be forced to surrender after Johnston and Sherman finally agreed to terms on April 26. St. George Tucker Mason and Robert L. Judkins of the 13th Virginia Cavalry, for example, appeared on a parole list of staff officers and men serving with the headquarters of the Army of Tennessee's Cavalry Corps.[77]

Even after Johnston's surrender, some diehards refused to give up. Such was the case for Capt. William Frederic Pendleton, a soldier from the Army of Northern Virginia who had been convalescing since an injury at Cedar Creek the previous October. April 6 found him with Confederate forces in Augusta, Georgia. News of Richmond's fall had not discouraged him. On the contrary, it enlivened his spirits. "We have too much to lose by failure; and too much to gain by success, to basely to submit to a ruthless foe," he wrote in his diary. It would be another ten days before he learned of Lee's surrender, yet he remained determined "to do my duty to the last" and departed for Charlotte for orders. On April 27, Maj. Gen. Ambrose Wright directed Pendleton to Ware County, Georgia, where he was to collect and forward "all officers and men belonging to Genl. Lee's Army now on furlough or who may have straggled" to Augusta.[78]

Back in Virginia, at least some cavalrymen continued to resist. By late April, Rosser had gathered nearly 500 men at Swope's Depot, ten miles west

Caroline E. Janney

of Staunton.[79] Even though a great many cavalrymen had voluntarily sought out paroles, upon learning that Johnston had surrendered his army Rosser issued a second proclamation on April 28 urging his men "to continue the struggle for Liberty as long as there is hope of success." He directed "all true men who are determined to never abandon our sacred cause" to meet him at Staunton on May 10 for the purpose of reenlisting, reorganizing, and heading west to join whatever forces might still be in the field.[80] The following morning he departed from the city in the company of William Lowther Jackson, who had commanded a cavalry brigade in Lomax's division. By May 2, locals had heard reports that Rosser, Jackson, and "a few followers" had headed for the Southwest.[81]

When his efforts to rally more men to head south faltered, Rosser concluded that the time had come to quit the fight.[82] On May 4 he sent word to U.S. authorities that his men would gather in Staunton on the tenth to sign paroles and turn over their arms.[83] Yet rumors continued to swirl that Rosser, now accompanied by the one-armed brigadier general Robert Doak Lilley, were planning a raid with 3,000 to 5,000 men on Union lines near Philippi, West Virginia. After the strike, the men would disband and disappear.[84] In Washington, Grant likewise heard rumors, albeit ones that claimed Rosser had been captured near Richmond. Telegraphing Maj. Gen. Henry Halleck on May 9, Grant ordered the cavalry general brought to Washington "to be tried for deserting his command after it had been surrendered."[85] There would be no lenient terms for those who had absconded. Halleck quickly reassured Grant that Rosser had come voluntarily within Union lines to surrender himself and arrange for the parole of his command at Staunton.[86]

In fact, Rosser had made little effort to arrange for the surrender of his men. There would be no single paroling of his command, the greater portion of the men already having either turned themselves in or returned to their homes without paroles. Indeed, they would continue to arrive at provost marshal stations only in small detachments or as individuals over the next few weeks. Moreover, Rosser had made no attempt to turn over Confederate property, though he did admit to Union officials that he had concealed thirteen artillery pieces between Staunton and Lexington and another eight near Pittsylvania Court House and had buried small arms near Charlottesville.[87]

The hiding of arms and dispersal of small bands of men into the countryside was precisely what Grant and others had feared most as Union forces finally ground down the Confederate armies throughout late April. In the wake of Lincoln's assassination, many Union officials remained especially wary of guerrilla forces. As he began surrender negotiations with Johnston's army, Sherman had warned Grant of such an outcome. "There is great danger that the confederate armies will dissolve and fill the whole land with robbers and assassins," he counseled, adding that "the assassination of Mr. Lincoln shows one of the elements in the rebel army which will be almost as difficult to deal with as the main armies."[88] Even after Appomattox, the prospect of continued guerrilla-style warfare motivated the Union high command to ensure that every Confederate soldier surrendered himself on parole. The Confederate States of America had not been declared defunct. There had been no peace treaty. And as of May 9, President Jefferson Davis remained on the run. If the United States hoped to end the war, it was imperative that *all* Confederate soldiers give up the fight, including those who had not been at Appomattox.

If the Union high command realized the importance of compelling the surrender of all those who had borne arms against the United States, Confederate soldiers likewise came to recognize that it was in their best interest to seek paroles.[89] Lee's soldiers continued to trickle into Union posts in Charlottesville, Louisa, Halifax Court House, King George County, Columbia, Fairfax Court House, Westmoreland County, and myriad other places in Virginia. Among them were Thomas A. Somers, Albert Somers, and James Prince of Company H, 33rd Virginia, who traveled from their Page County homes to Winchester seeking paroles on June 1.[90] Like these men, most of those who surrendered throughout May and into June had already returned to their families and finally concluded to seek out provost marshals nearest to their respective homes.[91]

But other parolees in May and June included some who had escaped the Union cordon at Appomattox. Perhaps after learning of Rosser's surrender or hearing threats that the Union army intended to "burn and destroy everything he had," Munford and two of his staff officers finally surrendered at Lynchburg on May 20. With them came Brig. Gen. Moxley Sorrel of Georgia, who had been absent from Appomattox recovering from a wound received at Hatcher's Run and had since been evading Union troops after learning of Lee's surrender.[92] Artillerist captain John J. Shoemaker had returned from North Carolina in April after Johnston refused to receive any of Lee's men, but it was not until May 22 that he sought a parole in his hometown of Lynchburg.[93] William Gordon McCabe had remained in North Carolina until mid-May, when he finally gave up the fight and resolved to go home. Having seen the U.S. army's order forbidding Confederates from donning their uniforms, he had thought it best to travel first to Richmond, where he hoped to get money and clothes from his father's family before venturing to his residence in Petersburg. Presumably after acquiring civilian clothing, on May 22 he too turned himself in to the local provost marshal and signed his parole.[94]

Many of Lee's men sought paroles beyond the borders of Virginia. Singly and in small bands, they ambled into provost marshal offices in Cumberland, Maryland; Charles Town, West Virginia; and even Washington, D.C. Others found themselves at paroling stations even farther from Appomattox. Some, like Ham Chamberlayne, remained die-hard rebels who held out in the hope that the Confederacy might yet keep fighting. Having tendered his services to the Army of Tennessee (which Johnston declined) and attempted to report to Secretary of War John C. Breckinridge in Augusta, Georgia, the artillerist finally signed a parole in Atlanta on May 12.[95] Others who had hoped to avoid the humiliation of surrender soon recognized that without paroles they would not be able to utilize government transports. Heading home to Alabama on horseback, Clayton Wilson made it to Bladen County, North Carolina, on April 23 when he discovered that his horse's back was in too bad of a condition to continue. He decided to rest for a week for the animal to heal, but a month later he remained in North Carolina. Finally, on May 22 he could wait no longer and decided to sign a parole so that he might catch a steamer out of Wilmington and draw rations.[96]

By mid-June, at least some white Southerners had begun to wonder about the number of Confederates who continued to arrive at paroling stations throughout the South. One man observed that the daily crowds at the Macon, Georgia, provost marshal's office seemed to exceed the entire active force of the Confederate armies. He wondered where they had come from, to which another quipped, "Why, don't you see from the mud on their sleeves and breeches, that they are just out of the swamp!" Although the newspaper described this comment as "facetious," perhaps it was closer to the truth than many former Confederates cared to acknowledge. The paper continued, "When a full return of all Confederates who have been paroled since the surrenders of General Lee and Johnston shall be made, it will present some curious statistics, more flattering, perhaps, to the numerical strength than the moral heroism of the Southern people. We shall then be able to learn, not what was the available, but the unavailable force of the South."[97]

An Army of Northern Virginia soldier's presence at Appomattox served as testament to his devotion to the cause—proof that he was among those who had either survived or remained in the ranks until that final day. In the decades following the war, veterans could point to the tattered and treasured parole passes bearing one of the three decorative designs printed only at Appomattox as evidence of their loyalty to the end. Additional verification appeared in 1887 when the *Southern Historical Society Papers* published what it described as a master list of the 26,950 men paroled at Appomattox.[98] Whether on the list or bearing a pass, those who surrendered at Appomattox could claim to be among those Lee described as the "brave survivors of so many hard fought battles."[99]

But for many of those who had escaped or eluded capture at the time of surrender, defiance served as proof of their status as die-hard rebels. Benjamin Washington Jones of the Surry Light Artillery Battery had been among those who had absconded across the James on April 9. Years later, he remained fiercely proud that he and several of his comrades "did not undergo the humiliation of a surrender; we were not paroled; and some have never assented to the 'oath of allegiance.'"[100] The 1932 obituary of Jones's comrade Charles Coker Richardson proudly asserted that he "never surrendered" but "left Appomattox without having laid down his arms."[101] When asked years later what the greatest moment of his military career was, Thomas Rosser responded "without hesitation" that it was his successful charge at Appomattox, after which he "left that fatal field in triumph, refusing to surrender either myself or my command to the enemy."[102] And in a piece for the *Confederate Veteran* in 1902, N. B. Bowyer observed that he did not know how many members of his old regiment surrendered at Appomattox; "I only know that I did not, nor have I surrendered yet." Whether it was a purposeful omission or the effects of old age on his memory, Bowyer had not been entirely honest. In fact he had turned himself in to Union authorities at Charleston, West Virginia, on May 26, 1865.[103]

In the years and decades that followed 1865, the debate about how many men Lee had fielded at Appomattox became a crucial component of the Lost Cause. In memoirs, veterans' speeches, and the pages of periodicals such as the *Southern Historical Society Papers* and *Confederate Veteran*, former Confederates pointed out that they had been vastly outnumbered, overwhelmed by superior Union resources and manpower rather than defeated in battle. The paradox was that in describing how few men remained in Lee's lines on April 9, they underscored how many were not there.

NOTES

I would like to thank the following individuals for their help with this essay: Gary W. Gallagher, Trevor Plante, Keith Bohannon, Patrick Schroeder, Ernie Price, Michael Musick, Allison Kraft, and Zachary Elledge.

1. N. B. Bowyer, "Reminiscences of Appomattox," *Confederate Veteran* 10, no. 2 (February 1902): 77–78.

Caroline E. Janney

2. David G. McIntosh Diary, April 9, 1865, Virginia Historical Society, Richmond (hereafter cited as VHS).

3. John H. Chamberlayne and C. G. Chamberlayne, *Ham Chamberlayne, Virginian: Letters and Papers of an Artillery Officer in the War for Southern Independence, 1861–1865* (Richmond, Va.: Dietz Print. Co, 1932), 320–22. Chamberlayne wrote two letters to his brother and sister on April 12. They are slightly different but contain similar sentiments. Both are quoted here.

4. U.S. War Department, *The War of the Rebellion: A Compilation of the Official Records of the Union and Confederate Armies*, 127 vols., index, and atlas (Washington, D.C.: Government Printing Office, 1880–1901), ser. 1, 46 (3): 665 (hereafter cited as *OR*).

5. *Wheeling (W.Va.) Daily Intelligencer*, May 13, 1865.

6. Confederate troop strength is very difficult to determine, especially because so many of the records were destroyed during the final campaign. My numbers are based on a close reading of the *OR* along with the work of other historians. Gary W. Gallagher argues that on April 2, "the Army of Northern Virginia and miscellaneous units from the Richmond defenses (including a battalion of sailors) almost certainly approached, and perhaps exceeded, 60,000 men of all arms." Gary W. Gallagher, "An End and a New Beginning," in *Appomattox Court House*, by the U.S. National Park Service (Harpers Ferry, W.Va.: Division of Publications of the National Park Service, 2003), 42, 56. Chris M. Calkins estimates Lee's strength at 58,400 at the beginning of the Appomattox campaign. Chris M. Calkins, *The Final Bivouac: The Surrender Parade at Appomattox and the Disbanding of the Armies, April 10–May 20, 1865* (Lynchburg, Va.: H. E. Howard, 1988), 208. Finally, William Marvel states that "between 51,200 and 57,200 men should have begun the retreat." He observes that thousands deserted during the evacuation but that when Lee united the Confederate units that had occupied the defenses around Petersburg with those from Richmond at Amelia Court House, "he probably collected about 45,000 men . . . not counting the naval battalion that joined him there." These numbers do not include detached units such as Mosby's. For an in-depth analysis of Lee's troop strength, see William Marvel, *Lee's Last Retreat: The Flight to Appomattox* (Chapel Hill: University of North Carolina Press, 2002), 201–6. For the 11,530 Confederate casualties between Sutherland Station (April 2) and the final battle at Appomattox Court House (April 9), see Chris M. Calkins, *The Appomattox Campaign, March 29–April 9, 1865* (Lynchburg, Va.: Schroeder Publications, 2008), 201–02. It is likewise unclear precisely how many men Union authorities paroled at Appomattox. The numbers range from 26,000 to 28,231. *OR*, ser. 1, 46 (3): 851–53, 1279.

7. For more on the spiraling morale and rising desertions in Lee's army throughout the winter of 1864–65, see Joseph T. Glatthaar, *General Lee's Army: From Victory to Collapse* (New York: Free Press, 2008), 440–51. Glatthaar points out that "although Lee picked up an almost equal number through prisoner exchange in late February, most of those men were unfit for field duty."

8. Marvel, *Lee's Last Retreat*, 202; *OR*, ser. 1, 46 (3): 529.

9. Robert L. Stewart, *History of the One Hundred and Fortieth Regiment Pennsylvania Volunteers* (Philadelphia: published by authority of the Regimental Association, 1912), 274.

10. Joseph H. Prime to Darling, April 8, 1865, item DL1247, John L. Nau III Civil War Collection, Houston, Tex. Historian William Marvel likewise notes that "the farther

away Lee's soldiers lived from the campaign theater, the less likely they were to leave the ranks," pointing out that "the Virginia regiments suffered the greatest average attrition." Marvel, *Lee's Last Retreat*, 205–6.

11. Benjamin Sims Journal, April 1–2, 7, 1865, North Carolina Division of Archives and History, Raleigh.

12. William Andrew Mauney, transcript of "A Diary of the War between the States," entries April 3–23, 1865, Museum of the Confederacy, Richmond, Va. (hereafter cited as MOC). A note to future researchers: the collections of the MOC are in the process of being moved to the Virginia Historical Society in Richmond as of January 2016.

13. Richard M. Coffman and Kurt D. Graham, *To Honor These Men: A History of the Phillips Georgia Legion Infantry Battalion* (Macon, Ga.: Mercer University Press, 2007), 420–21.

14. Armistead C. Gordon, ed., *Memories and Memorials of William Gordon McCabe*, 2 vols. (Richmond, Va.: Old Dominion Press, 1925), 2:292 (letter dated April 11, 1865).

15. *OR*, ser. 1, 46 (1): 1303–4; Edward G. Longacre, *Fitz Lee: A Military Biography of Major General Fitzhugh Lee, C.S.A.* (Boston: Da Capo Press, 2006), 185.

16. Marvel, *Lee's Last Retreat*, 177–78; Longacre, *Fitz Lee*, 185–86.

17. The precise number of cavalry that escaped is difficult to determine. For various estimates see, Gallagher, "An End and a New Beginning," 66; Calkins, *Appomattox Campaign*, 200; and Thomas L. Livermore, *Numbers and Losses in the Civil War in America, 1861–65* (1900; repr., Carlisle, Penn.: John Kallman, 1996), 137. Among the cavalry, only W. H. F. "Rooney" Lee's division did not escape in its entirety.

18. Festus P. Summers, ed. *Borderland Confederate* (Pittsburgh: University of Pittsburgh Press, 1962), 105–6 (diary entry for April 9, 1865).

19. Diary of Hiram W. Harding, April 9, 1865, MOC. There is no record of parole found in Hiram W. Harding's Compiled Service Record (hereafter cited as CSR), although this does not necessarily mean he was never paroled. CSR for Hiram W. Harding, M324, National Archives and Records Administration, Washington, D.C. (hereafter cited as NARA). All CSRs were accessed through Fold3, but I have also included the microfilm number from NARA.

20. Douglas Southall Freeman, *R. E. Lee: A Biography*, 4 vols. (New York: Charles Scribner's Sons, 1934–35), 4:130; Marvel, *Lee's Last Retreat*, 178–79. This included repatriated prisoners who were especially fearful of returning to the Union prisons should the parole terms not hold.

21. Samuel H. Gray and Richard B. Harwell, *A Confederate Diary of the Retreat from Petersburg, April 3–20, 1865* (Atlanta: Library, Emory University, 1953), 17 (diary entry April 9, 1865).

22. Lewis T. Nunallee, postwar memoir/diary, entries April 9–20, 1865, MOC. Nunallee's name is alternatively spelled "Nunnallee" and "Nunnellee." Shoemaker's Battery was also known as the Stuart Horse Artillery, Beauregard Rifles, and Lynchburg Beauregards.

23. Charles C. Richardson, "A Few Reminiscences of My Experience in the Civil War, as a Confederate Soldier and Member of the Surry Light Brigade," Appomattox Court House National Historic Park (hereafter cited as APCO) Going Home research files. I

Caroline E. Janney

would like to extend my sincerest thanks to Ernie Price and Patrick Schroeder at APCO for graciously sharing their research files with me.

24. J. E. Whitehorne Diary, April 9, 1865, Southern Historical Society Collection, University of North Carolina, Chapel Hill (hereafter cited as SHC). Numerous contemporary accounts suggest that there were approximately 8,000 to 10,000 "infantry with arms." See, for example, Robert E. Lee's report in *OR*, ser. 1, 46 (1): 1266–67; and Kena King Chapman Diary, April 9, 1865, SHC. Historian Joseph T. Glatthaar likewise notes that "only 7,892 infantrymen and a couple thousand artillery and cavalry kept up with the army." Glatthaar, *General Lee's Army*, 470.

25. Dewitt Boyd Stone Jr., ed., *Wandering to Glory: Confederate Veterans Remember Evans's Brigade* (Columbia: University of South Carolina Press, 2002), 244. Robertson incorrectly states the date of the 23rd South Carolina's arrival as April 7 rather than April 9.

26. John Walters, *Norfolk Blues: The Civil War Diary of the Norfolk Light Artillery Blues*, ed. Kenneth Wiley (Shippensburg, Pa.: Burd Street Press, 1997), 224 (diary entry April 9, 1865).

27. Frank Potts, *The Death of the Confederacy: The Last Week of the Army of Northern Virginia as Set Forth in a Letter of April, 1865* (Richmond, Va.: privately printed, 1928), 5.

28. Jedediah Hotchkiss, *Make Me a Map of the Valley: The Civil War Journal of Stonewall Jackson's Topographer*, ed. Archie P. McDonald (Dallas: Southern Methodist University Press, 1973), 266 (diary entry April 12, 1865).

29. *The Papers of Ulysses S. Grant*, ed. John Y. Simon and others, 32 vols. to date (Carbondale: Southern Illinois University Press, 1967–), 14:385 (hereafter cited as *PUSG*).

30. "Paroles of the Army of Northern Virginia: Statement of Brigadier General W. P. Roberts as to His Staff and Command," in *Southern Historical Society Papers*, ed. J. William Jones and others, 52 vols. (Richmond, Va.: Southern Historical Society, 1876–1959), 18: 386–88 (hereafter cited as *SHSP*); CSR for W. P. Roberts, M331, NARA.

31. *SHSP*, 15:448–49.

32. *OR*, ser. 1, 46 (3): 685.

33. Hancock received orders on April 10 from Secretary Stanton to print and circulate the correspondence between Grant and Lee on the surrender of the Army of Northern Virginia and to offer the same terms as given to Lee. *OR*, ser. 1, 3 (46): 699.

34. *Daily National Republican*, April 14, 1865; Richard R. Duncan, *Beleaguered Winchester: A Virginia Community at War, 1861–1865* (Baton Rouge: Louisiana State University Press, 2007), 252; "Diary and Recollections of I. Norval Baker," in Garland R. Quarles, *Diaries, Letters, and Recollections of the War between the States* (Winchester, Va.: Winchester-Frederick County Historical Society, 1955), 122.

35. *OR*, ser. 1, 46 (3): 685, 701. The negotiations between Mosby and Hancock proved extensive, with meetings between their respective aids occurring over several days.

36. The number of 2,231 is found in Record Group 109, Records of the War Department Collection of Confederate Records (hereafter cited as RG 109), Parole Rolls of Confederates, entry 212 (hereafter cited as entry 212), box 42, Farmville folder, NARA. Chris Calkins indicates that 2,383 men were paroled at Farmville, including 582 patients,

22 officers in the institute, 34 detailed hospital attendants, 4 hospital stewards, and 1,742 men "from the field at Appomattox." Calkins, *Final Bivouac*, 208.

37. CSR for John N. Barnett, M267, NARA. Barnett was released from the Federal hospital at Burkeville on May 30, 1865.

38. CSR for Wm. Gaston Lewis, M331, ibid. Several sources indicate that Lewis was wounded and "captured at Farmville, Virginia, on April 7, 1865." See, for example, Ezra J. Warner, *Generals in Gray: Lives of the Confederate Commanders* (Baton Rouge: Louisiana State University Press, 1959), 187. This appears, however, to be a misreading of the CSR. The service record indicates that he was paroled at some point between April 11 and 21 and that he appeared on a roll of prisoners at the U.S. Hospital in Farmville from April 7 to June 15, 1865. A register for the CSA General Hospital in Farmville notes that he was admitted on or prior to April 10, 1865.

39. RG 109, entry 212, box 42, Farmville folder, NARA; CSR for S. S. Keeling, M347, NARA.

40. RG 109, entry 212, box 42, Farmville folder, NARA.

41. Ibid.; CSR for Bradford Ivy, M266, NARA.

42. RG 109, entry 212, box 42, Farmville folder, NARA; CSR for J. B. O'Neal, M270, NARA; CSR for T. J. Howell, M324, NARA.

43. Calkins, *Final Bivouac*, 208.

44. *OR*, ser. 1, 46 (3): 796. My survey of 2,839 parolees from Lynchburg between April 12 and April 17 indicates that least 1,085 were able-bodied men — more than an entire regiment even in the earliest days of the war. RG 109, entry 212, box 43, NARA.

45. RG 109, entry 212, box 43, Lynchburg folder, NARA.

46. Ibid.; *SHSP* 15:56–57.

47. Thomas Rosser to Veterans of the Old Dominion broadside, April 12, 1865, Scrapbook of Betty Winston Rosser, Thomas L. Rosser Papers, Accession #1171, a-b, box 2, Albert and Shirley Small Special Collections Library, University of Virginia, Charlottesville (hereafter cited as UVA); Millard K. Bushong and Dean M. Bushong, *Fightin' Tom Rosser, C.S.A.* (Shippensburg, Pa.: Beidel Printing House, 1983), 182–83; Thomas L. Rosser, *Riding with Rosser*, ed. S. Roger Keller (Shippensburg, Pa.: Burd Street Press, 1997), 73–74.

48. There is an extensive literature on Confederate nationalism. See, for example, Richard Beringer, Herman Hattaway, Archer Jones, and William N. Still Jr., *Why the South Lost the Civil War* (Athens: University of Georgia Press, 1986), 36–62; Drew Gilpin Faust, *The Creation of Confederate Nationalism: Ideology and Identity in the Civil War South* (Baton Rouge: Louisiana State University Press, 1988); Gary W. Gallagher, *The Confederate War: How Popular Will, Nationalism, and Military Strategy Could Not Stave Off Defeat* (Cambridge, Mass.: Harvard University Press, 1997), 63–111; Jacqueline Glass Campbell, *When Sherman Marched North from the Sea: Resistance on the Confederate Home Front* (Chapel Hill: University of North Carolina Press, 2003), 12–13, 15, 71–74, 91–98, 101–4; Anne Sarah Rubin, *A Shattered Nation: The Rise and Fall of the Confederacy, 1861–1868* (Chapel Hill: University of North Carolina Press, 2005), 2–7; Aaron Sheehan-Dean, *Why Confederates Fought: Family and Nation in Civil War Virginia* (Chapel Hill: University of North Carolina Press, 2007), 9–10, 59–62, 70–71; and Paul Quigley, *Shifting Grounds: Nationalism and the American South, 1848–1865* (New York: Oxford University Press, 2012).

Caroline E. Janney

49. Major Thomas J. Rowland letters, April 12 and 28, 1865, MOC.

50. On die-hard rebels, see Jason Philips, *Diehard Rebels: The Confederate Culture of Invincibility* (Athens: University of Georgia Press, 2007).

51. Gray and Harwell, *Confederate Diary of the Retreat from Petersburg*, 19 (diary entry April 12, 1865).

52. Benjamin W. Jones, Lee A. Wallace, and Barbara Long, *Under the Stars and Bars: A History of the Surry Light Artillery: Recollections of a Private Soldier in the War between the States* (Dayton, Ohio: Morningside Bookshop, 1975), 266–72; CSR of George C. Holmes, M324, NARA. Holmes would not be released until July 1, 1865.

53. Jones, Wallace, and Long, *Under the Stars and Bars*, 266–72.

54. Richardson, "Few Reminiscences of My Experience in the Civil War."

55. *OR*, ser. 2, 8:488.

56. CSR of George C. Holmes, M324, NARA.

57. Jones, Wallace, and Long, *Under the Stars and Bars*, 274–76.

58. John Kerr Oakes Reminiscences, Collected by the Virginia Sesquicentennial of the American Civil War and the Danville Local Sesquicentennial Committee, Virginia file, APCO Going Home research files.

59. *OR*, ser. 1, 49 (1): 551.

60. Diary of Caldwell Calhoun Buckner, entries April 9–May 16, 1865, in Papers Chiefly Pertaining to Virginia, 1803–1904, Accession #8995, UVA; Richard L. Armstrong, *7th Virginia Cavalry*, 2nd ed. (Lynchburg, Va.: H. E. Howard, 1992), 120. Buckner's CSR does not indicate whether he ever received a parole (CSR for C. C. Buckner, M324, NARA), but his diary notes that he had decided to take the oath on May 16, and his papers show that he did so on May 31.

61. RG 109, entry 212, box 41, Burkeville folder, NARA.

62. Ibid., box 43, Richmond folder.

63. For example, on April 17, General Orders No. 27 from the District of Eastern Virginia announced that the same terms of capitulation would be extended to any of Lee's officers and soldiers who were not present at Appomattox. All they need do was come within the lines of the U.S. forces "at or near Norfolk, Va., laying down their arms and receiving their paroles." *OR*, ser. 1 46 (3): 816.

64. Hotchkiss, *Make Me a Map of the Valley*, 267.

65. RG 109, entry 212, box 43, NARA. Included among the 1st Maryland Cavalry (CSA) were Companies A, B, D, E, and K.

66. Berkeley and Jefferson Counties both refused to recognize their inclusion into the state of West Virginia. An 1866 mandate by Congress and a Supreme Court case ultimately forced them to become part of the new state. Mark A Snell, *West Virginia and the Civil War* (Charleston, S.C.: History Press, 2011), 187.

67. RG 109, entry 212, box 44, NARA; *OR*, ser. 1, 46 (3): 897, 904; Jeffery D. Wert, *Mosby's Rangers: The True Adventures of the Most Famous Command of the Civil War* (New York: Simon and Schuster, 1990), 281–91. Wert notes that "at least 779 members of the 43rd Battalion were paroled out by the end of June 1865." Mosby would likewise finally surrender in late June.

68. Fitz Lee had recommended a brigadier's rank for Munford, but the Confederate Congress had not yet confirmed the appointment. Edward G. Longacre, *Lee's*

Cavalrymen: A History of the Mounted Forces of the Army of Northern Virginia, 1861–1865 (Mechanicsburg, Pa.: Stackpole Books, 2002), 322.

69. Thomas T. Munford, Special Orders No. 6, April 21, 1865, Confederate Military Leaders Collection, MOC.

70. "Diary and Recollections of I. Norval Baker," 122–23.

71. RG 109, entry 212, box 41, District of Eastern Virginia folder, NARA.

72. CSR of Benjamin Sims, M324, NARA.

73. RG 109, entry 212, box 42, NARA.

74. Gordon, *Memories and Memorials of William Gordon McCabe*, 1:292–93 (letter dated April 25, 1865).

75. For examples of Army of Northern Virginia men announcing Lee's surrender to Johnston's army, see Mark L. Bradley, *This Astounding Close: The Road to Bennett Place* (Chapel Hill: University of North Carolina Press, 2000), 150, 152, 153.

76. Lt. Lewis T. Nunallee, postwar memoir/diary, entry April 20, 1865, MOC.

77. Daniel T. Balfour, *13th Virginia Cavalry* (Lynchburg, Va.: H. E. Howard, 1986), 45; CSR for R. L. Judkins, M324, NARA; CSR for St. George T. Mason, M324, NARA; RG 109, entry 212, boxes 30 and 35, NARA.

78. Constance Pendleton, ed., *Confederate Memoirs: Early Life and Family History [of] William Frederic Pendleton [and] Mary Lawson Young Pendleton* (Bryan Athyn, Pa.: n.p., 1958), 16–21 (diary entries April 5–22, 1865), 78–80.

79. Rosser describes the place as "Swope's Depot," while others refer to it as "Swoope's." Rosser, *Riding with Rosser*, 74.

80. George W. Munford to Mrs. Elizabeth T. Munford, April 28, 1865, Munford-Ellis Family Papers, William R. Perkins Library, Duke University; General Orders No. 4 issued by Thomas L. Rosser, April 28, 1865, Confederate Military Leaders Collection, MOC.

81. *Journal of Capt. Jed Hotchkiss* reprinted in *OR*, ser. 1, 46 (1): 522–23. Hotchkiss's published diary, *Make Me a Map of the Valley*, ends with the diary entry for April 18, 1865. For material that goes through May 8, 1865, readers should consult the *OR*.

82. *OR*, ser. 1, 46 (3): 1095.

83. RG 393, part 1, entry 2076, Military Division of the James, Letters Received, April–June 1865, NARA; *OR*, ser. 1, 46 (3): 1088–89.

84. *OR*, ser. 1, 46 (3): 1104.

85. Ibid., 1117.

86. *PUSG*, 15:31.

87. *OR*, ser. 1, 46 (1): 1324.

88. *PUSG*, 14:419.

89. As of May 11, Union soldiers were no longer authorized to search the countryside for Confederate soldiers who had not surrendered. *OR*, ser. 1, 46 (3): 1136.

90. RG 109, entry 212, box 43, Various Locations file, NARA; CSR for Thomas A. Somers, Albert Sommers, and James H. Prince, M324, NARA.

91. RG 109, entry 212, boxes 41–44, NARA.

92. George W. Munford to Mrs. Elizabeth T. Munford, May 9, 1865, Munford-Ellis Family Papers; RG 109, entry 212, box 43, Lynchburg folder, NARA; Bell Irwin Wiley, ed., *Recollections of a Confederate Staff Officer* (Jackson, Tenn.: McCowat-Mercer Press, 1958), 276.

93. Lewis T. Nunallee, postwar memoir/diary, entry April 20, 1865, MOC; CSR, John J. Shoemaker, M324, NARA.

94. Gordon, *Memories and Memorials of William Gordon McCabe*, 1:294 (letter dated May 21, 1865); CSR for William Gordon McCabe, NARA. In response to the number of paroled (and likely unparoled) Confederates congregating in Washington, D.C., and Baltimore on April 22, Attorney General James Speed issued an opinion stating in part that Confederate soldiers who appeared in public in uniform were violating their paroles and therefore could be arrested and detained. *OR*, ser. 1, 3 (46): 918–20.

95. Chamberlayne and Chamberlayne, *Ham Chamberlayne*, 324, 327.

96. Diary of Clayton Wilson, April 23–May 22, 1865, APCO Going Home research files.

97. *Macon Journal* reprinted in the *Columbia Daily Phoenix*, June 24, 1865.

98. Elizabeth R. Varon, *Appomattox: Victory, Defeat, and Freedom at the End of the Civil War* (New York: Oxford University Press, 2013), 111; John M. Coski, "We Are All to Be Paroled," *Museum of the Confederacy Magazine*, Fall 2011, 5–9. Historians have noted numerous problems with the *SHSP* list, including men counted twice and others who were omitted. For the most thorough list, see William G. Nine and Ronald G. Wilson, *The Appomattox Paroles, April 9–15, 1865* (Lynchburg, Va.: H. E. Howard, 1989).

99. General Orders No. 9, Lee's Farewell to the Army of Northern Virginia in Calkins, *Final Bivouac*, 1.

100. Jones, Wallace, and Long, *Under the Stars and Bars*, 263–64.

101. Unidentified newspaper clipping, Charles Coker Richardson materials, Virginia, APCO Going Home research files.

102. Quoted in *Fightin' Tom Rosser*, 184.

103. Bowyer, "Reminiscences of Appomattox," 77–78; CSR of N. B. Bowyer, M324, NARA.

Sheridan's *Personal Memoirs* and the Appomattox Campaign

Stephen Cushman

"Dear Sir: / I beg to introduce you to Mr. C. L. Webster, who may not succeed with the conspiracy which he has in mind, but I very much hope he *will*." Dated December 26, 1884, in Hartford, Connecticut, this brief letter from Mark Twain to fifty-three-year-old Philip H. Sheridan apparently envisioned the writing of what would become the two-volume *Personal Memoirs of P. H. Sheridan*, published in New York by Twain's firm, Charles L. Webster and Company, in 1888, each spine bearing the general's four-star insignia, each cover stamped with a gilt image of hat-waving Sheridan on galloping Rienzi.[1] Seventeen months before Twain penned this letter, the *North American Review* had published Sheridan's brief essay "The Last Days of the Rebellion," consisting of ten pages of text and a full-page map.[2] Covering the six-day period from April 4 to April 9, 1865, Sheridan's essay—presumably among the promptings for Twain's query—formed the basis for the general's expanded narrative of the Appomattox campaign in the second volume of his *Memoirs*, where it runs for about eighty pages, from the fifth through the eighth chapters. Sheridan's narrative of the Appomattox campaign will occupy the second part of this discussion, but fuller understanding and appreciation of both that narrative and its narrator can begin productively with some remarks about Sheridan's first volume and the context in which he undertook, at Twain's instigation, to write it.

Sheridan's *Personal Memoirs* was the last of the memoirs published by the triumphant triumvirate of the U.S. Army high command. D. Appleton and Company had published William T. Sherman's *Memoirs of General William T. Sherman* in 1875, and Charles L. Webster followed with Ulysses S. Grant's *Personal Memoirs of U. S. Grant*, issuing the first volume in 1885 and the second in 1886, the same year in which Sherman brought out a second, expanded edition of his work.[3] Of the three memoirs, Grant's sold best and continues to sell best, with Sherman's coming in second. Both are still available in various editions, and the Library of America offers them together in a boxed set. Sheridan's memoirs have had a different, not so radiant career. One can offer several explanations for the more temperate reception of Sheridan's memoirs, both at the end of the nineteenth century and now, including the argument that Grant and Sherman were and are the more important historical figures or that Grant's and Sherman's memoirs have more literary merit. Despite the opening disclaimer of Sheridan's preface, "I make no pretension to literary merit" (*Memoirs*, 1:xiii), I hope to show that his memoirs have considerable literary merit, too, as they offer readers many richly textured glimpses of moments and subjects that have no counterparts in Grant's and Sherman's accounts. More important for the moment is the formulation that in the case of these memoirs by the three most famous architects of U.S. victory, one cannot separate the shaping of Civil War memory from the realities of book publishing and market demand at the end of the nineteenth century.

No one was more finely tuned to those realities than Mark Twain. Hoping to build on the success of Grant's *Personal Memoirs*, Twain courted Sheridan by sending him a special presentation copy of Grant's recently published book. In a notebook entry of November 1885, Twain jotted, "Send full morocco to Sherman & Sheridan, with their names printed in gilt on them." This gift followed one that Twain had given Sheridan eight months earlier, a copy of the first American edition of *Huckleberry Finn*, also published by Webster and Company. It bore this inscription:

> To the General's boys
> this book is offered
> with the compliments of
> The Author
> New York, March 21, 1885.[4]

In betting that Sheridan's memoirs would succeed in the same market as Grant's, Twain was not alone. The late 1880s appeared to be Sheridan's moment, as the "Publisher's Note" to *"Little Phil" and His Troopers: The Life of Gen. Philip H. Sheridan: Its Romance and Reality* (1888), written by Frank A. Burr and Richard J. Hinton, made clear:

> The story of the life of General Sheridan seemed to the publishers of this volume a matter of public interest well worth recording. He had

had a great and romantic career. At the time the work was first contemplated there was a possibility of his being the candidate of a great
political party for President of the United States, if not in '88, perhaps
in '92. However this might be, the publishers believed that the public
would fully appreciate a Life of Sheridan, and that it would meet with
a substantial sale. They therefore entered upon the work of furnishing
it. It was the intention to have thus honored Sheridan while he was
living. There was no popular life written that the publishers knew of,
nor any intimation of one, and the General's *Memoirs* had not been
announced.

In other words, the publishers of *"Little Phil" and His Troopers* smelled the
same potentially lucrative return that Twain did at precisely the same moment. With the death of Sheridan on August 5, 1888, at the age of fifty-seven,
the publishers "deemed it wise to delay the work to enable them to include the
events in the last sad chapters of the General's career," adding that they had
"considered the life and services of General Sheridan, as they would those of
Washington, Lincoln, or Grant, a matter of public record and of public interest, and have endeavored to do the work with honor to the General and credit
to themselves—and without detriment to others."[5]

Sheridan is no longer grouped with Washington and Lincoln on anybody's list, but that he once was associated with these two presidents, and
considered a possible successor to them, shows the risk of our twenty-first-
century perspective contracting into myopia. Still, high as Sheridan's star
may have risen by 1888, his book would have to compete in a market that
was quickly becoming saturated by Civil War memoirs, as Frederick J. Hall,
assistant to Charles L. Webster and later one-third partner of the company,
warned Mark Twain. Like Twain, Hall was aware of the potential benefits of
giving Sheridan's book the same *Personal Memoirs* title as Grant's, thereby
linking the two works in the minds of book buyers. But in a letter of May 19,
1887, he also wrote that "the way we handle [Sheridan's book] will either increase the good reputation made on the 'Grant Memoirs' or destroy it." Hall
continued that "people are so tired of 'war-literature' that something extraordinary is required to command large sales," adding that "General Sheridan
will probably take Grant's 'Memoirs' as the standard by which to judge of the
success of his own."[6] In a letter of October 15, 1888, Hall compounded this
sour dose of the reality principle: "There is one thing this trip has convinced
me of viz: *war literature of any kind and no matter by whom written is played
out*. We have got to hustle everlastingly to get rid of 75,000 sets of Sheridan.

Stephen Cushman

I had set my mind on 100,000 sets but am forced to lessen this figure. There is not a man today who could write another book on the war and sell 5000 in the whole country."[7]

Those tempted to dismiss Sheridan's memoirs—sometimes without reading them—as less important than Grant's or Sherman's might sharpen their historical awareness of that dismissal by pondering the extent to which it simply repeats and continues Gilded Age fatigue with books by Civil War generals. Then, as now, some will read Grant's 1,200 pages (its length in the original Webster edition) with absorbed eagerness; some fewer will tackle 800 more by Sherman. But only a resilient remnant will then move on to another 1,000 by Sheridan. The timing of Sheridan's death meant that he did not live to see whether Fred Hall's pessimistic sales predictions were fulfilled. Like Grant, Sheridan barely had time to finish his memoirs, sending them off to Webster on March 23, 1888, and suffering a severe heart attack, the first of many, two months later on May 22.[8] The preface in which he denies all pretension to literary merit was dated a mere three days before his death. But knowingly or not, he did fulfill Hall's prophecy that he would take Grant's *Personal Memoirs* as his standard, if not for judging the success of sales he did not see, then as a model for how to write his memoirs. True, he had other models available to him as well, including George B. McClellan's *McClellan's Own Story* (1887), for a copy of which Sheridan thanked Webster in a letter of December 7, 1886.[9] But when Twain sent Sheridan the morocco-bound, gilt-stamped copy of Grant's book, he gave him a star by which to steer.

Sheridan the writer went about the business of writing in much the same way that Sheridan the soldier went about the business of soldiering. In a letter of December 21, 1886, he acknowledged receipt of a contract for the memoirs and told Webster, "I am going right along with the book + will push it especially after the new year. I have a pretty good start on it now."[10] This tone of confident competence echoed the emerging, and dominant, can-do tone of the memoirs. By the time Sheridan's most recent readers arrive at his narrative of the Appomattox campaign, they will have seen instance after instance in which he found himself faced with a new challenge, developed a strategy or technique for meeting it, and implemented that strategy or technique effectively. Examples are legion, but some of the most intriguing involve—not surprisingly in the case of someone teaching himself how to tell his own story—successful uses of languages or methods of communication. While serving in Texas at Fort Duncan during 1854, for example, Sheridan's "constant association" with a Mexican guide enabled him "to pick up in a short time a smattering of the Spanish language, which was very useful to one serving on that frontier" (*Memoirs*, 1:20). Likewise, when in negotiations with hungry Coquille Indians living near Yaquina Bay, Oregon Territory, in the summer of 1856, Sheridan "talked in the Chinook language all the day long," having "learned at an early day to speak Chinook (the 'court language' among the coast tribes) almost as well as the Indians themselves" (1:102, 106).

This picture of Sheridan teaching himself fluent Chinook, along with many passages in which he observes, often with fascination or sympathy or both, the customs and behavior of northwestern tribes between 1853 and 1861, should complicate, if not correct, the later, reductive image of Sheridan the Indian killer. This simplistic caricature derives from a remark attributed to him by Edward Sylvester Ellis in 1869 at Fort Cobb, in what later became Oklahoma: "The only good Indians I ever saw were dead."[11] Usually, and infamously, rendered, "The only good Indian is a dead Indian," such a remark was certainly not beyond Sheridan, who, as Burr and Hinton remarked, was "restless, full of the combative quality, not politic in language." But his apocryphal remark at Fort Cobb should be considered alongside a sentence from the memoirs such as this one, about the Rogue River Indians: "When I saw them, fifteen years later, transformed into industrious and substantial farmers, with neat houses, fine cattle, wagons and horses, carrying their grain, eggs, and butter to market and bringing home flour, coffee, sugar, and calico in return, I found abundant confirmation of my early opinion that the most effectual measures for lifting them from a state of barbarism would be a practical supervision at the outset, coupled with a firm control and mild discipline" (*Memoirs*, 1:119–20).[12] The phrase "lifting them from a state of barbarism" may not strike twenty-first-century sensibilities as reassuringly enlightened, but this carefully controlled, complex sentence shows that Sheridan could be thoughtful and politic in language when it suited him.

To put it another way, Sheridan was a man of many tongues. He could speak the language of humor, often self-deprecating, as in the two-page story of his astonishment ("a mild way of putting it") upon learning that two women, disguised as soldiers, had been serving under him and were discovered only when "these Amazons . . . secured a supply of 'apple-jack' by some means, got very drunk, and on the return had fallen into Stone[s] River and been nearly drowned" (*Memoirs*, 1:254). He could also speak the lyrical language of aesthetic appreciation, as in his description of watching the 26th Ohio and 15th Indiana moving at dusk during the battle of Missionary Ridge, November 25, 1863: "Just as they reached the crest of the ridge the moon rose from behind, enlarged by the refraction of the atmosphere, and as the attacking column passed along the summit it crossed the moon's disk and disclosed

Stephen Cushman

to us below a most interesting panorama, every figure nearly being thrown out in full relief" (1:315).

An especially noteworthy instance of Sheridan's polyglot shape-shifting came with an anecdote that can serve as a larger parable for his various capabilities, verbal and otherwise, an anecdote of his working with oxen while engaged in the "tedious and laborious" toil of building a road (the double adjective connected by "and" is a Sheridan signature) "across the coast mountains from King's Valley to the Siletz [River]" sometime after he was assigned to Fort Haskins (his consistent version of "Hoskins") in July 1856. The road freshly completed, Sheridan set out to "demonstrate its value practically" by starting "a Government wagon over it loaded with about fifteen hundred pounds of freight drawn by six yoke of oxen." After the wagon had gone about seven miles, the sergeant in charge reported to Sheridan that he could go no farther. "Taking up a whip myself, I directed the men to lay on their gads," Sheridan recalled. This personal intervention had no effect on "the demoralized oxen," however. At this point Sheridan's narrative took an illuminating turn: "but following as a last resort an example I heard of on a former occasion, that brought into use the rough language of the country, I induced the oxen to move with alacrity, and the wagon and contents were speedily carried to the summit." The key, it turned out once again, was language: "The whole trouble was at once revealed: the oxen had been broken and trained by a man who, when they were in a pinch, had encouraged them by his frontier vocabulary, and they could not realize what was expected of them under extraordinary conditions until they heard familiar and possibly profanely urgent phrases" (Memoirs, 1:96–97).

A signal achievement of Sheridan's Personal Memoirs, one of distinct literary merit, was the creation of its protagonist, Phil Sheridan. "Camerado, this is no book, / Who touches this touches a man." These lines come from Walt Whitman's 1860 poem "So Long!," but they could serve aptly as an epigraph for Sheridan's Personal Memoirs.[13] Not only did he offer his readers many homely, personal, flesh-and-blood details, such as his enjoyment of a good night's sleep or a particular meal when keenly hungry (for example, Memoirs, 1:17, 39, 64, 199, 288); Sheridan could also be boldly and disarmingly frank about himself, and with the anecdote of the demoralized oxen, he established his credentials as a speaker of—in addition to Spanish and Chinook—"possibly profanely urgent phrases" under "extraordinary conditions." The sly wink of nineteenth-century circumlocution still does its work effectively, and one has no trouble imagining that in high gear Sheridan could sear the auditory nerve, whereas one faces many obstacles in imagining, say,

Joseph E. Johnston doing the same after a reading of his always decorous, tamped-down *Narrative of Military Operations*, published by D. Appleton and Company in 1874. Like a skilled novelist, once he had characterized his protagonist Phil Sheridan this way, Sheridan the writer could later call up plentiful resonance by lightly touching the same chord, as when, in volume 2, he described exchanging "hot words" with William W. Averell, commander of the Cavalry Second Division, whom Sheridan subsequently relieved because of Averell's apparent indifference to following up the victory at Fisher's Hill on September 22, 1864 (*Memoirs*, 2:43). Similarly, the anecdote of the oxen enhanced, by implication, the acoustics of Sheridan's "acrimonious interview" with George G. Meade in a "peppery temper" over the proper use of U.S. cavalry in the Overland campaign that began in May 1864: "Meade was very much irritated, and I was none the less so. One word brought on another, until, finally, I told him that I could whip Stuart if he (Meade) would only let me" (1:368–69).[14]

A familiar convention of Gilded Age memoirs by Civil War generals was self-justification, which came in various hues and intensities, and no memoir stayed wholly free of it, not even Grant's. But by comparison with Sherman or Johnston, for example, Sheridan served up refreshingly small helpings of self-justification, at least in the first volume.[15] Much more likely to second-guess another officer, whether Union or Confederate, he did so frequently, with prominent examples from volume 1 including critiques of Henry Halleck for not ordering more vigorous pursuit of P. G. T. Beauregard in northern Mississippi during the spring of 1862 (*Memoirs*, 1:152); of Braxton Bragg's failure "to utilize the chances falling to him" during his advance into Kentucky in the fall of 1862 (1:191); of Don Carlos Buell for his mismanagement of the battle of Perryville, "an example of lost opportunities," on October 8, 1862 (1:200); of "the enemy," presumably Jefferson Davis, for "the serious fault of detaching Longstreet's corps — sending it to aid in the siege of Knoxville in East Tennessee — an error which has no justification whatsoever" in the fall of 1863 (1:303); and of J. E. B. Stuart for "his error" of concentrating his troops at Beaver Dam before the battle of Yellow Tavern, where Stuart was mortally wounded by Sheridan's troops on May 11, 1864 (1:375).

Lest one think that Sheridan merely rerouted self-justification through criticism of others, it is only fair to note that he also candidly censured himself, most often for his tendency toward stubborn willfulness, if not downright insubordination. Again, examples are bountiful, the first one coming a mere eleven pages into the first chapter, with the story of Sheridan's "quarrel of a belligerent character in September, 1851, with Cadet William R. Terrill"

Stephen Cushman

at West Point in the fall of his fourth year as a member of the class of 1852: "Terrill was a Cadet Sergeant, and, while my company was forming for parade, having given me an order, in what I considered an improper tone, to 'dress' in a certain direction, when I believed I was accurately dressed, I fancied I had a grievance, and made toward him with lowered bayonet, but my better judgment recalled me before actual contact could take place" (*Memoirs*, 1:11). This incident, neatly recounted in a single, well-regulated sentence, resulted in Sheridan's one-year suspension from West Point by the secretary of war and placed him with the class of 1853, which included James B. McPherson, John M. Schofield, and John B. Hood. In his summation Sheridan did not spare himself: "Though the mortification I then endured was deep and trying, I am convinced that it was hardly as much as I deserved for such an outrageous breach of discipline" (1:12).[16]

This was no conversion story; Sheridan did not tell it in order to show that he learned a hard lesson about a tendency he never again indulged. Rather, he told it as part of a pattern of other instances of his unruliness, among them disobedience of a direct order by Samuel R. Curtis, commander of the Army of Southwest Missouri, to which Sheridan had been assigned as chief commissary on December 26, 1861. Without full knowledge of the situation, Curtis had ordered Sheridan to make payments for stolen horses dishonestly proffered to the army for purchase, and Sheridan had refused point-blank, bringing on himself a court-martial. Relieved by Halleck at his request and ordered to St. Louis, "forlorn and disheartened" (again, the double adjective), Sheridan avoided the court-martial (*Memoirs*, 1:134–35). Less spectacular than the incidents with Terrill and Curtis, though tending in the same direction of insisting on his own autonomy, were the "acrimonious interview" in May 1864 with Meade, his commanding officer, over the proper use of cavalry, and his earlier interview with Grant, in Corinth, Mississippi, in September 1862. Grant wanted Sheridan and his command to remain with him, but, not surprisingly, Sheridan had his own ideas: "Since I was of the opinion that the chief field of usefulness and opportunity was opening up in Kentucky, I did not wish him to retain me, which he might have done, and I impressed him with my conviction, somewhat emphatically, I fear" (1:182). Sheridan wrote this sentence after reading Grant's version of the same interview, and his closing admission, "somewhat emphatically, I fear," tacitly acknowledged the irritation he had caused his future friend, who recalled in his own memoirs, "I felt a little nettled at his desire to get away and did not detain him."[17]

Like his fluency with profanity, his desire "to get away" and be his own boss had two sides, one that could produce unquestionably positive results and one that could get him into trouble, and Sheridan owned them both. But what is more remarkable about these potentially volatile characteristics is that they throw into even sharper relief what made Sheridan such an effective leader. It was not simply that he could swear majestically, and it was not simply that he strongly preferred operating independently to being under anybody's thumb; it was that while exhibiting these high-tempered, hot-blooded characteristics, he demonstrated repeatedly his deep concern and solicitude for any person or animal of whom or which he was in charge. At a moment in its social history when the twenty-first-century United States is flooded by the products of the leadership-training industry—schools, programs, courses, retreats, books, articles, online encapsulations of various kinds—Sheridan still embodies a natural, homegrown gift for, and a profoundly simple theory of, effective leadership. Throughout his *Personal Memoirs*, especially in volume 1, he articulated, directly and without fanfare, the principles and assumptions that made him the leader who would contribute so significantly to the Appomattox campaign.[18]

Sheridan's first statement of his understanding of leadership appeared in his memoirs three pages before the anecdote of the demoralized oxen. In the summer of 1856 the men of Sheridan's small command were ordered elsewhere, while he himself was assigned to Fort Haskins. In recounting this separation, Sheridan admitted, as he often did, his strong feeling on the occasion: "I regretted exceedingly to see them go, for their faithful work and gallant service had endeared every man to me by the strongest ties" (*Memoirs*, 1:93). The effusive sentence that followed could not be mistaken for one in either Grant's or Sherman's memoirs: "Since I relieved Lieutenant [John B.] Hood on Pit River, nearly a twelvemonth before, they had been my constant companions, and the zeal with which they had responded to every call I made on them had inspired in my heart a deep affection that years have not removed" (1:93). What accounted for the zealous responsiveness of his men? Did they warm to Sheridan from the start? No, they had to be won over: "When I relieved Hood—a dragoon officer of their own regiment—they did not like the change, and I understood that they somewhat contemptuously expressed this in more ways than one, in order to try the temper of the new 'Leftenant,' but appreciative and unremitting care, together with firm and just discipline, soon quieted all symptoms of dissatisfaction and overcame all prejudice" (1:93).

Appreciative and unremitting care, together with firm and just discipline: Sheridan's style, or at least his representation of it, in a nutshell. Many a leader insists on discipline, often firm, not always just. But Sheridan's touch was the addition of the appreciative and unremitting care, the constant vigilance for the welfare of his men and their horses. His memoirs repeated this theme throughout the first volume, with the next instance following his assumption of brigade command in Mississippi in June 1862: "Although but a few days had elapsed from the date of my appointment as colonel of the Second Michigan to that of my succeeding to the command of the brigade, I believe I can say with propriety that I had firmly established myself in the confidence of the officers and men of the regiment, and won their regard by thoughtful care. I had striven unceasingly to have them well fed and well clothed, had personally looked after the selection of their camps, and had maintained such a discipline as to allay former irritation" (*Memoirs*, 1:153).

The point is not that Grant and Sherman did not care for their men; of course they did. For that matter, so did the much less effective Joseph E. Johnston and George B. McClellan. The point is that Sheridan the writer considered this aspect of his leadership significant enough to return to it throughout his narrative, as he labored to create an image of himself that would account for a large part of his celebrated success at the battle of Cedar Creek in October 1864 or in the high-speed climax of the Appomattox campaign six months later. Again, a sentence such as the second of the following does not appear in the memoirs of Grant or Sherman: "Men who march, scout, and fight, and suffer all the hardships that fall to the lot of soldiers in the field, in order to do vigorous work must have the best bodily sustenance, and every comfort that can be provided. I knew from practical experience on the frontier that my efforts in this direction would not only be appreciated, but requited with personal affection and gratitude; and, further, that such exertions would bring the best results to me" (*Memoirs*, 1:153–54). According to this formulation, Sheridan's appreciative and unremitting care for his soldiers made them personally affectionate toward and grateful to him, and their personal affection and gratitude made them more effective warriors. Grant and Sherman did not write as though the personal affection and gratitude of their men factored into their offensive strategies in any significant way, although clearly Sherman basked in his soldiers' affection for him; Johnston and McClellan did not write like leaders who thought of personal affection and gratitude primarily as things to be converted into offensive capability. Did Sheridan calculate this way because he had also served as an effective quartermaster, or was he an effective quartermaster because he calculated this way? Either way, his fullest, most moving enunciation of the deep ties between himself and the men in his charge came in one of the great paragraphs of his memoirs, with the account of his transfer to the Eastern Theater in the spring of 1864:

I was not informed of the purpose for which I was to proceed to Washington, but I conjectured that it meant a severing of my relations with the Second Division, Fourth Army Corps. I at once set about obeying the order, and as but little preparation was necessary, I started for Chattanooga the next day, without taking any formal leave of the troops I had so long commanded. I could not do it; the bond existing between them and me had grown to such depth of attachment that I feared to trust my emotions in any formal parting from a body of soldiers who, from our mutual devotion, had long before lost their official designation, and by general consent were called "Sheridan's Division." When I took the train at the station the whole command was collected on the hill-sides around to see me off. They had assembled spontaneously, officers and men, and as the cars moved out for Chattanooga they waved me farewell with demonstrations of affection. (1:340)

Whatever the vicissitudes of the Gilded Age market for Civil War memoirs, Twain could not have hoped for better writing than this exquisite balance of historical narrative and emotional charge. The moment captured perfectly Sheridan's distinct sensibility, one that combined resolute commitment to pragmatism, realism, and discipline, on the one hand, with, on the other, loyalty, affection, and an instinctive tendency to identify closely with those working beside him. These latter impulses extended to animals, too, as we have heard in the phrase "demoralized oxen." Who else would think to describe the morale of six yoke of oxen? It would be excessive to try to paint Sheridan as a military Saint Francis of Assisi, and he did not try to paint himself that way. But when it came to "appreciative and unremitting care," Sheridan's exertions did not limit themselves to men. In his *Personal Memoirs* a reader will find far more explicit concern for horses and mules than in the 2,000 pages of Grant and Sherman combined. What the same reader will not find is contradictory evidence that when it came to the Overland campaign of 1864, the real Sheridan, not the creation of his memoirs, could be very hard on horses, too.[19]

The etymology of the Greek name "Philip" is "lover of horses," and Sheridan's narrative showed him living up to that name many times over. Also an excellent horseman, Grant rode, among others, Cincinnati, Jack, Fox, Kangaroo, and Jeff Davis, while Sherman rode Lexington, Sam, and Dolly. But readers of their memoirs will find nothing like Sheridan's two full pages on Rienzi, the jet black Morgan gelding, "excepting three white feet" (*Mem-*

Stephen Cushman

oirs, 1:177), given to him by Capt. Archibald P. Campbell of the 2nd Michigan Cavalry, shortly after an August 1862 brush in northern Mississippi with William Faulkner's great-grandfather, a colonel in the 7th Mississippi Cavalry, also called the 1st Mississippi Partisan Rangers.[20] The extended description of Rienzi, who did not appear by name again in the memoirs until the events leading up to the battle of Cedar Creek on October 19, 1864 (2:65), showed the attentive and sympathetic assessment of a subordinate by his leader, or, in this case, master: "I never observed in him any vicious habit; a nervousness and restlessness and switching of the tail, when everything about him was in repose, being the only indication that he might be untrustworthy." Sheridan let this suggestive judgment linger in his readers' minds for only the brief typographic space between sentences before he moved swiftly and firmly to correct it: "No one but a novice could be deceived by this, however, for the intelligence evinced in every feature, and his thoroughbred appearance, were so striking that any person accustomed to horses could not misunderstand such a noble animal" (1:178).

The description of Rienzi, renamed Winchester after Cedar Creek, culminated in a sentence that reflected the high value Sheridan placed on the contributions and comforts of those who served him most productively, whether men or animals: "Although he was several times wounded, this horse escaped death in action; and living to a ripe old age, died in 1878, attended to the last with all the care and surrounded with every comfort due the faithful service he had rendered" (*Memoirs*, 1:180). Although Rienzi received the only prolonged attention given to any animal in his narrative, Sheridan included numerous references throughout his memoirs to the condition and service of horses and mules. In his account of the first day of the battle of Stones River (December 31, 1862; referred to in *Memoirs* as "Stone River"), he even included the exact number, among his casualty figures — "Eighty of the horses of Houghtaling's battery having been killed" (1:230) — when he could have said simply, "All," the precise number suggesting instead the leader's keener recognition and appraisal of the loss.

Of course he paid close attention to horses, the response might go; he served the last year of the war as a cavalryman. But again the issue is the difference between what the cavalryman paid attention to — Grant and Sherman could not have succeeded if they had been oblivious to the condition of their horses and mules — and what the writer chose to include in his narrative. In his note "To the Reader" at the beginning of *Look Homeward, Angel* (1929), Thomas Wolfe offered an aphoristic formulation that is relevant here: "Fiction is fact selected and understood, fiction is fact arranged and charged with pur-

pose."[21] If for the word "fiction" in this formulation we substitute "memoir,"
we can begin to get at the significance of Sheridan's selections and arrangements, as well as the purposes with which he charged them. In his account of
reviewing his new command at Brandy Station, Virginia, in April 1864, for example, the purposeful charging of fact, selected and arranged, is not difficult
to detect. Having reviewed the 12,000 officers and men of the Cavalry Corps,
Army of the Potomac, their new commander noted, "The corps presented a
fine appearance at the review, and so far as health and equipment of the men
were concerned the showing was good and satisfactory, but the horses were
thin and very much worn down by excessive and, it seemed to me, unnecessary picket duty" (*Memoirs*, 1:353). The phrasing "excessive and, it seemed to
me, unnecessary" purposefully prepared the way for the confrontation with
Meade, on the next page, during which Sheridan stoutly, and possibly profanely, maintained his point of view about the most productive use of cavalry: "As the effectiveness of my command rested mainly on the strength of
its horses, I thought the duty it was then performing was both burdensome
and wasteful" (1:354).

Sheridan valued effectiveness as highly as anything, and he pushed himself tirelessly to assure it. Whoever or whatever enhanced effectiveness, he
fostered and cultivated; whoever or whatever did not, he discarded without
ceremony or sentiment. This ethic clearly guided his approach to leadership,
and it came into play starkly and harshly in his remarks on an especially controversial phase of his Civil War service, the desolation of the Shenandoah
Valley during the summer and fall of 1864. The rhetorical framing of these
remarks in the memoirs was particularly significant. Unlike the ever-forensic
Sherman, Sheridan tended to avoid extensive primary documentation, ap-
proximating instead Grant's more modest ratio of quotation-to-narration,
although he often included the order of battle for a major engagement or
campaign, such as Stones River or Chickamauga or Missionary Ridge or the
Overland campaign, as well as the occasional order or letter of commenda-
tion from a superior. Usually, however, he let his story do the talking. The
major exception in volume 1 was the appearance of nearly four consecutive
pages of small-type excerpts at the end of the chapter on the battle of Missionary Ridge, as Sheridan, proceeding like Sherman, worked to discredit
William B. Hazen's claim that he was entitled to guns captured by Sheridan's
men because his, Hazen's, had reached the crest of Missionary Ridge first
(*Memoirs*, 1:320–24).[22]

But when Sheridan turned to the Shenandoah Valley campaign, the ratio
changed dramatically, especially in the case of a single, unusually long para-

graph in which he stepped back to meditate on the nature of war. This paragraph ran to four pages because so many messages from Grant appeared in the footnotes, which at one point squeezed Sheridan's own account to a mere four lines at the top of a page (*Memoirs*, 1:485–88). But Sheridan did not include Grant's orders to him merely to justify his own actions in the Valley or to shift from himself to Grant any blame arising from those actions. To be sure, the narrative moment was clearly a large one for the author, and its magnitude led to one of the few authorial, or editorial, stutters in the memoirs, the repeated printings, twenty pages apart, of Grant's order of August 5, 1864, to David Hunter, commander of the Department of West Virginia, which contained a key formulation that subsequently guided Sheridan: "In pushing up the Shenandoah Valley . . . it is desirable that nothing should be left to invite the enemy to return" (*Memoirs*, 1:465, 484). But instead of including Grant's various orders to show he was only acting under them as the obedient agent of destruction, not as its originator, Sheridan adopted a very different approach: "I endorsed [Grant's] programme in all its parts, for the stores of meat and grain that the valley provided, and the men it furnished for Lee's depleted regiments, were the strongest auxiliaries he possessed in the whole insurgent section" (1:487).

Endorsement usually flows the other way, with the commander endorsing the suggestion of a subordinate, a subordinate's endorsement of his commander wholly beside the point; it is for the subordinate to carry out the orders, not to presume to endorse them. But in this case the subordinate's explicit endorsement of Grant's program, presumptuous and insubordinate as it may sound, cleared the way for a unique moment in Sheridan's narrative, his shift, in the final chapter of the first volume, to a large and memorable formulation about the nature of war:

> Hence, as I have said, I endorsed Grant's programme, for I do not
> hold war to mean simply that lines of men shall engage each other in
> battle, and material interests be ignored. This is but a duel, in which
> one combatant seeks the other's life; war means much more, and is
> far worse than this. Those who rest at home in peace and plenty see
> but little of the horrors attending such a duel, and even grow indiffer-
> ent to them as the struggle goes on, contenting themselves with en-
> couraging all who are able-bodied to enlist in the cause, to fill up the
> shattered ranks as death thins them. It is another matter, however,
> when deprivation and suffering are brought to their own doors. Then
> the case appears much graver, for the loss of property weighs heavy

with the most of mankind; heavier often, than the sacrifices made
on the field of battle. Death is popularly considered the maximum of
punishment in war, but it is not; reduction to poverty brings prayers
for peace more surely and more quickly than does the destruction of
human life, as the selfishness of man has demonstrated in more than
one great conflict. (*Memoirs*, 1:487–88)

What makes this wide-angle meditation especially valuable is that in
addition to letting us hear yet another of the many languages Sheridan could
speak—here the language of the philosopher or social critic—there is nothing else as ambitious and comprehensive in either volume of his memoirs.
Unlike Grant or Sherman, Sheridan was not given to aerial perspectives and
pronouncements. Narrating the outbreak of the war, for example, Sheridan said nothing—not a word—about the causes behind it. Whereas Grant
traced these to the Mexican War and Sherman to the slavery question arising
from the acquisition of California, Sheridan, the only one of the three actually in the army when the war began, remained sublimely indifferent to larger
questions:

On the day of the week that our courier, or messenger, was expected
back from Portland, I would go out early in the morning to a commanding point above the post, from which I could see a long distance
down the road as it ran through the valley of the Yamhill, and there I
would watch with anxiety for his coming, longing for good news [in
the aftermath of First Manassas–Bull Run]; for, isolated as I had been
through years spent in the wilderness, my patriotism was untainted
by politics, nor had it been disturbed by any discussion of the questions out of which the war grew, and I hoped for the success of the
Government above all other considerations.[23] (*Memoirs*, 1:123)

Sheridan's claim to simple patriotism, undisturbed by any of the vast
questions out of which the war grew, made all the more remarkable the vast-
ness of his assertion that war means much more and is far worse than a duel
between lines of men engaged in battle. A cousin of Sherman's famous statement of September 12, 1864, to the mayor and councilmen of Atlanta, "War
is cruelty, and you cannot refine it," Sheridan's formulation focused on the
strategic efficacy of enlisting human selfishness on behalf of peace. Having
completed the desolation of the Shenandoah Valley in the name of such efficacy, Sheridan turned over command of the Middle Military Division to
Alfred T. A. Torbert on February 28, 1865, destroyed Jubal Early's army at the

Gen. Philip H. Sheridan's memoirs reveal much about his personality
and help explain his decisions during the Appomattox campaign.
(Library of Congress Prints and Photographs Division,
reproduction number LC-USZ62-131934)

battle of Waynesboro, March 2, 1865, and set out to rejoin Grant at Petersburg, "feeling that the war was nearing its end" and desiring his cavalry "to be in at the death" (*Memoirs*, 2:119).

In the fifth chapter of his second volume, Sheridan took up narration of the Appomattox campaign. Although at least one reader has claimed to prefer the 1883 account of the campaign published in the *North American Review*, those who have not followed Sheridan through his memoirs up to this point risk missing the sonority of accumulated echoes rolling through the 1888 version.[24] To begin with, if Sheridan had been dutifully subordinate, in both letter and spirit, he might not have taken part in the Appomattox campaign at all; or, to put it differently, if Sheridan had been dutifully subordinate, the Appomattox campaign, as we know it, would not have unfolded when it did, the way it did. Instead, we might well be talking about the final, and later, Lynchburg campaign or Chatham campaign or Danville campaign. These points cannot be made too emphatically. The opening sentence of the chapter quickly established Sheridan as the initiator of his shift eastward: "The transfer of my command from the Shenandoah Valley to the field of operations in front of Petersburg was not anticipated by General Grant; indeed, the despatch brought from Columbia by my scouts, asking that supplies be sent me at the White House, was the first word that reached him concerning the move" (*Memoirs*, 2:124). Here Sheridan's use of the passive voice ("was not anticipated by General Grant") neatly muffled the true state of affairs, which amounted to "I wanted to be in at the death of the rebellion and moved accordingly." In case his reader missed this point, he restated it more bluntly in the final sentence of the first paragraph: "The reunited [cavalry] corps was to enter upon the campaign as a separate army, I reporting directly to General Grant; the intention being thus to reward me for foregoing, of my own choice, my position as a department commander by joining the armies at Petersburg" (2:125).

Archival evidence shows the handwritten words "foregoing of my own choice" inserted above a caret mark in the heavily edited typescript that succeeded Sheridan's clerk's handwritten manuscript, in which the corresponding phrase read, less pointedly, "the intention being to thus reward me for sacrificing my position."[25] Critics of Sheridan who argue that his willful insistence on getting his own way inevitably compromised his integrity and value as a military leader have a strong case. A soldier's duty, whatever his rank (or, now, hers), is to obey orders or, where orders are lacking, to seek them. Furthermore, the phrase "of my own choice" was misleading at best and wholly disingenuous at worst. Grant did not give Sheridan a choice between

Stephen Cushman

retaining command of the Middle Military Division, on the one hand, or of forfeiting it in order to transfer his force to Petersburg, on the other, in which case he was to be rewarded with autonomy apart from Meade. Sheridan made the move on his own, having acknowledged that "Grant's orders were for me to destroy the Virginia Central railroad and the James River canal, capture Lynchburg if practicable, and then join General Sherman in North Carolina wherever he might be found, or return to Winchester, but as to joining Sherman I was to be governed by the state of affairs after the projected capture of Lynchburg" (*Memoirs*, 2:112–13). Although one could maintain that Grant's orders to his subordinate were discretionary, Grant's larger intention could not have been clearer. As he wrote to Meade from City Point on February 21, 1865, "Sherman has but little over 4,000 cavalry, and Schofield none. The main object is to re-inforce Sherman in that arm of service."[26]

But fulfilling Grant's main object by moving southwest to serve Sherman was the last thing Sheridan wanted, as he recounted at length. Through ten pages of his memoirs — one-eighth of the space he devoted to the Appomattox campaign — he fretted quite openly, especially after Sherman himself appeared on the scene at City Point to make his own case: "Well knowing the zeal and emphasis with which General Sherman would present his views, there again came into my mind many misgivings with reference to the movement of the cavalry, and I made haste to start for Grant's headquarters" (*Memoirs*, 2:131). The reader who has followed Sheridan from the opening of his memoirs to this point, and who recollects his account of the 1862 interview with Grant in Corinth, can anticipate the story of what followed in the shanty where Sheridan found Grant and Sherman in conversation: "My uneasiness made me somewhat too earnest, I fear, but General Grant soon mollified me, and smoothed matters over" (2:133).[27]

If one needed further confirmation of Grant's superlative skills as a leader, the image of him mediating between the prickly self-interests of Sherman and Sheridan in his City Point shanty should provide it abundantly. Sheridan was unstinting in his summary praise of Grant, to whom he allotted the final two pages of the Appomattox section, giving to him the kind of encomium Grant and Sherman gave to Lincoln in their respective memoirs. By the time of his writing in 1887 or 1888, Sheridan's encomium for Grant doubled as a moving eulogy, ending with three sentences that showed keen awareness and appreciation of how Grant had managed him and others:

During [the Overland campaign] and in the siege of Petersburg he met with many disappointments — on several occasions the shortcomings of generals, when at the point of success, leading to wretched failures. But so far as he was concerned, the only apparent effect of these discomfitures was to make him all the more determined to discharge successfully the stupendous trust committed to his care, and to bring into play the manifold resources of his well-ordered military mind. He guided every subordinate then, and in the last days of the rebellion, with a fund of common sense and superiority of intellect, which have left an impress so distinct as to exhibit his great personality. When his military history is analyzed after the lapse of years, it will show, even more clearly than now, that during these as well as in his previous campaigns he was the steadfast centre about and on which everything else turned. (*Memoirs*, 2:204)

To the everlasting credit of "the steadfast centre"—a phrase that first appeared in the typescript to replace "the planet about which everything revolved" in the clerk's manuscript—Grant's superiority of intellect and fund of common sense enabled him to know when to let Sheridan have his way. Recounting a meeting with his feisty lieutenant early in the Appomattox campaign, Grant claimed he felt "glad to see the spirit of confidence with which he was imbued," knowing as he did "from experience, of what great value that feeling of confidence by a commander was." [28] Spirit of confidence or insubordination? The line between them is not always clear, especially in Sheridan's case, but Grant saw the former where others might see only the latter. Critical as some may be about Sheridan's willfulness, Grant knew what he had in this particular subordinate, as he testified to, among many others, Mark Twain's daughter Susy Clemens, in memory of whom the bereaved father began "A Family Sketch" soon after her death on August 18, 1896, at the age of twenty-four: "When Susy was twelve years old General Grant described one or two of Sheridan's achievements to her, and gave his reasons for regarding Sheridan as the first general of the age." [29] The point here is not whether everyone agrees that Sheridan was the first general of the age or whether he should have done what Grant originally wanted and gone southwest to serve under Sherman or whether his version of events is wholly reliable; the point is that Sheridan the writer could strike the rhetorical pose he adopted in his memoirs, and particularly in his narrative of the Appomattox campaign, because he had triumphed as the hero of that campaign. He could afford to admit his tendency toward willful insubordination throughout his memoirs because, in the case of the Appomattox campaign, it produced victory. [30]

In this respect Sheridan the writer drew heavily on credit accrued from what Thomas Nagel has called "moral luck," and specifically from one of Nagel's four types of moral luck, that pertaining to the results or outcome of one's actions or projects. Arguing that "whether we succeed or fail in what we try to do nearly always depends to some extent on factors beyond our control" and "what has been done, and what is morally judged, is partly determined by external factors," Nagel summarized his idea of moral luck this way: "Where a significant aspect of what someone does depends on factors beyond his control, yet we continue to treat him in that respect as an object of moral judgment, it can be called moral luck. Such luck can be good or bad." Nobody understood this kind of moral luck better than Abraham Lincoln, who explained in a letter to Albert G. Hodges, written April 4, 1864, exactly a year before the opening day of Sheridan's 1883 account of the Appomattox campaign, "I claim not to have controlled events, but confess plainly that events have controlled me." This admission was not merely humility, true or false, on Lincoln's part; it was an instance of his shrewd, lawyerly appraisal of the role external factors play in moral judgments. If external factors had turned out to Lincoln's disadvantage—if in the fall of 1864, for example, Sherman had not taken Atlanta and Sheridan had not subdued the Shenandoah Valley, so that the president had lost his bid for reelection, as he fully expected to as of August 1864—the moral judgment of controversial actions such as suspending habeas corpus or issuing the Emancipation Proclamation or initiating a draft might have gone against him and his moral luck been much worse.[31]

The Sheridan of the memoirs had good moral luck, too. If we take as comparative examples the insubordination or noncompliance of two leaders, such as Sheridan before the Appomattox campaign and Joseph E. Johnston during the later stages of Grant's Vicksburg campaign—when Johnston failed, from Jefferson Davis's point of view, to comply with his orders and fulfill his duties as commander of the Department of the West—we tend to praise the former and condemn the latter largely on the basis of results or consequences: Sheridan's noncompliance contributed to Lee's surrender at Appomattox, Johnston's to the Confederate loss of Vicksburg.[32] What matters most here is that if the positions were reversed—if Sheridan's noncompliance had led to Lee's escape and reunion with Johnston somewhere between Appomattox and Greensboro, or Johnston's noncompliance had led to Grant's failure to capture Vicksburg—the two generals' memoirs most likely would have turned out to be very different. Presumably, Johnston could have done something else with the many pages he spent refuting Davis's censure of his performance, and Sheridan might have had to resort to much more of the self-justifying rhetorical strategy of extensive documentation that he adopted in the chapters devoted to his tumultuous service in New Orleans as military governor of Texas and Louisiana during the early years of Reconstruction (*Memoirs*, 2:235–80). Then again, if his noncompliance had led to Lee's escape at Appomattox, the *North American Review* might have been much less interested in publishing his account, and Mark Twain might never have suggested his writing his memoirs at all. Unlike Lincoln, however, Sheridan gave no hint in his memoirs that he spent substantial time in contemplating his subordination to external factors.

A particularly urgent and complicated example of moral luck emerged in Sheridan's account of his relieving Gouverneur Warren from command of the Fifth Corps during the battle of Five Forks, April 1, 1865: "It was therefore necessary to protect myself in this critical situation, and General Warren having sorely disappointed me, both in the moving of his corps and in its management during the battle, I felt that he was not the man to rely upon under such circumstances, and deeming that it was to the best interest of the service as well as but just to myself, I relieved him, ordering him to report to General Grant" (*Memoirs*, 2:165). The controversy that followed Sheridan's bold action—some have maintained it an unjust one—cast the only large shadow over the Appomattox portion of the memoirs. For seventeen pages, or between a fifth and a quarter of the whole, Sheridan told the story of the battles of Dinwiddie Court House (March 31, 1865) and Five Forks not by focusing exclusively on his case against Warren's alleged slowness and apathy but certainly by including more than enough details along the way to explain his decision.[33]

Like everyone else involved in the race west from Petersburg, Warren had to cope with, among other things, the heavy rains and extreme muddiness of the roads, which almost led Grant to suspend operations—until Sheridan, in combination with John Rawlins, argued him out of doing so (*Memoirs*, 2:144–45)—and which caused Sheridan to choose over Rienzi "a powerful gray pacing horse called Breckenridge" to carry him through the immobilizing muck (2:143). But Sheridan gave none of his narrative to Warren's challenges. True to form, even though by the time of writing he had succeeded Sherman as commanding general of the United States and might have rehearsed the events of April 1865 with the coolly secure detachment of that high eminence, Sheridan instead chose to describe candidly his own agitations in the moment: "That we had accomplished nothing but to oblige our foe to retreat was to me bitterly disappointing. . . . I was disappointed. . . . At last I expressed to Warren my fears. . . . My patience was almost worn out . . . General Warren having sorely disappointed me" (*Memoirs*, 2:158, 160, 161, 165).

What made this unguarded self-portrait of agitation particularly revealing was that it showed little or no attempt to answer controversy by pretend-
ing to level-headed objectivity. Instead, Sheridan the writer gambled that because his action against Warren was part and parcel of all the actions that led
to victory on April 9, when his cavalry delayed the final Confederate push
west from Appomattox long enough for lead elements of Edward O. C. Ord's
Army of the James to arrive and block it, his own subjective state was justification enough for Warren's relief. The language we have seen could not
have been more telling: "Deeming that it was to the best interest of the service *as well as but just to myself,* I relieved him" (emphasis added). Grant's
order of March 31, 10:15 P.M., had instructed Meade to urge Warren "not to
stop for anything," and Grant had given Sheridan authority to relieve Warren,
as he would not have done unless he had anticipated some version of what
later happened (*Memoirs,* 2:155, 160). There was something almost defiant in
Sheridan's account, as though he were saying, I had the power to relieve Warren, so when he disappointed me, I relieved him, and the positive ending justified the controversial means to it.

Not quite willing to let it go so brazenly at that, however, Sheridan sought
to strengthen his position and jumped ahead to the 1879 Court of Inquiry
given to Warren. This flash-forward actually took him eight years beyond the
narrative boundary of his memoirs, which concluded, after many pages of
what often reads like pleasure-seeking travel literature, with his return in 1871
from observing the Franco-Prussian War. Having pointed out that the court
found against Warren on two counts and for him on two counts, Sheridan
took the fifty-fifty split as vindication and ended his sixth chapter of the second volume with the assertion — one that appeared neither in typescript nor
manuscript and must have been added at a later stage — "That I was justified in
this is plain to all who are disposed to be fair-minded" (*Memoirs,* 2:169). Then,
in a final clinching move tinged by some irony after the reluctance to serve
under him in the spring of 1865, Sheridan gave the last word to Sherman, commanding general of the army in 1879, the authority and eloquence of whose
judgment were powerfully persuasive, as Sheridan himself knew very well.

Familiar to readers of his own memoirs as capable of both passionate
enthusiasm and passionate disgust, Sherman delivered his opinion on Sheridan's relief of Warren with a sagacious tact and finely calibrated precision
worthy of Solomon. One can imagine without difficulty that Sheridan quoted
Sherman's opening statements with a firm conviction that they had been designed specifically with him in mind, as they captured his style of leadership
exactly:

It would be an unsafe and dangerous rule to hold the commander of an army in battle to a technical adherence to any rule of conduct for managing his command. He is responsible for results, and holds the lives and reputations of every officer and soldier under his orders as subordinate to the great end — victory. The most important events are usually compressed into an hour, a minute, and he cannot stop to analyze his reasons. He must act on the impulse, the conviction, of the instant, and should be sustained in his conclusions, if not manifestly unjust. The power to command men, and give vehement impulse to their joint action, is something which cannot be defined by words, but it is plain and manifest in battles, and whoever commands an army in chief must choose his subordinates by reason of qualities which can alone be tested in actual conflict. (*Memoirs*, 2:169–70)

Sherman's assertion that the conditions of battle compel us to subordinate judgment of a leader's actions to "the great end" of victory offered yet another version of moral luck. Where a leader's impulses, convictions, and actions combine with external events to produce victory, they "should be sustained," or judged morally acceptable. What Sherman did not say, but what his assertion left implicit, is that the same impulses, convictions, and actions could be judged unacceptable where they fail to combine with external events to produce victory. This unspoken side of the argument led one of Sheridan's early readers to call Sherman's rationale "a monstrous theory."[34] Sheridan's account of the Appomattox campaign was an account of nothing so much as his exertions, under extraordinary conditions, to "give vehement impulse" to the joint action of the men under his command and, by doing so, to produce victory. That Sherman did not find the effects of Sheridan's exertions "manifestly unjust" became clear in the deliberate, discriminating language of what followed: "'No one has questioned the patriotism, integrity, and great intelligence of General Warren. These are attested by a long record of most excellent service, but in the clash of arms at and near Five Forks, March 31 and April 1, 1865, his personal activity fell short of the standard fixed by General Sheridan, on whom alone rested the great responsibility for that and succeeding days.'" One might wonder what role Grant played in Sherman's understanding of the Appomattox campaign, if such great responsibility rested on Sheridan "alone," but with or without acknowledgment of Sheridan's own subordinate position, Sherman's final word could not have been more welcome: "'My conclusion is that General Sheridan was perfectly justified in his

Stephen Cushman

action in this case, and he must be fully and entirely sustained if the United States expects great victories by her arms in the future'" (*Memoirs*, 2:170).

If "the standard fixed by General Sheridan" during the Appomattox campaign could be compressed into one word, that word, his word, was "celerity," from the Latin for swiftness. Speed was the key to the vehement impulse Sheridan sought to give the joint actions of the men he commanded. The word "celerity" appeared five times in the two volumes of his memoirs, the first time in orders issued by Andrew A. Humphreys to James H. Wilson on June 21, 1864: "'The success of your expedition will depend upon the secrecy with which it is commenced, and the celerity with which its movements are conducted'" (*Memoirs*, 1:441). Within the next twenty pages Sheridan used the word twice more, both times in a phrase that echoed Humphreys, "celerity of movement" (1:458, 459), leading to the reasonable conclusion that quoting Humphreys brought the word to his attention, and he liked it enough to employ it on his own. But even though the word did not appear in the first volume before the quotation from Humphreys, Sheridan had used it years earlier in "The Last Days of the Rebellion," specifically with respect to events of April 7, 1865: "A detachment ordered to move with the greatest celerity, via Prince Edward's Court-house, reported that Lee had crossed the Appomattox at and near Farmville, and that Crook had followed him" (11). Sheridan's single-minded focus on celerity, swiftness, or speed found its way from his memory of 1865 into the writing of 1883, as he entrusted multiple adverbs, appearing on the same page, with the work of conveying the breathlessness of the pace in the last forty-eight hours of the campaign: "He immediately started. . . . I swung off to the left, and moved quickly. . . . My command was instantly turned north" (11). In the final version of 1888, he did not retain any of these particular phrases to describe these particular moments, but he did retain the language of speed, which he now enhanced and extended over his account of April 7, 8, and 9: Crook "promptly attacked. . . . The intelligence as to the trains was immediately despatched to Crook. . . . Custer having the advance, moved rapidly. . . . These regiments set off at a gallop. . . . Without halting to look after the cars further, Custer attacked. . . . That the Confederates might have no rest . . . after a hasty consultation . . . but hastily galloping back . . . I decided to attack at once" (*Memoirs*, 2:188–93).

Framing and intensifying the narrative speed of these pages was an anecdote missing from the earlier 1883 version, the anecdote of what Sheridan dubbed "Lincoln's Laconic Despatch." Lincoln made only three personal appearances in Sheridan's memoirs, and none of the three constituted the stuff of myth-making hero worship. The first appearance came when Sheridan, newly transferred to the East in April 1864, went to see the president after an interview with Edwin Stanton, and Lincoln "wound up our short conversation by quoting that stale interrogation so prevalent during the early years of the war, 'Who ever saw a dead cavalryman?'" (*Memoirs*, 1:347). In the second, in August 1864, Sheridan, in company with Stanton, went to see Lincoln again, and again the connection between the soldier and president was less than lustrous: "During a short conversation Mr. Lincoln candidly told me that Mr. Stanton had objected to my assignment to General Hunter's command, because he thought me too young, and that he himself had concurred with the Secretary," although the president now had decided to back Grant's selection of Sheridan and hope for the best (1:463–64). Of their third and final meeting, aboard the steamer *Mary Martin* at City Point in March 1865, Sheridan sketched a telling portrait, one that showed the strain of recent events on the chief executive: "On the trip the President was not very cheerful. In fact, he was dejected, giving no indication of his usual means of diversion, by which (his quaint stories) I had often heard he could find relief from his cares" (2:130). In the clerk's manuscript "dejected" replaced and softened Sheridan's original, darker word, "gloomy."

Lincoln did not come through as an inspiring personal presence in any of these accounts, but with the inclusion of his "laconic despatch," sent sometime during the early hours of April 7, 1865, Sheridan suggested that the president's words played a significant part in the final push for celerity. Near midnight on April 6, Sheridan telegraphed Grant about the victory at Sailor's Creek that day, adding, "'If the thing is pressed, I think that Lee will surrender.'" Grant transmitted the message to Lincoln, who replied to Grant, simply and sufficiently, with five words that, Sheridan's narrative arrangement implied, were all the fiat he needed to hear: "'Let the thing be pressed'" (*Memoirs*, 2:187). Sheridan's account did not say how he came to know of Lincoln's dispatch, nor did Grant mention it in his memoirs, but Sheridan's narrative management of the anecdote made it seem as though Lincoln were authorizing him directly. From the recounting of Lincoln's reply on, Sheridan accelerated both his actions and his descriptions of them toward the surrender at Appomattox.

An especially valuable assessment of Sheridan's standard of celerity during the Appomattox campaign came from someone who was not an unqualified supporter of his, someone who opposed and criticized his treatment of Warren. In his posthumously published *The Passing of the Armies* (1915), Joshua Lawrence Chamberlain recounted the evening of April 1, after the battle of Five Forks, when "a compact form" emerged from the shadows "with vigorous stride unlike the measure and mood of ours, and a voice that would itself have thrilled us had not the import of it thrilled us more." It was Sheridan, come to offer his apologies for speaking harshly to some of the officers in the Fifth Corps during the battle. Having gushed, "And this is Phil Sheridan! . . . All the repressed feeling of our hearts sprang out towards him," Chamberlain settled into a paragraph comparing Sheridan's style with that to which they had been accustomed under Warren: "We had had a taste of his style of fighting, and we liked it. In some respects it was different from ours. . . . We had a habit, perhaps, drawn from dire experience, and for which we had also Grant's quite recent sanction, when we had carried a vital point or had to hold one, to entrench. But Sheridan does not entrench. He pushes on, carrying his flank and rear with him — rushing, flashing, smashing. He transfuses into his subordinates the vitality and energy of his purpose; transforms them into part of his own mind and will."[35]

Brandishing an auditory bravado fully worthy of the man it described, Chamberlain's apt phrase "rushing, flashing, smashing" caught something essential about Sheridan at the height of his powers during the Appomattox campaign. It caught the quicksilver quality of his inspired, inspiring impulsiveness and opportunism, along with the relentless destructiveness that went with it. Sheridan was not the first or only military commander to insist on speed and mobility to keep an enemy off-balance. Antecedents and analogues extend from the ancient world through his Confederate counterparts Stonewall Jackson, Nathan Bedford Forrest, and John Singleton Mosby — not to mention the Indian warriors he faced in the Northwest and, later, on the Plains, especially the Cheyennes, "the most warlike tribe of all" (*Memoirs*, 2:287) — and on to those influenced by the twentieth-century ideas of John Boyd, the fighter pilot whose presentations led to the U.S. Marine model of maneuver warfare.[36] But Sheridan was the first commander to bring speed, mobility, and the quick reactions of self-reliant autonomy to the Army of the Potomac, as Chamberlain's testimony confirmed. Not everyone liked or admired his early prototype of maneuver warfare, which he could not have developed without Grant's understanding and support, and criticisms of Sheridan for insubordination or ill breeding unbecoming to an officer sometimes masked, and continue to mask, discomfort with the innovations he introduced and embodied. But at least one of his enemies, the straight-talking artillerist Edward Porter Alexander, also recognized something undeniable about the power of "Sheridan's presence & personality," referring unequivocally to the Union cavalry commander as Grant's "best general."[37]

For all his insistence on speed, when it came to narrating the events of April 9, Sheridan the writer slowed down his pace considerably, giving eleven pages to the hours beginning with the sleepless night of April 8, during which "everybody was overjoyed at the prospect that our weary work was about to end so happily" (*Memoirs*, 2:191), and ending with Lee, after his meeting with Grant in the McLean house, riding "his chunky gray horse" through "the bivouac of the Army of Northern Virginia," his progress audible by the varying loudness of his soldiers' cheering (2:202). Along the way Sheridan recounted Ord's predawn arrival with news that John Gibbon's Twenty-fourth Corps was approaching; the moment when John B. Gordon's advancing "gray lines instinctively halted" upon reaching the crest from which they could "see Ord's men emerging from the woods, and the hopelessness of a further attack" (2:192); and word from George A. Custer, "'Lee has surrendered; do not charge; the white flag is up'" (2:194). After five pages devoted to the unsettled period before Grant's arrival, during which Confederates continued to fire on Sheridan and others before Sheridan managed to meet with Gordon and Cadmus M. Wilcox, the story finally brought Grant onstage.

The memoirs had prepared the ground for this moment seventy pages earlier, with a sentence describing the commanding general's manner with his subordinates: "General Grant was never impulsive, and always met his officers in an unceremonious way, with a quiet 'How are you?' soon putting one at his ease, since the pleasant tone in which he spoke gave assurance of welcome, although his manner was otherwise impassive" (*Memoirs*, 2:126). With this brief, deft characterization, Sheridan equipped his readers to savor the understated power of this unadorned exchange near the village of Appomattox Court House:

> He remaining mounted, spoke first to me, saying simply, "How are you, Sheridan?" I assured him with thanks that I was "first-rate," when, pointing toward the village, he asked, "Is General Lee up there?" and I replied, "There is his army down in that valley, and he himself is over in that house (designating McLean's house) waiting to surrender to you." The General then said, "Come, let us go over," this last remark being addressed to both Ord and me. (*Memoirs*, 2:200)

At this weighty moment it was as though Sheridan the writer chose to surrender the rushing, flashing, smashing of Sheridan the warrior to the calm, quiet manner of Grant. The lean, spare quality of the writing amounted to an act of imitative homage, a voluntary act of authorial subordination to the composed taciturnity of the steadfast center.

Proceeding from this moment, Sheridan's 1888 account omitted some details of the 1883 one in "The Last Days of the Rebellion," forgoing, for example, an inventory of U.S. officers who entered the McLean house with Grant ("as nearly as I can recollect, Ord, Rawlins, Seth Williams, Ingalls, Babcock, Parker, and myself"). The version in the memoirs also dropped the parenthetically inserted information that Sheridan bought from McLean the "elliptical-shaped table" on which Grant had written out the terms of surrender, later presenting it to "Mrs. G. A. Custer," as well as a sentence about Lee: "He had on his face the expression of relief from a heavy burden" (17–18). A perfectly good sentence, and one that offered readers a moving glimpse of the Confederate chief, it may have struck Sheridan later as tending toward cliché or overly sympathetic attentiveness to the icon of the Lost Cause. Whatever his reason for dropping it, he did retain quotation of Lee's one direct statement to him. Earlier in the day, Sheridan had fired off two dispatches to Lee, protesting the withdrawal of a portion of the Confederate cavalry in violation of the truce agreement. Having had no time to make copies of the dispatches, Sheridan had asked to have them returned. Handing the dispatches back to Sheridan in the McLean house, Lee apologized, with the small but suggestive change from "possible" in the 1883 version and memoir manuscripts (both Sheridan's original and his clerk's copy) to "probable" in the typescript and 1888 final version: "'I am sorry. It is probable that my cavalry at that point of the line did not understand the agreement'" (*Memoirs*, 2:201).

Then, after the moment that ended the 1883 version, with the image of hearing the cheers for Lee on Traveller, Sheridan spent a short paragraph assessing the Confederate general before concluding his account of the Appomattox campaign with his two pages in praise of Grant. Sixty pages earlier, Sheridan had subjected Lee to the critical second-guessing familiar to readers of the first volume: "Lee made no effort to hold Dinwiddie, which he might have done with his cavalry, and in this he made a fatal mistake" (*Memoirs*, 2:141). When it came to his parting assessment, however, he waived all criticism in favor of a short, matter-of-fact appraisal with which few could quarrel: "For four years his army had been the main-stay of the Confederacy; and the marked ability with which he directed its operations is evidenced both by his frequent successes and the length of time he kept up the contest." As it turned out, this relatively muted approbation — acknowledging a record of "frequent" successes was hardly the same as bowing to the unparalleled achievements of military genius — simply prepared the way for Grant to receive the last word: "Indeed, it may be said that till General Grant was matched against him, he never met an opponent he did not vanquish"

(2:202), a statement that dismissed Meade's victory at Gettysburg. After the summary encomium for Grant, Sheridan turned briefly to the assassination of Lincoln ("dastardly deed") and then to missing the Grand Review in Washington because of Grant's insistence that he go west immediately "to force the surrender of the Confederates under Kirby Smith" (2:205, 209). With that, Grant faded into the background of Sheridan's memoirs, which moved on to the border with Mexico during the downfall of Maximilian, New Orleans during Reconstruction, the Plains during the campaign against hostile tribes, and Europe during the Franco-Prussian War. Those primarily interested in Sheridan in the context of the Civil War may have already ended their reading with Appomattox, however.

Sheridan's style of fighting may have shaped the victorious Appomattox campaign, but his *Personal Memoirs* did not shape commercial victory for Charles L. Webster and Company. Bound in green boards to match the other works in Webster's "Great War Library," Sheridan's two volumes joined those by or about Grant, Sherman, McClellan, Samuel Crawford, Winfield Scott Hancock, and Custer. In 1891 the publisher followed a cheap, two-dollar edition of Sherman's memoirs with one of Sheridan's. But by this point the financial health of the company was steadily deteriorating. For years Mark Twain had been pouring the profits into another commercial venture, the Paige typesetting machine. When the machine proved a failure, and when financial panic struck the markets in 1893, Charles L. Webster and Company did not survive. News of the bankruptcy, formally declared the day before, appeared in the *New York Times* on April 19, 1894. Eight years later, when Michael Sheridan brought out an enlarged edition of his brother's memoirs, continuing the story from 1871 through his death in 1888, he did so with Sherman's original publisher, D. Appleton and Company. This enlarged edition, now out of print, has not replaced the original in the literary and military history of the Civil War; Sheridan's original continues to maintain its independent command.[38]

NOTES

1. Samuel L. Clemens (Mark Twain) to Philip H. Sheridan, December 26, 1884, MSS 7.60, series B, Samuel L. Clemens Papers, Vassar College Archives and Special Collections Library. It has been published in *Mark Twain: Business Man*, ed. Samuel Charles Webster (Boston: Little, Brown, 1946), 288, where the editor introduced it with the statement, "The following letter seems not to have been delivered." Clearly, some subsequent version of the letter must have been delivered, or Webster and Company would not have published Sheridan's *Personal Memoirs of P. H. Sheridan*, 2 vols. (New

York: Charles L. Webster, 1888). For quotations from Sheridan, this will be the edition throughout. Subsequent citations will appear parenthetically in the text as *Memoirs*, followed by volume and page numbers. I am grateful to Robert H. Hirst, general editor, Mark Twain Papers, Bancroft Library, University of California at Berkeley, and to Dean Rogers, special collections assistant, Vassar College Archives and Special Collections Library, for their generous assistance.

2. Philip H. Sheridan, "The Last Days of the Rebellion," *North American Review* 137, no. 320 (July 1883): 8–18. Subsequent page references to this article will appear parenthetically in the text.

3. *Memoirs of General William T. Sherman*, 2 vols. (New York: D. Appleton, 1875); *Personal Memoirs of U. S. Grant*, 2 vols. (New York: Charles L. Webster, 1885–86).

4. *Mark Twain's Notebooks and Journals*, ed. Frederick Anderson (gen. ed.), Robert Pack Browning, Michael B. Frank, and Lin Salamo, 3 vols. (Berkeley: University of California Press, 1975–79), 3:212; Samuel L. Clemens (Mark Twain), *Adventures of Huckleberry Finn (Tom Sawyer's Comrade)* (New York: Charles L. Webster, 1885). This copy resides in the Albert and Shirley Small Special Collections Library, University of Virginia, Charlottesville. Twain's inscription to "the General's boys" raises some questions, as Sheridan had three daughters and only one son, Philip Jr., who was born in 1880 and who wrote his name in pencil on the rear flyleaf. It may well be that Twain was referring to Sheridan's soldiers or some other group identified with him.

5. Frank A. Burr and Richard J. Hinton, *"Little Phil" and His Troopers: The Life of Gen. Philip H. Sheridan: Its Romance and Reality: How an Humble Lad Reached the Head of an Army* (Providence, R.I.: J. A. and R. A. Reid, 1888), 3–4.

6. *Twain's Notebooks and Journals*, 3:388n.

7. Ibid., 3:430n.

8. Paul Andrew Hutton, *Phil Sheridan and His Army* (Lincoln: University of Nebraska Press, 1985), 371.

9. George B. McClellan, *McClellan's Own Story: The War for the Union, the Soldiers Who Fought It, the Civilians Who Directed It and His Relations to It and to Them* (New York: Charles L. Webster, 1887 [c. 1886]). Philip H. Sheridan to Charles L. Webster, December 7, 1886, MSS 30.35, Series HH, Samuel L. Clemens Papers.

10. Philip H. Sheridan to Charles L. Webster, December 21, 1886, MSS 30.43, Series HH, Samuel L. Clemens Papers.

11. See, for example, John Bartlett, *Familiar Quotations*, ed. Emily Morison Beck, 14th ed. (Boston: Little, Brown, 1968), 742. For background on Sheridan and the Plains Indians, see Burr and Hinton, *"Little Phil" and His Troopers*, 343–47; Richard O'Connor, *Sheridan the Inevitable* (New York: Bobbs-Merrill, 1953), 293–306; Hutton, *Phil Sheridan and His Army*, 180–200; Roy Morris Jr., *Sheridan: The Life and Wars of General Phil Sheridan* (New York: Crown, 1992), 297–328; and Joseph Wheelan, *The Terrible Swift Sword: The Life of General Philip H. Sheridan* (Cambridge, Mass.: Da Capo, 2012), 229–47. For Hutton's and Morris's comments on Sheridan's notorious statement, see pp. 180 and 328 of their books, respectively. Any close reader of Sheridan's own account of his role in the Indian wars of 1868 and 1869 (*Memoirs*, 2:281–347) cannot help but have a nuanced view of his attitude toward the Plains Indians, as when, for example, he referred throughout to George A. Custer's scouts as "friendly Osages" (e.g., *Memoirs*, 2:313) or

concluded, "After this fight [on the Republican River in early May 1869] all the Indians of the southern Plains settled down on their reservations, and I doubt whether the peace would ever again have been broken had they not in after years been driven to hostilities by most unjust treatment" (*Memoirs*, 2:346). This last sentence could not have been written by someone who endorsed no policy but the extermination of Indians.

12. Burr and Hinton, *"Little Phil" and His Troopers*, 18.

13. Walt Whitman, "So Long!," *Complete Poetry and Collected Prose* (New York: Library of America, 1982), 611.

14. The theme of swearing reappeared in Sheridan's account of observing the battle of Gravelotte (August 18, 1870) during the Franco-Prussian War. In that account he described King Wilhelm I of Prussia, whom he called "William," berating fugitive German soldiers with an energy that reminded Sheridan "forcibly of the 'Dutch' swearing that I used to hear in my boyhood in Ohio" (*Memoirs*, 2:377). In November 1888, *Scribner's Magazine* published an excerpt from Sheridan's *Personal Memoirs* titled "From Gravelotte to Sedan," 515–35. The publication of this excerpt resulted from contractual wrangling between Webster and Scribner's. For background on negotiations between the two publishers, see *Twain's Notebooks and Journals*, 3:387n. The excerpt in *Scribner's Magazine* includes an illustration, on p. 524, of Wilhelm I, in Sheridan's words, "dressing down" the shirkers. Frederick C. Newhall, one of Sheridan's principal staff officers in the Appomattox campaign, tried to dispel the "popular idea" that his commander "was an exceedingly profane man," admitting that he could use "some lusty oaths" to "buffet back the panic and retrieve disorder" of men in combat. See Frederick C. Newhall, *With Sheridan in the Final Campaign against Lee*, ed. Eric J. Wittenberg (1866; repr., Baton Rouge: Louisiana State University Press, 2002), 2–3.

15. Sheridan's second volume included two extended self-justifications, one with respect to the controversies arising from his relieving Gouverneur Warren from command of the Fifth Corps during the battle of Five Forks, April 1, 1865 (*Memoirs*, 2:154–70), the other from his collision with Andrew Johnson over the implementation of the Reconstruction Laws in New Orleans after a riot there, July 30, 1866 (2:233–80). See n. 22 below.

16. See Eric J. Wittenberg, *Little Phil: A Reassessment of the Civil War Leadership of General Philip H. Sheridan* (Washington, D.C.: Brassey's, 2002), 171, for criticism of Sheridan's "wide streak of insubordination." Although I agree with Wittenberg about the width of that streak, it should be apparent that I cannot agree wholly about what he calls Sheridan's "hypocrisy" about his insubordination. As I have tried to show here, his memoirs suggest considerable self-awareness and candor about his tendency toward insubordination.

17. *Personal Memoirs of U.S. Grant*, 1:402.

18. Not everyone has celebrated Sheridan or his leadership. George Crook, who first appeared in Sheridan's narrative at Fort Reading in California in 1855 (*Memoirs*, 1:37), later fought beside him in the Shenandoah Valley as head of the Army of West Virginia. Resenting the credit he felt Sheridan took for his, Crook's, achievements at the battles of Cedar Creek and Winchester, Crook fumed retrospectively, in a diary entry for December 26, 1889, "The adulations heaped upon him by a grateful nature for his supposed genius turned his head, which, added to his natural disposition, caused him to bloat his little

Stephen Cushman

carcass with debauchery and dissipation, which carried him off prematurely." See *General George Crook: His Autobiography*, ed. Martin Schmitt (Norman: University of Oklahoma Press, 1946), 134n; and David Coffey, *Sheridan's Lieutenants: Phil Sheridan, His Generals, and the Final Year of the Civil War* (Lanham, Md.: Rowman and Littlefield, 2005), 142–43. In the booklet-sized *Notes on the Personal Memoirs of P. H. Sheridan* (St. Paul, Minn.: Press of William L. Banning Jr., 1889), Carswell McClellan, a brevet lieutenant colonel, U.S. Volunteers, challenged many moments in Sheridan's memoirs from the Wilderness on. In *Glory Enough for All: Sheridan's Second Raid and the Battle of Trevilian Station* (Washington, D.C.: Brassey's, 2001), 304–9, Eric J. Wittenberg summarizes various negative assessments of Sheridan's performance in that battle. But Wittenberg also admits, "In spite of their commander's poor performance, Sheridan had a true gift for inspiring the men who served under him" (308–9). Wittenberg has continued his bracing though balanced critique of Sheridan in *Little Phil*.

19. See, for example, Wittenberg, *Little Phil*, specifically these sentences from Sheridan's report of operations from April 6 to August 4, 1864, which Wittenberg reprints as appendix A (176–95): "The horses which failed were shot by the rear guard, as they could have been easily recuperated and made serviceable to the enemy. I think the actual number lost would not exceed 300, perhaps not more than 250" (183). Although Sheridan claimed, "We lost but few horses, considering their condition when we started" (183), the official numbers of horses sent to him strongly suggest that this policy of shooting failed horses, here carried out during his raid on Richmond (May 9–24, 1864), could not have been an isolated one. Consider Henry W. Halleck's letter of June 4, 1864, written from Washington, D.C., to Ulysses S. Grant: "In the month of May we sent to the Army of the Potomac 6,683 cavalry horses in addition to the cavalrymen remounted here. About 1,000 more cavalry horses are being shipped to White House." For Halleck's letter, see *The War of the Rebellion: A Compilation of the Official Records of the Union and Confederate Armies* (Washington, D.C.: Government Printing Office, 1880–1901), ser. 1, 36 (3): 569 (hereafter cited as OR). Sheridan started the Overland campaign with 12,000 mounted cavalrymen, so the need for 7,700 new horses would suggest a loss of 64 percent. I am grateful to Robert E. L. Krick for pointing out his letter.

20. In his narrative (*Memoirs*, 1:176), Sheridan spelled William Clark Falkner's name incorrectly as "Faulkner," anticipating the novelist's later change in the spelling of his surname, but he did spell it correctly in his official report of the action. See OR, ser. 1, 17 (1): 42. Sheridan dated his report August 27, 1862, and referred to the action as having taken place "yesterday," August 26, although he dates it August 27 in the memoirs (*Memoirs*, 1:175). For Falkner's unit affiliation, see *List of Field Officers, Regiments and Battalions in the Confederate States Army, 1861–1865* (Macon, Ga.: J. W. Burke, 1912), 42.

21. Thomas Wolfe, *Look Homeward, Angel* (1929; repr., New York: Charles Scribner's Sons, 1957), xv.

22. Defending his actions, Sheridan included documentation related to the relieving of Warren during the battle of Five Forks and to the implementation of the Reconstruction Laws in New Orleans. See n. 15 above.

23. I have compared Grant's and Sherman's accounts of causes of the war in *Belligerent Muse: Five Northern Writers and How They Shaped Our Understanding of the Civil War* (Chapel Hill: University of North Carolina Press, 2014), 166–67, 170–72.

24. In a note to his reprinting of Sheridan's 1883 essay "The Last Days of the Rebellion," in *Battles and Leaders of the Civil War*, vol. 6 (Urbana: University of Illinois Press, 2004), 6:526–35, editor Peter Cozzens offered this puzzling judgment: "This account of the Appomattox Campaign is longer, markedly superior to, and much more personal than Sheridan's treatment of the subject in his memoirs" (598). In fact, the 1883 version, which corresponds to *Memoirs*, 2:175–202, is shorter than the later version (approximately 4,300 words to 5,800); it omits a description of the battle of Sailor's Creek, April 6, 1865; and it leaves out Lincoln's "laconic despatch" of April 7, 1865, to Sheridan. In fairness to Cozzens, the earlier version included two or three colorful touches that did not make it into the memoirs, such as a jocular quip by Confederate Cadmus M. Wilcox at Appomattox: "'Here, Sheridan, take these saddlebags; they have one soiled shirt and a pair of drawers. You have burned everything else I had in the world, and I think you are entitled to these also'" ("Last Days of the Rebellion," 17). But otherwise it would be hard to defend as "markedly superior" locutions such as "sanguinary engagement" ("Last Days of the Rebellion," 13) to "spirited fight" (*Memoirs*, 2:190) or "'I am very well, thank you'" (Sheridan's response to Grant's "'Sheridan, how are you?'" in "Last Days of the Rebellion," 17) to "I assured him with thanks that I was 'first-rate'" (*Memoirs*, 2:200). Finally, it is unclear how such passive constructions in the earlier version as "Orders were at once given to General Crook" and "Orders were given to complete the formation" ("Last Days of the Rebellion," 8, 15) helped to make it "much more personal" than the first-person, active constructions Sheridan used later in the memoirs. At one point Cozzens undertook to correct Sheridan's Latin, changing *in statu quo* ("Last Days of the Rebellion," 17) to "in status quo" (*Battles and Leaders*, 6:533). Sheridan's version is grammatically correct. Cozzens has published two volumes (vol. 5 [Urbana: University of Illinois Press, 2002] and vol. 6 [Urbana: University of Illinois Press, 2004]) supplementing the original four volumes of *Battles and Leaders of the Civil War*, ed. Robert Underwood Johnson and Clarence Clough Buel, 4 vols. (New York: Century, 1887–88).

25. Philip Henry Sheridan Papers, Library of Congress, box 104, reel 98, shelf no. 19,308. In the letter of December 21, 1886, cited above (n. 10), Sheridan asked Webster to send him a check for $100 each month to pay his clerk for work on the memoirs. The clerk's manuscript followed Sheridan's handwritten first draft, which is often difficult to read. All subsequent discussion of changes in the typescript or the clerk's manuscript refers to this microfilm reel.

26. *OR*, ser. 1, 46 (2): 609. For background on Grant's repeated attempts to get Sheridan to destroy the Virginia Central Railroad and Sheridan's noncompliance, see Morris, *Sheridan*, 222–37.

27. This was another moment revised in the clerk's manuscript, where "I fear" has been inserted above a caret mark and "earnest" has replaced "emphatic."

28. *Personal Memoirs of U. S. Grant*, 2:438.

29. Mark Twain, Livy Clemens, and Susy Clemens, *A Family Sketch and Other Private Writings*, ed. Benjamin Griffin (Oakland: University of California Press, 2014), 40.

30. Even Wittenberg concedes that the Appomattox campaign was Sheridan's "finest moment" and showed him "at his best"; see Wittenberg, *Little Phil*, 149.

31. Thomas Nagel, "Moral Luck," in *Mortal Questions* (Cambridge: Cambridge

University Press, 1979), 25–6; Abraham Lincoln, letter to Albert G. Hodges, April 4, 1864, in *Collected Works of Abraham Lincoln*, ed. Roy P. Basler, 9 vols. (New Brunswick, N.J.: Rutgers University Press, 1953–55), 7:282. For Lincoln's expectation that he would lose the election of 1864, see his "Memorandum Concerning His Probable Failure of Re-election," August 23, 1864, in *Collected Works*, 7:514.

32. For a balanced discussion of Johnston's performance as commander of the Department of the West and Davis's censure of that performance, see Craig Symonds, *Joseph E. Johnston: A Civil War Biography* (New York: Norton, 1992), 187–218.

33. An especially passionate defender of Warren has been Eric J. Wittenberg, who dedicated his edition of Newhall's *With Sheridan in the Final Campaign against Lee* to "the brave men" of the Armies of the Potomac and Northern Virginia and "to the memory of Maj. Gen. Gouverneur K. Warren, whose many contributions to the Union victory in the Civil War have been largely forgotten by history as the result of an injustice" (v). Wittenberg reprinted as appendix B to this edition Warren's 1866 pamphlet defending his actions, "An Account of the Operations of the Fifth Corps, Commanded by Maj. Gen. G. K. Warren, at the Battle of Five Forks, April 1, 1865, and the Battles and Movements Preliminary to It, by G. K. Warren, Late Major General Volunteers" (147–88).

34. McClellan, *Notes on the Personal Memoirs of P. H. Sheridan*, 54.

35. Joshua Lawrence Chamberlain, *The Passing of the Armies: An Account of the Final Campaign of the Army of the Potomac, Based upon Personal Reminiscences of the Fifth Army Corps* (1915; repr., New York: Bantam Books, 1993), 115–16.

36. For background on John Boyd, see Grant T. Hammond, *The Mind of War: John Boyd and American Security* (Washington, D.C.: Smithsonian Institution Press, 2001); and Robert Coram, *Boyd: The Fighter Pilot Who Changed the Art of War* (Boston: Little, Brown, 2002). See especially Hammond's chapter "From Patterns of Conflict to Maneuver Warfare" (136–54), which includes this formulation: "Two concepts underlie Boyd's analysis and synthesis of warfare. They are time and movement, or, more precisely, speed and maneuver. If one moves and constantly presents an opponent with a changing situation and does so quickly, one has a tremendous advantage" (151). Boyd contrasted maneuver warfare with attrition warfare, which students of the Appomattox and Overland campaigns can readily associate with Sheridan and Grant, respectively.

37. Edward Porter Alexander, *Fighting for the Confederacy: The Personal Recollections of General Edward Porter Alexander*, ed. Gary W. Gallagher (Chapel Hill: University of North Carolina Press, 1989), 512.

38. *Twain's Notebooks and Journals*, 3:612n, 614n. Webster and Company had been selling a two-volume set of Sherman's memoirs since September 1890. For background on the failure of the company, see *Mark Twain: Business Man*, vii–viii; and Albert Bigelow Paine, *Mark Twain: A Biography*, 3 vols. (New York: Harper and Brothers, 1912), 2:983–87. News of the bankruptcy appeared in the *New York Times*, Thursday, April 19, 1894, 9. For the later edition of Sheridan's book, see *Personal Memoirs of P. H. Sheridan*, 2 vols., enlarged and ed. Michael V. Sheridan (New York: D. Appleton, 1902). The only available print edition of this book seems to be one published in 2012 by General Books LLC, an imprint of Books LLC of Memphis, Tennessee. General Books LLC scans public domain material and sells it on a print-on-demand basis.

The Last Hour of the Slaveholders' Rebellion

African American Discourse on Lee's Surrender

Elizabeth R. Varon

◇ ◇ ◇ ◇
◇ ◇ ◇ ◇

On January 2, 1888, the Reverend E. K. Love, a Georgia Baptist, addressed a gathering of African Americans in Savannah, convened to celebrate the anniversary of Lincoln's January 1, 1863, Emancipation Proclamation. He began by noting that "this day's celebration necessarily calls up the past"—and he then solemnly evoked the brutality of slavery, "with all its inhuman hardships, wounds, bruises, cowhides, bull-whips." Love turned next not to Lincoln or to the fateful year of 1863 but instead to 1865, when "the mighty God said to the raging billows of slavery thus far shalt thou go and no further." It was "at Appomattox," he explained, "amidst the awful clash of arms," that the "child of liberty was born." The war itself was the "crimson stream" that washed away the "stain of slavery."[1]

In highlighting the place of Appomattox in the story of emancipation, Love acknowledged a powerful tradition among African Americans—a strong belief that Gen. Robert E. Lee's defeat marked the demise of slavery. This chapter will elucidate how that belief took shape in the moment of Union victory and the myriad ways it found expression in the postwar era. The enshrinement of Appomattox as a "freedom day" rested on three interconnected claims: that the Union army's victory over Lee dramatized the manly heroism and agency of African American soldiers; that the surrender brought many slaves their first consciousness and experience of liberation; and that the magnanimous terms of surrender that Lt. Gen. Ulysses S. Grant offered Lee symbolized the promise of racial reconciliation between whites and blacks. These ideas found expression in a wide array of texts, including speeches, newspaper articles and editorials, memoirs, WPA narratives, and works of history, sociology, and literature. And Appomattox was commemo-rated in a wide array of public settings — not only on anniversaries of the sur-render but also at other sorts of civic events.

Lest it seem self-evident that blacks should link freedom and the surren-der, one should note that modern-day historians, almost without exception, have missed this connection. In his pathbreaking account of wartime emanci-pation, *Been in the Storm So Long*, Leon Litwack observed, based on a few tell-ing examples, that "only with 'the surrender,' as they came to call it, did many slaves begin to acknowledge the reality of emancipation." Despite this prom-ising lead, recent scholarship on the demise of slavery has overlooked the sig-nificance of Lee's surrender.[2] Scholarly syntheses by Bruce Levine, Stephanie McCurry, and James Oakes have underscored that emancipation was a pro-cess, not a moment, emphasizing, as Levine has put it, that "a war launched to preserve slavery succeeded instead in abolishing that institution more rapidly and more radically than would have occurred otherwise." Southern blacks hastened and shaped that process: roughly half a million achieved freedom during the war, leaving behind farms and plantations to head to Union lines or coming under Union occupation, and some 150,000 men joined the Union army. Freedom remained elusive, however, for the vast majority — three and a half million bound laborers were still formally enslaved in the spring of 1865. While these scholars acknowledge that only the final defeat of the Con-federacy could guarantee that freedom would prevail over slavery, they have little to say about Appomattox.[3] Meanwhile, a burgeoning literature on black commemorations of emancipation, by scholars such as Mitch Kachun and Kathleen Ann Clark, tends to mention Appomattox only in passing, high-lighting instead the other ceremonial days — such as July 4, January 1, and Juneteenth — on the commemorative calendar.[4]

Such oversight is symptomatic of a broader problem — the tendency of historians to see Lee's surrender as a moment of reconciliation rather than of contestation. On the face of it, what transpired on April 9, 1865, seems simple enough. The patrician Lee met the commoner Grant at Wilmer McLean's parlor at Appomattox Court House, Virginia, to yield up the tattered Con-federate army; Grant, to Lee's surprise, extended a hand of clemency to the prostrate rebels, paroling them and sending them to their homes on the promise that they would never again take up arms against the United States. Lee stoically accepted the terms and rejected calls from his own ranks to prolong the war as a guerrilla conflict. In the days that followed, the remain-ing Confederate armies in the Deep South, too, capitulated. Thus ended the American Civil War, without reprisals.

Two distinct interpretations have structured the scholarship, each influential in its own right. The dominant interpretation, what we might call the triumphalist one, is dramatized by Ken Burns's documentary *The Civil War* and given a patina of scholarly legitimacy by such historians as Bruce Catton and Jay Winik. This is the argument that the surrender "saved America," to use Winik's formulation from his acclaimed 2001 book, *April 1865*. Grant's magnanimity to Lee at Appomattox and Lee's resignation in defeat, enactments of the simple goodness of these two men, unified the country and assured America's rise as a great power on the world stage. By crediting Americans with ending their Civil War far more civilly than any other society ever had ended such a bitter conflict, this interpretation "nourishes the American sense of exceptionalism," the historian Gary Gallagher has noted. Grant and Lee's great achievement at Appomattox was to guarantee that Americans would never again turn against each other.[5]

In a second, revisionist, interpretation, the peace that Grant and Lee tried to conjure came at a terrible price. Their gesture of mutual forgiveness at Appomattox was a harbinger of the overthrow of Reconstruction and the ascendance of the "Lost Cause" mythology, which romanticized the Confederacy. This view is articulated most forcefully by the historian David Blight, whose *Race and Reunion* charts how "Grant's lenient terms" had "transfigured" by the turn of the century into "a slow surrender of a different kind": in their determination to reconcile with white Southerners and restore "order" to the unstable South, Northern whites abandoned their commitment to black citizenship, capitulated to "Jim Crow" segregation, and embraced the gospel of white solidarity. This long retreat, which was well underway by the time Reconstruction formally ended in 1877, "drained the war of political meaning."[6]

Neither the triumphalist interpretation nor the revisionist one (which has prevailed in academic circles) acknowledges the symbolic role Appomattox has played as a black freedom day.[7] This chapter will offer an alternate interpretive framework. Lee's surrender neither transcended politics nor was drained of political meaning but figured as a prominent symbol in the bitter and protracted debates over what, exactly, had been won and lost in the Civil War.

"WE THE COLORED SOLDIERS, HAVE FAIRLY WON OUR RIGHTS"

Beginning in April 1865 and continuing well into the twentieth century, countless African American commentators, including veterans, ministers, politicians, reformers, editors, and historians, depicted Appomattox as the

Regimental flag of the 127th U.S. Colored Troops, emblazoned
with the motto "We Will Prove Ourselves Men." The 127th
was one of seven USCT regiments present at Appomattox.
(Library of Congress Prints and Photographs Division,
reproduction number LC-USZ62-23097)

apogee of black military heroism. They were keenly aware of, and eager to
call the nation's attention to, the fact that seven different regiments of the
United States Colored Troops (USCT) participated in the Appomattox campaign and were present at the surrender. In the last clash of Grant and Lee, at
the end of a fabled and desperate chase across the Virginia countryside from
Petersburg to Appomattox, Lee's army had tried on the morning of April 9 to
break free of a Federal trap, only to find that its last escape route was blocked

by black soldiers in blue: the 8th, 29th, 31st, 41st, 45th, and 116th regiments of the USCT. These troops, with one other USCT regiment (the 127th) waiting in the wings, fought back the advancing Confederates and left Lee no choice but to surrender.[8]

The USCT regiments had just been reassigned from the Twenty-fifth Army Corps of Maj. Gen. Edward O. C. Ord's Army of the James to its Twenty-fourth Corps. The Twenty-fifth Corps, the brainchild of Ord's predecessor, Maj. Gen. Benjamin Butler, had the distinction of being the only corps consisting solely of African American regiments; white officers commanded the black troops. In the last stages of the Appomattox campaign, the Twenty-fifth Corps had been split up, and two of its prime brigades, under Col. Ulysses Doubleday and Col. William W. Woodward, were attached to Maj. Gen. John Gibbon's Twenty-fourth Army Corps to fight alongside the white troops there. Doubleday's brigade was folded into the First Division, under Brig. Gen. Robert S. Foster, and Woodward's brigade joined the Second Division, under Bvt. Maj. Gen. John W. Turner.[9]

These troops had been rushed to the front, marching nearly twenty hours straight and covering some thirty miles on April 8, so they could reinforce Maj. Gen. Philip H. Sheridan's cavalry, which was starting to bend under the force of the Confederate infantry attack that had been launched in the early morning hours of April 9. The Union infantry, marching at the double-quick, arrived at the front at approximately 9:30 A.M. While Ord thought they intervened "barely in time" to save the flustered cavalry, Sheridan believed that his plan had worked like clockwork—on his orders, the cavalry fell back purposefully, gradually, "to give time for the infantry to form its lines and march to the attack." The Federals, in other words, baited the Confederates with a seeming retreat and then sprang the trap: as the Confederates advanced into the breach, they "could see Ord's men emerging from the woods" to the south and pushing up toward the Lynchburg stage road. Gibbon directed Foster's First Division of the Army of the James to form across the road and Turner's division to move forward on Foster's right.[10]

Doubleday's brigade went into action first. Three of its regiments— the 8th, 41st, and 45th USCT (a fourth, the 127th, was posted to the rear)— clashed with Confederate cavalry on Foster's left flank, in the edge of the woods parallel to the Lynchburg stage road. These units then hung back while Woodward's brigade, consisting of the 29th, 31st, and 116th USCT, moved forward to take its place along the Union's main battle line, between Foster's and Turner's white brigades, astride the stage road. These were the units that blocked Lee's escape route and convinced those of the Confederate

Elizabeth R. Varon

high command of the hopelessness of their "break-out" strategy. When they heard confirmation of Lee's surrender, the black troops' "exultation knew no bounds." "They shouted, danced and sang" and "embraced each other" with exuberant joy, a white Union private observed.[11]

The seven black regiments at Appomattox, numbering 2,000 men in all, were a microcosm of black life in America. They included ex-slaves trained at Kentucky's Camp Nelson and free blacks trained at Philadelphia's Camp William Penn. They included men who would become race leaders in the postwar era, such as renowned historian George Washington Williams, influential AME minister William Yeocum, South Carolina judge and legislator William J. Whipper, and Baptist editor William J. Simmons, who was the journalistic mentor to none other than Ida B. Wells. We are only just beginning to recover the stories of still others, more obscure, who filled out the ranks — men such as William H. Costley, whose mother, Nance, had been freed in an 1841 Illinois court case argued by a young upcoming lawyer named Abraham Lincoln, and George Edmondson of the 127th USCT, a descendant of the Hemings family of Thomas Jefferson's plantation Monticello.[12]

For all of these men, regardless of their backgrounds, their presence on the battlefield was itself the culmination of a long struggle. The Federal army had initially turned away black volunteers, on the grounds that African American men did not possess the attributes of patriotism and courage; even after the Union, midway though the war, endorsed emancipation and black enlistment, it granted to black troops only a second-class status within the ranks and shunted them into noncombat roles under white officers. When blacks finally got the chance to fight, they showed their mettle at dozens of engagements such as the charge on Fort Wagner, in the summer of 1863. But African American soldiers were keenly aware that their march toward equality could still be turned back, so long as powerful Confederate armies were in the field. Indeed, the Confederate government viewed all black Union soldiers as so many rebellious slaves and "left it to state authorities either to return captured [soldiers] to owners or execute them as insurrectionaries." Black soldiers were aware too that white Northerners viewed their enlistment as a social experiment — testing the capacity of blacks for citizenship — and that many of those whites hoped and expected that the experiment would, in the end, fail.[13]

It is little wonder, then, that black soldiers quickly seized on the USCT's critical role in Lee's surrender as a vindication of their manhood and claim to citizenship. As William McCoslin of the 29th Regiment USCT put it in a May 1865 letter, "We the colored soldiers, have fairly won our rights by loyalty and bravery." He was echoed by a veteran of the 41st USCT, who in a June 1865 letter to the *Christian Recorder*, the very influential organ of the AME church, noted that it was the "remarkable courage" of black troops that made possible the "capturing of Lee's army."[14]

Black heroism in the last major engagement of the war would long remain a point of pride among African Americans, thanks in part to the efforts of veterans to keep the story in the public eye. No one was more important in this regard than George Washington Williams. Having served with one of the USCT regiments present at the surrender, Williams established a public reputation after the war as a minister, an editor, a Republican politician, and ultimately the leading African American historian of the nineteenth century. Indeed, he was the originator of the postbellum literary genre of "race history." Race histories took the distinctive civilizationist discourse of the nineteenth century—which emphasized the stages of advancement of Western society—and reworked it to chart the process of emancipation. The premise of such histories, to quote the modern-day historian Stephen G. Hall, was that "if African Americans could prove they were a progressive race, it would be impossible to deny them full entry to the body politic." According to George Washington Williams, the role blacks played in Lee's surrender offered unimpeachable proof of the race's progress. In his Reconstruction-era speeches and his landmark *History of the Negro Race in America*, Williams repeatedly insisted that at Appomattox, in the "last hour of the Slave-holders' Rebellion," the "brilliant fighting" of black troops had ensured the triumph of the Union. Black soldiers had "purchased their citizenship," as he put it, "by the sword"—and in so doing proved they could "endure the sharp competition of American civilization." Another USCT veteran, Congressional Medal of Honor recipient Christian A. Fleetwood of the 4th Regiment, likewise celebrated the role of African American troops in the war's climactic campaign, observing in 1895 that "they were one of the strong fingers upon the mighty hand that grasped the giant's throat at Petersburg and never flexed until the breath went out at Appomattox." The pioneering historian Carter G. Woodson would recall in a February 1944 reminiscence that one of his early mentors, while he was working as a coal miner in West Virginia in the 1890s, was a USCT veteran named Oliver Jones. Jones, Woodson remembered fondly, loved to talk about all aspects of black military service in the Civil War but especially about "those veterans who, like himself, were in battle array to attack Lee's army the morning he surrendered at Appomattox Court House."[15]

The fact that black soldiers had defeated *Lee* lent additional symbolic meaning to "the surrender." For Lee and his Army of Northern Virginia typi-

Elizabeth R. Varon

A veteran who became the first African American member of the
Ohio legislature, George Washington Williams proved instrumental in helping
keep alive the memory of black heroism in the Appomattox campaign.
(Courtesy Ohio History Connection, Columbus, Ohio)

fied in the eyes of the USCT the haughty slaveholding elite and its pretense of racial superiority. According to Thomas Morris Chester, the black correspondent embedded with the Army of the James during the Appomattox campaign, the Confederate capitulation was especially sweet because it was a rebuke to the "F.F.V.'s" or "first families of Virginia"—whom he wryly dubbed, after the surrender, the "Fleet-Footed Virginians." This view was echoed by veterans such as Joseph T. Wilson, himself a noted scholar (he published an influential military history, *The Black Phalanx*, in 1887). Only after USCT troops had proven their mettle elsewhere, Wilson noted, were they allowed to fight in the critical Virginia theater; by defeating the "flower" of Confederate manhood at Appomattox, the USCT had answered unequivocally the question of whether black soldiers were the equals of the white master class.[16]

Moreover, Appomattox was aligned in black commentary with another great Virginia battle—the triumph of the Continental army at Yorktown during the American Revolution. "While our hearts swell with pride on the Fourth of July, on this sacred day we feel additional pride and joy in the thought that the glorious flag made independent at Yorktown, was purged of its greatest stain at Appomattox," George Washington Ellis (a midwestern lawyer and social scientist) declared in an Independence Day address in the 1890s. Booker T. Washington, too, made this connection, likening Yorktown's eclipse of British tyranny with the "great surrender at Appomattox" of the slaveholding "aristocracy."[17] For others, the Virginia setting of the surrender mattered not because the state was the birthplace of the Revolution but instead because it was the birthplace of slavery itself. Thus Roscoe Simmons, columnist for the *Chicago Defender*, reminded his readers in 1924 that "slavery began in Virginia" and that, fittingly, "it ended in Virginia" with Lee's capitulation; this made Appomattox, in his view, blacks' "place of salvation."[18]

In short, black commentators made the bold claim that in defeating Lee's army, on Virginia soil, African American troops had dealt a death blow to all that that army stood for. "Servitude" was a "corpse . . . wrapped in the rebels' fallen stars and broken bars for a shroud" and "buried at Appomattox," as the 1892 narrative of William Walker, who had been a slave in Virginia, put it. So deeply did the case for USCT heroism at Appomattox resonate that George Washington Williams's epigram—"the last guns fired at Lee's army were in the hands of Negro soldiers"—became a recurring motif in black public discourse, invoked in the name of uplift and social justice. For example, at an 1885 Philadelphia meeting to promote education, AME church officials called upon African Americans to vanquish the foe of illiteracy by showing the same courage as the heroic black soldier who "fired the last gun at Lee's army."

Elizabeth R. Varon

And it wasn't only men who seized upon this epigram. Leila Amos Pendle-ton, an eminent educator, clubwoman, and race historian, also invoked the "last shots" in her textbook *A Narrative of the Negro*. Animated by the "high-est sentiments of courage and patriotism," as Pendleton put it, USCT soldiers had "won for themselves lasting glory."[19]

In the eyes of black troops, the final campaign of the war in Virginia mat-tered: the fate of the Union still hung in the balance on the morning of Palm Sunday, April 9, 1865 — and their own agency tipped the scales. In highlight-ing the contingencies in the "last hour of the Slaveholders['] rebellion," Afri-can Americans offered a counternarrative to an influential Confederate ar-gument about the outcome of the war: this was the view, articulated most memorably by Lee in his final address to his troops at Appomattox, that the Confederacy lost not because of any moral defect but because it faced the "overwhelming numbers and resources" of the industrial North. For Lee, Union military might signified the ruthless efficiency and unbridled force of modernization itself, while the outnumbered Confederates embodied the traditional — and in his mind, endangered — masculine values of "courage and fortitude."[20] In the African American counternarrative, by contrast, the Union army's victory emanated from its superior morality and courage and manhood — and black troops in particular exemplified how military prowess was animated by moral purpose. In the last hour, Providence had favored the righteous.

In other words, the Appomattox narrative highlighted black agency in two overlapping registers, national and millennial. Black soldiers were agents of the state: they were, Williams wrote, the "muscle and sinew of the Re-public." But they were also the agents of Providence. "The Civil War was a black man's war and it was brought about to redeem both whites and blacks from the curse of slavery," noted Pendleton, succinctly stating the case. The image of blacks as the "redeemer race" had its roots in the efforts of the ante-bellum free black elite to counter whites' pseudoscientific claim that racial differences were inherent and biological. Much of antebellum black ethnol-ogy had decried the aggressive, belligerent, brutal nature of the Anglo-Saxon race and attributed to blacks superior civility and piety. The Civil War reori-ented black ethnology toward an emphasis on African Americans' attributes as warriors. And thus for writers such as Williams and Pendleton, Appomat-tox was the grand culmination of an epic and indeed providential story — the long struggle against slavery — that featured a panoply of freedom fighters, from Crispus Attucks, to Toussaint L'Ouverture, to Nat Turner, to the regi-ments that fired the last shots at Lee. It was no accident that the black soldier

became the "determinative factor in the problem of war," Williams wrote —
"in the Universe of God there are no accidents." "From the first slave-hunt
in unhappy Africa to the surrender of General Lee at Appomattox," the Reverend P. Thomas Stanford, pastor of the Zion Congregational Church in
Haverhill, Massachusetts, wrote in 1897, slavery's "blood-stained hand" had
"defied God and the inexorable law of righteousness." But the "War of Emancipation" had brought "Jehovah's judgment" on the sinning nation. "Let this
never be forgotten," the reverend intoned.[21]

It was not forgotten. Throughout the "nadir" period in race relations that
spanned the late nineteenth and early twentieth centuries, African American writers and orators kept the memory of Appomattox alive as a rhetorical weapon against waves of reactionary proscription. In the wake of World
War I, for example, with a new generation of black veterans demanding recognition of its service, only to face violent reprisals by white supremacist mobs,
black intellectuals invoked Appomattox to renew their faith that the forces
of reaction would, in the end, fail. A memorial to Congress by the "Commission on After-War Problems of the African Methodist Episcopal Church" declared that "the archaic and vicious dogma, 'This is a white man's country,'
which of late has been resurrected," would not prevail — for "when Lee surrendered his sword to the commander of the triumphant armies of freedom
at Appomattox, that dogma fell a shattered idol." The heroic deeds of African American soldiers, from "Bunker Hill to Metz," the petition continued,
had made blacks an "integral part of the body politic." In the same spirit, the
eminent sociologist Kelly Miller claimed in his 1919 study *The Negro's Place
in the New Reconstruction* that not just slavery but the institution's underlying
conceit — "the right of the strong to own the weak" — was "shot to death at
Appomattox." That "righteous judgment" could not be overturned.[22]

That same year, Bishop Levi Jenkins Coppin of the AME Church published his memoir, *Unwritten History*. He wrote of Appomattox, "The war
finally came to a close by the surrender of Lee and the fall of Richmond.
There was no longer any doubt then about the final issue. Slavery, the 'sum of
all villainy,' was crushed. Its ghost has appeared in different and many forms
since General Lee gave up the struggle on the field of battle; but at most, it
is but a ghost."[23]

"SEE WHAT FREEDOM MEANT"

Appomattox signified collective race pride for African Americans and served
symbolically as a wellspring of hope in the fight against racism. But for many

blacks it also symbolized, on the personal level, the consciousness and experience of freedom. Virginia slaves were the first to hear the tidings of the surrender and to fathom the significance of the event. The Reverend Peter Randolph's *From Slave Cabin to The Pulpit* described Lee's surrender as the day on which the slaves in his native Virginia became free; by congregating where Union soldiers were quartered, he observed, these slaves could at last "see what freedom meant." None other than Booker T. Washington, in his classic autobiography, *Up from Slavery*, remembered how "when the war closed, the day of freedom came" to southwestern Virginia; the sight of Confederate soldiers who had deserted Lee's army or been paroled by Grant dramatized for the slaves—as much as a U.S. officer's belated reading of the Emancipation Proclamation did—that the April surrender brought the long-awaited moment of deliverance.[24]

Federal Writers' Project interviews with African Americans who had been slaves in Virginia echo these published reminiscences. Charley Mitchell, remembering his boyhood in Lynchburg, told an interviewer in 1937 that after the surrender, slaves in the area were summoned to the city's fairgrounds to hear the news of their emancipation, for the first time, announced. Joseph Holmes recalled seeing General Grant's legions on the march though the Virginia countryside; it was after the Yankees came through, and after "de Surrender," that Holmes's mistress told him he was free. William Harrison, a native of Richmond, got an early taste of war when his master enlisted in the Confederate army and brought Harrison along with him as his body servant. After the master was captured at Bull's Gap, Tennessee, in November 1864, Harrison joined the Union army. More than 100 years old at the time of his WPA interview, he recalled of his service as a USCT soldier, "I was with General Grant when Lee surrendered at Appomattox. That was freedom." Fanny Berry, for her part, remembered that slaves in Pamplin, Virginia, burst into spontaneous song when they learned that Lee, his escape blocked by the USCT, had raised the white flag—for they at that moment "knew dat dey were free."[25]

As news of the surrender traveled throughout the South, slaves far away from the events at Appomattox also experienced Grant's final triumph as the end of their enslavement. Wesley John Gaines, in his 1897 book, *The Negro and the White Man*, describes the "beautiful and enrapturing" moment he "heard the first tidings proclaiming liberty to the captive":

> I was ploughing in the fields of Southern Georgia. The whole universe seemed to be exulting in the unrestraint of the liberty where-

with God has made all things free, save my bound and fettered soul, which dared not claim its birthright and kinship with God's world of freedom. . . . Suddenly the news was announced that the war had ended and that slavery was dead. The last battle had been fought, and the tragedy that closed at Appomattox had left the tyrant who had reigned for centuries slain upon the gory field. In a moment the pent-up tears flooded my cheeks and the psalm of thanksgiving arose to my lips. "I am free," I cried. . . . Oh! The rapture of that hour![26]

Ruby Lorraine Radford, who interviewed thirty Georgia slaves for the Federal Writers' Project, concluded that "although the Emancipation Proclamation was delivered on January 1st, 1863, it was not until Lee's final surrender that most of the negroes knew they were free." This was a recurring theme in former slaves' reminiscences. For example, James H. Johnson of South Carolina lamented that after "President Lincoln's freedom proclamation in 1863," the "status quo of slavery kept right on as it had." It was only when "General Lee surrendered," he observed in his WPA interview, that "we learned we were free."[27]

For some former slaves, the date of Lee's surrender structured their very sense of time and of history. Eliza Washington told her WPA interviewer, S. S. Taylor, that "the first thing I remember was living with my mother about six miles from Scott's Crossing in Arkansas, about the year 1866. I know it was 1866 because it was the year after the surrender, and we know the surrender was in 1865. I know the dates after 1866. You don't know nothin' when you don't know dates." For Della Harris of Petersburg, too, the passage of time came into focus in 1865. "I don't know just how old I is," she told Susie Byrd in 1937. But Harris remembered with certainty that "I was 13 years old at de time of Lee's surrender." Among the earliest memories of Easter Jones of Georgia was that her brother was born the Sunday that Lee surrendered—and that he was named, after the fallen Confederate capital, "Richmond." Fannie Dorum of Arkansas, ninety-four years old when she was interviewed, began by observing that "I was here in slavery time. The third year of the surrender (1868), I married—married Burton Dorum." For Dorum, the surrender brought the consciousness, and the prerogatives, such as legal marriage, of freedom. And when Lucy Redman Crawford turned 100 years of age in 1939, the *Pittsburgh Courier* featured a story explaining how she had endured slavery in Virginia and built a new life in the North. "Her mind is clear and she has a very retentive memory," the reporter noted, adding that she dated almost every milestone in her life from the time of the surrender.[28]

Elizabeth R. Varon

Just as Appomattox persisted in the memory of many ex-slaves, it was an enduring presence on the commemorative calendar of the freedpeople. The same premise that underlay the reminiscences — that Lee's surrender fulfilled the promise of Lincoln's proclamation — animated the anniversary celebrations. "Surrender Day" festivities began in southern Virginia as early as 1866. Blacks in Mecklenburg County, on the border with North Carolina, commemorated April 9 because, as they saw it, "if Lee had never been beaten . . . the [Emancipation] [P]roclamation would have been to no avail." The date had resonance for black communities well into the twentieth century. For example, a notice published in the *Baltimore Afro-American* for the 1905 "Surrender Anniversary" in Dinwiddie County, Virginia (southwest of Petersburg), promised that "the affair will be an elaborate one and many societies will participate."[29]

Such Appomattox anniversary celebrations were not restricted to Virginia. On April 9, 1914, the black congregation of Philadelphia's Miller Memorial Baptist Church gathered to celebrate "the Emancipation of the Ethiopians from American slavery, by the surrender of General Robert E. Lee to General U. S. Grant at Appomattox." Eleven years later in the same city, the Reverend W. H. Powell gave a sermon at the Shiloh Baptist Church on the sixtieth anniversary of Lee's defeat. The sermon explained that the surrender made effective Lincoln's Emancipation Proclamation — and thus "for all practical purposes the 9th day of April, from that time forward, became the greatest historical event in the history of the race."[30]

The idea that Appomattox signified freedom surfaced even at events commemorating the Emancipation Proclamation itself. At an Emancipation Day celebration in Knoxville, Tennessee, in the winter of 1910, the orator said not one word about Lincoln and his proclamation but instead praised Grant as the herald of freedom. When he "reached his noonday at Appomattox," Grant "pointed out a clear sky . . . saying 'There is still a way'" to Zion. Five years later, on the fifty-second anniversary of the Emancipation Proclamation, the *Baltimore Afro-American* featured an article by N. Barnett Dodson entitled "Milestones in Our History" — and the milestone Dodson highlighted was Appomattox. It was fitting to celebrate Lincoln's proclamation, he explained, but it must be placed in historical context — for it was not "until after the surrender of Lee . . . that the act of Jan. 1, 1863 became truly effective and a general freeing of the slaves throughout the country took place."[31]

African Americans' interpretation of Appomattox as a freedom day incorporated the themes not only of race pride and liberation but also of clemency, which was the keynote of surrender. Judging by the WPA interviews, the comportment of Lee and Grant themselves figured prominently in the black folklore of Appomattox. Eliza Washington, for example, noted of the surrender terms that "General Lee said there wasn't any use doing any more fighting," while "General Grant let all the rebels keep their guns. He didn't take anything away from them." In Cornelius Garner's vivid account, "Grant had Lee all bottled up. Lee couldn' go back, he couldn' go forward, an' he couldn' go sideways. Grant gave him five minutes to surrender. Then Grant told the rebels to go home and be good citizens."[32]

An enduring myth of the surrender was that Grant and Lee met and negotiated the peace under an apple tree in an orchard outside the village of Appomattox. This image was popularized by engravers and lithographers who churned out prints of Grant and Lee under the apple tree, as a pastoral fantasy to grace American homes and public spaces. This piece of folklore, too, appears in African American accounts. Former slave Jeff Stanfield of Virginia claimed in his WPA narrative that Lee and Grant met "up under an apple tree" and they "kissed" and then rode off toward Richmond together.[33]

While one might conclude that blacks shared whites' inclination to romanticize the surrender, or that the ex-slave narrators were telling their white interviewers what they wanted to hear, the WPA interviews take on new meanings when read against nineteenth-century black public discourse on the surrender terms. "Lee surrendered at Appomattox under the shade of the old apple tree," intoned the Reverend G. V. Clark at an 1895 meeting of a black literary association in Memphis, Tennessee, "leaving our brave black heroes covered with glory and crowned with imperishable laurels." "A race with such indomitable courage," he assured his listeners, "must have under God a future, inspiring and glorious." (Clark himself had been born into slavery in Georgia, and first learned of his freedom after the surrender.) This juxtaposition of images, of the apple tree and the USCT, represents an attempt to fuse two modes of black thought — the reconciliationist mode with the emancipationist one (to use David Blight's nomenclature). The reconciliationist mode, which found its most influential champion in Booker T. Washington, promulgated the view that the Civil War's divine purpose was the national reunion itself (and that all white soldiers, Confederate and Union, had played a noble role in the drama); as an accommodation to white culture, this mode was, Blight has argued, a "license to forget" the achievement and promises of emancipation. The emancipationist mode, by contrast, championed by Frederick Douglass and W. E. B. Du Bois, held that the demise of slavery and the slaves' attainment of freedom should rest at the center of the nation's understanding of the war.[34]

Blight and those scholars who have tried to build upon and amend his influential paradigm have drawn stark distinctions between these two modes — perhaps too stark.[35] For in their discourse on Appomattox, blacks attempted to inscribe a civil rights message *into* the magnanimous terms of the surrender. Emphasizing the promise of Appomattox, advocates of civil rights depicted the freedpeople, and black soldiers in particular, as agents not only of their own liberation but also of national healing. George Washington Williams's 1888 *History of the Negro Troops in the War of the Rebellion* praised black soldiers for treating the vanquished Confederates with "quiet dignity and Christian humility." He wrote, "After the Confederate army had been paroled the Negro troops cheerfully and cordially divided their rations with the late enemy, and welcomed them at their campfires on the march back to Petersburg. The sweet gospel of forgiveness was expressed in the Negro soldiers' intercourse with ex-rebel soldiers, who freely mingled with the black conquerors. It was a spectacle of magnanimity never before witnessed."[36] To be sure, this account was wishful and a poor reflection of Confederate hostility toward USCT soldiers. But such memory making was designed to incorporate blacks figuratively into the victors' circle, among those whose generosity had earned them gratitude. T. Thomas Fortune, editor of the influential *New York Age*, struck a similar note in an 1890 address to the National Afro-American League. He paid homage to the black veterans of the Civil War who *"came from Appomattox and its famous apple tree"* and who "like their white comrades went back to their homes after the toils of war and mingled in the pursuits of peace." Their comportment had vindicated "the right of every man born on this soil to be free indeed."[37]

Kelly Miller, too, sustained the belief that the black heroes of the Civil War were heralds of racial harmony. A professor of mathematics and sociology at Howard University, Miller was also a widely read contributor to the black press. In his 1918 book, *An Appeal to Conscience*, he reflected on the 1915 Appomattox "semi-centennial" commemoration in Washington, D.C., in which "white and black veterans, broken with the weight of years," marched in "friendly reunion." Blacks' participation in such an event, he observed, testified to their spirit of forgiveness and their "altruistic patriotism."[38]

Williams, Fortune, and Miller were no accommodationists; indeed, their evocations of Lee's surrender came in the context of impassioned pleas for full equality. In their eyes, the image of black troops as heralds of interracial brotherhood was in no way incompatible with the image of them as fierce warriors. These images corresponded to stages in the process of redemption. As Williams explained, the black soldier had "first swept away the bitter prejudice of the Northern army," then "convinced the Southern soldier that he was his equal in arms," and then proved himself to be a merciful conqueror. The alliance of white and black Union troops, and their shared impulse of magnanimity toward the South, made possible a new narrative of cross-racial unity; that narrative, of which Williams was the principal author, arrayed the black race, in defiance of longstanding prejudice, with the forces of order and progress and civilization.[39]

The ideal of cross-racial unity had long been an animating principle of the abolitionist movement. African Americans elaborated in the early nineteenth century their own narrative of an "unfulfilled" union, an imagined community dedicated to the principle of the "universal brotherhood of man." Black leaders from Richard Allen to James Forten to David Walker to Frederick Douglass invoked this unfulfilled union to refute anti-abolitionist claims that emancipation would open a Pandora's box of racial recrimination and social chaos. But abolitionists were unable, as sectional tensions escalated, to dispel the pervasive fears among whites that any disruption of the racial caste system would embolden slaves to seek vengeance against their masters. Indeed, secessionists cannily played on that fear, arguing that abolition and race war were inseparable.[40]

This antebellum discourse linking emancipation and retribution is essential context for understanding why the Union was so slow to enlist black troops during the war, why the Confederacy was so quick to label black soldiers as insurrectionists, and why the presence of black troops at the moment of peacemaking, on April 9, 1865, was so rife with meaning: for the victors, the Appomattox surrender repudiated, in a way that no other event could, the longstanding charge that emancipationists were disunionists who sought war, chaos, and vengeance. White abolitionists, no less than African American ones, felt vindicated by the way the surrender had been conducted. For example, Horace Greeley's *New York Tribune*, in an April 11, 1865, article titled "Magnanimity in Triumph," declared that blacks, including newly freed slaves, were "on the side of Clemency—of Humanity" and were thus ready to exercise the full prerogatives of citizenship. Moreover, the civility of African American troops in victory seemed all the more remarkable when contrasted with the wartime barbarity of Confederates, whose "no quarter" policy had resulted in the wholesale slaughter of black troops when they had tried to raise the white flag over battlefields such as Fort Pillow. Blacks had proven their valor in the face of "every conceivable indignity," G. V. Clark's 1895 speech titled "Our Fallen Heroes" noted; through it all, they had "always been loyal to the old flag which now floats over a united people."[41] In short, the USCT's courage had redeemed the country from slavery; the purpose of its clemency was to redeem the country from racial hatred.

This discourse of black civility, which took its shape in the moment of the surrender and then inflected the race histories of the late nineteenth century, must be understood as part of a broader reconsideration of black masculinity and citizenship in the postwar period. As scholars such as Craig Thompson Friend and Michele Mitchell have noted, "beginning with Reconstruction, a new purposefulness characterized definitions of manhood" in both the North and South. Men in both sections tried to harmonize what had been competing antebellum ideals of manhood: the ideal of restrained manhood, or of the "Christian gentleman," emphasized pious self-control and the exercise of conscience, while the ideal of martial manhood emphasized physical courage and daring and the defense of honor. While both ideals were in evidence in each region, the restrained manhood image seemed to have prevailed in the antebellum North and that of the martial man in the South.[42]

After the war, with the citizenship status of white Southerners and of blacks in flux, Americans intent on maintaining the racial caste system celebrated those men who seemed to blend the two ideals of manhood—men who thus could restore the link between whiteness and citizenship. As the historian Craig Friend has noted, the man who more than any other came to typify for Southern whites the perfect balance of heroic manliness and self-restrained piety was none other than Robert E. Lee, who had been peerless in battle and gracious in defeat.[43]

Even as they deified Lee, whites opposed to black citizenship rights derided African American men as "inherently lascivious and degenerate," as utterly lacking in courage or self-control. African American soldiers, as part of an unwelcome army of occupation, were singled out, portrayed by opponents of Radical Reconstruction as the very essence of lawless violence and criminality. "This was the fiction" to which race historians such as George Washington Williams "felt obliged to respond." Black leaders of the post-emancipation period thus "considered it critical that . . . men embody controlled manliness," to quote Mitchell.[44]

The determination of race leaders to find their own exemplars of masculinity—men who embodied both courage and self-restraint—helps explain why the surrender of Lee to Grant had such lasting resonance among African Americans. For black veterans of the Appomattox campaign, proven warriors and Christian gentlemen, could be such exemplars. The story of William J. Simmons is a case in point. Simmons was born a slave in Charleston, South Carolina, in 1849. He joined the Union army in 1864, at age fifteen, and was present as a member of the 41st USCT at Appomattox on April 9, 1865. After the war, Simmons rose to prominence as pastor of the First Baptist Church of Lexington, Kentucky, and then as president of State University in Louisville. He often discoursed on the topic of "true masculinity," and he penned an influential race history on that topic, *Men of Mark: Eminent, Progressive and Rising*. Simmons himself was widely regarded, as an 1890 eulogy by a fellow Baptist pastor explained, as a shining model of black masculinity: of a "heroic indomitable spirit" and of "Christian self-control and patience and magnanimity."[45]

One might ask where this valorization of black manhood left black women. There is considerable scholarly dispute on this question. Some historians argue that black politics became more masculinist, patriarchal, and gender exclusive in the late nineteenth century, while others contend that black men and women saw each other as allies, fellow citizens, working at the multiple sites — electoral, reform, and religious — of African American politics. The middle position in this debate holds that efforts by black men to base citizenship claims on manhood never went uncontested by women. And that position accords well with the Appomattox evidence. It is true that race histories by Williams and other men emphasized male heroism. But women such as Leila Amos Pendleton were able to inscribe female heroines into the narrative; in Pendleton's race history, Phillis Wheatley and Harriet Tubman played their own part in the march of progress, setting the stage for the soldiers who fired the last shots at Lee.[46]

The key point is this: in African American race histories, black magnanimity at Appomattox was not a reflection of some innate docility (as ascribed to blacks in romantic-racialist stereotypes) but rather the exercise of moral authority — a conscious effort by men like Williams and Simmons, *as purposeful as Grant's own act of clemency to Lee*, to break the cycle of violence that slaveholders had so long perpetuated.

THE "LOST CAUSE"

But could the cycle be broken? African Americans who invoked Appomattox as a signifier of hope were fighting a rearguard action against a determined and ruthless foe, armed with its own distinct interpretation of the meaning

Elizabeth R. Varon

of Lee's surrender. In the decade after the war, defeated Southerners began to elaborate the Lost Cause tradition, a mythology that romanticized the Old South and the Confederacy; demonized Radical Reconstruction as corrupt and punitive; and justified vigilante violence as a legitimate means to restore the old order. Extensive modern scholarship has charted how such Confederate apologetics achieved cultural hegemony in the late nineteenth century: by emphasizing the essential heroism and nobility of all white soldiers, those in gray and in blue, the Lost Cause mythology fused white supremacy and sectional reconciliation.[47]

But scholars have overlooked the key symbolic function that Appomattox played in this tradition. Needless to say, for champions of the Lost Cause, there were no black heroes in the Appomattox story; there was no liberation from tyranny and no promise of interracial reconciliation. Instead, unreconstructed rebels such as the Confederate major general John B. Gordon interpreted a key line in Grant's surrender terms—the stipulation that paroled Confederate soldiers would "not be disturbed" by the U.S. authorities—as a promise that although slavery was defunct, the racial caste system would remain undisturbed. In the view of men like Gordon, Radical Republicans had broken that promise by according civil rights to ex-slaves, and white Southerners in turn fulfilled the promise when they "redeemed" the region from Northern misrule. Northerners opposed to racial equality too argued that Congressional Reconstruction was a "blight ... upon the apple tree of Appomattox," as one Democratic paper put it; only by forsaking radicalism could the North be reconciled with the South.[48]

White supremacists, in effect, seized Appomattox as a symbol of Confederate righteousness. We can read all of the sorts of African American rhetoric I have quoted as a collective effort to say, in effect, "Appomattox is our moment of triumph, not yours." But while black rhetoric invoked Appomattox to signify a just peace, white supremacists used it to call forth violence. For example, Gordon (who headed Georgia's Ku Klux Klan and represented the state in Congress) credited Lee's army and Grant's with sheathing the "sword of vengeance" and indicted Southern blacks, whom he regarded as criminal and insurrectionary, for unsheathing it. He declared in the U.S. Senate in 1875 that "deluded, ignorant negroes ... with arms to murder and hearts for plunder" perpetrated "crimes not to be described on this floor"—leaving white men no choice but to resort to violence in self-defense. In Gordon's view, blacks had no place whatsoever in the "fraternity" of "once opposing soldiers" who had tried to "inaugurate an era of peace"; the former slaves were beyond the pale of American public opinion and of civilization itself.[49]

The tragic implications of this ideology are starkly illustrated by the WPA reminiscence of Lucinda Elder. Elder was born into slavery near Concord Depot, Virginia. After the war, her master, John Caldwell, announced to his slaves that they were free but could continue to work for him for wages. Lucinda's family accepted this offer. Some years later, she was hired to work as a nursemaid for the family of one Will Jones.

One day this Jones announced to the family that they were going to Appomattox to spend the day and that Lucinda and the children could come too. The significance of the site was well known to Lucinda. "Course, I was tickled mos' to pieces," she told her WPA interviewer, at the prospect of this trip. But Jones had not told her why they were going to Appomattox.[50]

The purpose of the Jones family outing was to witness a lynching—"to see a nigger hung," in Elder's words. She was told he was being punished because he had "kilt a man." "I never saw so many people 'fore, as the number there to see him hang," she recalled. "I jes' shut my eyes." But the macabre lesson was not over. After the lynching, Jones took the family to the famous apple tree of Appomattox lore. Elder described it as a "big tree that had all de bark strip off it and de branches strip off." Jones turned to her and said, "Lucinda, dis de tree where Gen. Lee surrendered." She put her two hands on the tree. She would never ever, as long as she lived, she told her interviewer, forget that one day.[51]

Whatever Jones's intentions in orchestrating this grim excursion, the message was clear: the South had not surrendered white supremacy at Appomattox. This message reverberated in black public discourse on the meaning of April 9. Faced with the malevolent power of the Lost Cause mythology to renew the cycle of violence, some black Americans reluctantly concluded that the effort to read a civil rights message into the surrender was itself a lost cause.

"WHO WON THE CIVIL WAR?"

In the first decades of the twentieth century, an alternative, more somber interpretation of the surrender began to gain currency among black opinion makers. Some commentators insisted that Lee and the South had never accepted defeat; Grant had been too lenient, and thus the spirit of Southern defiance had survived the surrender intact. Decrying "lynching, disfranchising, intimidation, and the present effort of eliminating almost wholly Negro education," a writer in the *Baltimore Afro-American* lamented in 1902 that white Southerners had revived an argument over black inferiority that "we imagined we had won at Appomattox."[52] In 1912, with the Lost Cause cult at a peak of popularity, an article in the *Pittsburgh Courier* bemoaned that "southern thought is conquering the entire country on the race question." The article quoted a poem called "Appomattox" by the black poet Charles Dinkins in which Lee addresses his defeated army with the following charge:

> When falls the sword, the better way
> Becomes the soldier's part to play
> The south will whip the north some day
> With ink and pen

Lee's prophecy, the article noted, had come to pass: the unrepentant South had struck down the doctrine of social equality and "revolutionized the sentiment, doctrines and practices of the north."[53]

Precisely the same point was made by an editorial in the *Afro-American* on the fiftieth anniversary of the surrender in 1915. With the establishment of "Jim Crow" segregation, the South had "gained all it fought for and more," while the North meekly allowed "the South to bend and break at its own sweet will" all of the gains that emancipation had promised. These, alas, were "the results growing out of Appomattox."[54]

Such laments testify to the waning of a once-proud tradition—of the "fondly cherished" belief, as one black journalist put it, that Appomattox had consigned the regime of racial subordination to "the things of the past." The significance of Appomattox as a frame for analyzing race relations, and the difficulty of sustaining it as an emblem of hope, is summed up cogently in a 1939 article in the *Pittsburgh Courier*. That year (the very year *Gone with the Wind*—that ultimate Lost Cause artifact—hit movie screens), when Marian Anderson was refused the opportunity to sing at Constitution Hall, the *Courier* protested, with an article titled "Who Won the Civil War?" "For years now," the article's author, P. L. Prattis, began, in deference to tradition, "we have been taught to celebrate the surrender of Lee at Appomattox on April 9, 1865." But "when Miss Anderson complains that she can sing in every capital in the world except the capital of her own country," he went on, one could be "pardoned for wondering whether it was General Grant who surrendered to General Lee at Appomattox Courthouse."[55]

The waning belief in Appomattox as a "freedom day" can be understood as part of a broader reorientation of African American culture. The 1920s and 1930s brought "unmistakable changes in the form and content of black collective memory," to quote Fitzhugh Brundage. His work on Southern commemorations, along with Mitch Kachun's on black festive culture, charts the shift: celebrations of emancipation did not disappear, but they did dwindle, as a new generation of black activists and scholars rejected what they deemed the sentimental approach to commemorating American history. The "civilizationist" ideology, with its emphasis on Anglo-European ideas of progress, lost ground, while the "New Negro" movement popularized the message that blacks should take pride in their African heritage. New types of mass art forms, such as cinema, emerged as vehicles of cultural expression. And institutions such as the NAACP were established to provide "a structure from which to work for the reinstatement of blacks' civil and political rights."[56]

In the case of Appomattox, the passing from the scene of ex-slaves and black veterans who had firsthand memories of April 9 surely contributed to the decline of the tradition; so too did the fact that World War I and then World War II supplanted the Civil War as the test cases for how America would reward black patriotism. While all of these developments were factors in the fading of Appomattox from black memory, it was ultimately the "long absence of any real freedom," Kachun has cogently observed, that caused the demise of emancipation celebrations. In that light, it is noteworthy that Appomattox seems to have persisted on the black commemorative calendar longest in Chicago, where a strong and assertive black political elite had institutionalized the commemoration of the surrender in its "Appomattox Club." Established in 1900, this civic organization soon emerged as a prominent vehicle for the city's black political leadership. Deeming Lee's surrender an "epoch making event," the club held an annual "monster celebration" to mark the Appomattox anniversary and to renew the hope that "millions of white and black men" might "bridge the chasm of political, social and economic prejudice and in universal brotherhood shake hands as did Grant and Lee." In addition to commemorating the surrender, the club held an annual memorial service in honor of two heroes of the antislavery cause, Abraham Lincoln and Frederick Douglass. For this organization, racial reconciliation was premised not on forgetting emancipation but on remembering it as a complex process that linked the two iconic days of January 1, 1863, and April 9, 1865.[57] In 1943 a proclamation by the Illinois General Assembly, introduced by black assemblyman Charles J. Jenkins of Chicago, designated April 9 as a holiday in the state to be observed as "Freedom Day." No other states followed suit.[58]

It is noteworthy, too, that as evocations of Appomattox as a moment of emancipation dwindled in black discourse, Juneteenth emerged, nationally, as the most important festive marker of freedom. The Juneteenth commemorative tradition reflected the experience of slaves in the southwestern theater of the Civil War, where there was sporadic combat after Lee's surrender. The date of June 19, 1865, marks the liberation of Galveston, Texas, the last major port in Confederate control, by the Union army under Bvt. Maj. Gen. Gordon Granger. Granger promulgated General Orders No. 3, informing Texas slaves of the passage of the Emancipation Proclamation and thus belatedly granting them freedom. In the years after the war, Texas freedpeople celebrated this moment of liberation with elaborate festivals, and civic groups began purchasing land where the celebrations could be held; for example, citizens of Mexia bought a ten-acre plot for their Juneteenth events and designated the site Booker T. Washington Park. The Juneteenth tradition soon spread to Louisiana, Arkansas, Oklahoma, and beyond.[59]

The black press in the Northeast covered such events somewhat quizzically; "it seemed strange to Northern and Eastern visitors," the *New York Amsterdam News* opined, to see emancipation "celebrated this time of year." Like other emancipation festivities, Juneteenth lost momentum in the middle decades of the twentieth century. But unlike Appomattox, it experienced a dramatic revival, as a consequence of the modern-day civil rights movement. In 1968 the Poor People's March organized by the Southern Christian Leadership Council, the Urban League, and other civil rights organizations culminated with a massive Juneteenth rally in Washington, D.C. And in 1973, the Reverend C. Anderson Davis, former president of the Houston NAACP, began a campaign to revive Juneteenth as "Emancipation Day" in Texas and establish it as a state holiday. As the historian Elizabeth Hayes Turner has explained, "The civil rights movement accomplished what all the years of Juneteenth celebrations could not"—it "legitimated black history." What had once been a southwestern tradition was now capturing the national imagination. Texas declared Juneteenth a state holiday in 1979, and to date some thirty other states and the District of Columbia have followed suit.[60]

While a detailed history of Juneteenth is beyond the scope of this essay, I would like to suggest that by acknowledging the role Appomattox played in black remembrance, we can gain insight into why Juneteenth has emerged as such a compelling day. In some sense, Juneteenth represents an alternative to Appomattox, as a day free of the negative connotations and bitter contestation associated with Lee's surrender: Juneteenth has not been claimed by Confederate apologists and incorporated into Lost Cause mythology, and there is no way to read Granger's declaration of emancipation in Texas as a story of white Southern heroism or resurgence.

But at the same time, Juneteenth as a historical moment shares some of the symbolic power, for the freedom struggle, as Appomattox. Juneteenth celebrations typically have featured readings of the Emancipation Proclamation and have extolled the leadership of Abraham Lincoln, the role of the Union army in actuating emancipation, and the heroism and sacrifices of black soldiers; thus Juneteenth represents, as Lee's surrender once did for blacks, a counter-memory to the Lost Cause tradition. Both moments, coming as they did long after the Emancipation Proclamation, speak, too, to the depth of slaveholder treachery (in withholding the news of emancipation) and the reality of freedom deferred.[61]

Indeed, in the fall of 1935, the *Chicago Defender*, America's most influential black newspaper, ran a piece titled "Emancipation Day: When Is It?" The piece began with a description of a Juneteenth celebration in Texas, an event that featured a band, a parade, a baseball game, and a "big dance." But the author, Roberta Clay, then moved on to contextualize Juneteenth among the many other "dates commemorating the freeing of the slaves." Those dates included April 9, 1865; January 1, 1863; September 22, the date of the preliminary proclamation of 1862; and August 1, which signified the 1834 abolition of slavery in the British West Indies. Together these dates signify clearly that emancipation was not an event but a process.[62]

While the enshrinement of Juneteenth as a freedom day suggests that Americans may be recovering from the "historical amnesia" that has blunted the nation's memory of emancipation, unless we remember Appomattox, too, as a moment of liberation, we are granting the "Lost Cause" mythology too much power to obscure the past. The story of black commemoration of Lee's surrender reminds us that the rise of the white supremacist version of national reunion was neither swift nor inexorable. Long after that mode of reconciliation had supposedly trumped the emancipationist vision, African Americans insisted that the Union defeat of Lee was theirs; that it had enduring meaning as a moment of deliverance; and that they had a vital role to play in the process of national healing and regeneration.[63]

NOTES

1. Rev. E. K. Love, "Oration Delivered on Emancipation Day, January 2, 1888" (Savannah, Ga., n.p., 1888), 2–3, accessed through "African American Perspectives: Pamphlets from the Daniel A. P. Murray Collection, 1818–1907," http://memory.loc.gov/ammem/aap (hereafter cited as AAP).

2. Leon Litwack, *Been in the Storm So Long: The Aftermath of Slavery* (New York: Knopf, 1979), 171–72.

3. Bruce Levine, *The Fall of the House of Dixie: The Civil War and the Social Revolution That Transformed the South* (New York: Random House, 2013), 289, 295; Stephanie McCurry, *Confederate Reckoning: Power and Politics in the Civil War South* (Cambridge,

Elizabeth R. Varon

Mass.: Harvard University Press, 2010), 283; James Oakes, *Freedom National: The Destruction of Slavery in the United States, 1861–1865* (New York: Norton, 2012).

4. Mitch Kachun, *Festivals of Freedom: Meaning and Memory in African American Emancipation Celebrations, 1808–1915* (Amherst: University of Massachusetts Press, 2003), 118; William Blair, *Cities of the Dead: Contesting the Memory of the Civil War in the South, 1865–1914* (Chapel Hill: University of North Carolina Press, 2004), 137, 163; Kathleen Ann Clark, *Defining Moments: African American Commemorations and Political Culture in the South, 1863–1913* (Chapel Hill: University of North Carolina Press, 2005).

5. Jay Winik, *April 1865: The Month That Saved America* (New York: HarperCollins, 2001). For a concise and illuminating analysis of the "exceptionalist" view of the surrender, see Gary W. Gallagher, "There Is Rancor in Our Hearts . . . Which You Little Dream Of," *Civil War Times Illustrated* 39 (May 2000): 68–72. See also the National Park Service sponsored pamphlet by Noah Andre Trudeau, *The Campaign to Appomattox* (Eastern National, 1995), 56.

6. David W. Blight, *Race and Reunion: The Civil War in American Memory* (Cambridge, Mass.: Belknap Press of Harvard University Press, 2001), 214, 356. For an index of the influence of Blight's argument, see Alice Fahs and Joan Waugh, eds., *The Memory of the Civil War in American Culture* (Chapel Hill: University of North Carolina Press, 2004), in which Blight is cited some fifty times. On the literature of reunion, see also Nina Silber, *Romance of Reunion: Northerners and the South, 1865–1900* (Chapel Hill: University of North Carolina Press, 1993); Carol Reardon, *Pickett's Charge in History and Memory* (Chapel Hill: University of North Carolina Press, 1997); and John R. Neff, *Honoring the Civil War Dead: Commemoration and the Problem of Reconciliation* (Lawrence: University Press of Kansas, 2005).

7. This framework is elaborated in my *Appomattox: Victory, Defeat, and Freedom at the End of the Civil War* (New York: Oxford University Press, 2013). My interpretation aligns with those in two recent studies that question the Blight thesis: Caroline E. Janney, *Remembering the Civil War: Reunion and the Limits of Reconciliation* (Chapel Hill: University of North Carolina Press, 2013); and Barbara Gannon, *The Won Cause: Black and White Comradeship in the Grand Army of the Republic* (Chapel Hill: University of North Carolina Press, 2011).

8. Chris M. Calkins, *The Battles of Appomattox Station and Appomattox Court House, April 8–9, 1865* (Lynchburg, Va.: H. E. Howard, 1987), 88–90; Joseph T. Wilson, *The Black Phalanx: African American Soldiers in the War of Independence, the War of 1812 and the Civil War* (1887; repr., New York: Da Capo, 1994), 458–59.

9. Edward G. Longacre, *Army of Amateurs: General Benjamin F. Butler and the Army of the James, 1863–1865* (Mechanicsburg, Pa.: Stackpole Books, 1997), 243–44; Calkins, *Battles of Appomattox Station*, 88–93.

10. Report of Maj. Gen. Edward O. C. Ord, April 26, 1865, U.S. War Department, *The War of the Rebellion: A Compilation of the Official Records of the Union and Confederate Armies*, 127 vols., index, and atlas (Washington: Government Printing Office, 1880–1901) (hereafter cited as *OR*), 46 (1): 1162; Report of Maj. Gen. Philip H. Sheridan, May 16, 1865, *OR* 46 (1): 1109; Report of Maj. Gen. John Gibbon, April 24, 1865, *OR* 46 (1): 1175.

11. Calkins, *Battles of Appomattox Station*, 19, 79, 88–93, 100–101; Wilson, *Black Phalanx*,

458–59; "Too Exuberant Joy," in *War Anecdotes and Incidents of Army Life*, ed. Albert Lawson (Cincinnati: E. H. Beasley, 1888), 142.

12. On Williams see John Hope Franklin, *George Washington Williams* (Chicago: University of Chicago Press, 1985); on Yeocum, *Christian Recorder*, August 25, 1887; on Whipper, see Eric Foner, *Freedom's Lawmakers* (Baton Rouge: Louisiana State University Press, 1996); on Simmons, see "Eulogy on William J. Simmons," in W. Bishop Johnson, *Sermons and Addresses* (Lynchburg, Va.: Virginia Seminary Steam Print, 1899), 4–5, accessed through AAP, and Miriam DaCosta-Willis, ed., *The Memphis Diary of Ida B. Wells* (Boston: Beacon Press, 1995), 121–27; on Costley, see Carl M. Adams, "The First Slave Freed by Abraham Lincoln: A Biographical Sketch of Nance Legins (Cox-Cromwell) Costley, circa 1813–1873," *For the People: A Newsletter of the Abraham Lincoln Association* 3 (Autumn 1999): 1–2; on Edmondson, see Lucia C. Stanton, *"Those Who Labor for My Happiness": Slavery and Thomas Jefferson's Monticello* (Charlottesville: University of Virginia Press, 2012).

13. For background on the USCT, see, for example, Dudley Taylor Cornish, *The Sable Arm: Black Troops in the Union Army, 1861–1865* (Lawrence: University Press of Kansas, 1956); James M. McPherson, *The Negro's Civil War: How American Blacks Felt and Acted during the War for the Union* (New York: Pantheon, 1965); Joseph T. Glatthaar, *Forged in Battle: The Civil War Alliance of Black Soldiers and White Officers* (Baton Rouge: Louisiana State University Press, 2000); John David Smith, ed., *Black Soldiers in Blue: African American Troops in the Civil War Era* (Chapel Hill: University of North Carolina Press, 2002); and John Cimprich, *Fort Pillow, a Civil War Massacre and Public Memory* (Baton Rouge: Louisiana State University Press, 2005), 62 (quotation).

14. McCoslin quoted in Noah Andre Trudeau, *Like Men of War* (New York: Little, Brown, 1998), 423; *Christian Recorder*, July 29, 1865. On black soldiers' conceptions of citizenship, see Chandra Manning, *What This Cruel War Was Over: Soldiers, Slavery, and the Civil War* (New York: Knopf, 2007), 193–98.

15. George W. Williams, *History of the Negro Race in America from 1619 to 1880* (New York: G. P. Putnam's Sons, 1883), 341–44; Stephen G. Hall, *A Faithful Account of the Race: African American Historical Writing in Nineteenth-Century America* (Chapel Hill: University of North Carolina Press, 2009), 155; Christian A. Fleetwood, *The Negro as a Soldier* (Washington, D.C.: Howard University Print, 1895), 13–14, AAP; C. G. Woodson, "My Recollections of the Veterans of the Civil War," *Negro History Bulletin*, February 1, 1944, 116.

16. R. J. M. Blackett, ed., *Thomas Morris Chester, Black Civil War Correspondent* (Baton Rouge: Louisiana State University Press, 1989), 302, 313, 332; Wilson, *Black Phalanx*, 378, 392, 406, 458.

17. George Washington Ellis, "G. W. Ellis' Oration" (n.p.: n.p., 189–[?]), 1, AAP; Booker T. Washington, *A New Negro for a New Century* (1900; repr., New York: Arno Press, 1969), 149. This idea persisted—as late as 1931 the *Chicago Defender* ran an article celebrating the two great surrenders in Virginia: "one was that of majesty to independence; the other of slavery to FREEDOM.... Yorktown was the beginning of the nation. APPOMATTOX saw it fixed to a divine purpose." *Chicago Defender*, October 24, 1931.

18. *Chicago Defender*, July 26, 1924.

Elizabeth R. Varon

19. *Christian Recorder*, September 10, 1885; Thomas S. Gaines, ed., *Buried Alive (behind Prison Walls) for a Quarter of a Century: Life of William Walker* (Saginaw, Mich.: Friedman and Hynan, 1892), 208, accessed through the Documenting the American South website, http://docsouth.unc.edu (hereafter cited as docsouth); Leila Amos Pendleton, *A Narrative of the Negro* (Washington, D.C.: R. L. Pendleton, 1912), 90, 157–67.

20. On Lee's farewell address, see Michael Fellman, *The Making of Robert E. Lee* (Baltimore: Johns Hopkins University Press, 2000), 190–93.

21. George Washington Williams, *A History of the Negro Troops in the War of the Rebellion, 1861–1865* (New York: Harper and Brothers, 1888), 326; Pendleton, *Narrative*, 157–65; P. Thomas Stanford, *The Tragedy of the Negro in America: A Condensed History of the Enslavement, Sufferings, Emancipation, Present Condition and Progress of the Negro Race in the United States of America* (Boston: Charles W. Wasto, 1897), 49. On the literary tradition of blacks as the "redeemer race," see, for example, Mia Bay, *The White Image in the Black Mind: African-American Ideas about White People, 1830–1925* (New York: Oxford University Press, 2000).

22. Charles Spencer Smith, *A History of the African Methodist Episcopal Church* (Philadelphia: Book Concern of the A. M. E. Church, 1922), 395–97 (docsouth); Kelly Miller, *The Negro's Place in the New Reconstruction* (Washington, D.C.: Howard University Press, 1919), 10.

23. Bishop L. J. Coppin, *Unwritten History* (Philadelphia: A. M. E. Book Concern, 1919), 100.

24. Peter Randolph, *From Slave Cabin to the Pulpit: The Autobiography of Rev. Peter Randolph: The Southern Question Illustrated and Sketches of Slave Life* (Boston: J. H. Earle, 1893), 57–58; Booker T. Washington, *Up from Slavery* (1901; repr., New York: Penguin, 2000), 13.

25. Mitchell, Texas Narratives, vol. 16, pt. 3, 112; Holmes, Alabama Narratives, vol. 1, 195; Harrison, Arkansas Narratives, vol. 2, pt. 3, 185–86, accessed through the "Born in Slavery: Slaves Narratives from the Federal Writers' Project, 1936–1938" website, http://memory.loc.gov/ammem/snhtml, 110, 186, 195 (hereafter cited as FWP); Charles L. Perdue Jr., Thomas E. Barden, and Robert K. Phillips, eds. *Weevils in the Wheat: Interviews with Virginia Ex-slaves* (Charlottesville: University Press of Virginia, 1976), 39. For background on the WPA interview process and on both the shortcomings and the richness of the interviews as a window into "black folk thought," see Bay, *The White Image in the Black Mind*, 115–16.

26. Wesley John Gaines, *The Negro and the White Man* (Philadelphia: A. M. E. Publishing House, 1897), 71–72.

27. Radford, Georgia Narratives, vol. 4, pt. 4, 346–47; Johnson, South Carolina Narratives, vol. 14, pt. 3, 45, all in FWP.

28. Washington, Arkansas Narratives, vol. 2, pt. 7, 49; Harris, Virginia Narratives, vol. 17, 24; Jones, Georgia Narratives, vol. 4, pt. 4, 345; Dorum, Arkansas Narratives, vol. 2, pt. 2, 180, all in FWP; *Pittsburgh Courier*, May 20, 1939.

29. Kachun, *Festivals of Freedom*, 118 (Mecklenburg quotation); see also W. Fitzhugh Brundage, *The Southern Past: A Clash of Race and Memory* (Cambridge, Mass.: Harvard University Press, 2005) 80. On the Dinwiddie event, see the *Baltimore Afro-American*, March 17, 1905.

30. *Philadelphia Tribune*, April 18, 1914; June 13, 1925.

31. *Chicago Defender*, February 19, 1910; *Baltimore Afro-American*, January 2, 1915.

32. Washington, Arkansas Narratives, vol. 2, pt. 7, 55–56, FWP; Perdue, Barden, and Phillips, *Weevils in the Wheat*, 29, 103.

33. Perdue, Barden, and Phillips, *Weevils in the Wheat*, 280. On the origins and expressions of the apple tree myth, see Harold Holzer, Gabor S. Boritt, and Mark E. Neely Jr., "Images of Peace," *Civil War Times Illustrated*, January 2006, 74–80.

34. G. V. Clark, "Our Fallen Heroes," in James T. Haley, *Afro-American Encyclopedia; or, the Thoughts, Doings, and Sayings of the Race* (Nashville, Tenn.: Haley and Florida, 1895), 378; Blight, *Race and Reunion*, 300, 324–25.

35. Articles by M. Keith Harris and Andre Fleche argue that the emancipationist view of the war was stronger among Union veterans, white and black, than Blight's interpretation had suggested, but they too emphasize that the emancipationist mode was fundamentally at odds with the reconciliationist one. M. Keith Harris, "Slavery, Emancipation, and Veterans of the Union Cause: Commemorating Freedom in the Era of Reconciliation, 1885–1915," *Civil War History* 53 (2007): 264–90; Andre Fleche, "'Shoulder to Shoulder as Comrades Tried': Black and White Union Veterans and Civil War Memory," *Civil War History* 51 (2005): 175–201. See also Gannon, *Won Cause*.

36. Williams, *History of the Negro Troops*, 289–93.

37. T. Thomas Fortune, "It Is Time to Call a Halt," in *Lift Every Voice: African American Oratory, 1787–1900*, ed. Philip S. Foner and Robert J. Branham (Tuscaloosa: University of Alabama Press, 1998), 713–28.

38. Kelly Miller, *An Appeal to Conscience: America's Code of Caste a Disgrace to Democracy* (New York: Macmillan, 1918), 77.

39. George Washington Williams, "Centennial: The American Negro from 1776–1876; Oration Delivered at Avondale, Ohio, 1876," AAP.

40. Elizabeth R. Varon, *Disunion! The Coming of the American Civil War, 1789–1859* (Chapel Hill: University of North Carolina Press, 2008).

41. *New York Tribune*, April 11, 1865; Clark, "Our Fallen Heroes"; Cimprich, *Fort Pillow*.

42. Craig Thompson Friend, ed., *Southern Masculinity: Perspectives on Manhood in the South since Reconstruction* (Athens: University of Georgia Press, 2009), x. See also Philip Brian Harper, *Are We Not Men? Masculine Anxiety and the Problem of African American Identity* (New York: Oxford University Press, 1996); Michele Mitchell, *Righteous Propagation: African Americans and the Politics of Racial Destiny after Reconstruction* (Chapel Hill: University of North Carolina Press, 2004); and Hannah Rosen, *Terror in the Heart of Freedom: Citizenship, Sexual Violence, and the Meaning of Race in the Postemancipation South* (Chapel Hill: University of North Carolina Press, 2009).

43. Friend, *Southern Masculinity*, xi–xii.

44. Rosen, *Terror in the Heart of Freedom*, 45–49; Harper, *Are We Not Men?*, xvi; Mitchell, *Righteous Propagation*, 11.

45. Johnson, *Sermons and Addresses*, 7; William J. Simmons, *Men of Mark: Eminent, Progressive and Rising* (Cleveland: Geo. M. Rewell, 1887), 49–57.

46. On this debate, see Rosen, *Terror in the Heart of Freedom*, 306n103; and Martha S. Jones, *All Bound Up Together: The Woman Question in African American Public Culture*,

1830–1900 (Chapel Hill: University of North Carolina Press, 2007), chap. 4; Pendleton, *Narrative*.

47. On the Lost Cause, see, for example, Blight, *Race and Reunion*; Gaines Foster, *Ghosts of the Confederacy: Defeat, the Lost Cause, and the Emergence of the New South* (New York: Oxford, 1987); Gary W. Gallagher and Alan T. Nolan, eds., *The Myth of the Lost Cause and Civil War History* (Bloomington: Indiana University Press, 2000); Fahs and Waugh, *Memory of the Civil War*, and Caroline E. Janney, *Burying the Dead but Not the Past: Ladies' Memorial Associations and the Lost Cause* (Chapel Hill: University of North Carolina Press, 2008).

48. See, for example, Gordon's testimony in *Report of the Joint Select Committee Appointed to Inquire into the Condition of the Affairs in the Late Insurrectionary States* (Washington, D.C.: U.S. Congress, 1872), 316–17, and *Valley Virginian*, February 21, 1866, February 27, 1867; for the last quote, see *Brooklyn Eagle*, April 9, 1875. For context, see George C. Rable, *But There Was No Peace: The Role of Violence in the Politics of Reconstruction* (Athens: University of Georgia Press, 1984), esp. 93–94.

49. *Congressional Record*, 43rd Cong., 2nd sess., 1875, 269–71.

50. Elder, Texas Narratives, vol. 16, pt. 2, 17–20, FWP.

51. Ibid.

52. *Baltimore Afro-American*, July 12, 1902.

53. *Pittsburgh Courier*, April 27, 1912.

54. Ibid.; *Baltimore Afro-American*, April 17, 1915.

55. *Baltimore Afro-American*, April 15, 1899; *Pittsburgh Courier*, March 11, 1939.

56. Brundage, *Southern Past*, 102–4; Kachun, *Festivals of Freedom*, 257–58.

57. *Chicago Defender*, February 11, 1911; April 12, 1913; April 11, 1914. See also Paula J. Giddings, *Ida: A Sword among Lions* (New York: Amistad, 2009), 636.

58. Kachun, *Festivals of Freedom*, 258; *Chicago Defender*, April 10, 1943.

59. For the history of Juneteenth, see, for example, Elizabeth Hayes Turner, "Juneteenth: Emancipation and Memory," in *Lone Star Pasts: Memory and History in Texas*, ed. Gregg Cantrall and Elizabeth Hayes Turner (College Station: Texas A&M University Press, 2007), 143–75; Brundage, *Southern Past*; William H. Wiggins Jr., "Juneteenth: A Red Spot Day on the Texas Calendar," in *Juneteenth Texas: Essays in African-American Folklore*, ed. Francis Edward Abernethy (Denton: University of North Texas Press, 1996), 237–50; Kathlyn Gay, *African-American Holidays, Festivals, and Celebrations* (Detroit: Omnigraphics, 2007), 250–57.

60. *New York Amsterdam News*, June 27, 1936; on the Poor People's March, see *Chicago Daily Defender*, June 17, 1968, and *Baltimore Afro-American*, June 22, 1968; on Davis, and for quotation, see Turner, "Juneteenth," 163.

61. Turner, "Juneteenth," 150–60, 164; Wiggins, "Juneteenth," 248–50. On contemporary developments, see the National Juneteenth Christian Leadership Council's press releases at http://www.njclc.com and *Washington Post*, June 19, 2009. There is a tangible connection between the two freedom days, as the seven USCT regiments that fought at Appomattox were sent, in May 1865, to Texas, both to roust the last pockets of Confederate troops there and to guard against possible incursions by the puppet government that the French had set up in Mexico. While these troops

were not attached to Granger's corps as he entered Galveston (they were sent to points farther south on the Gulf Coast), they were part of the Union's army of liberation and surely helped to spread the word of freedom in the Lone Star State. On the Twenty-Fifth Corps's service in Texas, see Longacre, *Army of Amateurs*, 319–20.

62. *Chicago Defender*, September 14, 1935.

63. On the persistence of the emancipationist legacy, see Julie Roy Jeffrey, *Abolitionists Remember: Antislavery Autobiographies and the Unfinished Work of Emancipation* (Chapel Hill: University of North Carolina Press, 2008).

Elizabeth R. Varon

Bibliographic Essay

Readers hoping to further explore the final months of the war in the Eastern Theater should first consult the notes for each of the essays, which collectively cover a wide range of primary and secondary sources.

As with all of the books in the Military Campaigns of the Civil War series, the best source for published primary material on the armies is the U.S. War Department, *The War of the Rebellion: A Compilation of the Official Records of the Union and Confederate Armies*, 127 vols., index, and atlas (Washington, D.C.: Government Printing Office, 1880–1901). For materials that cover January–June 1865, see series 1, volume 46, parts 1–3. As Keith Bohannon's essay in this volume explains, coverage of the respective armies is unbalanced, with far more Federal than Confederate reports and correspondence. Volumes 7–8 of part 1 of *Supplement to the Official Records of the Union and Confederate Armies*, ed. Janet B. Hewett and others, 95 vols. and 5-vol. index (Wilmington, N.C.: Broadfoot, 1994–2001), also contain some pertinent material.

For the Union high command, volumes 13–15 of *The Papers of Ulysses S. Grant*, ed. John Y. Simon and others, 32 vols. to date (Carbondale: Southern Illinois University Press, 1967–), are essential regarding the general-in-chief's decisions and actions. For the general's postwar reflections, see *Personal Memoirs of U. S. Grant*, 2 vols. (New York: Charles L. Webster, 1885–86). For a convenient modern edition, with some correspondence added, see Ulysses S. Grant, *Memoirs and Selected Letters*, ed. Mary Drake McFeely and William S. McFeely (New York: Library of America, 1990). On the Army of the Potomac's commander, see George Gordon Meade, *The Life and Letters of George Gordon Meade, Major-General United States Army*, 2 vols. (New York: Scribner's, 1913).

Robert E. Lee's letters and other documents can be found in *The Wartime Papers of R. E. Lee*, ed. Clifford Dowdey and Louis H. Manarin (Boston: Little, Brown, 1961). Closest to a memoir from Lee are his postwar conversations with William Allan, William Preston Johnston, and Edward Clifford

Gordon, published as "Testimony of R. E. Lee" in Gary W. Gallagher, ed., *Lee the Soldier* (Lincoln: University of Nebraska Press, 1996). Walter Taylor's *Lee's Adjutant: The Wartime Letters of Colonel Walter Herron Taylor, 1862–1865* (Columbia: University of South Carolina Press, 1995) offers a view from Confederate headquarters through the eyes of a member of Lee's staff.

For firsthand views from within the armies, readers can select from numerous titles. Among Union letters and diaries, artillerist Charles S. Wainwright's *A Diary of Battle: The Personal Journals of Colonel Charles S. Wainwright, 1861–1865*, ed. Allan Nevins (New York: Harcourt, Brace and World, 1962) and *The Civil War Letters of General Robert McAllister*, ed. James I. Robertson Jr. (New Brunswick, N.J.: Rutgers University Press, 1965) are essential. Theodore Lyman contributed two excellent accounts: *Meade's Headquarters, 1863–1865: Letters of Colonel Theodore Lyman from the Wilderness to Appomattox*, ed. George R. Agassiz (Boston: Atlantic Monthly, 1922), and *Meade's Army: The Private Notebooks of Lt. Col. Theodore Lyman*, ed. David W. Lowe (Kent, Ohio: Kent State University Press, 2007). For materials from men in the ranks, see John W. Haley, *The Rebel Yell and the Yankee Hurrah: The Civil War Journal of a Maine Volunteer*, ed. Ruth L. Silliker (Camden, Maine: Down East Books, 1985); Elisha Hunt Rhodes, *All for the Union: The Civil War Diary and Letters of Elisha Hunt Rhodes*, ed. Robert Hunt Rhodes (New York: Random House, 1985); and Wilbur Fisk, *Hard Marching Every Day: The Civil War Letters of Private Wilbur Fisk, 1861–1865*, ed. Emil Rosenblatt and Ruth Rosenblatt (Lawrence: University Press of Kansas, 1992; originally published privately in 1983 as *Anti-rebel: The Civil War Letters of Wilbur Fisk*).

On the Confederate side, a sampling of diaries and letters that cover the period from January through April 1865 include John H. Chamberlayne and C. G. Chamberlayne, *Ham Chamberlayne, Virginian: Letters and Papers of an Artillery Officer in the War for Southern Independence, 1861–1865* (Richmond, Va.: Dietz Print. Co., 1932); Alex L. Wiatt, ed., *Confederate Chaplain William Edward Wiatt: An Annotated Diary* (Lynchburg, Va.: H. E. Howard, 1994); John Dooley, *John Dooley's Civil War: An Irish American's Journey in the First Virginia Infantry Regiment*, ed. Robert Emmett Curran (Knoxville: University of Tennessee Press, 2012); and Oscar Hinrichs, *Stonewall's Prussian Mapmaker: The Journals of Captain Oscar Hinrichs*, ed. Richard Brady Williams (Chapel Hill: University of North Carolina Press, 2014).

For firsthand views from behind the lines, readers can select from a significant number of titles. Among women's diaries, two stand out: *"Journal of a Secesh Lady": The Diary of Catherine Ann Devereux Edmondston, 1860–1866*, ed. Beth Gilbert Crabtree and James W. Patton (Raleigh: North Carolina

Division of Archives and History, 1979), and Judith W. McGuire's *Diary of a Southern Refugee: During the War* (1867; repr., Salem, N.H.: Ayer, 1986). Three other titles notable in covering the last few months of the war include John B. Jones, *A Rebel War Clerk's Diary at the Confederate States Capital*, 2 vols. (Philadelphia: Lippincott, 1866); Michael Bedout Chesson and Leslie Jean Roberts, eds., *Exile in Richmond: The Confederate Journal of Henri Garidel* (Charlottesville: University of Virginia Press, 2001); and volume 3 of *The Diary of George Templeton Strong*, ed. Allan Nevins and Milton Halsey Thomas, 4 vols. (New York: Macmillan, 1952).

Veterans wrote extensively about the Appomattox campaign, but like most retrospective accounts, theirs often reveal more about the postwar world than about wartime events and interpretations. Such is certainly the case with Joshua Chamberlain's *The Passing of the Armies: An Account of the Final Campaign of the Army of the Potomac, Based upon Personal Reminiscences of the Fifth Army Corps* (1915; repr., New York: Bantam, 1993). For an account of the evolution of Chamberlain's postwar descriptions of the surrender ceremony at Appomattox, readers should turn to chapter 5 of Stephen Cushman's *Belligerent Muse: Five Northern Writers and How They Shaped Our Understanding of the Civil War* (Chapel Hill: University of North Carolina Press, 2014). As Cushman's essay in this volume reminds us, among the most revealing of the Union accounts remains Philip H. Sheridan's *Personal Memoirs of P. H. Sheridan, General United States Army*, 2 vols. (New York: Charles L. Webster, 1888). Andrew A. Humphreys, who served as chief of staff to George G. Meade and later as commander of the Second Corps, contributed *The Virginia Campaign of '64 and '65: The Army of the Potomac and the Army of the James* (New York: Scribner's, 1883), a book of lasting value that used records from the War Department as well as correspondence with officers from both sides. For Union rank and file, see such accounts as Henry E. Tremain, *Sailor's Creek to Appomattox Court House, 7th, 8th, 9th April, 1865: Or, the Last Hours of Sheridan's Cavalry* (New York: C.H. Ludwig, 1885).

Among Confederate memoirs, readers should begin with Edward Porter Alexander's *Military Memoirs of a Confederate: A Critical Narrative* (New York: Scribner's, 1907) and *Fighting for the Confederacy: The Personal Recollections of General Edward Porter Alexander*, ed. Gary W. Gallagher (Chapel Hill: University of North Carolina Press, 1989), the latter of which offers one of the best military overviews of the Army of Northern Virginia. Readers consulting James Longstreet's *From Manassas to Appomattox: Memoirs of the Civil War in America* (Philadelphia: Lippincott, 1896) should keep in mind that the First Corps commander wrote his memoirs in large part as a response to postwar critics such as Jubal Early. John B. Gordon's *Reminiscences of the Civil War* (1903; repr., Baton Rouge: Louisiana State University Press, 1993) offers a counterpart to Chamberlain's account of the surrender ceremony at Appomattox.

As with the memoirs, five multivolume sets include valuable postwar testimony, which should be read with some caution. *Southern Historical Society Papers*, ed. J. William Jones and others, 52 vols. (1876–1959; repr., with 3-vol. index, Wilmington, N.C.: Broadfoot, 1990–92), and the *Confederate Veteran*, 40 vols. (1893–1932; repr., with 3-vol. index, Wilmington, N.C.: Broadfoot, 1984–86), are foundational for Confederate topics. Equivalent Union material resides in the *Papers of the Military Order of the Loyal Legion of the United States*, 66 vols. and 3-vol. index (Wilmington, N.C.: Broadfoot, 1991–96). Read before the state commanderies of the Military Order of the Loyal Legion of the United States, many of these papers illuminate aspects of operations in June and July 1864. Union and Confederate veterans contributed to volumes 4 and 5 of *Papers of the Military Historical Society of Massachusetts*, 14 vols. (1895–1918; repr. in 15 vols. with a general index, Wilmington, N.C.: Broadfoot, 1989–90), and to volume 4 of *Battles and Leaders of the Civil War*, ed. Robert Underwood Johnson and Clarence Clough Buel, 4 vols. (New York: Century, 1887–88).

For overviews of the Appomattox campaign, readers should consult William Marvel, *Lee's Last Retreat: The Flight to Appomattox* (Chapel Hill: University of North Carolina Press, 2002); Gary W. Gallagher, "An End and a New Beginning," in *Appomattox Court House*, by the U.S. National Park Service (Harpers Ferry, W.Va.: Division of Publications of the National Park Service, 2003), 27–81; Burke Davis, *To Appomattox: Nine April Days, 1865* (New York: Hold, Rinehart, and Winston, 1959); and Chris M. Calkins, *The Appomattox Campaign, March 29–April 9, 1865* (Lynchburg, Va.: Schroeder, 2008). Burke Davis's *The Long Surrender* (New York: Random House, 1985); J. Tracy Power's *Lee's Miserables: Life in the Army of Northern Virginia from the Wilderness to Appomattox* (Chapel Hill: University of North Carolina Press, 1998); Noah Andre Trudeau's *Out of the Storm: The End of the Civil War, April–June 1865* (Baton Rouge: Louisiana State University Press, 1994); editors Mark Grimsley and Brooks D. Simpson's *The Collapse of the Confederacy* (Lincoln: University of Nebraska Press, 2001); Joseph T. Glatthaar's *General Lee's Army: From Victory to Collapse* (New York: Free Press, 2008); and Perry D. Jamieson's *Spring 1865: The Closing Campaigns of the Civil War* (Lincoln: University of Nebraska Press, 2015) are more general titles containing lengthy sections on the final campaign in the East.

Several of the campaign's individual battles have received detailed attention. On the fall of Petersburg, readers should consult A. Wilson Greene, *The Final Battles of the Petersburg Campaign*, 2nd ed. (Knoxville: University of Tennessee Press, 2008); Earl J. Hess, *In the Trenches at Petersburg: Field Fortifications and Confederate Defeat* (Chapel Hill: University of North Carolina Press, 2009); and Noah Andre Trudeau, *The Last Citadel: Petersburg, June 1864–April 1865* (1991; reprint, El Dorado Hills, Calif.: Savas Beatie, 2014). For the fighting at Five Forks, Edwin C. Bearss and Chris Calkins's *The Battle of Five Forks* (Lynchburg, Va.: H. E. Howard, 1985) remains the best full-length study. On Sailor's Creek, see Derek Smith, *Lee's Last Stand: Sailor's Creek, Virginia, 1865* (Shippensburg, Pa.: White Mane Books, 2002).

Several notable books take a close look at what happened on and immediately after April 9. On the morning's battle, see Chris M. Calkins, *The Battles of Appomattox Station and Appomattox Court House, April 8–9, 1865* (Lynchburg, Va.: H. E. Howard, 1987). Elizabeth R. Varon's award-winning *Appomattox: Victory, Defeat, and Freedom at the End of the Civil War* (New York: Oxford University Press, 2013) examines the bitter and contested meaning of the surrender as understood by Grant, Lee, their respective soldiers, and African Americans. Chris M. Calkins's *The Final Bivouac: The Surrender Parade at Appomattox and the Disbanding of the Armies, April 10–May 20, 1865* (Lynchburg, Va.: H. E. Howard, 1988) details the surrender parade and the Federal occupation of Southside Virginia in the six weeks after the surrender, while Robert M. Dunkerly's *To the Bitter End: Appomattox, Bennett Place, and the Surrenders of the Confederacy* (El Dorado Hills, Calif.: Savas Beatie, 2015) provides brief overviews of the Confederate surrenders beginning with Appomattox and continuing through the Trans-Mississippi. Finally, William B. Holberton's *Homeward Bound: The Demobilization of the Union and Confederate Armies, 1865–66* (Mechanicsburg, Pa.: Stackpole Books, 2001) traces the demobilization of both the Union and Confederate armies.

In 1887, the *Southern Historical Society Papers* published a list of Confederates paroled at Appomattox. Historians have noted numerous problems with this list, including men counted twice and others who were omitted. For the most thorough list of paroles, see William G. Nine and Ronald G. Wilson, *The Appomattox Paroles, April 9–15, 1865* (Lynchburg, Va.: H. E. Howard, 1989).

For photographs, readers should consult William A. Frassanito, *Grant and Lee: The Virginia Campaigns, 1864–1865* (New York: Scribner's, 1983). Although it offers fewer iconic photographs than the author's earlier books on Gettysburg and Antietam, this one also juxtaposes modern photographs alongside period views of numerous sites and provides a useful analytical text. For more illustrative material, including color reproductions of paintings, see Jerry Korn and the Editors of Time-Life Books, *Pursuit to Appomattox: The Last Battles* (Alexandria, Va.: Time-Life Books, 1987).

A trio of books completes this short review of worthwhile literature. For the broadest strategic picture of the war in the late winter and early spring of 1865, readers should go first to Herman Hattaway and Archer Jones, *How the North Won: A Military History of the Civil War* (Urbana: University of Illinois Press, 1983). Parts of trilogies by Bruce Catton and Douglas Southall Freeman continue to engage those hoping for fine narrative treatments. The third volume of Freeman's *Lee's Lieutenants: A Study in Command*, 3 vols. (New York: Charles Scribner's Sons, 1942–44), describes and analyzes Confederate leaders, and Catton's *A Stillness at Appomattox* (Garden City, N.Y.: Doubleday, 1953) remains one of the most poignant treatments of the Army of the Potomac's final campaign.

Contributors

WILLIAM W. BERGEN is an independent scholar living in Charlottesville, Virginia.

KEITH BOHANNON is a member of the Department of History at the University of West Georgia and teaches courses on the Civil War and the history of Georgia. He is the author of a number of essays and articles in scholarly journals and popular magazines and a coeditor of *Campaigning with "Old Stonewall": Confederate Captain Ujanirtus Allen's Letters to His Wife*.

PETER S. CARMICHAEL is the Fluhrer Professor of History and the director of the Civil War Institute at Gettysburg College. He is the author and editor of four books, including *The Last Generation: Young Virginians in Peace, War, and Reunion* and *Audacity Personified: The Generalship of Robert E. Lee*.

STEPHEN CUSHMAN is Robert C. Taylor Professor of English at the University of Virginia and on the advisory board of the Nau Center for Civil War History at the University of Virginia. He has written several volumes of poetry and literary criticism, as well as *Bloody Promenade: Meditations on a Civil War Battle*, which focuses on the battle of the Wilderness, and *Belligerent Muse*, which examines the narrative artistry of Abraham Lincoln, Walt Whitman, William T. Sherman, Ambrose Bierce, and Joshua Lawrence Chamberlain.

WILLIAM C. DAVIS recently retired as the executive director of the Virginia Center for Civil War Studies at Virginia Tech. His most recent books are *Inventing Loreta Velasquez: Confederate Soldier Impersonator, Media Celebrity, and Con Artist* and *Crucible of Command: Ulysses S. Grant and Robert E. Lee — The War They Fought, the Peace They Forged*.

WAYNE WEI-SIANG HSIEH is an associate professor of history at the U.S. Naval Academy. He has also served as a State Department political officer in Iraq between July 2008 and June 2009, where he managed civilian U.S. government efforts in Tuz, Iraq. He is the author of *West Pointers and the Civil War: The Old Army in War and Peace* and a coauthor of *A Savage War: A Military History of the Civil War.*

CAROLINE E. JANNEY is a professor of history at Purdue University and the past president of the Society of Civil War Historians. She is the author of *Burying the Dead but Not the Past: Ladies' Memorial Associations and the Lost Cause* and *Remembering the Civil War: Reunion and the Limits of Reconciliation,* as well as a coeditor with Gary W. Gallagher on the previous Military Campaigns of the Civil War volume *Cold Harbor to the Crater: The End of the Overland Campaign.*

SUSANNAH J. URAL is a professor of history and a codirector of the Dale Center for the Study of War and Society at the University of Southern Mississippi. She is the author of several books and articles on the U.S. Civil War era, including most recently *Hood's Texas Brigade: The Soldiers and Families of the Confederacy's Most Celebrated Unit.*

ELIZABETH R. VARON is Langbourne M. Williams Professor of American History and the associate director of the Nau Center for Civil War History at the University of Virginia. Her most recent book, *Appomattox: Victory, Defeat, and Freedom at the End of the Civil War,* won the 2014 Library of Virginia Literary Award for Nonfiction.

Index

Page numbers in *italics* refer to illustrations.

recommended by, 171, 172; in Sheridan's memoirs, 239–40, 244, 247; African Americans and surrender by, 254–78; Union strength viewed by, 263

Lee, William H. F. "Rooney," 95, 98, 104, 131, 214n17

Lee's Lieutenants (Freeman), 87

Levine, Bruce, 255

Lewis, Harriet C., 68

Lewis, W. G., 199

Lewis's Farm (Quaker Road), battle of, 90

Lieber, Francis, 184–85

Life and Campaigns of Robert E. Lee (McCabe), 84–85

Lightfoot, C. E., 196

Lilley, Robert Doak, 209

Lincoln, Abraham, 3, 20, 23, 239, 240, 276, 278; reelection of, 13, 14, 17, 18, 22, 27, 29, 33, 139; McClellan's suspicions of, 16; Meade's reassignment blocked by, 19, 118; Butler relieved by, 22; assassination of, 111, 174, 205, 206, 209, 248; Confederate peace overture to, 143–44, 146, 151, 160, 163–64; in Richmond, 156–57; in Sheridan's memoirs, 243–44; as trial lawyer, 259

Littlefield, J. H., 53–54

"Little Phil" and His Troopers (Barr and Hinton), 221–22

Little Round Top, 72

Litwack, Leon, 255

Lockett, James, 179

Lomax, Lunsford L., 195, 209

Long, A. L., 185

Longacre, Edward G., 31

Longstreet, James, 43, 44, 52, 89, 131–32, 140, 173, 178, 180, 226; consolidation opposed by, 50; Grant-Lee meetings proposed by, 148

Look Homeward, Angel (Wolfe), 231

Lost Cause, 7, 84, 87, 107, 212, 247, 256, 272–75, 277–78

Love, E. K., 254

Lowery, Robert, 73

Lyman, Theodore, 170

Lynchburg, Va., 4, 131, 208, 237; Confederate supplies in, 157, 171–72, 195–96; paroles issued in, 200, 204, 207, 210

Lynchburg Beauregards. *See* Army of Northern Virginia, units in

Macon Light Artillery, 195

Magruder, John Bankhead, 74

Mahone, William, 180, 183

Manassas, first battle of (first battle of Bull Run), 26, 55, 234

Manassas, second battle of, 21, 41, 42, 43, 70, 74, 88

Marshall, Charles, 184, 185

Martin, Martha E. Gallemore, 79n58

Martin, William "Howdy," 56–58, 71, 72, 74

Marvel, William, 194, 213n6, 213–14n10

Mason, St. George Tucker, 208

Mattocks, Charles, 179–80

Mauney, William Andrew, 194

Maximilian, emperor of Mexico, 248

May, W. C., 65

Mayo, Joseph, Jr., 98, 103–4

McCabe, James D., Jr., 84–85

McCabe, William Gordon, 95, 182, 195, 207–8, 210

McClellan, Carswell, 250–51n18

McClellan, George B., 19, 26, 112, 121, 123, 229, 248; excessive prudence of, 15–16; as presidential candidate, 20, 25, 34; as cavalry authority, 113–14, 115; Franklin linked to, 118; cavalry mismanaged by, 119; Stoneman promoted by, 120; memoirs of, 223

McClernand, John A., 20

McCoslin, William, 259–60

McCurry, Stephanie, 255

McDonald, Greenberry, 42, 46

McGowan, Samuel, 99

McGraw, Joseph, 207

McGregor, William Morrell, 95

McIntosh, David, 192–93

McKinnon, R. J., 69

McLean, Wilmer, 5, 182, 246, 247, 255

McPherson, James B., 110, 227

Meade, George G., 2, 21, 23, 30, 32, 120, 121, 129, 170, 180–81, 248; replacement of, 15, 18, 19, 24; Griffin viewed by, 16–17, 27; Army of the Potomac reorganized by, 18–19; Warren viewed by, 25; Sheridan vs., 27, 115–16, 123, 226, 227; academic accomplishments of, 28; as prospective Shenandoah Valley commander, 118–19; Fitz Lee's surrender to, 197

Men of Mark (Simmons), 272

Mercer, Alfred, 49–50

Merritt, Wesley, 123, *128*, 129, 131, 178

Mexican War, 18, 121, 234

Middle Military Division, 118, 198, 234, 237

Milam County Greys. *See* Army of Northern Virginia, units in

Military Division of the Missouri, 21

Miller, Kelly, 264, 269–70

Millican, E. B., 76n12

Missionary Ridge, battle of, 27, 224–25, 232

Mississippi Partisan Rangers (7th Mississippi Cavalry), 231

Mitchell, Charley, 265

Mitchell, Michele, 271

Mixon, Charles, 54–55

Mobile, Ala., 30, 33

Monocacy, battle of, 184

Monroe Doctrine, 144

Moorman, Marcellus N., 196

Mordecai, Emma, 174

Mosby, John Singleton, 198–99, 204, 205–6, 245

Mosby's Rangers (43rd Virginia Battalion), 198–99, 205–6

Moseley, Sidney E., 48–50

Mount Jackson, Va., 205

Munford, Thomas T., 205, 207; at Five Forks, 94–95, 100–101, 102, 103; at Warren court of inquiry, 98; surrender rejected by, 195, 206; surrender of, 210

Murray, Asa, 72

Murray, James, 71–72

Murray, John David, 71–72

Murray, Owen, 72

Murray, Robert Washington, 71–72

Murray, Sarah, 72

Myers, Gustavus A., 141

NAACP, 276

Nagel, Thomas, 239

Napoleon I, emperor of the French, 111

Narrative of the Negro, A (Pendleton), 263

Nashville, battle of, 28, 117

Negro and the White Man, The (Gaines), 265–66

Negro's Place in the New Reconstruction, The (Miller), 264

Newhall, Frederick C., 133, 250n14, 253n33

New Market, battle of, 20

New Market, Va., 205

New Orleans, La., 248

Ninth Corps, Army of the Potomac. *See* Army of the Potomac, units in

9th Maine Volunteer Infantry Regiment, 72

9th Virginia Infantry. *See* Army of Northern Virginia, units in

North American Review, 220, 236, 240

North Carolina Cavalry, 197

Oakes, James, 255

Oakes, John Kerr, 204

Old, Robert, 194

O'Neal, J. B., 199

Ord, Edward O. C., 32–33, 133, 148, 241, 246, 247; African American soldiers led by, 4, 258; political opposition to, 22, 27–28; Butler replaced by, 22, 117; Army of the James strengthened by, 31

Otey's Battery. *See* Army of Northern Virginia, units in

Overland campaign, 2, 7, 14, 16, 23, 111, 126; heavy casualties of, 6, 45; Sigel's and Butler's shortcomings during, 17; Sheridan in, 27, 115, 119, 130, 226, 230; McClellan's shortcomings during, 115; cavalry raids during, 116, 119, 226; in Sheridan's memoirs, 230, 237–38

Packard, Joseph, 177

Page, Charles A., 174

Parke, John, 23–24, 27, 28, 30, 33

Parker, Ely S., 247

Passing of the Armies, The (Chamberlain), 244–45

Patrick, Marsena R., 37n18

Patterson, James, 65

Pea Ridge, battle of, 146

Peebles Farm, battle of, 91

Peeks, W. W., 48

Pegram, William R. J., 92, 95, 101, 207

Pendleton, Leila Amos, 263, 272

Pendleton, William Frederic, 208

Peninsula campaign, 120

Petersburg, Va., 2, 14, 19, 27, 30, 32, 84, 110, 118, 175; trenches surrounding, 3, 33, 46, 88, 90, 91, 94, 99, 131, 193, 194; Richmond's fate linked to, 3, 83, 89, 153; Grant's mistrust of Butler and, 21, 117; Grant's anxiety at, 30; Confederate morale at, 47; conditions in, 88; rail links to, 89; Lee's constraints at, 91–92, 131

Pettigrew-Kirkland-MacRae Brigade, 55–56

Phelps, Charles R., 196

Pickett, Charles F., 174

Pickett, George E., 3, 6–7, 86, 91–92, 101, 178; historical judgments of, 83–87; Sheridan vs., 89–90, 94; gun placement by, 95; Lee's "at all hazards" order to, 96, 98; blunders by, 98–106; Anderson criticized by, 104–5

Pickett, LaSalle Corbell, 108n23

Pickett's Charge, 55, 83–84

Pickett's Men (Harrison), 85

Pittsburgh Courier, 266, 275

Pleasonton, Alfred, 7, 114, 119, 121–22, 123

Poor People's March, 277

Pope, John, 21

Porter, Horace, 129–30, 169n68

Potts, Frank, 181, 197

Powell, Robert M., 63

Powell, W. H., 267

Prattis, P. L., 275

Prince, James, 210

Quaker Road (Lewis's Farm), battle of, 90

R. E. Lee (Freeman), 87

Race and Reunion (Blight), 255

Radford, Ruby Lorraine, 266

Radical Republicans, 17, 18

Randolph, Peter, 265

Ransom, Matt W., 94–95, 100, 101, 102, 106

Rawlins, John, 240, 247

Reagan, John H., 43, 58, 157, 162

Reams Station, battle of, 24, 91

Reconstruction, 111, 240, 248, 256, 271, 273

Red River campaign, 17

Reynolds, John, 121

Rhett, Robert Barnwell, 139

Richardson, C. B., 185

Richardson, Charles Coker, 202, 212

Richmond, 17, 48; evacuation of, 3, 8, 14, 89, 131, 138–39, 170–75, 184, 193, 264; Petersburg's fate linked to, 3, 83, 89, 153; Lee's defense of, 33, 88, 110, 139, 156, 157; late surrenders in, 204

Richmond & Danville Railroad, 3–4, 89, 105, 204

Richmond Whig, 68

Rives, William C., 151

Roberts, William P., 105, 197–98

Robertson, Jerome B., 43, 44, 53

Robertson, John Forrest, 196–97

Robinson, L. D., 207

Rogers, Jefferson C., 48

Rosecrans, William, 20–21

Rosser, Thomas, 98, 101, 102, 106, 196, 201, 204; fish fry episode linked to, 6, 83, 85–87; surrender rejected by, 195, 200, 205, 206, 208–9; surrender of, 209, 212

Rowland, Thomas J., 202

Russia, 113

Sabers, 111–13

Sailor's Creek, battle of, 3, 8, 132, 133, 158, 179, 180–81, 194–95, 244

Salisbury, N.C., 30

Sandy Point Mounted Rifles. *See* Army of Northern Virginia, units in

"Sanitary Camps," 75n4

Scales, Alfred North, 99

Schadt, Caroline, 68–69

Schadt, William, 68–69

Schofield, John M., 172, 227

Scott, Robert N., 186

Scott, Winfield, 27

Searle, Edwin, 54

Second Corps, Army of Northern Virginia. See Army of Northern Virginia, units in

Second Corps, Army of the Potomac, 19, 24, 31, 100, 105, 131, 179, 180. See Army of the Potomac, units in

2nd Maryland Battery (Baltimore Light Artillery). See Army of the Potomac, units in

2nd Michigan Cavalry, 124, 231

2nd Virginia Cavalry. See Army of Northern Virginia, units in

Seddon, James A., 51, 53, 141, 146

Sedgwick, John, 26, 27, 28

17th Tennessee Infantry Regiment, 200

17th Virginia Cavalry. See Army of Northern Virginia, units in

7th Mississippi Cavalry (Mississippi Partisan Rangers), 231

Seward, William H., 143, 180

Sharpe, George H., 193

Sharps carbine, 124

Shelby, Joe, 74

Shenandoah Valley, 17, 19, 26, 33, 123, 184, 195; Sheridan's commands in, 7, 18, 110–11, 113, 116, 117, 118, 122, 125, 130, 132, 232–33; Confederate operations in, 117, 141; Confederate operations in, 117, 141; after surrender, 205, 206, 207

Shepley, George, 174

Sheridan, Michael, 248

Sheridan, Philip H., 4, 20, 30, 128, 235, 258; Early routed by, 2, 126–27, 234, 236; Lee's right flank attacked by, 3, 131; aggressiveness of, 7, 9, 25–26, 27, 33, 105, 110–11, 122, 127, 129, 134; leadership style of, 7, 9, 110–11, 126, 134, 228–29, 241–42; memoirs of, 9, 125, 220–48; rebellious streak of, 9, 127, 129, 227, 236, 239–40, 245; at Shenandoah Valley, 18, 113, 116–27,

130, 132, 134, 232–33; Warren dismissed by, 25–26, 98, 115, 122, 240–43; American Indians and, 26, 223–24, 245; at West Point, 26–27, 226–27; Meade vs., 27, 115–16, 123, 226, 227; undistinguished academic record of, 28; Ord's deference to, 32; at Five Forks, 83–84, 87, 89–90, 91, 92, 94, 98, 99, 101, 105–6, 115, 129, 130, 134; shortcomings of, 115; Stoneman compared to, 120, 121; as Michigan Cavalry commander, 124; confidence of, 125–26; in Appomattox campaign, 129–33, 181, 194, 236–47; death of, 222, 223; reputation of, 222; self-criticism by, 226–27; empathy of, 228–30; as horseman, 230–31; effectiveness esteemed by, 232; on nature of war, 233–34; Grant praised by, 237–38, 246, 247–48; during Reconstruction, 240; celerity stressed by, 243–46

Sherman, William T., 2–3, 20, 27, 68, 156; memoirs of, 9, 220–21, 223, 226, 229, 248; Grant's trust in, 17–18; march to sea of, 30, 33; Johnston's surrender to, 111, 162–63, 164, 208; at Atlanta, 116, 117; amnesty granted by, 162–63; guerrillas feared by, 210; war viewed by, 234; leadership viewed by, 242–43

Sherrill, D. M., 48

Shoemaker, John J., 196, 210

Shoemaker's Battery. See Army of Northern Virginia, units in

Sigel, Franz, 17, 20, 117

Simmons, Roscoe, 262

Simmons, William J., 259, 272

Simms, William E., 147

Sims, Benjamin, 194, 207

Singleton, James W., 140–41, 143, 145

16th North Carolina Battalion, 197

Sixth Corps, Army of the Potomac. See Army of the Potomac, units in

61st Pennsylvania Infantry. See Army of the Potomac, units in

Skinner, William, 205

Slavery, 9, 49, 143, 151, 234, 254–55, 259, 260, 262–73, 276–78

Smith, E. Kirby, 74, 248
Smith, James J., 180
Smith, John, 48
Smith, William Farrar, 27
Sither, Mark, 63
Somers, Albert, 210
Somers, Thomas A., 210
Sorrel, Moxley, 210
Southern Christian Leadership
   Conference, 277
Southern Historical Society Papers, 212
South Side Railroad, 83, 87, 89, 90, 105, 204
Speed, James, 219n94
Spencer repeating carbine, 7, 111, 112–13,
   124, 126, 127, 132, 133–34
Spotsylvania, battle of, 27, 28, 55
Stagg, Peter, 130
Stanfield, Jeff, 268
Stanford, P. Thomas, 264
Stanton, Edwin M., 19–20, 23, 30, 172, 184–
   85, 198, 205, 244; document retention
   ordered by, 8, 172, 174, 181; Meade
   defended by, 18; command for Hancock
   crafted by, 24
Staples, J. D., 65
Steele, Frederick, 23
Stephens, Alexander H., 140, 143, 144, 151
Steuart, George H., 101, 102, 103, 120–21
Stevens, Walter H., 181
Stoneman, George, 30, 119, 120–21, 123
Stones River, battle of, 27, 231, 232
Stonewall Brigade (Virginia's First
   Brigade), 55–56
Streetman, Sam, 48
Stuart, J. E. B., 112, 115, 116, 124, 226
Stuart Horse Artillery. *See* Army of
   Northern Virginia, units in
Supplement to the Official Records, 186
Surry Light Artillery Battery, 196, 202–3,
   212
Sutherland Station, 90

Talcott, Thomas M. R., 179
Taylor, Erasmus, 182
Taylor, R. C., 56

Taylor, S. S., 266
Taylor, W. C., 207
Taylor, Walter H., 177, 184, 191n44
Terrill, William R., 226–27
Terry, William, 48, 171
3rd Arkansas Infantry. *See* Army of
   Northern Virginia, units in
3rd Delaware Infantry, 54
3rd Virginia Infantry. *See* Army of
   Northern Virginia, units in
3rd Virginia Reserves, 200
Thirteenth Amendment, 143
13th Virginia Cavalry, 207, 208
Thomas, George H., 28, 34, 116
Tilden, John Newel, 49
Tiner, James, 41, 42, 45
Tiner, Margaret, 41
Tom's Brook, battle of, 127
Torbert, Alfred T. A., 123, 126, 127, 234
Toussaint L'Ouverture, 263
Tubman, Harriet, 272
Turner, Elizabeth Hayes, 277
Turner, John W., 258
Turner, Nat, 263
Twain, Mark, 220, 221, 222, 223, 238, 240,
   248
12th Virginia Cavalry. *See* Army of
   Northern Virginia, units in
Twenty-fifth Corps, Army of the James. *See*
   Army of the James, units in
Twenty-fourth Corps, Army of the James
   See Army of the James, units in

United States Colored Troops (USCT),
   194, 257–63, 265, 268, 269, 271, 272
University Publishing Company, 185
Unwritten History (Coppin), 264
Up from Slavery (Washington), 265
Upton, Emory, 127
Urban League, 277

Vest, George G., 146, 151–52, 153, 164
Vicksburg, battle of, 15, 20, 23, 61, 116, 117,
   239
Virginia Central Railroad, 28, 127, 237